Fodor's

EXPLORING
THAILAND

FODOR'S TRAVEL PUBLICATIONS, INC.

NEW YORK • TORONTO • LONDON • SYDNEY • AUCKLAND

HTTP://WWW.FODORS.COM/

Revised third edition 1997
First published 1993
Copyright © The Automobile Association 1997
Maps copyright © The Automobile Association 1997

Published in the United States by Fodor's Travel Publications, Inc.
Published in the United Kingdom by AA Publishing.

Fodor's and Fodor's Exploring Guides are registered trademarks of Fodor's Travel Publications, Inc.

ISBN 0-679-03477-3
Third Edition

Fodor's Exploring Thailand

Authors: **Tim Locke, Martin Clutterbuck, Dick Wilson**
Original Photography: **Rick Strange**
Series Editor: **Nia Williams**
Cartography: **The Automobile Association**
Copy Editor: **Diana Payne**
Cover Design: **Louise Fili, Fabrizio La Rocca**
Front Cover Silhouette: **Bob Krist**

Special Sales
Fodor's Travel Publications are available at special discounts for bulk purchases (100 copies or more) for sales promotions or premiums. Special editions, including personalized covers, excerpts of existing guides, and corporate imprints, can be created in large quantities for special needs. For more information, contact your local bookseller or write to Special Markets, Fodor's Travel Publications, 201 East 50th Street, New York, NY 10022.

PRINTED IN ITALY by Printer Trento srl
10 9 8 7 6 5 4 3 2 1

How to use this book

This book is divided into five main sections:

❏ Section 1
Thailand Is
discusses aspects of life and living today, from traditional ways to modern streetlife

❏ Section 2
Thailand Was
places the country in its historical context and explores those past events whose influences are felt to this day

❏ Section 3
A to Z Section
covers places to visit, arranged region by region, with suggested walks and drives. Within this section fall the Focus On articles, which consider a variety of topics in greater detail

❏ Section 4
Travel Facts
contains the strictly practical information that is vital for a successful trip

❏ Section 5:
Hotels and Restaurants
lists recommended establishments in Thailand, giving a brief description of what they offer

How to use the star rating
Most places described in this book have been given a separate rating:

►►► **Do not miss**

►► **Highly recommended**

► **Worth seeing**

Not essential viewing

Contents

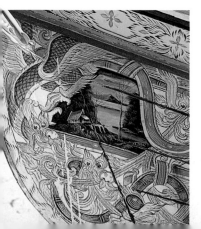

This quick-reference guide highlights the elements of the book you will use most often: the maps; the introductory features; the Focus-on articles and the drives.

My Thailand by Tim Locke

Whenever I revisit Thailand, I savor my first impressions. The hectic taxi ride from Bangkok Airport into the city feels like half of Asia is on the move, but away from the major din it's a different world. A temple compound provides an oasis of peace, but the glinting gold dazzles; I take off my shoes and enter the cool, dark wiharn, where the Buddha image smiles inscrutably. Back outside, I buy a coconut, which the vendor cuts open and sticks a straw into. I hand over a few baht for a sticky rice pancake and smile inwardly at the prospect of weeks of Thai cuisine. It's nice to know that compared to many other Asian countries, I won't have to worry—Thais are fastidious about hygiene and food preparation.

From Bangkok's Noi station a third-class only train with wooden carriages rattles through the jungly fringes of the city. Kanchana Buri, at the end of the trip, seems incredibly sleepy after Bangkok. Outside the station a sinewy bicycle rickshaw "driver" conveys me to my favorite guesthouse, by the river, where I find my "room"—a bamboo cabin perched above the Kwai, looking across to a dreamy, serpentine chain of hazy limestone peaks. A flotilla of rafts resembling a street of thatched cottages glides along the river to the accompaniment of tinny disco music.

On the east coast I hitch a lift from a fishing boat to the island of Ko Si Chang. I scramble among the ruins of the summer palace, now running riot with cacti and frangipani and frequented by dazzlingly colored, over-sized butterflies. Alongside a ruined temple a pair of turtles idle in a lily pond. At the center of the island I scale some 500 steps to a dizzily sited hilltop temple.

In a remote town in western Thailand, I alight from a long ride on a songthaew. I have no idea where to head for, but I am immediately taken into hand by a man who turns out to be the local headmaster. We head on to a rockface where a Buddhist monk has set up his own hermitage in a cave entrance. He lights a lantern and silently leads us through a labyrinth of chambers, the floors soft with bat droppings.

The great temples of Bangkok, the ruins of Sukothai, and the dreamlike beaches of the south are among the most celebrated tourist attractions of Thailand. Yet most visitors will find that this country is more than a package of scenery, sand, and sights. For me, the pleasure is just being there, riding a bus or giving impromptu English lessons to a gang of Thai student monks, or watching a game of takraw in a side street. More perhaps than most countries, Thailand repays the effort to get off the beaten track, and to try to learn a few words of the language; Thai is not easy, but a little goes a long way. Above all, try to keep *jai yen*—a cool heart. Be open to the country and her people, be patient and allow events take their course.

Tim Locke

THAILAND IS & WAS

THAILAND

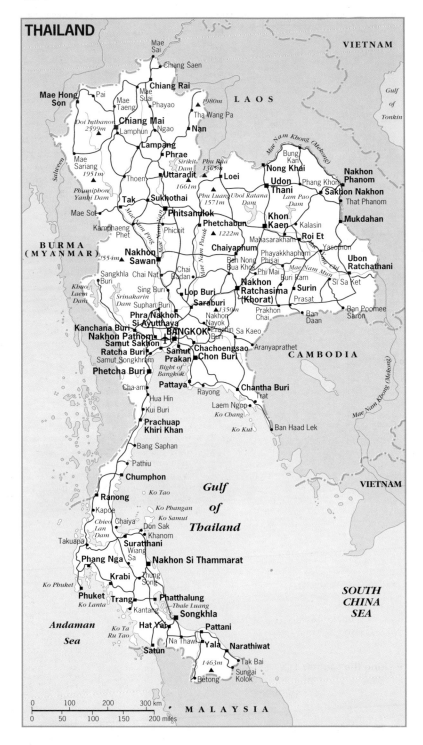

■ **Thailand is a country of tropical abundance, inhabited by gentle and courteous people mostly professing Buddhism. "Land of the free" is the literal meaning of Thailand, and the Thais consider themselves, with justification, to have one of the more free societies in Asia. They have borrowed from both Chinese and Indian civilizations, and the resultant mix is most distinctive and interesting. The Thais are happy-go-lucky, spontaneous, and carefree. ■**

Something for everyone To the Western visitor, Thailand is not just another land; it's another way of life. Tradition and development rub shoulders here as nowhere else. In Bangkok, wooden houses built on stilts over the water stand in the shadows of gleaming condominium blocks. The air is filled with different smells: stir-fried food, *tuk tuk* (motorized trishaw) fumes, dried coconuts, incense, canal water .... Exotic *wats* (temples) glimmer in the sunlight, their cool interiors a welcome refuge from the city din.

A bus ride into the countryside brings a vivid glimpse of Thai variety. Buses equipped with hi-fi and videos also have their mirrors draped with garlands of everlasting flowers for good luck. Instead of pinups, there are photos of venerable monks above the driver's seat. The driver tears along the road, blaring his horn, passing the occasional ox-drawn cart. Women board the buses to sell Coke from plastic bags and sticky rice concoctions wrapped in banana leaves to the passengers—who include immaculate schoolchildren, saffron-robed monks and hill-tribe women in dazzling home-embroidered clothes and grubby, Western-style running shoes.

Visiting the country Thailand has a huge amount to offer, endowed with resorts well-attuned to the needs of Western tourists as well as many places that are still remote in character. Visitors can get a good idea of the range of experiences by staying in Bangkok for a few days and taking a few side trips into the surrounding areas. Many stay on for months. The Thais' gentle and laid-back nature, coupled with the ease of getting around and making one's own discoveries, contribute to Thailand's popularity. This country has dazzling temples and some extraordinary historic sights. Beyond the great rice plains, where farmers bend over in their lampshade hats to tend the crops, rise mountains harboring hill-tribe cultures. In the south are some of the loveliest beaches anywhere, with squeaky white sands backed by lofty limestone cliffs and fringed with palm trees.

Thailand is its people: in spite of spiraling economic change, they have kept their traditions, festivals, and essential Thai qualities. It would take a great deal to change all that.

A Thai classical dancer

■ **Thailand has a distinctive shape on the map, tailing away in the south into a long, narrow strip of land. Some people have likened the outline of the country to an elephant's head, with the trunk curling down toward Malaysia. With a land area of 198,400 square miles, Thailand is no small state—it is, in fact, roughly the same size as France or Texas—and it has a population of 60 million.** ■

How the land lies Thailand has Malaysia as its neighbor in the south, Burma (Myanmar) in the west, and Laos and Cambodia in the northeast and east.

❏ In the 19th century, French and British cartographers left a narrow stretch of Burmese and Laotian territory on Thailand's eastern border in order to cordon off Thailand from China. ❏

The north of the country is mountainous and hilly, with outriders of the Himalayas separated by narrow valleys, notably formed by the Nan, Yom, Wang and Ping rivers. The high ground gradually rises toward the west and north, where Doi Inthanon (8,512 feet/2,595m), Thailand's highest mountain, is to be found. The rivers flowing down these north–south valleys come together to form the Chao Phraya, Thailand's principal river, the floodplain of which constitutes the central plateau of the country. The **central plain** is Thailand's rice bowl, and the area where population is most dense. Most of the political, economic, and intellectual life of Thailand goes on in this central area.

The east is dominated by the Khorat Plateau, shut off from the central plain by the Phetchabun range. The Khorat Plateau is drained by the Mun and Chi rivers and by the Mekong, into which they ultimately flow, and which forms Thailand's border with Laos. A large shallow basin, the Khorat Plateau is 656 feet above sea level, encircled by hills; its rolling terrain gives way to swampland at the approach to the Mekong River.

A long cordillera, the Tennasserim range, runs from northern Thailand down the **western border** to connect with peninsular ranges that continue down the center of the Thai isthmus into Malaysia. This **southern peninsula** is rich in rubber, tin and tropical vegetation.

The main coastline is around the Gulf of Thailand, which merges into the South China Sea and thus gives Thailand a window onto the Pacific. There is also a shorter coastline on the Andaman Sea, on the other side of the peninsula, which makes Thailand an Indian Ocean state as well.

Weather and natural resources Tropical forest used to cover much of Thailand, supporting a variety of animal and plant life, but over the past 50 years forests have disappeared at an alarming rate, with a consequent decline in the natural resources to be found in those areas. In 1945, over 90 percent of Thailand was forested; now estimates are nearer 15 percent.

Until recently, farmers made use of the natural nutrients brought down by annual floods of streams and rivers in order to grow rice. On the hill farms of **northern Thailand** elaborate systems of irrigation— ditches, dikes and terraces—can still be seen.

Population The rapid increase in population, especially between 1950 and 1970, unnaturally swelled the size of the capital city, Bangkok, which is now about 40 times bigger than any other Thai city.

Population growth has now been brought down to about 1.5 percent a year, largely as a result of a successful campaign by the government to popularize family

❏ Thailand is in the tropical belt, standing in the path of monsoon storms that boil up from the South China Sea. There is heavy rainfall from July through October, cool, dry weather from November through February, and dry heat from March through June. ❏

The image presented to the world: two girls in formal Thai dress

planning, especially through the use of condoms. But today the population faces a bigger threat in AIDS, which some Thai experts believe may reach disastrous proportions by the year 2000.

Three-quarters of Thailand's inhabitants are ethnic Thais, with the Chinese providing about 15 percent and the remaining 10 percent comprising Malays, Khmers, Laotians, Mons, Shans and numerous hill tribes.

❏ The Chinese population in Thailand is said to be the largest outside China itself. Some go so far as to dub Thailand China's number-one colony. ❏

13

■ **Thailand is a constitutional monarchy with a democratic government under a prime minister elected by the national assembly, which in turn is elected by universal suffrage. However, military dictatorships seem to occur approximately every decade. The military junta that staged a *coup d'état* in February 1991 introduced an interim constitution under which elections were held in March 1992. These lead to the formation of a democratic civilian government (see also pages 68–71). ■**

14

Working with change During the greater part of 1991, there was a caretaker government whose prime minister, Anand Panyarachun, was appointed by the military junta. Anand, himself a former diplomat and businessman, chose a largely technocratic cabinet of former bureaucrats and businessmen, which was praised for resolving a number of problems inherited from the previous government.

Normally the Thai prime minister operates very much like counterparts in Western democracies, though he is responsible ultimately to the king in matters of grave importance involving national interest and morality. But the army has frequently intervened if dissatisfied with the government's behavior, always appealing for the king's approval or acquiescence in order to gain popular legitimacy. There is then pressure from liberal quarters for the army to return power to civilians, and to reinstate democracy. Unlike the army in some other Asian countries, the

❏ The main issues between the army and civilian politicians are excessive corruption in big infrastructure projects requiring ministerial approval; the handling of senior army appointments; the army's right to be represented in the cabinet; and the former system of holding elections, which involved money changing hands. ❏

Thai army has always done this, though it sometimes takes a while.

The main parties Chart Thai (Thai Nation Party) was the party with most seats in the national assembly before the coup of 1991. Its then leader, General Chatichai Choonhavan (a former cavalry officer and wealthy businessman), became prime minister from 1988 to 1991. After the coup, the Chart Thai party reoriented itself to align with the very military leaders who had deposed it.

By the end of 1991 there were two new parties reflecting the ambitions of senior generals: the New Aspiration Party (NAP) of General Chaovalit Yongchaiyudh and the Samakki Tham. (In 1992, General Chatichai Choonhavan formed a new party, the Chat Pattana, or National Development Party.)

In a typically Thai compromise, therefore, the generals were competing with one another on democratic lines to become "civilian" prime ministers. Samakki Tham and Chart Thai (which merged) and the NAP dominated the new 1992 parliament.

The Thai system of elections makes it easy for candidates to bribe voters, but actually makes it hard for any politician to succeed without having large sums of money to pay out to supporters, godfathers and the like.

The 1992 elections The constitution drawn up after Thailand's 17th coup in modern times allowed the army to appoint General Suchinda Krapayoon as prime minister. His unelected status caused immediate unrest and dissatisfaction. Tens of thousands of demonstrators took to the streets to voice their protest in May 1992; the militia responded with water cannons at first, then hastily resorted to live ammunition in an action claiming possibly hundreds of lives. In September 1992, a coalition government under the premiership of Chuan Leekpai survived for a record two years seven months. It was succeeded in June 1995 by a return of the Chart Thai party under Banharn Silipa-archa, who was brought down in September 1996 by yet more corruption scandal. In November 1996, the New Aspiration Party was reelected under ex-army leader Chaovalit Yongchaiyuah.

Rural politics Local political institutions and systems have lagged behind national developments. The villages used to be uninvolved in politics, receiving decisions rather than making them. Then Phibul (see pages 60–61) set up *sapha tambol*, or village commune councils, which provide a means for rural inhabitants to take part in the political system. These are much under the influence of the village headman, who normally has the respect of the villagers and can bring them together to work with local authorities in socioeconomic and political developments.

The 1991 junta wanted the headman to be appointed by the local officials instead of being elected by the villagers. The villagers are insufficiently experienced—for example, in financial, managerial or administrative matters—to go against a determined district officer who represents the forces of bureaucracy in the area and who may be a political science graduate.

The *sapha tambol* are under the control of the Ministry of the Interior, and this at once brings in both a bureaucratic and, ultimately, a political party intervention. Democracy is easy to legislate through the national assembly, but not so easy to establish effectively and healthily on the ground.

Government House, Bangkok

15

■ **King Bhumiphol Adulyadej was born on December 5, 1927, in Cambridge, Massachusetts, where his father was a hospital doctor. He came to the throne unexpectedly in 1946 when he was only 18, after his elder brother, King Ananda Mahidol, was found dead with a bullet in his head. The mystery of that death has never been explained.** ■

16

King Bhumiphol has now become the longest-reigning king in Thai history, and one of the most respected. The 50th anniversary of his accession was celebrated in 1996 with great splendor. The Thai royal family is one of the very few remaining in Asia, succeeding in increasing the *de facto* authority of the monarchy within the political system of Thailand.

In his early years on the throne, Bhumiphol cultivated a dilettante image, gaining fame as the king who played the saxophone well enough to accompany Benny Goodman and

❑ King Bhumiphol won a gold medal for Thailand in the Southeast Asian Peninsular Games in 1967. His musical compositions include *Blue Day* (revue song of the 1950s), the Thai national anthem and a ballet, *Manohra*. ❑

Louis Armstrong in Dixieland numbers.

In his youth, the king was an enthusiastic sailor, building his own boats and winning many trophies. He painted in oils, published translations from English and exhibited much-admired photographs. His queen, Sirikit, was one of the great Thai beauties of her day. Gradually the king's interests shifted to the more serious concerns of rural, social and political reform. In a country where the pace of economic growth swamped the interests of traditional farmers and tribespeople who found it hard to adapt, Bhumiphol used his mystique as king to good effect.

Practical involvement The king took the lead in putting rural development programs firmly on the Thai agenda, jogging the government into giving them higher priority. He regularly tours rural areas to see the problems for himself and has become something of an expert on small irrigation projects and the introduction of better farming practices as well as reforestation.

In the political arena, the king found a place as a focus of national unity, a mediator and a source of stability. While generals, prime ministers and dictators rose and fell from power, he supplied the balancing role. No *coup d'état* has sought to overthrow him; on the contrary, the prospective *coup* leaders have always sought to gain his approval, if necessary by moderating their program.

The immense popularity and adoration that the king has built up with the ordinary people of the kingdom during over 50 years on the throne enable him to play this role to the utmost, sometimes tipping the balance in a power

Celebrating the king's birthday

struggle or actually preventing a *coup* in the making. The king lives with his family in the Chitladda Palace close to the center of Bangkok. Queen Sirikit

> ❏ Bhumiphol once calculated 14 chemical formulas for seeding clouds to produce rain, paying for the research himself and sending up specially equipped light aircraft to test the formulations. ❏

also carries out a wide range of social duties including the leadership of the Girl Guides and the very successful promotion of peasant handicrafts

The succession Bhumiphol's health is not good, and there is likely to be a controversy over the succession when that occurs. His eldest daughter, Ubol Rattana, now lives in the United States, where she married an American engineer.

The only son and heir to the throne, Crown Prince Vajiralongkorn, does not share his father's popularity. Trained as an air force pilot, he has a reputation for bad temper and has

The ceremonial royal barges

not shown any interest in politics.

Some Thais would like to see Princess Sirindhorn, the King's second daughter, succeed instead, but a woman has never taken the throne in Thailand, and the prevalent male chauvinism would probably stand in the way, despite her great popularity and capability.

Bhumiphol is a very wealthy man, with properties including a controlling share of the Siam Cement Corporation as well as many banks and other companies. These are managed by the Crown Property Bureau, which is a major asset holder and investor in Thailand. Dividends from these investments supplement the king's government budget allocation and help him play a larger part in the political arena.

The king has a strong scientific bent, having studied science in Lausanne in Switzerland. His quick reaction to the arrival of artificial rain-making in Western science has led to a regular scheme and program within the Ministry of Agriculture. King Bhumiphol has undoubtedly built up goodwill for the monarchy, which should last for some time to come. Without a monarch in the middle, Thai politics would be much more unstable.

■ **Thai society is built on the family, though there is also scope for individualism; group discipline is not one of the country's strong points. Nowadays modern middle-class children usually choose their own marriage partners and parents usually approve, but rural fathers expect deference to their wishes, and rural society teaches loyalty to parents. Even in the towns, family solidarity continues to be the norm.** ■

Housing In Bangkok the relatively affluent middle class lives increasingly in a style similar to its counterparts worldwide. Some of the wealthier elite prefer to live in traditional spacious wooden houses, with high roofs and large gardens, including a fish pond. Such houses are cool and breezy and can also be moved to another place if necessary. Now, however, new estates of Western-style white-walled houses with stone balconies and red tiles are springing up.

A modern Thai wedding

❑ Many Thai men have two or more wives. The first wife of General Sunthorn, the leader of the 1991 coup, took his second wife to court to prevent her using his surname. In response, the general invited the press around to meet his lover. ❑

The fashion for the rich Thais is to buy, say, two traditional houses-on-stilts (the stilts protect against wildlife and floods) in the countryside, dismantle them, take them by truck to a quiet suburb of Bangkok and reassemble them as old-fashioned bedroom wings of a modern concrete house—thus gaining the advantages of both styles.

Life is considerably more basic and simple in the countryside, but a TV, refrigerator and other modern appliances are commonplace.

Marriage, customs, equality
A wedding is usually celebrated in stages, the couple being ceremonially blessed in the morning at the bride's house, and having holy water poured into their hands (a Brahmin ritual in origin) in the afternoon. That is usually followed by an informal party. In rural areas ceremonies can last for two or three days, during which time the groom is not supposed to touch the bride.

Women rank below men in the traditional order of things and do not get equal treatment in the legal aspects of marriage and divorce. In practice, however, they can pursue successful careers. Thailand was the

first Asian country to give women the vote (in 1933), and several big corporations have women at their head. There is one woman priest, who was ordained outside Thailand.

Education Six years of primary school are compulsory, but only a small number of children go beyond to secondary or higher education, something that will place Thailand at a disadvantage in the long run compared with some other Southeast Asian countries. In the schools there is a morning ritual of flying the Thai flag and singing the national anthem.

Buddhist groups are opposing the new government curriculum, which cuts down the hours devoted to Buddhism in favor of the sciences. The two best-known universities are Chulalongkorn, the oldest, and Thammasat, which is traditionally the more radical. Both are in Bangkok. There are many others, in the capital as well as in the provinces.

Health and family planning Health facilities in Bangkok are generally good, but those in the more distant provinces are very poor. One area of public health where Thailand excels is family planning: children in many primary schools sing a family planning song, promising not to have more than two children when they grow up, and not to marry before 25 (girls) or 30 (boys). Buddhist monks will even bless contraceptives.

The rate of increase of the population is only about 1.5 percent, lower than in most Third World countries. The person most

❏ When the first American condoms to arrive in Thailand proved to be too big, Mechai Viravaidya hired five "massage-parlor girls" to measure more than 500 of their customers in order to produce a Thai national size for the manufacturers to meet. ❏

responsible for this low population growth is Mechai Viravaidya, a tough, imaginative, bold and determined man. He is a remarkable publicist who has championed the controversial issues of population growth and AIDS with great enthusiasm and some success (see page 8).

Mechai's plain speaking about the need for condoms, vasectomies and sterilization has made him so much a part of the health education scene that condoms in Thailand are often referred to as "Mechais." In publicizing their use he has employed unorthodox but effective methods, such as making them into balloons, filling them with water and introducing them at festivals. He also invented catchy slogans to put on T-shirts.

❏ Meatball vendor Tek Kop lives in a house with seven wives and 22 children. Mechai Viravaidya offered to pay for the children's education if Tek had a vasectomy. He refused, and Mechai acknowledged his worst failure. ❏

■ **Thailand has now joined the second wave of emergent Asian economies, or NICs (Newly Industrializing Countries). The "dragons" (Thailand, Malaysia, Indonesia and the Philippines) are racing to catch up with the richer "tigers" (Hong Kong, Singapore, Taiwan and South Korea). Despite rapid recent growth, Thailand's standard of living remains low—about $2,000 per head in annual national income.** ■

Agriculture Thailand has always been a rich agricultural producer, especially of rice. More than 20 million tons are normally harvested every year—and of better quality than that of other countries. Not only rice, but also rubber (about a million tons a year), corn, cassava, sugar, soybeans, coconuts, fish and shrimps are produced in large quantities.

Spectacular increases in crop yields have been won in recent years through the use of chemical fertilizers and pesticides and irrigation canals. Unfortunately some of the new strains of high-yielding rice that were introduced have proved vulnerable to insects and other pests.

This has resulted in a new trend toward what some Thais call "Buddhist farming," where natural organic fertilizer and herbal sprays are used to deter rather than kill pests. On some farms the natural balance has been restored under this regime, so birds have returned to prey on the insects that eat the crops. This is praised as being consistent with Buddhism and with the Thai tradition, although it is still only a minority system.

Some Thai **exports** are restricted. The European Union made Thailand cut its exports of tapioca, although it gave funds for the development of alternative crops. Thai textiles and garments are restricted in most Western markets, and British manufacturers once demanded restrictions on Thai TV sets.

One of every two cans of pineapple opened in America comes from Thailand, while a Thai company now stands as Asia's largest exporter of tuna, commanding one-

❑ Textiles are currently the biggest export, followed by rice, rubber, precious stones and jewelry, tapioca, sugar, integrated circuits and canned fish. ❑

fifth of the world market and having absorbed one of the largest American companies.

Today traditional farming is beginning to give way to agribusiness, in particular the production of broiler chickens and shrimps. This is symbolized by Charoen Pokphand, the Chinese-founded agribusiness conglomerate.

Manufacturing industry A more recent development, this now accounts for over a third of the gross national product, while service industries account for almost half. Tourism alone supplies a tenth. The manufacturing industry benefits from the pool of cheap unskilled labor (newly landless poor farmers) that can be supplied from the Thai rural areas. Two out of three Thai workers are in agriculture, yet they account for only one-sixth of the national production. Many multinationals and manufacturers from Japan, Northeast Asia, Europe and America are attracted by this, and electronics and textiles in particular are flourishing as a result. These developments are pursued by private enterprise, the government taking a back seat in the economy. This results in some problems, such as the inadequacy of the infrastructure (especially transportation and communications)

❏ Charoen Pokphand is the world's largest prawn feed producer, the fifth-largest feed-mill producer and the largest Southeast Asian investor in China. It has the tallest skyscraper on Bangkok's Silom Road and a turnover of more than $2.5 billion a year. ❏

and the inferiority of higher education, technology and technical training. There is a severe shortage of engineers.

Steel and petrochemical industries are in evidence, and exports to markets as far afield as Africa have been established. Several companies are assembling cars, notably Mitsubishi Motors, and some of these have been exported with almost 60 percent locally produced parts.

The country is blessed with mineral deposits, notably tin, lead, zinc and lignite. The relatively recent discovery and exploitation of offshore natural gas has rendered Thailand less dependent on oil imports.

Thai silk is one of the best dollar-earners of the traditional textiles, a business developed initially by Jim Thompson, an American who stayed in Thailand after World War II. He built a major industry of Thai silk by introducing modern dyes and designs to the hand-loom workers.

❏ Jim Thompson started by selling silk in the foyer of the Oriental Hotel, and later introduced it to Hollywood costume designers with great success. Jim Thompson silk is still considered the best in this billion-dollar export industry. ❏

Working conditions These are appalling in many of the smaller Thai factories. Safety records are poor, and several cases of illegal child

workers have been exposed.

Only one worker in 10 is organized in a trade union, although that is mainly because Thais prefer to retain their individual freedom. The unions are relatively strong in public enterprises. There is a minimum wage, which has been raised more than once in the past three or four years. It is now about $5 per day.

Finance There is an active finance center, with more than 30 commercial and foreign banks in the Bangkok market, and over 100 finance and securities firms. The stock exchange is volatile but nevertheless attracts a good deal of Western custom; the baht is one of the stronger currencies in Asia. Exchange rates in 1996 gave approximately 25 baht to the U.S. dollar and 40 to the pound sterling.

One of the most popular vocations now for high school and college graduates in Bangkok is banking. The

biggest local bank is the Bangkok Bank, still controlled and largely owned by the Sophonpanich family, now second-generation Chinese immigrants. Thousands of young men and women in almost identical navy blue and white outfits flock into the headquarters on Silom Road and the myriad branches around the country every morning—and at lunchtime you will see them tumbling out to head for their favorite cafés and street stalls.

The Bangkok Bank is now the biggest commercial bank in Southeast Asia. There are many other successful local Thai banks, and the foreign banks are still kept out to some extent in order to protect these. Buddhism does not favor the collapse of bankrupt companies since that causes hardship for employees and shareholders.

Individuals are taxed on a sliding scale from 5 to 55 percent, while corporations pay 35 percent on profits (less for those publicly traded on the Securities Exchange).

Pepsi plant at Bangkok

Significant tax holidays and reductions are available for all approved new investments. A 7-percent value-added tax was implemented in 1992.

Looking to the future Financial liberalization is progressing, with currency exchange controls already ended. The government intends to loosen regulations and controls on many more aspects of Thailand's financial activities.

The economy Since the early 1990s, the Thai economy has slowed down dramatically, in response to the world recession, Gulf War, oil price increases and domestic overheating. It was once predicted to be one of the world's top eight economies by 2020, but many Thais believe the price is too high. Growth at that pace widens the gap between rich and poor, making for social unrest. The World Bank estimates there are about 14 million Thais below the poverty line.

Among many worries for the future are the decline in rice exports and the likelihood of Vietnam taking away some of Thailand's old markets at

23

A ruby mine in the southeast: gems were once a major export

the cheaper end. In the 1980s, Thailand was the world's leading rice exporter, supplying one-third of world exports, but that level may prove difficult to sustain.

Western managers in Thai factories have often carped about their work force. But the degree of hard work put in by Thais is evident: for proof, look at the many building sites in Bangkok, mostly manned by relatively new labor from the northeast.

Neither does the lazy image square with the $1 billion that some 300,000 Thais have sent home while under long-term contract in construction projects in the Middle East and other Asian locations.

None of the recent economic achievements of Thailand could have been attained if the typical Thai was shirking work.

The tourist industry now brings more than 7 million foreigners to Thailand every year. They arrive at

the rate of 800 an hour, and the average tourist spends over $1,000, which adds up to a total of $8 billion a year, about half of total Thai exports. One factor in this is sheer quality.

The natural attractions of Thai climate, scenery, historical sites, colorful festivals and exotic experiences add up to a powerful draw. Half of Thailand's tourists come from Western countries, the remainder from Asia—especially Japan, Taiwan, Korea, Malaysia and Singapore.

❑ The Oriental Hotel, beloved by Somerset Maugham, has been consistently voted "best in the world" in international travelers' polls every year for over a decade. ❑

■ The Thai mentality is shaped in part by the country itself. Its hot, tropical climate receives periods of intense heavy rain; it is a land of plenty, where food is bountiful. Buddhist philosophy has a strong hold on the Thai people, teaching them to put self-cultivation above social works. It does not offer a universal ethic, but rather it accepts the inequalities among men in their spiritual progress. ■

Social attitudes Thailand is a society of vertical hierarchy, where people respect the authority of those above them (fathers, the king, prime ministers, schoolteachers), but this is not quite the same system as is found in Japan. Even family ties are looser in Thailand than in Northeast Asia.

This also means that Thais are more receptive to foreign influences, something that was reinforced by their history of resisting colonialism during the 19th century. The inferiority complex that can be noted among former colonized states (such as India and Indonesia) is missing with the Thais, whose authority structure has been unbroken for centuries.

It is almost a taboo to contradict someone directly. Maybe national politics is an exception, where mud-slinging during election time is acceptable and enjoyed.

The self-respect of other people is normally considered so important that it must never be infringed upon. One story tells of the Thai who was hired to teach the Thai language to a foreigner, but never corrected the foreigner because he would not embarrass a person by drawing attention to his mistakes.

A Thai will make a big effort not to inconvenience or upset another person, and he expects to get the same treatment in return.

There is heavy reliance on the smile, but if that suggests an underlying gentleness of character it has to reconciled with the extraordinary violence that does occasionally break out. A servant may endure the rude treatment of his employer for many years without complaint, but then his patience might suddenly break, and he might even kill his persecutor. There are many *crimes passionnels*, and Thailand is said to have one of the highest murder rates in the world.

Becoming absorbed in self-cultivation, and dealing with the intricate problems of social relationships in such variety, has another consequence. Thais avoid

People at prayer

❑ The ideal man would have "…the moral principles of a *farang* (Westerner), the diligence of a Chinese and the heart of a Thai." Heart is: "Love of peace, contentment with little, concern for others and a sense of moderation."—From Botan's novel *Letters from Thailand.* ❑

Bangkok's Brahmin Erawan shrine

> ❑ During World War II, villagers in Thailand brought food to British POWs in a Japanese camp. When the Japanese surrendered in 1945, the villagers brought food for the Japanese prisoners with the same solicitude. ❑

> ❑ "The Thai way of life is an elegant sort of life, surrounded by benevolent and exuberantly plentiful nature, with adaptable morals and a serene detachment to the more difficult problems of life.... To a Thai, life itself is one long relaxation."—Kukrit Pramoj, Thailand's ex-prime minister and famous novelist. ❑

becoming involved in other people's problems. They are not "Good Samaritans." They normally avoid conflict and keep contacts with other people to a minimum.

There is a legitimate outlet for relaxation in *sanuk* (fun). *Sanuk* is a very old feature in Thai life. It means getting pleasure from carefree amusement with congenial friends or companions. No one is criticized for doing this; it has a positive value in the code of behavior.

Spontaneity is valued. Thais dislike planning, and interviews are often much better without an appointment because the impromptu encounter is more enjoyed.

It sounds idyllic, but for Westerners the Thai mentality can be difficult to work with.

Objectivity is an elusive quality in Thai life, even at the university level. If a professor gives an opinion on a matter under discussion, junior lecturers or students will rarely argue with him or express a different point of view. If they think it important enough, they might beard him privately afterward. It is not timidity, or fear, but a concern for the professor's self-respect that prevents what Westerners would regard as a normal productive discussion from opening up.

■ **Thais have a strong sense of hierarchy and take immense care in their behavior toward other people. Different gradations of respect or treatment need to be given, and this is reflected in the language. Learning Thai involves a system of "honorifics," where different pronouns are used according to social status. Speaking to a bus conductor, a teacher, a student or royalty all call for different words. To a Thai, these distinctions in social status are very important, and even a foreigner is expected to show some awareness of them. ■**

Getting it wrong Never touch a Thai, even a child, on the head. The Thais consider the head the most important part of the body, deserving the most honor – while the foot is the least honored. The head is the seat of the *khwan,* or vital spirit, which lives in the body. Students who have to pass in front of a seated teacher will instinctively lower their heads as they pass. A servant will do the same in a house.

❏ Traditionally, Thais should not stand higher than their royal family. A prince was unable to inspect the first printing press because there were residences over it whose occupants might walk over his head. When President Lyndon B. Johnson visited in 1966, police cleared the second and higher stories of buildings lining the route. ❏

Forms of greeting The traditional Thai form of greeting is the *wai,* in which both hands are raised slowly and gracefully, palm to palm and close to the body. More than a greeting, it is a way of paying one's respects. The higher the hands are raised, the greater the respect signaled.

The *wai* is the normal form of greeting between Thai people, but some more Westernized Thais are just as likely to shake hands with foreigners.

❏ It is still said that men are comparable to the front legs of an elephant, and women to the hind legs. Male chauvinists in Thailand like to say that the elephant seems to be walking backward these days. ❏

Women's rights and wrongs Women have traditionally deferred to men in society and are thought to have adverse *khwan.* Thai men will still refuse to walk underneath a clothesline where female garments are hanging, in case their heads are touched by them. For this reason women's clothes are usually hung out to dry on a very low clothesline that has to be walked around.

Do's and don'ts No one would ever enter a house or a temple without taking off the shoes first. Nowadays, although it is impractical to have everybody leaving shoes at the door

❏ "If you want to be somebody in this country, you have to dress like a European," complained Sulak Sivaraksa, the well-known critic and writer, after an incident when, wearing his usual traditional Thai dress, he was refused admittance to the Oriental Hotel in Bangkok to see the then German foreign minister, Herr Genscher. ❏

> ❑ Never sleep with your head facing to the west. That is where the sun sets, and the setting sun symbolizes death — Thai superstition. ❑

of a very large building, like a bank or department store, in temples or in private houses belonging to Thais, foreigners would be expected to take off their shoes and walk about inside in socks or in slippers provided by the host.

Never give a Thai friend or colleague a red pen with which to write a signature. Names are written in red at the side of coffins awaiting cremation.

Thai people do not touch each other and rarely hold hands or have physical contact in the same easygoing manner that Westerners do. In the northeast such behavior can even result in a fine. The traditional dance, the *Ramwong*, demonstrates how this avoidance of bodily contact does not inhibit a graceful dance movement in which neither partner touches the other.

You bet! The Thais are inveterate gamblers. They bet on horses, with cards, and on all kinds of contest— Thai boxing, cockfights, fish fights, bullfights...if they scent a competition, they will be there with a wager. Poker, mah-jongg, checkers and chess are all played with rising excitement for sums of money. The national lottery is a huge business; the generals who managed it became rich men. Thais will devote enormous time and energy to accumulating enough merit by their actions to get a lucky lottery number.

Thai boxing: a chance to lay bets

■ **Thailand is a predominantly Buddhist country. More than 90 percent of the population believe in some form or other of Buddhism, even though they may not perform the ceremonies or visit the temples frequently. The picturesque temples in every village and dotted about in each city are tranquil oases to which almost all Thais are drawn at some time in their lives.** ■

Buddhist traditions Thai Buddhism follows the Theravada tradition, which is based on the oldest Buddhist writings recorded in Pali, the ancient Indian language. **Theravada Buddhism** aims to preserve the way of life described in those early writings. The other important Buddhist tradition is the **Mahayana**, which spread to China, Korea, Japan and Vietnam and developed Buddhist philosophy while also trying to make the early teachings more accessible to lay followers. Buddhism was founded in the 6th century BC by Siddhartha Gautama, an Indian prince who turned ascetic. After years of fasting and meditation, he arrived at a unique vision of the world, centered on the Four Noble Truths. The Thais converted to Buddhism in the 7th century and can now boast the longest unbroken ordination chain in any of the Theravada countries. The millions of Buddha images that can be seen in Thailand in every house and temple, though not always approved of by Thai intellectuals, are deeply respected by ordinary men and women. Visitors must be very careful not to give offence by behaving disrespectfully toward Buddha statues, which are felt to represent the Buddha in person. Some tourists who were photographed sitting on the head of a big Buddha statue aroused a furor of criticism. It is forbidden to take Buddha statues out of Thailand without special permission from the Fine Arts Department. Shops will advise you and can sometimes get an export license.

Buddhist beliefs Buddhism does not involve a belief in any god or gods. The central feature of Buddhism is the concept of *karma*, which literally means "action." Every action, word or thought has a consequence, which becomes manifest sometime in the future. Evil acts produce evil consequences or suffering. Inequalities between people in the present are rationalized by the idea that *karma* can be carried over from previous lives.

The effort to achieve a high degree of spirituality is left on the whole to the monks in their monasteries or *wats* (temples). The central building of the *wat* is the most sacred and is known as the *bot*. It is here that the ceremonies of ordination, the daily morning and evening chanting of monks and services on days of fasting (on the first, eighth, 15th and 23rd days of the lunar month) take place. Lesser buildings, called *wiharn*, are often used for religious services for lay people and as living accommodations for the monks.

❑ The Four Noble Truths:
- *dukkha*, or suffering, is life's central problem
- the cause of suffering is desire
- the way to eliminate suffering is to eliminate its cause, desire
- the way to achieve this is to follow the Eightfold Way, which describes standards of morality and qualities to be encouraged in meditation to this end. ❑

Lay Buddhists gain merit by giving alms to the monks, as well as by following basic moral guidelines—not to kill or tell lies and to be moderate in physical indulgence. Every morning at dawn the saffron-robed monks go out with their begging bowls to ask for alms in the form of food, and traditionally every house will spare a little for them.

Religious hierarchy All monks are members of the *sangha*, the Buddhist order of monks. The *sangha* is supervised by an executive council headed by a supreme patriarch who is appointed by the king. There are two main sects in the Thai sangha: the **Mahanikai**, by far the larger of the two, and the **Thammayut**, which was formed in the last century and follows stricter rules—for example, taking only one meal a day.

The tradition survives of laymen spending a week or so as monks in a

The central mosque in Pattani, where Muslims have a strong presence (see page 31)

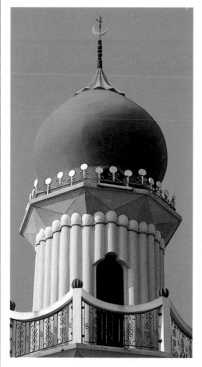

❑ The Buddhist teachings (*dharma*) are taught to every child in primary school; that is how Buddhist morality is diffused. ❑

monastery and subject to the same discipline and routine as the monks. Even King Bhumiphol took alms from the people on the streets of Bangkok when he performed this traditional act early in his reign.

Monks are greatly respected by the public. They get free food in the morning and travel free or half-price on the buses and trains. Some are involved in local development projects (for example, by helping to plan and build bridges, dams and schools, and to modernize farming methods).

Buddhist temples Bangkok has the greatest concentration of important temples. The most renowned is the **Wat Phra Keo**, which is also called the Temple of the Emerald Buddha, containing the mysterious Emerald Buddha statue, a Thai national symbol. Established in 1782, adjoining the Grand Palace, it is the ceremonial temple of the Thai kings. **Wat Mahathat** is the chief temple of Thailand's largest monastic sect, the Mahanikai. The national headquarters of the Thammayut sect is **Wat Bowonniwet** (Bowornives), which is where King Bhumiphol was ordained as a monk. **Wat Po** (Wat Phra Chetuphon) is the oldest and largest *wat* in Bangkok, containing the largest collection of Buddha images in Thailand.

Buddhist sects There is a general consensus that the *sangha* is becoming remote from everyday problems, and for this reason new

❑ Thai intellectuals were furious when a 13th-century carved stone lintel from the Khmer sanctuary of Phanom Rung turned up in a museum in Chicago. The lintel has now been returned. ❑

Muslim people in Narathiwat

sects have been founded. These frown on old-fashioned fortune-telling and the traffic in amulets and charms that are supposed to carry good luck. They try to teach a combination of Buddhist philosophy and meditation techniques suitable for the urban lifestyle. The best known of these is **Santi Asoke** (Peace and No Sorrow), founded by Phra Bodhirak. He is half Chinese and was a TV producer and singer before his ordination. His followers, strict vegetarians who wear white robes, were excommunicated from the sangha in 1989. The sect's major theme is that monks have to be involved with the people and cannot therefore remain distant from politics.

Dhammakaya (Body of Truth) is the other influential new sect. It is highly practical in its financial ideas, being founded by Phra Dhammachayo, a Thai Chinese and a graduate in economics. This sect holds many industrial investments, and its leaders will drive out in a Rolls-Royce or Mercedes to collect their morning alms. In a neat dovetailing of *karma*

and property management, Dhammachayo persuades his lay supporters to donate land to his monks with the promise that the merit acquired will ensure that they enjoy more land in their next life. There is also a sect called **Suan Mokh** (Garden of Liberation), which preaches "dharmic socialism," a decentralized and noncompetitive form of social cooperation among farmers that is free from greed.

> ❑ Phra Bodhirak once claimed that he had personally attained the same level of enlightenment as the Buddha himself, something that no Thai had ever dared to claim before. Although this led to his excommunication, he still has a popular following. ❑

Other religions There is an underlying element of Indian Brahmanism which the Thais acquired from the Indian-influenced societies that they conquered and absorbed as they settled into the present territory of Thailand. Some of the shrines with figures of deities to be seen in Bangkok are Brahman rather than Buddhist. One of these is the *naga*, a semidivine god and fertility symbol that often takes the form of a dragon-headed serpent.

Buddhism is a tolerant religion, and there are small minorities of other the countryside. There is a smaller minority of **Christians**. The Roman Catholic cemetery on Silom Road and the Protestant one on the riverbank are two of the historical sites of Bangkok. A few Thais have become Catholic or Protestant, and some of the refugees from Vietnam

faiths, notably the 2 million **Muslims** in the southern provinces adjoining Malaysia. They are mostly Sunni Muslims, although there has recently been some concern about the growth in numbers of fundamentalist Shiite adherents. Three provinces, Yala, Pattani and Narathiwat, are dominated by Muslims, especially in

Buddhist monks receive their alms

are Catholic, but they are all able to coexist in Thai society without difficulty. The Buddhist ideas of the "Middle Way," compassion and karma, still operate for them too, having become, as it were, part of the Thai national character.

❏ Women are not allowed to attend Buddhist schools, but they enter *bots* in large numbers. They can take eight or 10 precepts and wear the white robes of a nun, or *mae chi*. ❏

❏ Buddhism injects an element of fatalism into the Thai mentality. This accounts for the passiveness, acceptance and social calm that the outsider observes in Thai society. ❏

■ It is believed that the Thais first migrated to their country from China many centuries ago. That ancient connection has been reinforced by further large-scale immigration of Chinese into Thailand; an estimated 9 million Chinese may have crossed during the past hundred years, making the Chinese the largest minority group in Thailand. ■

Roots Archeological evidence in the past 35 years has raised the interesting possibility that prehistoric sites such as Ban Chiang, Mae Hong Son and Kanchana Buri could have predated the Chinese by several thousand years. If these theories are verified, it will call into question the present understanding of who came from where originally.

The Chinese coming into Thailand in the early days of commerce were merchants who traveled widely in Asia. The Thais were tolerant toward the Chinese immigrants, allowing them to settle and gradually become Thai, although there was a time in the 1930s when Thai nationalism made things difficult for the Chinese.

Further immigration was halted completely in 1950, but in the period following World War II the Chinese completed their assimilation into Thai society. They could be said to be responsible for much of Thailand's economic success.

The borders are blurred Most of those coming into Thailand were single males who married Thai women, starting a process of intermarriage that has gone on over many generations. It is almost impossible now to disentangle the ethnic origins of the mainly Chinese, the mainly Thai and the full Thai. Almost everyone in the ruling elite, from the royal family to the politicians, civil servants and army officers—and especially business leaders—admits to some degree of Chinese ancestry.

Many Chinese in Thailand no longer speak or read Chinese but still perform the occasional Chinese ritual. Thailand is their home and inspires their loyalty and patriotism, but many feel curious about China rather as many Americans take an interest in their ancestors' origins.

Trading places Coming in from outside, the Chinese immigrants had to fall into whatever niche was available in order to make a living. Many turned toward trade and industry and other forms of business. From fairly humble merchants and shopkeepers to major bankers and industrialists, the Chinese are well represented. Indeed, some very big names on the present scene are Chinese.

Virtually all of Thailand's industrialists and entrepreneurs are either recent Chinese immigrants or "Sino-Thais," as the mixed-lineage people are sometimes called. Dhanin Chearavanont is the most successful Chinese businessman, running the

❑ The best way to understand the motivation and early experiences of the migrant Chinese is to read the heartwarming novel *Letters from Thailand* by Botan (a pen name). ❑

Charoen Pokphand agribusiness group. Other famous Chinese business families are Sarasin, Sophonpanich (who own the Bangkok Bank) and Techapaibul.

Bangkok's Patpong Road, which many foreigners visit because of its red-light notoriety, was originally built by a typical Chinese immigrant, Poon Pat. He came to Bangkok from Hainan (a large island off the South

A glimpse of life in Bangkok's Chinatown

China coast) at the age of 12 and became a skillful buyer of rice who made his fortune supplying limestone for the king's new cement factory.

Integration The Chinese resemble the Thais physically in many respects —there are no distinctly typical Thai features—and the two can easily be confused. By now most have taken Thai names, and the fact that they were not made to adopt an alien religion, as the Chinese immigrants did in Malaysia and Indonesia, was a great help.

Nevertheless, there are differences, some of which are cherished by the Chinese. With typical Thai tolerance, these are generally accepted and respected. One of the few traits that distinguish the Chinese from the Thai is the Chinese respect for the family tree. Another is the practice of burying their dead, where Thais have traditionally practiced cremation. There also tends to be a greater practice of Christianity among the Chinese than there is among the Thais, who believe in reincarnation.

Dual identity Some of the Sino-Thais lead, in effect, a double life, being Thai in public but reverting to Chinese ways with their family. There are still some Chinese-language newspapers published, and there are several Chinese Christian churches. As time goes by, however, and certainly in recent years, the tendency is for more and more Chinese children to become completely integrated into the Thai way of life.

❑ All children, whether they be Thai, Chinese or another race, are expected to learn the Thai language from an early age in school. Until relatively recently, Chinese languages were not available for study at college level. ❑

A Chinese Taoist shrine in Bangkok

■ **Thais are natural and spontaneous about sex in private, though they can be somewhat reserved in public, especially where women are concerned. It is an open and tolerant society, and people tend to accept most things, as long as a degree of discretion is employed.** ■

Dictator Field Marshall Sarit's 100 or so mistresses did not shock the Thais. Older men hark back to the days of their youth when a man could have as many wives and/or mistresses as he could afford.

The public health ministry in Thailand estimates there are about 600 brothels in Bangkok, but until recently their existence was officially denied. Countless women and boys earn their living from sex. Girls, some younger than 13, are pressured into prostitution in provincial towns.

Recent moves to decriminalize prostitution have had the support of Mechai Viravaidya, who has campaigned hard for AIDS awareness. It is felt that making prostitutes carry health cards and legalizing brothels would make it easier to enforce health standards in a country where commercial sex is part of everyday life for Thai men.

The woman's point of view Within a marriage a woman overtly takes second place, but in practice she is often the keeper of the purse.

❑ Virtually every town in Thailand has a brothel. Usually it will have a "Thai only" clientele. Most "service girls" have never had sex with a *farang* (foreigner). ❑

Attitudes are changing slowly. Women are becoming more assertive and vocal. There are scores of capable women heading large corporations, trade unions and public offices.

The gay scene There are many gay bars and clubs in Thailand and a number of specialized magazines.

Although the Thais do not frown on homosexuality, AIDS is making everyone think hard. There is now anxious debate about the economic consequences of sexual permissiveness and who will pay the medical expenses of employees who contract AIDS.

❑ A Thai doctor describes AIDS as "…worse than any war. It will destroy every fiber of our social and economic life. We need a movement so intense that it can uproot men's sexual habits…" ❑

An AIDS awareness poster

■ **The army has been an extremely important group in Thai society and politics ever since the 1932 revolution, when it forced King Prajadhipok to abandon his absolute powers. Periods of civilian rule have often been interrupted by military coup attempts—17 in all since 1932.** ■

The military profile was kept high from the 1950s by the perception that Thailand was the "next domino" likely to fall to Communism in Southeast Asia and by the continual threat of Communist insurgency. The army runs its own bank, radio and television stations, and regional economic development programs. It is firmly part of the Thai establishment; the army chief of staff is chairman of the Telephone

❑ Thai military leaders commonly control private business concerns, sometimes through their wives, children or friends, a trend that reached its peak in the early 1970s when the military dictators Thanom and Praphas held 150 company directorships. ❑

Organization of Thailand. The air force commander has in the past doubled as the chairman of Thai Airways International, but the political and economic roles of the army are now under serious review.

The 1973 student revolution produced a sea change in Thai politics that permanently weakened the legitimacy of military rule in Thailand. The military, however, retained enormous influence and has made comebacks—first in the late 1970s as part of a rightist reaction to the weak and unstable civilian coalition governments of the mid-1970s, and most recently in the 1991 coup as a result of corruption and personality clashes with members of Chatichai Choonhavan's administration.

❑ The Thai armed forces are well equipped. A few years ago they purchased cheap Chinese arms, but on finding the reliability and quality poor, they placed orders again with the Americans for M60A1 and M48A5 tanks, Kaman SH2 antisubmarine helicopters and torpedoes. Some of these new arms are to be installed on the four Chinese frigates bought earlier by Thailand. ❑

Armed guard at Bangkok's National Assembly

In recent years With the ending of the Vietnam War, the subsiding of domestic Communist insurgency, and the withdrawal of Vietnamese troops from Cambodia, the Thai army has sensed a loss of purpose. The air force wants more F16 fighters, and the navy is lobbying for more powerful vessels, but these are hardly necessary for Thailand's current defense needs, and civilian bureaucrats have resisted the demands.

■ **With very fast economic growth in recent years and a culturally permissive attitude to life, Thailand now presents a very bad case of pollution of the natural environment.** ■

Forests Degradation of the environment can be seen most dramatically with the forests, which covered more than three-quarters of the land area 50 years ago but now cover somewhat less than 20 percent. Thailand used to be a famed exporter of teak, but today it is actually a net importer of wood. Reforestation campaigns did not begin until as recently as the mid-1980s. Tough measures against illegal logging were introduced only in 1986, when sawmills were shut down and concessions revoked, yet still it continues.

The military has been used to protect reserve forests threatened by villagers. The hill tribes used to practice "slash-and-burn" agriculture, staying on a given plot of ground for only a short time and burning the trees to make fertilizer. That is now illegal.

After the disastrous 1987–88 floods, commercial logging was banned. The loss of trees from

A coconut-picking monkey, trained to work for men in the forests that men are destroying

36

watershed areas in upland districts shifted the pattern of rainfall and actually reduced the water supply to farmers below. In that bad flood, hundreds of people were drowned in the south and whole villages washed away. The removal of the trees resulted in disastrous soil erosion; whole communities were buried in mudslides.

Legislation Unfortunately, legislation is hard to implement. The logging companies are politically powerful and do not find it hard to continue logging in remote areas of Thailand by bribing officials. Many logging companies, including army enterprises, negotiated alternative contracts across the border in the Burmese, Laotian or Cambodian forests, thus exporting Thailand's environmental problem. In Laos, Thai logging companies are building hotels in return for access to the local forest stands.

Positive progress Some constructive measures were started in the 1980s. One interesting conservation project is at Ban Sup Tai village on the edge of one of Thailand's last virgin forests. This forms a national park, sheltering 180 elephants and 50 tigers.

The villagers had been poaching and encroaching on the national park. In response to this, voluntary groups from Bangkok organized German finance and set up a number of measures including a credit cooperative, a cooperative store, animal husbandry activities, tree planting and conservation awareness sessions.

Now these villagers have stopped farming inside the park boundary, and the barking deer and elephants have returned to the fringes of the village for the first time in over a

❑ Bangkok was an idyllic "village of wild plum trees" when the Chakri kings founded their capital there 200 years ago. ❑

decade. In fact, wild pigs are now feeding freely on the villagers' rich corn and soybean crops and are not being killed as they were in the past —because villagers have caught the new conservation bug and do not like to shoot them!

Air pollution There were only 12,750 registered motor vehicles in the city when King Bhumiphol was born in 1927. By the 1980s, the number of cars on Thailand's roads was increasing by their original total figure every month. Today there are nearly 2 million on the roads. More than 5 tons of lead, not to mention quantities of other toxic matter, are released into Bangkok's air every day. The problem has been aggravated by the proliferation of factories in Bangkok since the 1960s: their number has increased more than a hundredfold.

Boom! In the 1960s and '70s the urban area in the capital doubled; it then doubled again during the first half of the 1980s. This rapid sprawling development swamped any ideas of planning for transportation or other infrastructure. More than half of the country's manufacturing takes place in Bangkok. Together with Bangkok's governmental and administrative functions, this has created a nightmarish problem of traffic congestion. The average speed of traffic in the central area is only 6mph. During the school term, or in the rainy season floods, it is even worse. Some 70 percent of Thailand's energy consumption is used in transportation.

That sinking feeling Bangkok is slowly sinking, at the rate of about an inch a year. It has been suggested by a city official that it might just collapse under its own weight one day. Little can be done about it; the city grew up over a riverine delta with what used to be a network of *khlongs*, or canals, reminiscent of Venice, but now these are mostly built over. Bangkokians await their doom with customary fatalism and will no doubt go and build a new city somewhere else when it happens.

Rivers The rivers are in a disastrous state. At the mouth of Bangkok's Chao Phraya River, the mercury contamination is between seven and 40 times the accepted safe level, and accumulated heavy metal in fish and shellfish is 10 to 20 times greater than safety standards.

Bangkok uses so much water that there is now talk of diverting a major northeastern river into the Chao Phraya. The booming tiger-prawn fishery business has caused the destruction of many of Thailand's

A traffic policeman equipped with respirator in Bangkok

> ❏ "The purpose of development is to create a liveable environment."
> —King Bhumiphol. ❏

ancient mangrove swamps. Things are no better in rural areas, where farmers have for decades been applying too much chemical fertilizer and insecticide. The malignant residue remains in canals, rivers and reservoirs. Once in the soil, it gets into the food chain and builds up to fatally toxic levels in animals. This will inevitably affect humans, too. Only when the enormity of the situation has sunk in will effective action take place, as has been the case in other parts of the world.

Alternatives There are some signs that the process has begun. An Eastern form of "green" response has been "Buddhist farming," a form of organic farming influenced by the Japanese pioneer Masanobu Fukuoka (author of *The One Straw Revolution*). Its main features include the abandonment of chemical pesticides and herbicides in favor of natural herbal sprays and the encouragement of natural predators such as birds. Soil fertility is maintained by natural leaf-based fertilizers and intercropping (the practice of growing a variety of crops in the same field). The West's growing interest in organic farming is giving Thai pioneers in this field, such as Prawase Wasi and Wibul Khemchalerm, renewed confidence.

Fighting back Some local lobbies have succeeded in protecting their environment against development damage. Popular opposition buried the important Nam Choan dam scheme in 1988, despite determined efforts of successive governments to launch it.

The $44 million tantalum plant at Phuket, constructed in spite of intense local objections, was burned to the ground in 1985 after 50,000 people had demonstrated outside it. The Phuket environmentalists maintained their militant reputation in 1990 with forceful protests against

Choking the city to death?
Bangkok's traffic

the encroachment of a new yacht club development onto public land, and also demanded that a massive planned development involving the construction of seven new hotels be abandoned. The Swiss consortium's offer to include an ecological research institute in the development did not impress the people. Many beaches are now severely polluted, with raw sewage pumped straight into the sea, and unfortunately not much is being done to remedy the situation.

Meanwhile, in the northeastern province of Maha Sarakham, 1,500 villagers clashed with police in a violent demonstration against pollution of their local river by rock-salt mining. The salination of the Siew River was killing fish and turning sparkling green rice land into a moonscape. According to the National Environmental Board, 15 percent of the soil in Isan (northeast Thailand) is already badly salinated.

Changing attitudes The climate of opinion is now moving in favor of environmentalism. Those leaders with influential opinions are not just talking: they are taking action. The Thai Environmental and Community Development Association, led by Chodchoy Sophonpanich, wealthy daughter of the founder of the Bangkok Bank, launched a program to clean up Bangkok's river and canals.

Future development There is a debate in Thailand over the pace of economic growth and whether Thailand should aspire to compete with Asia's other "tiger" economies. Some argue that Thailand's future does not lie in industrialization and all its associated environmental problems, but rather in an agricultural, food-processing and service economy.

■ **Thailand provides a very pleasant surprise when it comes to food. Meals are a great social event, and Thai food is one of the major Asian cuisines, quite distinct from Chinese, Indian and Indonesian culinary styles. And now Thai food, with its low meat and fat content and profusion of skillfully prepared vegetable dishes, has become increasingly popular in the West (see also pages 102–103).** ■

Fifty years ago, the dictator Field Marshal Phibul made the use of spoons and forks compulsory in his naive attempt to Westernize the country. Before this the Thais used to eat with their hands.

As Buddhists, Thais avoid eating too much red meat, so the main dish could be shellfish, game or fish, perhaps cooked with a sauce of *galingale* (mild ginger), tamarind, lemon grass and chili. The dishes are often washed down with chilled beer—Singha is a favorite local brand.

The introduction of spices into Thai cooking dates roughly from the time of King Mongkut, whose encouragement of openness to Western ideas and technology also extended to the import of spices from China, India and Java. Once introduced, they became subjected to the distinctive application, mixtures and measures of Thai taste.

Quintessentially Thai That taste begins with the five flavors that also lie at the root of Chinese cooking, namely bitter, salt, sour, hot and sweet; but the Thais use them in quite a different way from the Chinese.

❑ The staple food is rice, usually eaten with a spoon. One type, a fine long grain called *khao hom mali*, is so delicious that some Thais see it as a meal in itself. Thais grow many varieties of rice, and its pearly white rice grain is in particular demand for export. ❑

❑ At least six different types of *phrik* (chili pepper) are used. The smaller the chili, the stronger it is. The smallest variety, known as "mouse droppings" (*phrik kee noo*), should be handled with particular care. ❑

Some ingredients used in Thai cuisine are not found in either Chinese or Indian cooking. Lemon grass is a tall grass (totally unrelated to the lemon), the leaf and root of which are used to flavor soups and salads, as well as curries and stews. The *makrud* leaf comes from a large type of lime tree native to Thailand. Its juice and rough green skin add a strong, tart flavor to soups, sauces and curries.

There is almost a national obsession with sauces. *Nam phrik* is an extremely spicy sauce that often proves too fiery for the Western palate, but the Thais adore it. *Nam plaa* (literally "fish water") is a pungent fish sauce made from fermenting anchovies. It is as common a condiment on the Thai dining table as salt is in the West.

Tom yam, a spicy soup containing shrimp flavored with lemon grass, kafir lime leaves, fish sauce and lemon juice, is extremely popular. *Khao tom* is a clear rice soup flavored with vinegar or chilies with scraps of meat or poultry. It is regarded as a cure-all for fevers, colds and especially hangovers.

A typical dinner might include boiled rice; two soups; a bland

Chinese-style stir-fried vegetable; a pungent Indian-style curry; and boned chicken wings, stuffed with ground pork and spices and then steamed and subsequently fried, served with a sweet-sour plum sauce.

Thai curries (*kaeng*) are cooked with coconut milk or cream to thicken the stock at the end, thus softening the fierceness common in Indian curries. Red curries (*kaeng dang*) are made with Indian chili, garlic and onion laced with Thai lemon grass, makrud leaf and galanga root. Green curries are made with green chili, usually with chicken and beef. Sour curry is made with shrimp paste, used with seafood.

Coconut cream ranges beyond the curry pot to find uses in soups and desserts as well—such as spicy

An evening meal, Thai style

coconut cream and chicken soup (*tom kha gai*) or bananas in coconut cream with mango and sticky rice.

Chinese influence Thai chefs use the wok to stir-fry crispy green vegetables, sauté seasoned slivers of pork, beef and chicken, and prepare fried rice and fried noodles. Steaming fish (*plaa neung*) is another technique that the Thais have adopted from China. Thai cooking

❏ The harvest of many fruits is marked by annual pageants featuring beauty competitions to find "Miss Pineapple" or "Miss Mango." ❏

also mirrors in some ways the regional division of staple grains found in China. Rice predominates in the south, while dumplings and Chiang Mai noodles are a specialty of the north.

The Thais are extremely fond of fresh vegetables and salads (known as *yum* in Thai). Freshly cut cabbage and lettuce leaves, scallion stalks, coriander sprigs, chili pods and mint leaves are served with lightly poached seafood, eggplant, roast chicken or duck.

Fruit is by no means the least of Thailand's culinary pleasures. The tropical climate is ideal for the growing of a wide variety of fruits, such as mangos, durians, pineapples, guavas, longans, rambutans, custard apples, pomelos and jackfruits. Thailand produces about 7 million tons of fruit each year, and only about 1 percent of it is exported.

For the Thais, the "king of fruits" is the durian. Oval in shape, it is about 8–10 inches long and almost as wide. Its olive-green yellowish skin is covered with a fearsome armor of thick sharp-pointed spines up to half an inch or longer. Inside, the flesh is "custardlike"—creamy and yellow—and *extremely* pungent. Don't be put off by the smell; it really does taste good. There are at least five varieties of *mamuang* (mango), which is often eaten with glutinous rice and topped with coconut cream as a dessert. *Lamyai* is a marble-sized fruit with a hard brown skin that peels away to reveal a firm translucent flesh surrounding a black seed.

The litchi is similar to the lamyai but slightly larger with a pinkish flesh. The *mangkhut* (mangosteen)

season lasts from May until July. It is a small dark purple fruit with a white flesh that is sweet but slightly tart. Thais like to guess the number of seeds they will find inside.

Thais will eat bananas when they are fully grown but not yet ripe, fried and seasoned with sugar and salt, as a snack called *kluai chap*. If they are ripe, they can be made into all kinds of sweetmeats, including *kluai ping* (grilled banana soaked in syrup), *kluai*

> ❑ In May, the Songkhla festival has an annual fruit-carving competition. ❑

buat chi (pieces of banana boiled in coconut milk and seasoned with sugar and a pinch of salt) or *kluai khaek*, which Westerners may recognize as banana fritters.

That does not end the place of the banana in the Thai kitchen. It is turned into wrappings, cooking utensils or plates. The flowers can be put into a soup or a salad. The trunk and leaves are often borrowed for flower arrangements.

The presentation of food is extremely important. Meals are sometimes served with vegetables carved into the shape of blossoms and leaves. Desserts and salads may be garnished with roses or orchids.

Regional dishes The northeast specialty, *som tam*, is a salad made from grated unripe papaya mixed with sliced tomatoes, chopped garlic and chilies, pounded dried shrimps, fish sauce and lemon juice. Northeasterners usually like to have it with sticky rice and salted beef (the beef seasoned with pepper, marinated in garlic and soy sauce and dried in the sun).

The north is the best place to savor vegetables, eaten raw or very slightly cooked with *nam phrik ong*, which is a thick dipping sauce of tomatoes, ground pork, garlic and chili, seasoned with soy sauce and sugar and served with pork.

Many of the **central** Thailand dishes have already been described.

Mae Hong Son's early morning market, Northern Thailand

Chicken green curry is very typical, served with salted egg and yum, the Thai salad that does not use oil.

In the **southern** provinces there is an even wider range of curries, using all kinds of green, yellow or red curry paste. Some of them are very hot indeed. Southerners also enjoy fried fish, often coated with turmeric and other herbs and spices, deep fried and served with an aromatic sauce.

Western food is served in Thailand, along with many other cuisines, in restaurants and hotels, and there is a huge variety of Chinese restaurants to patronize.

But don't leave Thailand without trying Thai food. Even if you find your first Thai meal a little too hot, too spicy or too strong, don't give up. There are so many kinds of dishes that it is worth persevering—you will certainly find some that you really enjoy.

A mouth-watering market display

■ The Thai language is one of the oldest in the Orient, but Thai script is more recent. Thailand has epic folk tales drawn from mythology and modern award-winning writers. Classical works of art are often based on Buddhist religious texts, but modern works have experimented with abstract forms. Thai music is very different from the West's, using different instruments and tones. The classical orchestra accompanies the traditional *khon*, or masked dramas. ■

44

Language The spoken word is tonal: the same sound can have different meanings according to the tone with which it is pronounced. There are five tones—low, high, mid-pitch, rising and falling. Westerners find the language difficult to learn when one word—*ma*—can mean "horse," "dog" or the verb "to come," depending on intonation.

Epic tales Thai folk tales draw on Indian mythology, using themes of romance or the feats of divine heroes. They were usually written in verse form. *Khun Chang Khun Phan*

Painted fishing boat, Songkhla

is a Thai epic about a love triangle of a woman with two lovers and is often recited with a rhythmic percussion accompaniment.

Another classic is the *Ramakian*, the Thai version of the famous Indian epic *Ramayana*. The version current in Thailand today was written by the first two kings of the Chakri dynasty. It records the state ceremonies and traditions of the Thai royalty and is the theme of the large murals that adorn the walls of Wat Phra Keo, the Temple of the Emerald Buddha in Bangkok.

The *Jataka* are popular folk tales relating to the previous lives of the Buddha, mixing traditional folklore and pre-Buddhist legend with down-to-earth wisdom and high spirituality. One of the most popular, which teaches the virtue of generosity, is the tale of Prince Vessandan (a previous incarnation of the Buddha), who gives away everything, including his wife and children. Its thousand verses are usually chanted at temples over a three-day period in October, at the end of Phansa, a season of spiritual exercises and meditation.

Modern literature A journalistic heritage is reflected in modern social realism novels, which deal with problems such as poverty, prostitution and corruption, as well as the formulaic themes of cops and robbers, romance and ghost stories. Thailand's most famous novelist is Kukrit Pramoj, whose career as writer, critic and left-of-center politician eventually led him to become prime minister in 1975. One of his best-

❏ Thai script was developed by King Ramkhamhaeng in 1283. The king is said to have been responsible for the first Thai literary work, a famous stone inscription, supposedly of the late 13th century, extolling the glories of the Sukhothai kingdom. Thai script reads from left to right, although vowel sounds may be written after, before, above or below the consonant they follow. ❏

known works is **Red Bamboo**, the conflict between two boyhood friends in a remote village: one becomes a Buddhist monk, the other a Communist cell organizer. Both have a zeal for improving the village, but they disagree totally on how to do it. They finally unite to drive out a rapacious landowner.

One of the most celebrated of the new-wave writers is Pira Sudham, a Thai who writes in English about life in poverty-stricken Isan, in northeast Thailand. His *Monsoon Country* portrays the odyssey of Prem, an outcast in his own village. He is taunted by the other village children, who call him "Tadpole." Prem manages to escape his village to attend the university in Bangkok and wins a scholarship to study in England. His quest for knowledge leads him to become thoroughly Westernized, leading a life of luxury in Germany and even winning poetry prizes in Western languages. But Prem never forgets his roots in Isan. Eventually he rejects Western materialism, burns his Western clothes and goes back to his village to become a Buddhist monk.

Movies There is a trend toward social realism in recent Thai movies. One film, *American Surplus*, details the discrimination against a girl born of a Thai bar-girl and a black American G.I. *Thongpun Kokpoh* (*The Citizen*) portrays the struggles of a taxi driver from the northeast trying to make a living in Bangkok in the face of powerful and corrupt officials. *The Hunt* portrays the lives of a group of girls who have been raped and their quest for revenge against their assailants.

Painting The theme of much Thai painting is the *Tosachat*, the name given to the last ten of the Buddhistic *Jataka* tales. You see it on wall murals, temple banners, canvas paintings, manuscripts and carvings on bookcases. Some of the best examples are at Wat Suwannaram in Thonburi, where formal gestures and religious symbols are skillfully blended with naturalistic observations of people working, relaxing, gossiping and even flirting.

Modern art made its appearance with the heroic realism of the Italian sculptor Corrado Feroci. He was invited to the court of King Vajiravudh and commissioned in Thailand's first

❏ Recent research has shown that the Thais may have been the originators of many Oriental styles of ceramic design that later developed in China, not the other way around. Some pottery kilns date back to AD 900. ❏

flush of "democracy" to sculpt the Democracy Monument (1939) and the Victory Monument (1941).

During the 1960s and 1970s many Thai artists experimented with abstract forms. King Bhumiphol is an accomplished artist. The style of his more abstract works has been compared to that of Expressionist artists Edvard Munch and Oskar Kokoschka.

The arts

Lop Buri is famed as the birthplace of a distinctive and highly developed school of sculpture specializing in both Mahayana and Theravada figures of the Buddha in bronze and, later, sandstone. The best Lop Buri Buddhas are marvelously authoritative with diadems enclosing a conical *ushnisha* (the protuberance on the crown of the head symbolizing enlightenment).

Music Traditional Thai music, pentatonic in origin, is sometimes difficult for Westerners to appreciate. It is a rich polyphony of subtle variations in tone, texture and mood, tuneful and often played at a fearsome pace. Behind the strange melodies lies an eight-note scale, but unlike Western music the stress is on full-note intervals without semitones.

One common instrument is the *pi*, a woodwind instrument with a reed mouthpiece. You can hear it being played at Thai boxing contests. The

classical shadow theater (*nang*) and dance-dramas, *khon*.

Khon, or masked drama, is one of several traditional forms that were revived by the early Chakri kings. It is believed to be about 400 years old

> ❏ "…[In Thai music] not a single note between a starting note and its octave agrees with any of the notes of the European scale."
> —Sir Hubert Parry, 19th-century British composer. ❏

and is almost always an enactment of the *Ramakian*. It developed from the ancient Thai arts of *nang yai* ("shadow play") and *krabee-krabong*, which is a form of theatrical fencing. Originally all the actors wore masks and mimed one of the 138 *Ramakian* episodes to the music of a piphat orchestra. Over the centuries the costumes and headdresses have

Thai musicians

pin is similar to the Indian banjo (*vina*), while the *ranad ek* is like a woodblock xylophone. Bamboo-pipe instruments are common in the north and northeast. In some of them several bamboo pipes are bound together to form a sort of harmonica called a *khaen*.

The Thais have developed their own version of a classical orchestra, called a *piphat*, which can include as many as 20 players. The *piphat* was the traditional accompaniment to

become more and more stylized. There are also established musical idioms for moods such as anger and grief and actions such as weeping.

One of Thailand's most famous pop stars is not technically a Thai at all. Billy Ogan is the son of a Catholic Filipino father and Thai mother and still carries a Philippine passport, though he calls himself a Thai and appears onstage with jasmine garlands draped around his neck. He began as a model and film star, but made singing hits with "Billy, Billy" in 1987 and "Billy Khem" in 1988.

■ **The ancient art of Thai massage—**
nuat phaen boran—is quite an experience.
Like other Eastern forms of massage,
it balances the body's energies by
working on the acupressure points and
meridians—sen—in a similar way to
acupuncture. It can be quite vigorous,
but it feels wonderful and it's certainly
a great cure for sitting in any one place
too long. ■

The beach is a good place to find a massage. Pattaya and Phuket in particular are home to the bands of blue-shirted women who have cards of accreditation; most hire out their services individually. Hotels and guest houses will also provide facilities, and the larger ones, such as The Pearl in Phuket, will have specialized staff.

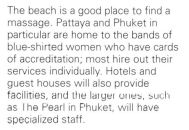

❏ *Caveat emptor!*
Watch out for the distinction between the ancient and "modern" massages. The latter is a quaint euphemism for sexual services, and some establishments, such as the Jansom Chumphon (sister of the famous Jansom Thara in Ranong), offer both! ❏

Where to go In Bangkok, traditional massage is available at many large hotels. The "jet-lag" massage in the Oriental's Health Spa will soothe fatigue. **The Two Doctors** apothecary shop is on Ha Prachan Road near Wat Mahathat. Here are preserved some traditions of the Thai masseur, such as the prayer to Jivaka Kumarabaccha, the Buddha's personal physician and early disciple. The scriptures mention practices that bear a striking resemblance to those of today.

The home of traditional healing, Wat Po, has two pavilions of 20 beds each and a cool marble floor. **Buatip Thai Massage** opposite the Landmark on Sukhumvit Road is among the modern-looking places that just do the ancient massage.

Several blind masseurs are employed for their heightened tactile sensitivity.

The Patpong area has **Vejakorn**, 37/25 Surawong Plaza and **Marble House** at Soi Surawong Plaza. Small cubicles are provided, and, at the latter, voluminous cotton trousers. The price for having your body pummeled may vary between 100 (or slightly less) and 200 baht, including a tip for the masseur. The supposedly higher-quality Buatip charges 300 baht.

Pleasure or pain? Thai massage

■ **Thailand is well served with internal flights—Thai Airways has a large number of flights to all important cities and major tourist resorts—and a railroad network extends into most regions of the country. Buses run in and between most towns and cities, but in city centers the traffic can be chaotic. Riverboats are the favorite means of travel from Bangkok upriver—to Ayutthaya, for example.** ■

48

In the early days The first rickshaw was introduced to Bangkok about 1871, and within a generation it became so popular that the government had to regulate its control and safety. Horse-drawn trams arrived in 1888, and were later converted into electric trams. Just after the beginning of the new century, Prince Rabi, one of King Chulalongkorn's sons, could be seen driving Thailand's first motorcar.

Railroads The first railroads were completed in 1900, between Bangkok and Nakhon Ratchasima.

On the road, Southern Thailand

Major railroad lines now connect the cities of Chiang Mai, Nong Khai and Ratchathani with Bangkok. Trains also run directly into Malaysia and Singapore. Before the Indo-China War there were trains to Cambodia too,

and these routes are being resumed. Trains are often more comfortable than buses over long distances—but tickets must be booked several days (at least) in advance.

Canals and rivers Bangkok was full of khlongs (canals) until the 1950s, with many small boats plying up and down. Although that network has collapsed, the mayor of Bangkok has organized a limited service of river and canal taxis along those waterways that remain. The Chao Phraya express service is great fun and can be picked up from many points on either side of the river. There are also long-tailed boat taxis, which are shared with other passengers. In northern Thailand, the boat trip from Tha Ton to Chiang Rai is highly recommended for its views, while Nong Khai offers scenic cruises on the Mekong River.

❑ Bangkok traffic averages only 2½mph. Hardened international travelers will tell you that only Lagos, in Nigeria, is worse. ❑

Buses running regular routes in the city are reliable and cheap, once you get the hang of how to use them. The conductor keeps tickets and loose change in a metal tube about 16 inches long. The hinged metal lid of the tube is used to clip off tickets from the roll.

Although buses are frequent, the signs are seldom in English and can be confusing. Local passengers will often help you if you get lost or confused.

There are three kinds of buses in Bangkok: the regular public buses which follow a more or less standard timetable along fixed routes; air-conditioned buses connecting the main bus stations and centers; and private air-conditioned bus services which are available at many hotels and offices with a deluxe service. Buses are inexpensive, but nearly always packed.

Alternatives in town Many *tuk tuks* —motorized trishaws (*samlors*)—are cheaper than taxis over short distances, provided you bargain a little. Most *tuk tuk* drivers rent their vehicles and work long hours to ensure that they at least break even. The original nonmotorized *samlors* still survive in the provinces, but

❏ People often complain that when Thai civil servants take out their scissors to cut red tape, "they cut it lengthwise." ❏

Samlors in the rush hour

were banned in Bangkok some years ago. In Chiang Mai and other regional centers there are *songthaews*— small pickup trucks with two rows of seats—which pursue a more or less fixed route.

Taxis, where all the windows can be tightly closed and some air-conditioning turned on, afford a little more comfort but can be expensive.

❏ Until the 1930s, trains and canal boats were the only means of communication between Bangkok and the provinces. ❏

The swampy nature of Bangkok's location prohibits the building of an underground transportation network, and long-standing plans for an overhead transit system have still not been realized. Thai red tape takes years to unravel; meanwhile, the traffic pileups get worse.

For practical advice on using public transportation see pages 114–115 and 270–272.

■ **The king is indisputably the most famous person in Thailand. His portrait appears everywhere, his name is endlessly invoked, his appearances attract huge crowds. Besides the king, there is a host of former prime ministers, military leaders and business men and women who have high profiles. Other well-known figures include authors, Buddhist monks, a beauty queen and a pop singer.** ■

Royalty and politics On one of his regular walks through remote villages, the king discovered that people knew in advance that he was coming and would "get things ready" for him. He decided not to tell anybody where he wanted to go, so that his fairly large retinue would set out with no idea of their destination. However, this proved too chaotic in terms of logistics, so now the king compromises. Half of the visits are a surprise, half are planned ahead—a very Thai solution!

The king's daughter, Princess Sirindhorn, who frequently stands in for him on public occasions, is also a celebrated figure, as are former prime ministers like Thanom Kittikachorn, Kukrit Pramoj and his brother Seni Pramoj, Prem Tinsulanonda and Chatichai Choonhavan. Prem was the epitome of the traditional-style consensus politician, ready to wait a long time to win unanimous approval before going ahead with any decision.

Chatichai's moment of fame, before his premiership in the late 1980s, was in defusing an Arab hijack of hostages from the Israeli embassy in Bangkok. Chatichai, then a Foreign Office official, persuaded the Arabs to change their Israeli hostages for Thai volunteers, including himself. He flew with the hijackers and Thai hostages to Cairo.

Chaovalit Yongchaiyudh, an energetic ex-general, suggested that corrupt politicians should be beheaded. He was elected Prime Minister in November 1996.

At a slightly lower level, General · Chamlong Srimuang, the mayor of Bangkok and a Buddhist ascetic, has endeared himself to the Bangkok population. He has foresworn sex, meat and liquor, sleeps on the floor and is regular in his Buddhist prayers.

❑ Kukrit Pramoj was a graduate of Queen's College, Oxford, where he was renowned for having a keg of beer always open in his room. He insists that he knows all the 2,000 fish in his fish pond by name. He is also very proud of the two chicks he reared personally when the mother hen died. ❑

Pop star Billy Ogan

The king visits his people

Popular entertainment In the world of Thai entertainment the name of Billy Ogan, a pop singer who has a Filipino father and a Thai mother, ranks very high. Ogan, who is Catholic, not Buddhist, was an extremely popular model during the late 1980s and became an adulated pop star.

Writers Thailand's most famous writers are Kukrit Pramoj, author of *Red Bamboo*, and the new-wave writer Kampoon Boontawee. Kukrit also wrote *Four Reigns*, a fictionalized story of the royal family, of which he is a minor son. Since he founded the newspaper *Siam Rath*, one of the few successful radical publications, he is also highly regarded among journalists. He also portrayed the prime minister of Sarkis in the 1963 movie *The Ugly American*, in which Marlon Brando was the star.

Well-known women Many of Thailand's famous women have made their name in the business world. Phornthip Narongdej is senior executive of Siam Motors; others include Lersak Sombatsiri, owner of the Hilton Hotel, and Sirilak Patanakorn, a graduate of the London School of Economics, who was president of the Bangkok Stock Exchange.

Religious figures Some Buddhist monks have become celebrities in Thailand, such as Phra Bodhirak, a former TV producer and singer, who is now the flamboyant and controversial leader of the radical Santi Asoke sect. Buddhadasa, the founder of the Suan Mokh movement, is well known throughout the country for preaching "dharmic socialism" (see page 30).

In the world of industry and commerce, Dhanin Chearavanont

❑ Phornthip Narkhirunkanok is Thailand's most successful beauty queen to date. She became a national heroine after winning the Miss Universe competition in 1988. The Thais did not seem to care at all that she had spent almost her entire life abroad in California. ❑

and Chatri Sophonpanich, heading the Charoen Pokphand group and the Bangkok Bank, respectively, are the leaders. In both cases their father emigrated from China, and they represent the first generation to be Thai-born. Both are famous for having key friends in the leadership of the political parties and the army, and they can swing very big deals indeed.

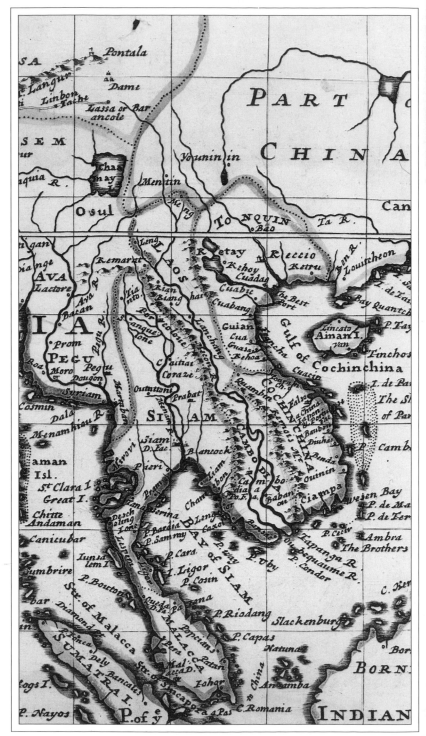

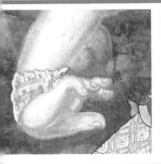

■ **The origins of the Thai people themselves are obscure. It is generally accepted that the ancestors of the Thais were, by the 7th century AD, living in the kingdom of Nanchao, in what is today China's Yunnan province. The slow migration southward began in about AD 900 and was probably hastened by the Mongol invasions of China in the mid-13th century.** ■

Beginnings Before the Thais reached Thailand, there had already been sophisticated Mon and Khmer civilizations, influenced by India, in the region. Some artifacts remain from these early cultures, in the form of Indian Gupta-style Buddhas, terracotta heads and some stucco reliefs on the walls of the few remaining buildings of antiquity.

Theravada Buddhism may have been introduced to these agrarian city-state cultures by Indian missionaries as early as the 2nd or 3rd century BC.

❑ Rama Tibodi I is noted for the promulgation of the first recorded Thai legal system. ❑

The early Thais practiced a rice agronomy. Their religion was a mix of Buddhism and animism. The country was ruled by a monarchy with periodic *corvée* (forced) labor; as yet there were no instances of peasant revolt or class warfare. In the 12th and 13th centuries, the Thai migrants from China, by now converted to Theravada Buddhism, set up little fiefdom states in the upper reaches of the Chao Phraya Valley. These began to impinge on the Khmer empire to the south and the Mons to the west in Burma.

The Sukhothai period Many histories mark the beginning of the Thais as a distinct people with King Phra Ruang's capture of Sukhothai in 1253 from the Khmers; and the

Khmer ruins in the Chao Phraya valley

Sukhothai period is often seen as the golden age in Thai history.

The Thais were strongly influenced by the Indianized culture of the Mons, especially their art, sculpture and literature. From the Khmers the Thais borrowed Brahmanical doctrines of political organization, a written script and improved agricultural technology. Sukhothai reached its peak with the late 13th-century reign of Ramkhamhaeng (the first Thai king to be called "the Great"), who extended his kingdom to the Bay of Bengal, Luang Prabang and the Malay Peninsula.

The second Thai capital was founded at Ayutthaya in 1350 by Rama Tibodi I, who captured Khmer and Sukhothai territories until his realm extended from Laos in the north and as far as the Strait of Malacca in the south.

❑ Paul Benedict (in *Austro-Thai Language and Culture*) has speculated on linguistic evidence that the Thais came from Indonesia and Southeast Asia before migrating northward into China. ❑

It was during the Ayutthaya period that elaborate royal rituals and the Khmer ideas of the king being a god were introduced. However, in spite of all the pomp and tribute, the Thai kings' power was actually quite limited until the great centralizing reforms of King Trailok (1448–88), who set up the Thai civil service and carefully stipulated the amount of land to which each rank of official was entitled. He also codified the confusing complexity of royal household etiquette and introduced the idea of having a second or vice-king to simplify succession problems.

From outside Thailand Thailand's first Western contact was with the Portuguese at the beginning of the 16th century. A century later, French, English, Japanese, Dutch and Spanish mercenaries, missionaries and traders were visiting Ayutthaya in considerable numbers. They were stunned by the wealth of the city. Thai tolerance of Westerners became strained after a charismatic Greek adventurer, Constantin Phaulkon, achieved such a high status in the Thai court that he began to take over Thailand's foreign policy, favoring the French at the expense of the Dutch. He was executed in 1688—probably the last and perhaps the only Westerner ever to have been executed in Thailand.

Throughout this period Thailand was fighting wars against the Burmese and Cambodians. After several defeats in the mid-16th century, Thailand became for a time little more than a vassal state of Burma. The Burmese invaded again in 1765. After a two-year siege, the Burmese razed the great Thai metropolis of Ayutthaya to the ground and carried off an immense amount of booty and 30,000 prisoners. The sack of Ayutthaya, with the loss of all its cultural treasures, was a terrible blow to the Thais, who have never completely forgiven the Burmese.

A temple mural from the 18th-century Wat Phra Keo, where the Emerald Buddha is contained

■ **Chao Phya Chakri became King Rama I of the new Chakri dynasty. His many achievements between 1782 and 1809 included the founding of a new royal palace and temple and the construction of Bangkok, originally designed to be an exact replica of Ayutthaya. He also reformed the Buddhist *sangha*. He repelled a full-scale invasion by Burma in 1785—and fought four more wars with Burma before his death in 1809.** ■

Before Rama I Phya Tak, or Taksin, was a general of mixed Thai–Chinese parentage, who showed great courage in fighting the Burmese. As King Taksin he established a new capital farther down the Chao Phraya River at Thonburi (on the opposite bank from Bangkok) and eventually brought the provinces and large areas of Laos under Thai control.

Taksin's descent into madness and increasing cruelty eventually led to a rebellion in Thonburi in 1782. The king's most trusted general, Tongduang (Chao Phya Chakri), was summoned back from military campaigning in Cambodia to take a lead. It was decided that both the

A Wat Phra Keo mural (below); and (above) King Rama I

❏ The first printing press was set up in Bangkok in 1835. The future King Mongkut (Rama IV) was the first Thai to set up his own press, which he used to print Buddhist books. ❏

king and the rebels should be put to death. Taksin was put into a sack and beaten to death with sandalwood clubs. So Chao Phya Chakri became King Rama I and founder of the Chakri dynasty.

The 19th century By the time Rama III was crowned, the Burmese were engrossed in fighting the British colonialists on their western frontier, leaving Thailand free to build up an empire to the east in Indochina. The early 19th century was also a time when European nations began to make a real impact on Thai life: trade treaties were signed with Britain (1826) and the United States (1833)—the first such American treaty with an Asian country.

By the late 1840s, there was increasing diplomatic and military pressure to revise earlier trade agreements, but Thailand scented the threat of Western imperialism, to which its neighbors were fast succumbing.

❏ During King Taksin's 1778 invasion of Laos, the 2,000-year-old sacred Emerald Buddha was recaptured and installed at Thonburi. ❏

■ **In 1851, King Mongkut ascended the throne of Thailand for a reign of 17 years, during which the foundations of the kingdom's modernization were firmly laid. He was succeeded by his 16-year-old son, Chulalongkorn, who instituted many reforms and succeeded in keeping the European colonial threat at bay.** ■

56

King Mongkut At the age of 20, Mongkut had been ordained as a Buddhist monk, and before becoming king he spent 27 years in the monkhood. This gave him the opportunity to tour the country, discovering the people's needs and complaints and learning much from the foreigners who had begun to reside in Thailand. In particular, he learned English from American missionaries, which he later used to advantage to correspond personally with Queen Victoria and President Lincoln.

Mongkut's achievements Mongkut had to agree to new treaties with Britain and the United States, giving foreigners extraterritorial immunity from the Thai courts. These treaties allowed Thai trade with the West to

> ❏ A *Bangkok Post* editorial called the movie *The King and I* "patronising, ignorant, stupidly comic and an affront to the Thai people." It is still officially banned, although videos circulate clandestinely in Bangkok. ❏

expand. He entirely reformed the taxation system, modernized the armed forces and police, and built roads and canals.

Mongkut was the king who hired Mrs. Anna Leonowens, an English widow from Singapore, to teach his 82 children in the palace in the 1860s. (It was her books, *An English Governess at the Siamese Court* and *The Romance of the Harem*, that formed the basis of the musical *The King and I*, in which Yul Brynner played the part of King Mongkut.)

Having studied astronomy, Mongkut astonished foreigners by correctly predicting the eclipse of the sun in 1868. It was while making the calculation in a remote part of southern Thailand that he caught malaria and died soon afterward. His 16-year-old son, Chulalongkorn, succeeded him.

King Chulalongkorn Once Anna Leonowens' star pupil, Chulalongkorn enjoyed a long reign (1868–1910) that allowed him to fulfill his father's plans and bring Thailand to the point of modernity. He traveled to Singapore, Java (in Indonesia) and India and twice to western Europe, intensifying his desire to continue the Westernization of his kingdom.

Chulalongkorn's achievements Chulalongkorn abolished the practice of perpetual prostration in the royal presence and simplified the court dress and hairstyle. He abolished slavery, reformed the Buddhist sangha, formed a council of state and privy council to regularize the government, and set up 12 departments to carry out government functions. He also wrote more than 200 books of history, archaeology, literature and public affairs. Modern schools were started, one of them destined to become Chulalongkorn University. Until then, boys—but not girls—used to study informally under the monks in the Buddhist temples.

The first railroad was opened, and currency was improved with modern minting. Everything in this absolute monarchy depended on a royal lead, so Chulalongkorn's reforming zeal was indispensable. The affection that Thais still feel toward this great king

may be observed every October 23, when they pay homage to his statue at the Royal Plaza.

Apart from the continuous and systematic modernization of the country along mainly French, British and German lines, the most important achievement during these two crucial reigns from 1851 to 1910 was the preservation of Thai independence. In the second half of his reign, Chulalongkorn was under constant pressure from the British and French colonial advance in neighboring territories. He had to cede Laos, parts of Cambodia and control of the four Malay states of Kedah, Perlis, Kelantan and Trengganu to those two European powers. This was agreed to reluctantly, and only because it fended off the threat of one or both of these European powers taking over the whole of Thailand.

This was the high tide of European colonialism. The British slowly nibbled away at the Malay states and

Opposite page: King Mongkut (Rama IV); and (above) King Chulalongkorn (Rama V)

had started to overrun Burma in 1824, while the French established a foothold in Vietnam. Thailand thus faced European imperialism on three sides: to the east, west and south.

The "open door" treaties of the 1850s postponed the threat to the kingdom's independence by satisfying the short-term commercial ambitions of the French, British and others. Luckily, the appetite for further conquest began to wane in the 1890s, and there was an agreement between Britain and France not to annex Thailand.

❏ "Never having been colonized, we can only blame ourselves for our problems."— former Prime Minister Kukrit Pramoj. ❏

■ **Chulalongkorn's immediate successors were neither as able nor as wise. The relative unpopularity of Prajadhipok led to discontent, which strengthened conspirators during the depression of the 1930s. When fighting broke out between democrats and loyalists in 1935, King Prajadhipok abdicated in disgust, leaving only his ten-year-old nephew as next in line.** ■

King Vajiravudh (reigned 1910–25) succeeded his father, Chulalongkorn. He tried to continue the reforms of his father and grandfather, although he lacked their charisma and character. The new king tried to promote nationalism by creating the Wild Tigers' Corps and the Village Scouts organizations. But this "praetorian guard" made him unpopular with the army and navy.

More changes Government ministries continued to be reformed, and Vajiravudh introduced surnames for Thai people—who had not hitherto felt the need for them. After his stay in Britain, he introduced soccer, Western-style dancing and Western hairstyles for women. He made Siam (as Thailand was then known) the first Asian country to bring in compulsory education, and opened the country's first private boarding school. He wrote copiously, under various pen names, translating many of Shakespeare's plays and giving his views on the Chinese in

❑ Vajiravudh was the first Thai king to be educated at Oxford University, where he wrote a book in English on the War of the Polish Succession. ❑

Thailand in a book called *The Jews in the Far East*. He was so generous and extravagant that the national budget was gravely overspent.

Sympathetic with the Allied cause in World War I, Vajiravudh declared war on Germany in 1917. In 1921, the Americans agreed to a new

treaty forgoing their former territorial demands, thus setting an example for other Western powers to follow in respecting Thailand's independence. This was King Vajiravudh's greatest achievement.

Whereas Mongkut had 39 wives and 82 children, and Chulalongkorn had 36 wives and 77 children, Vajiravudh preferred male company. Marrying late, he had only one child, a daughter; he was therefore succeeded by his younger brother, Prajadhipok (reigned 1925–35).

King Prajadhipok The new king, who had studied at Eton College in England, also lacked the strong will of his earlier predecessors, though he proved conscientious and thrifty and retrenched government officials by the hundreds to balance the books. When visiting the United States in 1931, King Prajadhipok shook hands with several Siamese students; this was the first time that any Siamese had ever touched his monarch without being punished.

The world depression of 1929–30 meant that the king had to reduce official salaries again, as well as raise taxes, and this emboldened a group of ambitious army and navy officers and civil servants to change the system.

The bloodless revolution On June 24, 1932, the People's Party, whose leaders were almost all European-educated, led a coup d'état to remove the absolute powers of the king and introduce democracy. The king agreed to become a constitutional monarch, and the revolution succeeded without bloodshed. A new constitution set up a national assembly, with power to name the prime minister. But the conspirators soon clashed. Their economic spokesman, Pridi Panomyong, a French-trained left-winger, was unable to persuade them to back his utopian plans to nationalize land and enterprises and put everyone on a state payroll.

When King Prajadhipok abdicated in 1935, retiring to exile in England, he left no son. The succession thus passed to his nephew, who was then a boy of 10 and in no position to withstand the ploys of the revolutionary democrats.

Offerings lie at the feet of the statue of reformer King Vajiravudh (Rama VI) in Bangkok

One of the early acts of the revolutionaries was to celebrate the arrival of democracy by changing the name of the country from Siam to Thailand. Nationalists among the "democratic" group argued that *Siam* was not a Thai word but one used by foreigners to describe Thailand and therefore unsuitable for a free and independent country. They also reasoned that the 23 million Thai-speaking people beyond the frontiers, in southern China, French Indochina and Burma, needed to be reflected in the kingdom's name. One of the coup leaders, Phibul, decided on Thailand as the new name, although many criticized it as being a bastardized compound—*Thai* meaning "free" and *land* being an English word.

■ **Two men dominated Thai public life during the quarter-century following the 1932 revolution—Pridi Panomyong and Phibul Songkram. Pridi was a brilliant Doctor of Law from the University of Paris, who served as regent while King Ananda Mahidol was a minor and then later as prime minister. Phibul became prime minister and army commander-in-chief, surviving difficult times to stay in power for some 20 years.** ■

Pridi Panomyong Part Chinese, Pridi had extremely egalitarian views —bordering on Marxist—although he was acquitted of being a Communist by a high-powered committee including a royal prince, the chief justice and a British legal adviser. He became foreign minister and tackled the further revision of treaties with foreign countries, something high on the agenda of the revolutionaries.

After Thailand declared war on Britain and the United States in 1942, Pridi organized an underground resistance movement against the Japanese. When the Japanese surrendered, Pridi, in his capacity as regent, officially repudiated the earlier declaration of war on the United States and Britain, which saved Thailand immense trouble in the postwar period. In the following year, Pridi became prime minister.

At this point Pridi seemed to be in the ascendant, triumphing over his conservative opponents. But an unexpected tragedy snatched the prize from his grasp. The young king, who had returned from Switzerland, where he had been studying, was found dead in bed in the Grand Palace on June 9, 1946, a revolver by his side and a bullet wound in his head. The story behind his death has remained a puzzle, in spite of public investigations. Meanwhile the economy had suddenly plunged, with high prices and scarcity of food, and this encouraged the right-wingers to act. There was another bloodless coup d'état in November 1947, as a result of which Pridi had to flee the country, leaving his rival, Phibul, as the new army commander-in-chief, poised for a prolonged domination of the country's politics.

Pridi Panomyong poses with his family during his years of exile

Phibul Songkram was one of the leaders of the 1932 revolution. He had led the army again in the coup d'état of 1933. In 1938, he was made prime minister on a platform of national reconstruction on progressive lines. In the immediate

> ❏ Phibul decreed that men and women should wear Western clothes, kiss each other in public, give up chewing betel nuts and learn Western dancing. ❏

aftermath of World War II, Phibul was in semidisgrace, having backed the Japanese side. But he soon made a comeback, being confirmed as army commander-in-chief in 1947 and resuming the premiership in 1948.

Phibul excluded Chinese from many occupations (including farming, taxi-driving and hairdressing) and made Chinese schools teach the Thai language and culture. Following a visit to many Western countries, his hitherto autocratic regime became more liberal; he had come back deeply impressed by the way in which democratic government was carried out in the West.

He encouraged public debate, passed many labor laws and recognized the Trades Union Congress. The result was that the government's manipulation of the general elections of 1957 was exposed and denounced, whereas before it would have been endured in silence.

Phibul himself was no money-grabber, but others in his cabinet were hugely corrupt, especially his minister of defence, Sarit Thanarat. In July 1957, disaffected army officers led by Sarit deposed Phibul, and he fled to exile in Japan.

Phibul's resilience was legendary. He was once shot in the neck and shoulder at a soccer match, but recovered. A couple of years later, his family dinner was poisoned, but again he recovered. He escaped from a ship where he was being held by rebels in the middle of the Chao Phraya River. His side strafed the vessel and everyone jumped overboard, but he swam to the bank held by rebel soldiers. Later, a prince who had witnessed the scene asked why he hadn't made for his own side. Phibul replied that no one

> ❏ Pridi's great memorial is Thammasat University, which he founded, and which remains a center of radical thinking in Thailand. ❏

would have recognized him in the dark, and anyway, those on his side were better shots!

Both of these leaders remained in exile. Pridi spent many years in Canton, in the People's Republic of China, and later lived just outside Paris. He made several attempts during successive Thai governments to return, but none of them felt the risk was worthwhile, given the former prime minister's powerful personality and radical views.

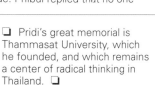

■ **The great international wars of the 20th century were crucial in the formation of Thai policy and the alignment of the kingdom in its regional and global setting. Thailand entered World War I on the side of the British and French; the position in World War II was more complicated; while the Vietnam War was far closer to home and much more dangerous.** ■

World War I In spite of the trouble it had experienced at their hands in the colonial period, Thailand backed the British and French in the Great War. This was largely because King Vajiravudh had become an Anglophile, with many English friends from his years at Sandhurst military college and at Christ Church, Oxford. The decision enabled Thailand to participate in the conference of Versailles in 1919 and to lobby effectively for the abolition of the unequal treaties with Western countries.

World War II saw fierce fighting going on in neighboring countries and a seemingly unstoppable Japanese advance. There was no reason for Thailand to become involved in the European war, but

Thai soldiers help a released prisoner of war in Vietnam

Thailand and Japan had the distinction of being the only Asian countries to be independently represented at Versailles, and they had naturally formed some ties.

When Japan sent its armies into China and Southeast Asia, attacking European colonies, the Thais had mixed feelings. The Japanese could hardly restrain themselves from occupying Thailand after their success in Vietnam, and there was no effective British or French force available to protect Thailand.

Temptingly, the Japanese offered to restore some of the territory that Thailand had had to give up to France earlier. The Thais actually had a short war with France in early 1941 and lost a naval engagement.

One of Phibul's advisers warned that Japan's intention was "to chase away the white men from Asia and put itself in their shoes." But Phibul's government declared war on the

Allies, though it allowed a degree of ambiguity as to whether the declaration had been effectively delivered to them. Thailand continued technically independent and sovereign throughout the war period.

The presence of more than 50,000 Japanese troops made it impossible for Phibul to act against Japan. All the same, he was no puppet: he would not enter the Japanese Co-Prosperity Sphere, or attend the Greater East Asia Conference, or

Japan was defeated in 1945, a new pro-Allied government was able to take over in Bangkok. This was the moment for Pridi, who was able to persuade the Allies not to treat Thailand as an enemy but almost as a friend. There was no formal occupation by the British army, as might have been expected.

The Vietnam War By 1954, the Thais had already joined Pakistan and the Philippines with the Western powers in the South East Asia Treaty

A U.S. pilot makes contact

send his children for schooling in Japan. A measure of real independence was maintained.

Meanwhile, Thais who disagreed

❏ "...like a fox arbitrating a dispute between two rabbits in a cabbage patch, preparing to fatten them before eating both of them."—An American critic of the Japanese offer.
"What would you do if you were a rabbit?"—A future Thai prime minister. ❏

with the Axis alignment started a Free Thai Movement in the United States that linked with pro-Allied agents within Thailand, so when

Organisation; under it, Thailand provided bases from which American bombers wreaked havoc on Vietnam in the 1960s and early 1970s.

Thailand had little option but to join the United States in contesting Vietnamese Communism, which was loudly hostile to Thailand. The Queen's Cobra Regiment of Thailand actually served in South Vietnam, fighting the Communists. Yet Thailand's other neighbors were mostly neutral in the conflict.

When the Vietnam War ended in 1975, it was followed by the Vietnamese invasion of Cambodia. This was also a threat to Thailand, and the Thais collaborated in helping those resisting Vietnamese occupation, including the Khmer Rouge, whose brutal treatment of their own population shocked the world.

■ **After the two dominating personalities of Pridi and Phibul came three more generals who tried to play the same role, though less successfully. Field Marshal Sarit Thanarat was succeeded by the weaker Field Marshal Thanom Kittikachorn and his portly, pugnacious deputy, Field Marshal Praphas Charusathien.** ■

Field Marshal Sarit Thanarat

Sarit was half Laotian. He had the temerity to bundle Phibul out of the country, largely because the former dictator had interfered with Sarit's improper profits from the state lottery. In spite of his corruption, however, he proved to be rather popular. He reversed many of Phibul's unpopular reforms, including those dictating the style of dress; he even tried to bring down the prices of electricity, sugar, charcoal and other items. The Chinese were encouraged, during his dictatorship, to feel that they were an accepted part of Thai society. He brought the young King Bhumiphol forward and gave him a bigger role in public affairs—something that the king fully exploited—as a symbol of Thai nationalism and traditional culture.

Sarit could also be tough: he closed down the weekly dance at the Lumphini Garden; arrested men with long hair, tight pants or flashy clothes; made rock-and-roll and the Twist illegal; and ordered summary executions of arsonists.

Sarit often expounded the idea that democracy needed to be adapted to the Thai genius in order to succeed. Political parties were abolished. Sarit governed without a parliament and managed to postpone indefinitely the writing of a new constitution. He set a new precedent in Thailand for open army rule. He never studied abroad and did not share the ideals of those who promoted Western-style parliamentary democracy. His direction of the economy proved invaluable, since he turned away from the state-enterprise ideas of both Pridi and Phibul to encourage investment of private capital, both domestic and foreign. Sarit's First Six-Year Plan (1961) provided the basis for the economic development that was to astonish observers later.

Everyone knew that Sarit had a strong appetite for sex and that he had many mistresses. Only after his death in 1963, however, did it come out that he maintained 100 mistresses in great style, using illegal income from various official funds and government influence for private financial gain. Sarit left an estate of $140 million on his death, and everyone knew that it could not have come from his salary.

Field Marshal Thanom Kittikachorn

Sarit's successor was reticent by comparison. Under Thanom's rule, from 1963 to 1973, the army had to come to terms with the idea of a constitution. After many years of drafting, a new constitution was proclaimed by the king in 1968. This made the prime minister responsible to parliament, and a general election was held in 1969. Thanom's party won a majority. But the various parliamentarians were so demanding and so unwilling to collaborate with the government in administering the country, and there was such insurgency in the border areas that

---

❑ Thanom's son, Narong, married Praphas's daughter and became particularly hated as a crude implementer of the dictators' commands. The three were nicknamed "father, son and wholly gross." ❑

Thanom abrogated the constitution and proclaimed martial law in 1971.

Thanom and his deputy, Field Marshal Praphas Charusathien, were then faced with renewed demands for democracy and a constitution, and this came to a head in a bloody confrontation in 1973.

The student uprising of 1973 (see also pages 66–67) The students' revolt was sparked by the refusal of Premier Thanom's government to speed up the drafting of a new constitution. When 25 democrats protested near Thammasat University, half of them were arrested, and this inspired about 100,000 students to take part in a rally and protest march to the police headquarters.

The explosion came on October 14, 1973, when the soldiers and students made bloody battle, leaving 69 dead and more than 800 wounded, while the police HQ was burned down. Thanom and Praphas resigned and were advised by the king to leave the country to prevent further violence.

The era of Thanom and Praphas was beneficial for Thailand in economic affairs and in many other respects. Sarit's policies were broadly followed, especially within the economy. But a harmful precedent was created in asserting the army's right to rule, and it did nothing for the concept of clean government.

Field Marshal Sarit Thanarat (center), one of the Thai generals

■ The students who had been so successful in 1973 sought to consolidate and extend their newfound power. They formed an alliance with workers and peasant groups and also, to some extent, with the Communist party of Thailand. The army leaders were demoralized by the exposure of corruption, and the new senior general showed no desire to enter government. The proliferation of political parties made democratic government ineffective. The king therefore filled the power vacuum. ■

King Bhumiphol came into his own after Thanom and Praphas fled, appointing as new prime minister a British-trained judge, Sanya Dharmasakdi. The first civilian head of government for more than two decades, Sanya and the king organized a large National Convention to elect a new Legislative Assembly.

The students and workers were forming groups and unions without police registration, contrary to the law, but Sanya persevered and a general election was held at the beginning of 1975. The first elected prime minister under the new

An anti-generals statement

constitution was Kukrit Pramoj, a minor royal who is also a brilliant editor and novelist. Kukrit's chief success was in diplomacy. He was the first Thai premier to visit the People's Republic of China, where he secured the opening of diplomatic relations between the two countries. But his parliamentary support was unstable, and another election was held in 1976, which led to his elder brother, Seni Pramoj, becoming prime minister.

A rash of strikes broke out in factories, often supported by the students. In rural areas, the new phenomenon of landless tenant farmers led to the formation of peasant organizations to lobby for improvement. The Farmers' Federation of Thailand was set up with student help and became a large and powerful body. In November 1974, about 50,000 students and farm laborers, led by young Buddhist monks, demonstrated in Bangkok.

While the army had been willing to take a back seat in the political arena after the scandals of previous military dictators, it was greatly concerned by the growth of radical and sometimes Communist-influenced pressure groups in the country. The students seemed oblivious of the backlash that their actions were inviting.

Right-wing backlash Just as the students had sponsored new radical groups, so now right-wing military officers countered by sponsoring or

supporting rightist movements. Some of them had wide popular support in the middle class and lower-middle class. The most famous of these was the Red Gaurs, organized by the controversial Major General Sudsai Hasdin, who commanded the army's Internal Security Operations Command. The Red Gaurs became in effect a paramilitary group, recruiting former mercenaries who had fought against the Communists in Laos. Other supporters for Red Gaur were vocational students in Bangkok, who

> ❏ A charismatic monk supported the right-wing group Navapol, preaching that it was not a sin to kill Communists. ❏

had distanced themselves from the more radical university students and were more concerned about jobs than political ideals.

Another group was Navapol, also established by right-wing army officers. It stood for a commitment to the Thai monarchy, nation and Buddhism.

In 1974–75, the leadership of the farmers' movement was systematically assassinated, and in 1976 some 30 leading personalities of left-wing parties were killed. The 1976 elections produced a weak civilian coalition government, which was not able to prevent the army from arranging for the former dictators, Thanom and Praphas, to

return to Thailand.

Two students distributing posters for the expulsion of Thanom were arrested in September 1976, and later found hanged. This sparked large scale student protest, and on October 5 a group of students staged a mock hanging to publicize the murder of their two comrades. The next day large numbers of Navapol, Red Gaurs and other right-wing organizations launched an assault on Thammasat University.

Massacre Many students were brutally murdered. Some were lynched, burned alive, beheaded or had their eyes gouged out. When the apparently gentle Thai turns nasty, the results can be horrifying. This prompted yet another coup d'état by armed forces leaders, and the king installed as the new prime minister a strongly anticommunist judge, Thanin Kraivixien. The right-wing reaction to student radicalism now set in.

The 1973 uprising

■ **Judge Thanin turned out to be the most repressive prime minister in Thai history and was soon ousted by the army leaders, who put one of their own men, the pipe-smoking moderate General Kriangsak Chomanan, into the premiership. He could not retain the support of the army and stepped down in 1980. Another general, Prem Tinsulanonda, took over, and he was to transform the face of Thai politics entirely.** ■

Judge Thanin was an ideological rightist who banned political parties and student groups, made strikes illegal, imposed strict censorship and made thousands of arbitrary arrests. He even ordered Thomas More's *Utopia* and George Orwell's books to be burned. Many of the student leaders involved in the 1973 uprising now left Bangkok in fear of their lives. They went "to the forest" (the jungle) to join Communist Party guerrillas. (See page 185.) There they

> ❑ General Kriangsak Chomanan invited the returned leftist students to his house and cooked breakfast for them. ❑

were disillusioned to find that the Communist leaders in Thailand were mostly Chinese and ardent Maoists, many of whom could not even speak Thai. Eventually, when the fury of the right-wing backlash had subsided, most came home to Bangkok.

The 1982 bicentennial of the Chakri dynasty—one of Prem's public relations successes

During this period of right-wing backlash in the late 1970s, Thailand had to cope with the withdrawal of the Americans from Vietnam and the fall of South Vietnam, formerly capitalist, to Communist control. It was a time of nervousness and danger, because the Vietnamese Communists, free from engagement with U.S. forces, were able to turn their attention to Laos and Cambodia on the Thai frontier.

When Thanin was ousted, **General Kriangsak Chomanan** came to power, and he returned to a more open style of government and removed many of the restrictions, even holding elections in 1979. But in spite of his efforts, General Kriangsak could not command the support of the army. He gave way to General Prem Tinsulanonda.

General Prem was no great intellect and had no strong power base of his own apart from the support of some other generals. Instead, he offered a style of leadership that was calm and consensus-based. He began as a serving officer heading the government and ended eight years later as a prime minister nominated by the elected National Assembly.

In the 1980s, the Thai economy first began to sprint—especially from 1987, when Thais sensed that they could become the next Newly Industrialized Economy in Asia—and double-digit growth was maintained for four years running.

Perhaps the vital thing for Thailand was that General Prem listened to the technocrats in the civil service

and followed their advice, particularly about the economy. Prem brought his senior planners and Finance Ministry officials into regular consultation with private businessmen, under his own chairmanship, to resolve disputes between the private and public sectors that were harming the economy. He agreed to a substantial devaluation of the baht, something that is always difficult for non-economists to accept.

He did not lack rivals and enemies within the armed forces. Two coups

General Prem sings for Thai TV

d'état were attempted during his premiership, and many physical attacks made on him. When General Arthit Kamlang ok opposed the baht devaluation and called Prem a liar, Prem dismissed the army commander.

Prem's genial manner endeared him to almost everyone, from the king down to ordinary citizens. He ensured the success of the double celebration in 1982 of the bicentennial of the Chakri dynasty and of the foundation of the new capital at Bangkok. Both events gave the king a great deal of publicity. The royal gratitude was expressed when King Bhumiphol gave his personal protection to General Prem during one of the unsuccessful coup attempts.

However, the king became gravely ill in 1982 and was out of public life for three months.

By allowing the constitutional political process to resume, providing him with an elected cabinet, Prem satisfied the liberals, while his stern attitude to crime and corruption pleased the right wing. This formula might have gone on for longer, but after almost a decade, one of the MPs threatened to reveal secrets of the bachelor Prem's private life. At that point, in 1988, he stepped down, leaving the political parties in the National Assembly to find their own candidates.

Prem will take his place in history as the man who served as the leader of a civilian administration longer than anyone else and who gave technocrats their head.

■ **The man who stepped into Prem's shoes as prime minister in 1988 was a former cavalry general turned diplomat and businessman, Chatichai Choonhavan, leader of the Chart Thai party, which was the largest in the elected Assembly. For three years Chatichai set a rather different style of government from that of the passive Prem.** ■

70

Under Chatichai the economy began to develop rapidly, with 10 percent annual growth and the private sector leading. Businessmen occupied many of the party leadership and cabinet positions during the Chatichai era. Many new development projects were started, and there was fierce controversy about alleged corruption.

Chatichai (above), and his deputy, General Chaovalit Yongchaiyudh, elected Thailand's Prime Minister in November 1996

By this time, the amounts of money involved in election-time vote-buying and bribery had multiplied. The political parties needed more funds to be sure of doing well in elections, and ministerial corruption—a bribe in return for official approval of a big project—was the easiest way to get them. The army in particular urged changes in the constitution to make elected MPs resign their seats if they joined the cabinet.

Coup In February 1991, the army leadership united to depose Chatichai, complaining of his bad treatment of the army and army interests, as well as the corruption that was rife in his cabinet. In the early morning of Saturday, February 23, 1991, soldiers left their barracks to take control of key government buildings. In most cases, they numbered only 50 or fewer. They were not resisted, and no blood was shed. Prime Minister Chatichai was arrested later that morning. The premier was later released unharmed and left for exile in England.

That afternoon, the supreme commander announced the total seizure of power by his armed forces. The constitution, Senate and House of Representatives were all summarily abolished. In the evening General Sunthorn and his deputy, General Suchinda, flew north to

❏ The supreme commander of the armed forces was well known for his tight-fitting uniforms and passion for flying helicopters. ❏

explain their action to the king. The king endorsed the coup in a slightly lukewarm manner, though he apparently sympathized with the criticisms of the civilian government's corruption. Yet he recalled Premier Chatichai from England to present him with a royal honor, and afterward the military junta gathered at Chatichai's house to pour holy water over his hands for the Thai New Year.

Chatichai and other politicians were later investigated for corruption, but the special investigators appointed by the military junta could not find the evidence they wanted.

The army installed a caretaker government under an ex-bureaucrat, Anand Panyarachun, who named a cabinet of technocrats and businessmen. This administration was able to clear some of the backlog of difficult decisions left by Chatichai.

The military junta held elections in March 1992, and army generals brains behind the 1991 coup, although ostensibly they had been supporting General Suchinda Kraprayoon. The Samakki Tham won 78 seats to become the biggest in the House of Representatives. The Chart Thai party of Sombun Rahong opted to make common cause with the group of generals around Suchinda. It came second with 73 seats.

Within months, demonstrators filled the streets of Bangkok to call for a democratically chosen prime minister, rather than one named by

General Suchinda Kraprayoon

formed political parties to contest them. One party (the New Aspiration Party) was the creation of General Chaovalit Yongchaiyudh, deputy prime minister in the Chatichai government. NAP became the third-largest party in the new 1992 parliament. Other senior army officers organized another party (the Samakki Tham). They were the

the military. In all, 52 pro-democracy demonstrators were killed in violent clashes with the army. The massacre resulted in Suchinda losing office. In September, a civilian government was elected, with Chuan Leekpai as prime minister. Chuan's democratic credentials enabled his unusually scandal-free administration to survive for over two and a half years, a record in modern Thai politics.

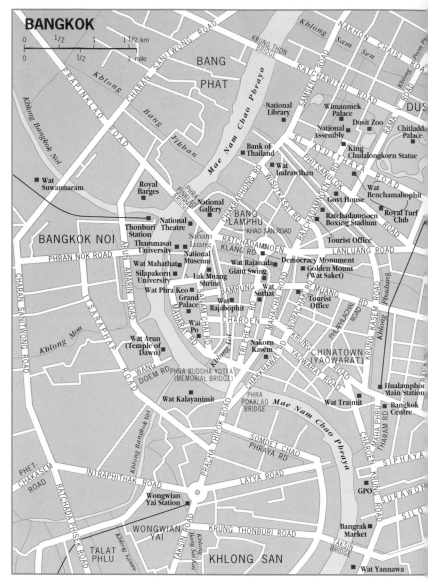

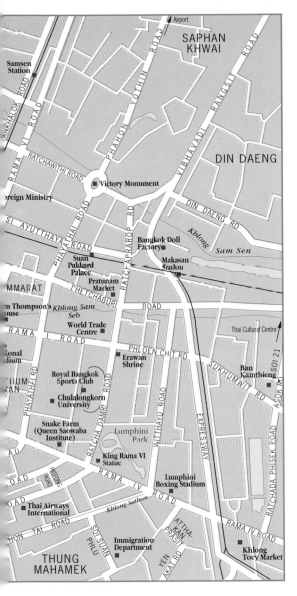

BANGKOK

Airport

SAPHAN KHWAI

Samsen Station

DIN DAENG

Victory Monument

Foreign Ministry

DIN DAENG RD

SI AYUTTHAYA ROAD

Khlong
Sam Sen

Bangkok Doll
Factory

Suan
Pakkard
Palace

Makasan
Station

MMARAT

PHETCHABURI

Pratunam
Market

Jim Thompson's Khlong Sam
House Seb

ROAD

Thai Cultural Centre

World Trade
Centre

RAMA ROAD

PHLOEN CHIT RD

National
Stadium

Erawan
Shrine

SUKHUMVIT RD

ASOK SOI 21

Ban
Kamthieng

Royal Bangkok
Sports Club

Chulalongkorn
University

Snake Farm
(Queen Saowaba
Institute)

Lumphini
Park

King Rama VI
Statue

Lumphini
Boxing Stadium

EXPRESSWAY

RAMA IV ROAD

RATCHADA PHISEK ROAD

Thai Airways
International

Khlong Sathon

Immigration
Department

THUNG
MAHAMEK

Khlong
Toey Market

RAMA IV ROAD

CITY HIGHLIGHTS ◄◄◄◄◄

GRAND PALACE AND WAT PHRA KEO *see pages 78–81*

JIM THOMPSON'S HOUSE *see page 87*

NATIONAL MUSEUM *see pages 88–91*

THONBURI *see page 91*

WAT ARUN *see page 76*

WAT PO *see pages 81–82*

WIMANMEK PALACE *see page 92*

Lumphini Park, one of Bangkok's traffic-free open spaces

The dancing policeman
Bangkok's traffic problems are chronic. Occasionally, the snail-pace lines snarl into a massive gridlock, causing delays of up to 20 hours. Pollution is so bad that the unfortunate traffic police have to wear face masks and breathing apparatus at busy inter-sections. Many suffer from loss of hearing and res-piratory diseases. In 1993, one policeman went temp-orarily berserk, switching all the traffic signals to green and dancing amid the chaos.

▶ ▶ ▶   **BANGKOK**

Sometimes it is hard to find a good word to say about Bangkok. The air is thick, and the roads clog up with traffic. The oppressive heat is unrelieved by trees or greenery, and after walking for half an hour you can become seriously dehydrated. Visitors ask themselves how it is possible to live in a place like this.

Yet amazingly a great many people come to love the capitol—or at least to develop a love–hate relationship with it. The basic rule to beat the heat is to remain calm. Bangkok does have its cool oases, and it is the focal point for the rest of Thailand, with which most people get on famously.

Contrasts Unlike old-established Western capitals, Bangkok has the exhilarating feeling of growth at a breakneck pace. The population will smash through the 10 million barrier by the end of the millenium, and foreign capital moves freely, creating employment. All of this contributes to Bangkok's vitality. It is a modern city

with extremes of wealth and poverty, and at the same time it has both a strong sense of history and an unmistakable identity.

The dark side of this is evident in the acres of leaky timber shacks that form a vista from the elevated expressway as it passes Khlong Toey port. The people are cheerfully resilient; out of the tourist areas they will always smile and say hello. The phrase *ot thon*, "to endure," finds an equivalent in the Buddhist lexicon: *ubekha*, "equanimity."

At just over two centuries, Bangkok may be relatively young, but it is firmly founded on the heritage of the 14th-century golden city of Ayutthaya (Bangkok's official designation of Manakhorn [Metropolis] once prefixed Ayutthaya). The Grand Palace, with its sumptuous spires and roof, is for outsiders the best-known symbol of Thailand; the Palace and all the major monuments are described in this section one by one.

But Bangkok is not just about buildings; it is vibrant, alive and full of hope. It gives a strange feeling that anything might be possible—and it usually is.

Bangkok is still growing fast, and its traffic grows at the same pace—making life in the city dirty and dangerous

Temples and shrines

Wat Arun, decorated with mosaics of broken porcelain

► ► ► **Arun, Wat**
Arun Amarin Road
Open: daily 8:30–5:30. Admission charge
The "Temple of Dawn" is built on the site of Wat Chang, the focus of King Taksin's Thonburi, the former capital. Taksin was paranoid about his status as an outsider king and he alienated the court, which had him executed. King Rama II and King Rama III raised the main *prang* (tower) to its present height of 243 feet.

As you come up the river, the glittering tower is an impressive sight. Nowadays dwarfed by skyscrapers, it still offers one of the city's finest views from halfway up the main *prang*, reached by a very steep and narrow staircase. A representation of Mt. Meru, center of traditional Indian cosmologies, it depicts the first 33 heavens immediately above it. The four small accompanying *prangs* are dedicated to Phra Phai, the god of the wind. Bizarre mosaics made of broken Chinese porcelain cover the prangs.

A pavilion in the compound has images of important stages in Buddha's life: birth, enlightenment, the first five disciples and his death or *Parinibbana*.

The locals frighten their children with a tale of the guardian *yaksha* of Wat Arun and Wat Po slugging it out in the Chao Phraya.

Wat Arun is best reached by river ferry from Tha Tien (the pier for Wat Po).

► **Benchamabophit, Wat**
Si Ayutthaya Road
Open: daily 9–5. Admission charge
Built of Carrara marble, this is also known as the "Marble Temple" and is the last *wat* of comparable size to Arun to be built in the modern era (1901). As at Wat Niwet Thamprawat, King Rama V commissioned stained-glass representations of Thai and Buddhist themes. The main image is a copy of the reputedly flawless *Phra Phuttha Chinnarat*, the original of which is in Phitsanulok.

The most interesting aspect of the temple is its bronze Buddha images—53 of them line an inner courtyard.

The temple is easily found on Si Ayutthaya Road near Chitladda Palace and could usefully fit within a day tour to Wimanmek and/or Dusit Zoo.

► **Erawan Shrine**
Ploen Chit Road
Open: daily 7 AM–11 PM
The Erawan Shrine, at a busy crossroads on Ploen Chit Road, is always milling with people. They come here to seek favor of the Brahman god Phra Pom; such favors may be as simple as help with winning a lottery. There is a resident dance troupe, which starts performing at 7am, and many of the supplicants commission the dancers to give a performance by way of an offering.

Spirits were said to inhabit the site of the shrine, built in 1956 at the same time as the Erawan Hotel—which has now been demolished and replaced with a much larger, modern structure.

Grand Palace see pages 79–81.

Indrawiharn, Wat

Wisut Kasat Road
Open: daily 9–5

Wat Indrawiharn (full name Wat Indra Mawasihara) on Wisut Kasat Road, a short way north of Banglamphu, has a huge (105 feet) statue of a standing Buddha dating from the mid-19th century. There is also a lifelike image of Luang Phor To, a venerated former abbot, cradling his alms bowl and housed in an air-conditioned, hollowed-out *stupa*. This is only a short bus ride north from Banglamphu (western end of Khao San Road) into Sam Sen Road.

▶ Mahathat, Wat

Sanam Luang
Open: daily 9–5

This extensive *wat* dating from the mid-19th century is centrally located on the west side of Sanam Luang near the National Museum and stretches back to Maharaj Road and the river. The home of Mahachulalongkorn Buddhist University, it is also renowned as a place where lay people can go to get instruction in meditation. The higgledy-piggledy *kuti*, or monks' quarters, make up most of the floor area.

What makes it especially worth visiting is the market that is held here on *wan phra*, the Buddhist holy days (full, new and half moons). Stalls offering herbal medicines, precious stones, amulets, old Buddhas and symbolic figures jostle with strange foods and fortune-tellers. Outside, by Sanam Luang, magicians perform bizarre acts, such as putting nails into their cheeks.

Meditation classes
The International Buddhist Meditation Center at Wat Mahathat offers classes in English lasting several hours every second Saturday. It specializes in the type of meditation known as *Vipassana*, in which enlightenment is taught by "mindfulness," involving a concentrated examination of internal physical sensations. (The other main type of meditation practiced in Thai monasteries is called *Samantha*.) Both novices and experienced practitioners are welcome. For more information, contact the monks in Section Five of the temple compound.

People gather around the Lucky Sara Tree (Buddha's Birth Tree) at Wat Mahathat, one of the most important centers of Buddhist teaching in Thailand

▶ Lak Muang Shrine (City Pillar)

Sanam Luang

Lak Muang dates from the time of the city's founding and was erected in 1782 by Rama I (and rebuilt under Rama VI). This pillar, containing the city's horoscope and protected by a little shrine, is across the road from the east wall of Wat Phra Keo.

The phallic pillar, or *lingam*, symbolizes the fertility and energy of the Hindu god Siva, and is accredited with the power to grant wishes. Originally made of wood, it is covered in gilt, as well as flowers and other offerings. All distances in Thailand are measured from here.

Likay performers—classical Thai dancers—are available to be commissioned to perform by Thai worshipers. As part of the ceremony, the people read their fortunes with the *siem sii* and light the obligatory joss sticks and candles to put themselves in the right mood.

There is a public park near the shrine, as well as several ministries; the Defence Ministry is easily spotted near the cannon outside at Sanam Luang's southeastern corner.

Inside and out, Wat Phra Keo glitters with ornamental gilded figures, including the strange, mythical birdlike creatures known as garudas and kinnarees

The **Sanam Luang** (Royal Field) is a huge open space adjacent to Lak Muang. It is a popular rendezvous for Bangkokites and a fascinating place to watch kite-fighting contests (see page 111) between March and May. It is also a haunt of fortunetellers and amulet vendors.

▶▶▶ The Grand Palace and Wat Phra Keo

Sanam Chai Road

The Grand Palace (*Open* daily 8:30–noon, 1–3:30. *Admission charge*) is one of the most dazzling sights in all Asia. It was once a city within a city, residence and last bastion of the Chakri dynasty. It covers 261,200 square yards and the perimeter walls are 1¼ miles long.

The harem Guarded by eunuchs, the harem could not be entered by any man but the king, on pain of severe punishment. Anna Leonowens's books (see page 56) give a rare inside picture of the harem, which played an important role in feudal politics.

Unlike the characters in the fanciful musical *The King and I*, Leonowens's books present an intellectual woman with a dry sense of humor. Although the harem was disbanded and the king moved out to Wimanmek, the buildings still stand, and some still have important ceremonial functions. (Closed to the public.)

Wat Phra Keo (The Chapel Royal) This is the building containing the image of the **Emerald Buddha** (see over), the holiest shrine in Thailand. The chapel was completed in 1784 and is unique among Thai temples because it has no resident monks; it also functions as the monarch's private chapel. To that end, there is a partition to either side of the image that serves as a retiring room. Murals inside the chapel depict the

This statue on a plinth by the rear wall of the bot at Wat Phra Keo represents the Hindu hermit credited with the invention of yoga and herbal medicine

Buddha's life, besides medieval cosmology and stories of the Buddha's former lives.

The Emerald Buddha was supposedly discovered in 1434 when a lightning bolt hit a temple in Chiang Rai, revealing the image. It remained in the possession of the northern Lanna kingdom until a Lao king was offered the vacant Lanna throne—from there, the Buddha went to Wiang Jan (Vientiane) in Laos. When Chao Phya Chakri, later to become King Rama I, made an expedition to Vientiane in 1779, the small, green jade image was the prize among the spoils. It may not be photographed.

A curiosity north of the chapel is a model of Cambodia's famous Angkor Wat, built by King Rama IV. Next to it are the Royal Pantheon (1903), the large *chedi* (pagodas where holy relics are kept) modeled on Phra Si Sanphet in Ayutthaya, and the Repository of Scripture.

The compound (*Open* daily to 4—tickets also gain access to Wimanmek Palace. *Admission charge*) is an eclectic and dazzling jumble that some have called the "Siamese Disneyland." Statues of white elephants vie with the reliquary chedis and mythological giants (*yuk*) and the half-bird, half-woman *kinnaree*. The entire epic story of the *Ramakian* is depicted in mural form along the galleries that enclose the chapel compound.

In the palace itself, the audience hall of Amarindra is open to view. It is part of the Mahamonthien, where kings are crowned in the room that is home to the country's guardian spirit, Phra Siam Deva Dhi Raj. Behind that is the Chakrabardiman, where kings traditionally stay the night after their coronation.

The audience hall of the Dusit Maha Prasa was the first brick building in the compound, completed in 1789. Built on a cruciform plan of pure Siamese design, the hall is where kings lie in state.

The Chakri Palace (1882) is of architectural interest for its efforts to combine Western and traditional Siamese styles (a trend taken to extremes at Bang Pa-In, in Ayutthaya). King Chulalongkorn, the creator of all this whimsy, conceived the Italian colonnades. A conservative faction at court insisted on the Thai roofs. The spires hold royal ashes—kings in the middle, princes to the left. Galleries depict diplomatic endeavors of the past, such as missions exchanged between King Narai and King Louis XIV of France and King Rama IV's delegation to Queen Victoria. Today, foreign ambassadors present their credentials here to the king.

The Grand Palace Museum, a stone building located northeast of the palace complex, provides invaluable explanations of the methods used in the construction and restoration of the various monuments. Upstairs an array of artifacts can be contemplated in air-conditioned silence. These include two detailed models that give a startling picture of how the palace has been changed and added to throughout the course of its 200-year history.

Visiting heads of state might banquet at the Sala Sahathai and stay in the Boromabiman building, which was richly decorated by King Rama VI with a square

The Emerald Buddha
The Emerald Buddha's robes are changed three times a year by the king to symbolize the passing of the seasons—cool, hot and rainy. Many of the yearly rites, such as the plowing ceremony (see page 94), start with his blessing.

The Temple of the Emerald Buddha bristles with a dazzling array of stupas, prangs, mondops and chedis (monumental towers), many covered in gold

Code of dress
Dress conservatively to visit the Grand Palace or Wimanmek. Shorts, sleeveless shirts, skimpy low-cut dresses, and open sandals are frowned on, and you may be refused admission if you are not dressed properly. If they are feeling good-humored, the guards may provide suitable clothing for you to borrow, but they may just direct you to a nearby clothes stall to purchase your own. Remember to remove your shoes before entering the main chapels.

A temple guard (above) and a young Buddhist (below) at Wat Phra Keo

dome and the written listing of the "ten kingly virtues." Numismatists may be interested in the **Coins and Royal Decorations Museum** (*Open* daily to 3:30. *Admission charge*) near the ticket office. Exhibits date from the 11th century onward.

▶▶▶   Po, Wat (Wat Phra Chetuphon)
South of the Grand Palace (entrance on Chetupon Road)
Open: daily 8–5. Admission charge
This large *wat* of 16th-century foundation took about 12 years for King Rama I to restore in the 1780s. Many come from far and wide to see the massive reclining Buddha, 150 feet long. The mother-of-pearl inlay on the feet represents the 108 "auspicious signs" whereby a Buddha is recognized. It is the oldest temple in Bangkok.

The 10 kingly virtues
giving, ethics, self-sacrifice, honesty, humility, concentration, patience, avoidance of wrongdoing, nonanger and nonviolence.

Amulets

Amulet-collecting is a great craze in Bangkok, with several specialist magazines devoted to the subject. Amulets are worn, especially by men, as both a protective force (against evil and misfortune) and to attract the opposite sex. Conversely, women sometimes wear amulets to ward off unwanted sexual advances. Taxi or *tuk tuk* drivers often hang amulets in their vehicles, then drive like demons, believing they are protected from all harm.

These comic-looking statues are Chinese caricatures of Europeans. Some of the statues reached Thailand in rice cargoes, where they were used as convenient ballast

More mother-of-pearl is used on the chapel doors to depict scenes from the Thai epic *Ramakien*. Scenes are also shown on Ayutthaya-period tapestries that were literally snatched from the flames when the city was destroyed by the Burmese in 1767. Rubbings are sold of the bas-reliefs around the chapel's base.

Inscriptions and treatises on medicine, botany and massage are left over from a host of other subjects formerly on public view, which earned this *wat* the epithet "great storehouse of knowledge" and made it a forerunner of the modern university.

Herbal medicine is still practiced and taught here, and Wat Po counts as the foremost institution in the training of Thai massage (courses available to Western foreigners last for ten or 15 days). By the east wall is a massage area where anyone feeling aches and pains can try the Wat Po version, which costs around 180 baht per hour (see page 47).

▶▶ Rajabophit, Wat

Off Atsadang Road
Open: 8–5. Admission charge

Half a mile south of the Lak Muang, this attractive *wat* of radical circular architecture was built around 1870 by King Rama V, or Chulalongkorn. The tall, gilded *chedi* is in a concentric cloister, and both are decorated with porcelain and chandeliers. Inside, the Buddha image is seated on a *naga*, or dragon-headed serpent, which originated in Lop Buri.

The *bot* (chapel) has mother-of-pearl doors and windows bearing the insignia of the five royal ranks conferred by the king. The interior is vaulted, and four chapels lead off from the central gallery. All in all, this is an unusual and interesting wat.

▶ Rajanada, Wat

Off Mahachai Road
Open: daily 9–5

A 19th-century *wat* graced with a curiously tiered roof, this temple is distinguished by its amulet market in an adjoining compound. The amulets, or *phra phim*, depict images of the Buddha, Thai deities and the more prominent or famous monks.

The amulets are often made of terracotta and are usually worn around the neck on a gold or silver chain. They reputedly have magical powers and can protect the wearer—the more expensive ones are worn by soldiers and these can cost thousands of baht, although not all are so expensive. There are various classes of amulet, each with its own special purpose: some are love amulets; some have many eyes to protect the wearer from all directions. The amulet market is not the cheapest place to buy amulets of any kind.

▶▶ Saket, Wat (Golden Mount)

Off Worachak Road
Open: daily 9–5. Admission free (charge for summit of the Golden Mount)

Once a charnel house, after a disastrous plague in the reign of King Rama II, this *wat* is distinguished by the

Phu Khao Thong (Golden Mount), 262 feet tall, which was started by King Rama III. Rama IV had 1,000 teak logs piled into the foundations to strengthen it because the underlying ground was too soft to support the original structure.

The chedi was added in 1863 by Rama V, and relics were brought from Nepal in 1897, a gift of the British viceroy. The spire is worth the climb—the view from the top affords a surprisingly panoramic vista over the Bangkok rooftops and beyond, but first you must negotiate the 318 steps.

Every November there is a large festival in the grounds of this chedi, during which there is a candlelit procession up the Golden Mount. Food stalls and stage shows appear by the dozen, and the mount is lit up with different colored lights.

▶▶ Suthat, Wat, and the Giant Swing

Bamrung Muang Road

Look closely at the doors here: they are said to have been personally carved by King Rama II.

There are some Jataka murals of an informal style, but most notable is the main meditating Buddha image, 26 feet tall, which comes from the ruins of Wat Mahathat in

The Golden Mount

The Golden Mount is an artificial hill composed of the earth dug out when the canal system was constructed. The only "mount" in pancake-flat Bangkok gives one of the best views over the city. Directly below lie the roofs of Wat Rajanada, with the multiple spires of the Grand Palace farther afield and the ceramic towers of Wat Arun glinting across the Chao Phraya River.

The metallic Burmese-style spires jutting from the elegant roofline of Wat Rajanada give it its alternative name— "Iron Monastery"

Sukhothai and was brought down the river by King Rama I. The peculiar statues of generals, scholars and sailors were brought in as ballast for Chinese rice hulks.

The Buddha image is housed in the tallest *wiharn* (*Open* 9–5, weekends and pubic holidays only) in Bangkok, and the bot (chapel) is impressively large.

Giant Swing Wat Suthat's most famous asset is the Sao Ching Cha, or Giant Swing. This was originally used for a Brahmin ceremony held once a year in which Siva and Vishnu were supposed to visit the temple. Every January up until the 1940s, men would grab for bags of gold off a 50-foot pole in an often fatal Sivaic rite.

Reclining at the feet of Wat Suthat's Golden Buddhas

The place where people used to hit the deck is now the "land of pigeons," with a Brahman temple (Wat Suthat) opposite.

▶▶ **Traimit, Wat**
East of intersection between Yaowarat and Charoen Krung roads
Open: 9–5. Admission charge

This *wat*, said to date from the 13th century, is a good place to visit if you have to wait for a train from nearby Hualamphong Station. Bags can be checked in at the station, and the Wat Traimit is a short stroll away down the road of the same name.

Vendors and schoolchildren crowd the entrance where the star exhibit, the Golden Buddha, is marked with signposts and a small entry fee is collected.

This Sukhothai-style Buddha is the largest solid gold image in the country; if it were melted down, its five and a half tons would be worth over $14 million at today's prices.

Its discovery is said to have been an accident. Like many valuable images in times of warfare and civil strife, it had been camouflaged in stucco. Only some 40 years ago the image was rediscovered when the stucco casing cracked while the image was being moved by crane after the East Asiatic Company took over the building. The plaster was removed to reveal a 12-foot Buddha cast from 5½ tonnes of solid gold.

The Giant Swing ritual
The Giant Swing ritual reenacted a Brahmin ceremony commemorating the Hindu god Siva's annual return to earth. The swinging action symbolized the rising and setting of the sun, tempered the force of the monsoon, and promoted good harvests. It also cost the lives of many brave, or foolhardy, young men who risked their necks in a terrifying attempt to wrench a bag of gold from a bamboo pole with their teeth.

■ **The Chinese quarter in Bangkok is of huge size and influence, tracing its beginnings to a river station—Bangkok—used for the building of Krung Thep. The identity of the Chinese Thais is blurred by intermarriage and assimilation, but most are only a few generations removed from the original immigrant Tia (Father). The predominant group speak *tae-jiw*, a branch of Cantonese, although Hokkien is also important. Around the turn of the century, the Chinese quarter gained a reputation for vice. ■**

Yaowarat Road, with its forest of Chinese signs, could be easily taken for Hong Kong or Singapore. Off the busy thoroughfare are timeless alleys and elaborate temples. Gold shops abound and others sell gaudy paraphernalia such as paper houses and the Benzes burned in the Kong Teck ceremony. Old men hang around the tea houses.

85

Because of the debilitating heat, the area is best explored on foot as the one-way streets are a nightmare. Soi Wanit 1 to the south—better known as Sampheng Lane—runs parallel to Yaowarat. Wat Patuma, at its eastern end, was once the execution ground for royal criminals. Continue east to *talat gao*, one of the oldest and most pungent Chinese markets. This is an early-morning experience. Ancient Wat Chakrawat, with its pond of crocodiles, is about halfway along Sampheng.

Catching up with the news in Chinatown

North from the old market is a new version, set up along Soi Issaraphap, which also leads to Wat Mangkon Kamalawat (Neng Noi Yee) on Charoen Krung (New) Road. This is the largest Mahayana temple in Bangkok, where laity can consult oracles and worship the Buddha Matreiya. A glimpse of the classically proportioned and decorated monks' quarters is permitted. Mayanist monks are vegetarian and do not collect alms.

Turn right down Plapachai Road behind this temple to reach Li Thi Miew. This is a Taoist shrine decorated in ancient style. Yaowarat is also home to the "Thieves' Market," up Boriphat Road near the canal. Soi Wanit leads across the canal to Pahurat, Bangkok's India town, which is famous for its textile markets.

Other sights

► Ban Khamthieng (Siam Society)

131 Soi Asoke (Soi 21), off Sukhumvit Road
Open: Tue–Sat 9–noon, 1–5. Admission charge

Originally constructed in Chiang Mai some 120 years ago, this fine old house was moved to Bangkok in the 1960s and rebuilt on its present site in attractive grounds.

There is also a museum of folk art, covering areas not represented in the national museum; exhibits tend to concentrate on humble aspects of daily life, such as fishing and cooking, as experienced 150 years ago. The house is the headquarters of the Siam Society, a scholarly organization devoted to researching obscure aspects of Thai culture. Their journal is a widely respected source material for academic writing of all disciplines. An invaluable venue for any serious study of Thailand, it has a reference library and books are on sale.

► Bangkok Doll Factory

85/2 Soi Rachada Phan
Open: Mon–Sat 8–5. Check for details of special exhibitions on 245–3008

Bangkok Doll Factory is situated on Soi Rachada Phan, winding down the *soi* half a mile from Ratchaprarop Road. It is entirely the creation of Khunying Thongkorn Chanvimol, who set up the current factory and show-room in 1961.

The attached international doll museum has over 700 exhibits that demonstrate the dollmaker's craft. Khunying Thongkorn has specialized in miniature representations of Thai life, from the colorful hill tribes to tableaux from the classics of Thai literature.

The delicate figurines are handmade from cloth and painstakingly detailed. They have received royal favor as gifts for foreign dignitaries. The most famous subjects are the Khon dancers, whose distinctive painted masks in small scale have become extremely popular in their own right.

Commissions and special occasions have, on the other hand, produced representations of figures as diverse as Miss Universe and the Pope. Other interesting themes covered include rural life, the history of Thai dress, the national dress of neighboring countries, and various regional dances.

Chitladda Palace

Sri Ayutthaya Road

This is the official residence of His Majesty the King: casual visitors are not welcome, and soldiers will not hesitate to shoot on sight. The wooden palace, built by Rama VI, is sited in the middle of spacious grounds and is therefore virtually invisible from the road. However, the imposing moat around the compound cannot be missed. The grounds are used for some of the present King's agricultural research projects.

Dusit

Open: daily 8–6. Admission charge

This area around the National Assembly contains Thailand's "corridors of power," being the headquarters of the powerful defense establishment. It is, unlike the

---

Jim Thompson's House
In Jim Thompson's House (see opposite) every room contains a treasure. Look for a 6th-century Buddha image in the study and a cute Chinese "mouse house" in the bedroom. The shop is highly recommended for its authentic souvenirs: paintings of Siamese cats, the rice goddess—even the whole Thai zodiac.

Royal white elephants
About a dozen rare white elephants enjoy a pampered existence in the Royal Stables at Dusit. These exotic albinos are sacred creatures in Thailand, and by law all found belong to the king. A white elephant is distinguished not so much by its color (a pale brown) as by its fastidious temperament. It is, of course, far too rare to work for a living, and the phenomenal cost of its upkeep gives rise to the phrase that describes an obsolete or burdensome possession.

rest of the city, spread out and leafy. The imposing Ananta Samakhom throne hall, the former National Assembly, has a big dome. Behind it is the current parliament building, while next door are the **Amphorn Gardens** (Open daily 8–6. Admission charge), frequently the site of exhibitions and the city's main zoo—**Khao Din**. It is more of a park than a zoo, and the entrance fee is modest.

►►► Jim Thompson's House
Soi Kasem San 2, off Rama I Road, opposite the National Stadium
Open: Mon–Sat 9–5. Guided tours available in English. All admission fees are donated to good causes
This is well hidden at the end of Soi Kasem San 2, but a delightful surprise awaits. This remarkable haven, overlooking a characterful if odor-laden canal, is one of the most appealing places in Bangkok.

The former owner, Jim Thompson, is something of a local legend (see page 101). Arriving with the U.S. Army in 1945, he soon adopted Thailand as his permanent home. He made both name and riches promoting Thai silk, but his interest was in the Thai fine arts, as these buildings, his monument, attest.

The ingenious structure, cobbled together out of six old red teak structures, is a series of small rooms, with a surprise in each. The place has a captivating charm, and the personality of its former owner still pervades the atmosphere. The collection is an outstanding one and a lesson in good taste.

Thompson's disappearance
The strange disappearance of Jim Thompson is one of the most intriguing mysteries of 20th-century Thailand. He vanished in 1967 on a jungle trek in the Cameron Highlands of Malaysia, but his body was never recovered. Rumors circulated that he was a spy and had been abducted or murdered by communists or the C.I.A. It is more probable that he met his fate under the wheels of a truck, and was quickly buried to hide the evidence.

The contents of Jim Thompson's House constitute a world-class collection of Southeast Asian art. Many artifacts were acquired from local markets in Chinatown or from rural temples

87

The National Museum
The National Museum's main collections of Thai and pre-Thai sculpture can be found in the two large modern wings that surround the older buildings. In the South Wing you will find art of the following periods: Dvaravati (6th–11th centuries), Srivichaya (8th–13th centuries), and Khmer and Lopburi (7th–14th centuries). In the North Wing are Chiang Saen (12th–20th centuries), Sukhothai (13th–15th centuries), Ayutthaya (15th–18th centuries), and Bangkok periods (18th–20th centuries).

Lumphini Park: a pleasure by day, a danger by night

► Lumphini Park
Between Rama IV and Sarasin roads
A smallish green space at the meeting of "port" and "downtown," Lumphini—named after the Buddha's birthplace—is distinguished by a standing statue of King Rama VI at its southwestern corner.

By day it is pleasant enough, with a fitness and recreation park used for tai-chi, jogging and *tagraw* (see page 112). There is also a boating lake. It is one of the places that stops moving when the national anthem is played at 8 AM and 6 PM.

Beware of Lumphini at night, however, when the story is different—the dark acres are irresistible to the violent and seedy element from Patpong to the south and Sarasin to the north.

► National Gallery
4 Chao fa Road (north of National Museum)
Open: Wed–Sun 9–4. Admission charge
This collection of 20th-century Thai art gives some insights into the Thai ways of seeing, although many of the exhibits are of minor artistic significance.

►►► National Museum (Pipitaphan)
Off the Na Phra That Road to the north of Sanam Luang, by Thammasat University
A few baht will get you into this treasure trove of art and culture. Excellent guided tours (free of charge) are available in several languages, lasting about two hours. Those in English take place on Wednesday and Thursday at 9:30. Topics covered include Thai and pre-Thai art and culture, and Buddhism.

The nucleus of the collection was first put on show in 1874 and was organized seriously as a national collection in 1933. The museum is housed in several different buildings, themselves fine examples of Thai architecture.

The oldest buildings in the compound date from the 1780s and were built as a palace for the second or deputy king. When the office of second king was abolished by King Rama V, the buildings became a museum.

The palace originally included an extensive park, which covered most of what are now the northern grounds.

The Pavilions The main acreage is spread out in pavilions behind the **Buddhaisawan Chapel** (1795–97). Built by the second king for his personal use, the chapel contains formal murals depicting 28 scenes from the Buddha's life. The main image, **Phra Buddha Sihing**, is anointed in the official celebrations of Songkran in April.

Halls behind the chapel are devoted to various themes; the large **Atsaraavinitchai Pavilion** is used for traveling and other temporary exhibitions. The emphasis is on artifacts and arts from Thai history. Gold, palanquins, shadow puppets, ceramics, mother-of-pearl, ivory, weapons, royal regalia, stone inscriptions, wood carving, textiles, Buddhist utensils and musical instruments each have their own room among the sprawling whitewashed cloisters. Of the ceramics, there are Chinese (Ming dynasty) examples and native Thai Benjarong (five-colored) ware.

The rear porch of this hall has models of ships and a large doll house. One prize exhibit is a model train presented to King Rama IV by Queen Victoria. The Textile Hall has examples of classical Thai patterns, including those picked out with gold thread. A portico at the end of this hall has some delicate silk embroidery—pictures of In-Jan, the original Siamese twins.

The Mahasurasinghanat Building, to the left of the main structure, is devoted to pre-Thai art and the work of non-Thai civilizations. The Mon-Indic culture of Lop Buri is to the fore, along with art from Dvaravati sites. The Mon are presumed heirs of Dvaravati culture, which appears to have been a peace-loving society occupying the Chao Praya basin some 900 years ago.

In the south at that time, the Javanese influence, as yet untamed by Islam, was very strong. Sumatra next door was center of the Srivijayan empire, which overran

Thai script origin
"The ruler does not collect *jagthorp* (a Khmer tax)"— Part of the inscription of King Ramkhamhaeng of Sukhothai from which, it is said, the Thai script is derived.

89

the Malay Peninsula, leaving a trail of cultural objects across southern Thailand.

The **Prapas Pipitaphan**, to the right, tells the story from the 13th- to 14th-century kingdoms of Lanna (Chiang Mai) and Sukhothai onward. The introduction of writing meant that Thai history could at last begin to be recorded. Various alliances and royal houses contested the supremacy of Siam.

Sivamokkhaphiman Pavilion is the main building and houses the proudest exhibit—the 1283 inscription of King Ramkhamhaeng of Sukhothai setting forth the

Bangkok's National Museum is one of the largest in Southeast Asia. A visit here gives an excellent introduction to Thai art and culture

Suan Pakkard Palace contains a superb collection of antiquities and works of art

Suan Pakkard Palace
The lovely old teak houses of Suan Pakkard Palace are some of the best examples of traditional Thai architecture in Bangkok. Rather than daunting royal residences, they are on a more approachable scale. The Lacquer Pavilion, originally a temple, was dismantled from its original site and brought to Bangkok as a 50th birthday present for the princess by her husband, Prince Chumbot.

prospectus of the Thai nation. It is referred to by some as the first Thai constitution.

A smaller gallery of Thai prehistory is located here at the back of the same building. The most interesting exhibits here are the Bronze Age whorl-patterned pots produced by the Ban Chiang civilization (see pages 194–195) and some unusually shaped Stone Age vessels.

Other small buildings are scattered across the compound. A fine collection of cremation chariots has its own pavilion on the right, and a Chinese house of the court service is tucked away behind exhibits of Thai art. Also of interest is the **Red House**, or **Tamnak Daeng**, (*Open* Wed–Sun 9–4. *Closed* for lunch. *Admission charge*) which was once the residence of the older sister of King Rama I. Once situated on the grounds of the Grand Palace, today it is home to a collection of furniture that was once used by royalty. A small bookstore in the foyer of the main gallery of Thai history has titles in English explaining the exhibits.

Guided tours in English start at 9:30 AM on Wednesday and Thursday. These concentrate on Thai and pre-Thai art and culture.

► ► **Suan Pakkard Palace**

352 Si Ayutthaya Road
Open: 9–4. Closed Sun. Admission charge

A *tuk tuk* ride from Jim Thompson's House, "the lettuce garden" is Bangkok's most serious rival, in sightseeing terms, to Jim Thompson's House. Five traditional houses were brought here in the 1920s by Prince and Princess Chumbhot Nagara Svarga and set in a landscaped garden.

The main reason to visit is the splendid **Lacquer Pavilion**, which was discovered in Ayutthaya, its inner walls portraying the life of the Buddha, among other themes.

Other noteworthy exhibits are the gold and lacquer manuscript cabinets, besides a good collection of elegant Ban Chiang pottery (see pages 194–195) and Khmer statuary.

► ► ► **Thonburi**

West bank of Chao Phraya River

Thonburi, Thailand's former capital city between the fall of Ayutthaya and the establishing of Bangkok in its place, occupies the west bank of the Chao Phraya River, just a ferry ride away from the Grand Palace and Wat Po. The great draws for the visitor are **Wat Arun**►►► (see page 76), the **canals**►►► and the **floating market**►► (see panel).

The floating market in Wat Sai, Bang Khun Thien district, was the first to attract tourists and has now become commercialized.

The left bank at Thonburi is gradually assuming the character of modern-day Bangkok. Wongwien Yai (Big Roundabout) boasts an impressive statue of King Taksin, Thonburi's founder. The immediate environs—the narrow streets, canal bridges and *wats*—preserve much atmosphere from King Taksin's temporary capital

Floating Market
Although run primarily as a tourist attraction, the Floating Market is nevertheless worth a look if you can't get to see the more authentic one at Damnoen Saduak (see page 124). Long-tail boat tours begin at 7 AM from Tha Chang and the Oriental Hotel pier.

Commercialized, but undeniably photogenic: Thonburi Floating Market

Teak
Once one of Thailand's greatest natural resources, teak made particularly good house-building material. The hardwood's naturally occurring oil made it durable and weather resistant. The teak forests have been felled drastically, but new propagation techniques are being tried (see pages 244–245).

The collection of state coaches at Wimanmek Palace reveals Rama V's interest in European culture. Many artifacts on display were imported after the king's foreign travels

▶▶▶ Wimanmek Palace (Phra Thi Nang Wimanmek)

Off Ratchawithi Road by the National Assembly
Open: daily 9:30–4. Last tour 3 PM. Free if you use a ticket already purchased for the Grand Palace

"The Palace in the Clouds" is claimed to be the world's largest structure made entirely of golden teak and contains over 80 rooms. On the orders of King Chulalongkorn (Rama V), the palace was dismantled and moved in sections in 1900 from Si Chang island in Chonburi province. The work was finished in seven months, and it set a trend that brought more royalty to the area to build their homes.

Wimanmek Palace was designed by Prince Naritsaranuwattiwong; two wings, each measuring 195 feet long, each contain three floors. There are 31 rooms, not including balconies. His Majesty would come here with his queens, favored concubines and daughters. The Amporn Sathan extension was added in 1907 to accommodate these influxes. The queen ordered it be made into a museum, and it now contains some of the king's personal effects and objets d'art.

After the reign of Rama VI, the palace was used merely to store things, and its condition deteriorated. It was opened to the public in 1982 to mark the 200th anniversary of Bangkok's founding.

It has the appearance of an island, being partly flanked by pools of water. A jade pool, green with vegetation, lies to the south, and beyond is a Thai house built for the use of visiting guests. The Silver Room has much detailed original work, such as a silver tree with woven leaves. On the wall are photos of various royals and aristocrats. There is a Metal Room with bronzes, models of warships and steamships belonging to King Rama VII. Two trophy rooms contain swords and guns and the traditional colonial elephants' feet.

■ **These ceremonial barges are brought out only on very special occasions. Intricately carved, they were once used in a traditional journey along the river when the king made his way to Wat Arun to present the krathin robes and a selection of gifts from the Grand Palace to the monks as a symbol to mark the end of the rainy season and Phrasa, a time of spirituality in Buddhism.** ■

A colorful spectacle Over 2,000 men straining at the oars, chanting ancient hymns and all dressed in brilliant costumes make quite a sight. The boats are now too frail for regular use, but are brought out to mark important events, such as the celebration of the 200th anniversary of the Chakri dynasty. Only a big occasion will get them out again. The spectacle is usually announced a year in advance; the last time was for the king's Golden Jubilee in 1996. They might well come out again in 1999 for his 70th or more probably 72nd (Thais mark age in 12-year cycles).

Principal barges The king's barge, *Sri Suphannahong*, is the biggest (about 145 feet long) and is also the oldest and most ornately carved. It takes the form of a golden swanlike bird called a *hongsa*, with a great bauble dangling from its beak, a national symbol used on coinage. His Majesty sits under a golden central canopy, tiered umbrellas of state set along the mid line. Ceremonially dressed crews pull the angular swan's head forward, and there is a special crew member who chants the rhythm of the oars.

The next biggest barge is *Anantanagaraj*. This has a seven-headed serpent prow and, like the others, elegant carvings along the sides. The full-blown ceremony uses 50 barges in all.

Sneak preview
Visitors can tour the Royal Barge Museum (*Open 8:30–4:30. Admission charge*) on the bank of Bangkok Noi Canal. It is best reached by boat (the regular long-tail from Tha Chang); vehicles can also gain access at 80/1 Rim Khlong, Arun Amarin Road.

93

Royal barges at night

Bangkok festivals

■ **Festivals and fairs are celebrated with gusto in Bangkok. Thais will celebrate at the drop of a firecracker, at almost any time of year, although dates will vary according to the lunar calendar. See also pages 228–229 and 226. Below are some significant occasions.** ■

The moon goddess

In September, the Chinese community makes offerings of food to the moon goddess. Special altars are crammed with goodies, including "moon cakes," which passersby are invited to try. There are also dragon dances and fireworks.

The king's birthday

On December 5, the Sanam Luang area becomes a feast of neon, and outdoor movies play all along Ratchadamnoen Klang Road. It is also "Father's Day" (the queen's birthday, on August 12, is "Mother's Day"). Every fifth year in the 12-year animal cycle is considered to be particularly auspicious; 1987 saw a fine spectacle.

Buddhist festivals Maga Puja, in mid-February, celebrates the spontaneous gathering of 1,250 disciples to hear the Buddha's sermon. There is mass merit-making and a candlelit procession. Wat Benchamabophit is a major venue.

Visaka Puja, in May, celebrates the Buddha's birth, enlightenment and death. This is the most fervently celebrated Buddhist festival; structures are erected in Sanam Luang for the faithful to listen to sermons. It immediately precedes the plowing ceremony for Maga Puja and Visaka Puja.

The plowing ceremony—*jarot hangkhai raek na Khwan*—has its roots in the Sukhothai period. The exact day is chosen by astrologers, usually in May, the start of the rains. After the procession, the king and queen appear and the "lord of the first field" comes out to greet them. A white bullock is then yoked to a plough and the lord makes three furrows in each direction. Astrologers can then predict the next year's harvest. Before leaving, the king asks the lord for some rice seeds to sow in a special patch at Chitladda Palace, to provide the new seed for the next year's ceremony.

Asalha Puja, in July, commemorates the Buddha's first sermon to his five original disciples. A few days after this festival, the Buddhist Lent, **Khao Phansa**, marks the start of the rains.

Kathin is held during the rainy season. Thais give "forest robes" to monks, and banknotes attached to "money trees" are presented to wats. **Ok Pansa**, in October, marks the end of the rains.

Wat Saket The "Golden Mount" hosts a lively fair in November. Typical of *wat* fairs all over the country. It has amusements and side-stalls, loud music and lots of people, even upstairs to the top of the *chedi*.

Right: making a splash at the Songkran Water Festival (Thai New Year, April)

94

River and canal tours

■ **Trips on the Chao Phraya River or its connecting canals (*khlongs*) give the visitor a glimpse of how the city must have appeared to the Europeans, who dubbed Bangkok "the Venice of the Orient." The picturesque *khlong*-side life with its glittering *wats* and cool palms is being replaced by the concrete mayhem that is Bangkok today.** ■

No visitor should miss a tour of what remains of the city's *khongs*. Either take an organized tour—some of these begin from the Oriental Hotel pier and feature trips on a narrow speedboat (known as a long-tail) along the *khlongs*, followed by a gentle cruise on a converted rice-barge. Or go to Tha Tien, Tha Chang or Maharaj piers, from where inexpensive canal "buses" (long-tails) leave regularly. It is possible to charter your own long-tail, but beware of being charged an extortionate rate.

Chao Phraya express boat service: central stops

Boat can get crowded, but it is a great experience for both views and local color. North of Krung Thon Bridge, the service heads under Rama VI Bridge and eventually reaches Nonthaburi (last boat returns at 5:45; if you get stranded, buses 64 and 203 get back to the Banglamphu area). The boat mainly stops along the east bank, but there are ferries crossing to the other side at certain points. There are three fare zones; fares are extremely cheap.

The great water trips around Bangkok include the river trip to Bang Pa-In and Ayutthaya, leaving from Maharaj pier at 8 AM, lunch is included in the price; and the floating markets at Thonburi (see page 91) and at Damnoen Saduak (see page 124).

Traveling by river

Pier (*tha*)	
Thewes	Just south of Krung Thon Bridge
Wisut Kasat	Samsen Road guest houses
Wat Samphraya	—
Phra Arthit	For Khao San Road guest houses
Maharaj	Just south of Phra Pin Klao Bridge; opposite Noi railroad station; canal bus; ferry for Royal Barges
Chang	Grand Palace; canal bus
Tien	Wat Po; river ferry for Wat Arun; canal bus
Rajinee	—
Memorial Bridge	Just north of Memorial Bridge
Rajawongse	For Chinatown
Harbour Department	—
River City	—
Si Phraya	—
Wat Muangkae	For GPO
Oriental	Oriental Hotel
Taksin	For Sathron Road

Outside Bangkok

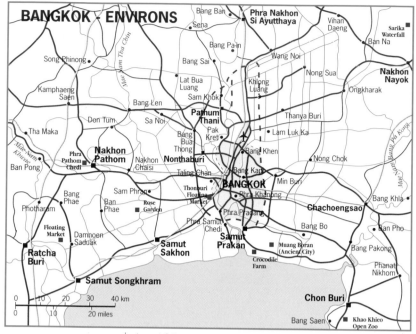

BANGKOK ENVIRONS

96

In addition to the places described below, many places mentioned in the chapter on Central Thailand can be visited on a day trip. Early risers should try to make it to the floating market at **Damnoen Saduak►►►** (see page 124). **Kanchana Buri►►►** (see pages 128–131) can be reached by train or bus; allow time to travel the Death Railway section to Nam Tok at the end of the line. The ancient remains of the former capital at **Ayuttaya►►** (see pages 119–122) can be visited by boat, train or bus; stop off on the way at **Bang Pa-In►►** summer palace►► (see page 123). A less hectic visit is by train to **Lop Buri►►** (see pages 138–139), which has impressive ruins.

There is no shortage of travel agents in Bangkok offering organized tours outside the capital.

►►► Muang Boran (Ancient City)

Sukhumvit Road, Bang Puu, Samut Prakan Province
Open: daily 8:30–5. Admission charge
What did Thailand's ruins look like when the buildings were new? This question may be answered at Muang Boran, a collection of reproduction buildings, most of them scaled down to one-third size.

Muang Boran is the brainchild of one man with a great love for the architectural heritage of his country. It is situated near the Crocodile Farm, 20 miles to the east of Bangkok; the drive out takes about two hours. Be careful when asking for "Muang Boran," as it means "ancient city" and this could be interpreted to mean a real ancient city like Ayuttaya. Numerous tour operators run trips from Bangkok.

This fascinating attraction presents models of Thailand's major monuments in around 200 acres of

---

Kanchana Buri
Start early if you want to visit Kanchana Buri on a day trip. The buses are faster, but less atmospheric than the trains. Special rail tours leave Bangkok soon after 6 AM (weekdays and holidays) and take you right to the end of the Death Railway line at Nam Tok, returning (with a stop) via Kanchana Buri in the evening. For a more leisurely visit, stop overnight in one of the raft houses on the River Kwae.

attractive gardens, which are laid out in the same shape as Thailand itself. Vehicles are available to explore the big site, so this could be a shortcut to appreciating the country's cultural diversity.

Hop from province to province in Muang Boran, from the distinctive That Phanom in Nakhon Phanom to Wat Mahathat in Sukhothai. Ayutthaya's Royal Palace, long ruined, has been re-created from old chronicles. The Muslim minority has not been forgotten: there is also a model of the famous Pattani mosque. More humble scenes abound, such as a floating market, and the overall attention to environment and detail is remarkable. A variety of refreshments are offered in a pleasing khlong-side ambience.

The Ancient City Company can give more details about the Ancient City; its office is at 78 Democracy Monument Circle, Ratchadamnoen Klang Road (tel: 222 8143/224 1057), in the shadow of the Democracy Monument, a reproduction of another famous structure. Weekend and holiday tours can be booked here.

▶ **Samut Prakan Crocodile Farm and Zoo**
19 miles south of Bangkok on Highway 3
Open: daily 7–6. Admission charge
This is the place to see domesticated saurian. Hundreds of individuals from a variety of both saltwater and freshwater species can be inspected or even fed here from a raised walkway. There is a croc-catching show daily and a shop selling crocodile-skin products, including handbags and belts. Stage shows are given—with audience participation. The place is emphatically *not* to everyone's taste!

▶▶ **Suan Sam Phran (Rose Garden)**
Off Highway 4, one hour west of Bangkok
Open: daily 8–6. Admission charge
The banks of the broad Thachin River in Nahkon Pathom provide the setting for the Rose Garden resort. Visitors pay a small admission charge to get into the landscaped gardens, lakes and bridges. Choose either to picnic, dine in the riverside restaurant, swim, play lawn-bowling, boat, waterski or look at the model village. A longish afternoon show, at extra charge, depicts some costumed aspects of Thai culture, rites of passage, dancing, with shows of Thai boxing and *krabee krabong* (sword and stave fighting). This is purely for the benefit of tourists, but it is done very well.

Captive crocs
The wild crocodiles that once infested the swamps of the central plains are now confined to zoos or farms like the one at Samut Prakan, but an occasional specimen has been known to escape into Bangkok's sewer system during the rainy season. The captive crocodiles are not farmed solely for their skins; crocodile meat is a popular delicacy on local restaurant menus, much as alligators are in Florida. The meat tastes a bit like salty chicken.

The savage crocodile
The endangered crocodile was among the most dangerous jungle predators during the "bad old days." Thai respect for this savage old monster can be found in the folk tale of *Kraithong*, the eponymous hero being the only "crocodile doctor" skillful enough to catch the diamond-toothed Chalawan.

A keeper entangled with a Siamese estuarine crocodile at the Crocodile Farm

Sarongs
Brightly colored *sarongs* make useful gifts. They are ideal garments to take to the beach and can double as a sheet. A man's *pha-khao-ma*, for bathing and generally lazing about the house, is identified by large checks.

A Bangkok street vendor carries her wares in traditional woven baskets, perfectly balanced from a pole on her shoulder

City for shoppers Whether you are shopping in the colorful, lively but sweltering hot markets or the glitzy space-age department stores, one thing is clear: a cornucopia beckons that can empty your purse more quickly than you can say *thii-raleuk*, the Thai term for "souvenir."

There are two tiers of prices in Thailand: basic and luxury. Basic goods cost about 30–40 percent of their equivalents in Western homes. Prices for luxury, imported goods are roughly comparable with those in the West.

Clothes These are obviously popular with visitors. Indeed, resourceful travelers could take just one change of clothes and purchase a vacation wardrobe as they go. Vacation clothes are of the casual, brightly patterned Hawaiian variety, but bargains do not stop at casual wear; Thailand is justly famous for the quality of its bespoke tailors. They might offer some standard styles to choose from, but it is possible to get any style run up from a sketch or photograph. A man's formal suit should cost upwards of 1,000 baht, and at least 48 hours should be allowed for fitting and adjustments. A word of caution: There are some tales of people being sold substandard workmanship, so be sure of your purchase.

The fabrics available for shirts and dresses are legion. **Cottons** come in brilliant hues and prints. Batik in particular is enjoying something of a boom. Some shops only sell cloth and are stocked with huge bolts of it waiting to be cut. The famous Thai **silk** is still cheap, and you will notice that it is, for many women in Bangkok, just everyday office wear (see page 203). Top-quality silk products are offered at Jim Thompson's Thai Silk Company, 9 Suriwong Road.

Souvenir shops Most people understandably want some souvenir proof of their visit. Although Oxfam has done sterling work promoting village handicrafts, major credit for the currently booming Thai handicraft scene should go to Queen Sirikit, whose "Support" foundation saved many of the traditional Thai crafts from extinction.

Common everywhere are baskets and furniture made of **bamboo and rattan**. These "wicker" goods are surprisingly cheap, and the *yan lipao* vine from the south can be woven into elegant accessories. The north is famous for intricate **woodcarving**—either figurines or scenes in bas-relief. It is unlikely that the average visitor will have space in their luggage for furniture, but it can be shipped anywhere in the world. Whether ornamental or functional, it is all very reasonable. However, it is important to remember that certain types of wood, especially hard woods which have an excess of moisture from the tropical climate, may shrink and crack once shipped back to a drier climate.

Markets These are everywhere. The streets of the city are in themselves one huge market, selling anything from silk flowers to a case of barbers' scissors. The granddaddy of them all is Chatuchak, up by the Northern

Bus Terminal on Phahon Yothin Road. Open only on Saturday and Sunday, it has become known as the "Weekend Market." China, wood, pets, books (including cheap secondhand paperbacks), fabulous food displays and, of course, clothes are sold cheek-by-jowl at countless stalls covering a huge area. It can get hot, but the experience is worth it.

Other popular markets include **Sampheng** in Chinatown, **Nakorn Kasem Road** by the canal, **Pahurat** and **Penang Market** in Khlong Toey, near the port. In Pratunam, a large covered area on Ratchprarop Road covers the downmarket clothes scene fairly comprehensively.

Department stores For shopping in comfort, try any of the air-conditioned department stores that have sprung up all over the place. These are great for Western food items and the more upmarket clothes.

The **Siam Center** and nearby **Mabunkhrong** on Rama I Road were among the first. The biggest is **Central** at Lard Phrao or perhaps the **Zen** on Ratcha Damri Road. **Pata Pin Klao** in Thonburi boasts a zoo and monkey theater!

Jewelry and handicrafts Jewelry is another of the luxury goods that Thailand exports in large amounts and that are correspondingly cheap locally. Thais love gold and still buy it by the baht, showing the origin of their money (a baht of weight is 15 grams of gold). Local production alone provides pearls (from farms in Koh Samui and Phuket), rubies and blue sapphires to be set into gold and made into jewelry. The factories are concentrated around **Soi Mahesak** to the west of Silom Road. Look for Tourist Authority of Thailand (TAT)

Appetizing shopping
New World department store in Chakraphong Road (in Banglamphu) is an eye-opening cross section of Thai consumerist aspirations. There is an enticing range of eateries on the top floor.

Silk
Every color of the spectrum is available in Thai silk, including some fabulous shot-silk that could be called the "Thai hologram," warp and weft shimmering in alternate colors. Enough to make a skirt will set you back anything from 500 baht upwards. The *mut mee* pattern is made by tie-dying the threads before they are woven. Not all of it is the real thing, so beware. Learn to distinguish between the real and the fake by feel.

*Lard Phrao
department store*

SHOPPING

Traditional crafts from all over Thailand can be found in Bangkok. This stall offers models and dolls. Shop around for quality, and don't forget to bargain

accreditation to make sure the stones are what they say they are; there are a lot of fakes about, and "amazing bargains" will probably turn out to be cons. To be on the safe side, ask for an independent test at the Asian Institute of Gemological Sciences, 484 Ratchadapisek Road (tel: 02/513 2112).

More downmarket, but still very attractive, is silver jewelry set with turquoise. Like woodcarving, it is considered to be a northern craft. Many hill tribespeople trek down to Bangkok to sell their distinctive tribal designs.

Another fine handicraft is lacquerware. After a block of teak has been transformed with the shiny black lacquer, patterns are either appliquéd in gold leaf or just painted on.

Other crafts Other Thai handicrafts include hand-painted blue celadon ware, a craft taught to the Thais by the Chinese. Cushions, whether the triangular *morn khwan* or the square *morn kit*, are ornately embroidered. Also from the north come hand-painted paper umbrellas and hill-tribe crafts (see page 162). On Khao San Road and Patpong Road there are numerous craft shops and market stalls.

Narai Phand, on Ratcha Damri Road, is a government-sponsored store with the widest selection of handicrafts from all over the country. Perhaps the saddest stalls of all are those selling paintings of rural scenes and dead insects in glass frames.

Unusual shops Banglamphu has some odd shops, the likes of which are not to be found elsewhere, as well as its wholesale clothes market. Handy snack stalls abound everywhere. The tourist emporiums on Khao San Road have the best selections of music tapes (although many are pirated). There is also one of Bangkok's few cooperatives, good for traditional cooking utensils, and also the Buddhist bookshop opposite Wat Boworn, with a selection of books in English. The traditional musical instrument workshop can be found on the corner of Tanao and Ratchdamnoen Klang roads, and a huge government school-supplies shop on Ratchdamnoen Klang by the bus stop is fascinating.

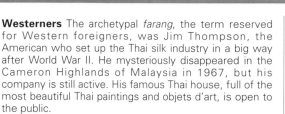

■ **Thailand is a hospitable country, and this is reflected in its attitude to foreigners (*farangs*). Almost every nationality can be found, especially in Bangkok's business community. Some businessmen, such as the Englishman David Tarrant of the Inchcape Group, can become very influential in the country's economy.** ■

Westerners The archetypal *farang*, the term reserved for Western foreigners, was Jim Thompson, the American who set up the Thai silk industry in a big way after World War II. He mysteriously disappeared in the Cameron Highlands of Malaysia in 1967, but his company is still active. His famous Thai house, full of the most beautiful Thai paintings and objets d'art, is open to the public.

Some Westerners are attracted by Buddhism and some become Buddhist monks. There is one *wat* in the remote forests of Ubon Ratchatahani that has 20 permanent monks and branches in England, Australia, Switzerland, Italy and New Zealand. A few foreigners teach at the universities and colleges.

Silk was Jim Thompson's fortune. His Thai silk company shop still offers silk of the highest quality

Asians Most foreigners living in Thailand are from other Asian countries. In addition to the Chinese, there is a big Indian community, many of whom used to work as butchers, because the Thais, as Buddhists, preferred to avoid this occupation.

Many Indians have become extremely successful in business, like Sura Chansrichawla, a second-generation Punjabi Sikh, whose real estate, valued at $650 million, makes him one of the biggest property owners in Bangkok.

Far Easterners Some 40,000 Japanese troops were based in Thailand during the Pacific War. Today there are probably 25,000 Japanese living in Thailand, mostly factory managers and technical advisers in joint enterprises.

Although there is little resentment against Japan's wartime activities, there are many left-wing critics of Japanese investment and management methods. The more negative segments of Japanese society also appear, notably the *yakuza*, or gangsters, who are quite active in Thailand.

The large refugee population of Vietnamese and Cambodians still living in the border areas of Thailand is a significant legacy from the Indochina War.

Food

Bangkok's produce markets are a cornucopia of amazing sights, smells and colors. Catch them early in the morning, and remember to take your camera

Bangkok is a great gastronomic experience. The Bangkok posting is a major prize for master chefs of the big hotel chains. Like any large city that opens its doors to all nationalities, it is host to a plethora of international cuisines. See also pages 40–43.

Thai food can be a real assault on the Western palate. To Thais, Western food is *jeuut*—tasteless. To Westerners, Thai food may be divided into varying degrees of difficulty.

Isan (northeastern) food is a good example of these variations. The *som tam*, or papaya salad, a specialty of the region, can be made sweet with sugar and peanuts and one chili. *Tam mthai* is made with tiny prawns, and cooked this way most Westerners would find it delicious. The average Bangkok Thai would move up to *tam puu*, with the diminutive freshwater crab and two or three extra chilies, whereas a northeasterner might add the vile-smelling fermented fish they call *plaa raa* and employ a "scorched mouth" policy with regard to the chilies! With this in mind, it might be a good idea to memorize the phrase *phrik neung met*—"one chili."

The most international Thai dish must be *khao phat* or fried rice. Made with beef, chicken, pork or squid and an egg, it can be found almost anywhere.

Shop-house restaurants These also do fried noodles with *phat sii iw* (soy sauce) and the *phat thai* of increasing international fame. The *phat gaprao* (sweet basil fry) on rice has a unique pungency, but it is probably best avoided by those with a sensitive stomach.

Much healthier and more traditional are the 1,001 varieties of *gup*—"with." With boiled rice, that is: the main food of the central plains. Gup restaurants are distinguished by rows of pots or aluminum trays. Pointing at the dish of your choice alleviates the language barrier; the order *raat khaao* will get your choices "on the rice" as one dish.

Upmarket eating places Those with a bit of money to spend can go to the class "restaurant" as Westerners understand the term. It can be interesting to order one of the exotic dishes and see what appears.

European sensibilities may be offended by *khai yio maa*—literally "horse-piss eggs"—which have been steeped in goodness-knows-what for so long that they are quite black when they hit the table!

This sort of restaurant charges upwards of 50 baht for a dish and is mainly frequented by the professional classes. Note the Thai tradition for picking up the tab: one person pays all. If a boss is dining with his underlings, "face" requires that he be the one who must oblige.

Street food In recent years, the profusion of street food stalls, night markets, charcoal burners, noodle shops and kitchenettes in Bangkok has turned the city into one huge open-air restaurant, and it is here that you will find some of the best regional and local food. The Thais enjoy wandering around to find out what is cooking in the next street.

Certain distinctly Chinese items have found their

special niche on the street. Boiled noodles, whether *nam* (soup) or *haeng* (dry), sell from carts that are often open all night. *Ba'mee*, the yellow wheat-flour noodles, are especially recommended.

From the many rich dishes, try *khao muu daeng* (red pork in a special sauce with hard-boiled egg) or *khao man kai*, white chicken in fatty rice with dark soy sauce.

The bone-shaped golden crispy *paa thong go* is a Thai version of hot buttered toast, often eaten after being dipped in sweet Thai coffee.

Sweetmeats The sweet-toothed have a bewildering choice of *khanom*, or sweetmeats. There are the cheap street kind, from the sticky Islamic *roti* to the delicate *khanom beuang*, a crisp wafer of coconut cream.

The restaurant diner may opt for the coconut milk/ sticky rice concoction; this is easily the best way to appreciate the notorious durian, while mangoes are better known. Try the *pheuak*—an Asian tuber called taro with a vanillalike flavor—or the honeydew melon, diced and covered with shredded ice.

The other way to round off a great meal is with fresh fruit. Most kinds are seasonal, like *ngo*, the red hairy rambutans, and *malagor*, the fleshy orange gourd papaya, but familiar fruits like pineapple and bananas appear all year round.

Freshwater crab is a great Bangkok delicacy. Beware of it in remote rural areas, though, where it may be contaminated with parasites

103

Nightlife

They say it was American soldiers looking for some recreation who got the petite farmers' daughters dancing to loud rock music, wearing bikinis and holding onto firemen's poles. That was some 20 years ago. Tourists may have more than made up for the departing G.I.s, but the fear of AIDS is changing the scene somewhat.

The area around Patpong Road and Soi Cowboy, off Sukhumvit Road, is full of murky dives, mainly catering to men. On the whole, this is a concentrated area of spectacular sleaze. The road is named after a Chinese millionaire, Phat Phong, who owns nearly everything in the area. The other side of the coin can be seen in the numerous victims of poverty, bad education, pimps, deserting husbands and illegal documents among a host of other woes. Patpong et al. represent the visible tip of an iceberg of suffering. While the women there enter into voluntary arrangements with the bars, in other establishments their rights are not nearly so well respected.

It is going to be a long time before Bangkok manages to shake off its reputation as "the brothel of Asia," but entertainment of the regular sort is booming right now, and women or men who don't care for degrading spectacles have a wide choice of venues for whiling the night away.

Food arrives on oiled wheels at Tum Nak Thai, the biggest restaurant in the world, seating around 3,000 guests at a time

104

Pubs and clubs Middle-class Thais thinking along similar lines opened the first "pub," **Brown Sugar**, on Sarasin Road. This proved to be a wild success, and pretty soon the area behind Lumphini Park—Lang Suan—was a festival of music and drink. Professional bands pump out jazz, rock, reggae and Latin rhythms. The drinks tend to be overpriced, however. Most establishments are open until around 2 or 3 AM. Particularly recommended are **Round Midnight** (mostly Latin) and **The Old West**

(Santana-type rock). If you want to talk, feel free to sit outside. Pubs have now opened in many other areas. The **Gypsy** in Banglamphu is near the New World department store. Sukhumvit Road, and Soi 55 (Thonglor) especially, has more than a few. One that helped popularize jazz here is **The Saxophone**, by the Victory Monument.

Not to be outdone, the women have "ladies' clubs" such as **Chippendales** in (fairly remote) Huay Khwang. Wealthy women tired of errant husbands get their revenge here with a selection of toyboys.

The neon signs advertizing Bangkok's steamy nightlife leave little to the imagination, especially in the red-light district at Pat Pong

105

Discos Another Western-inspired fixture on the night scene is the discotheque. While small and intimate dance halls thud in the basements of large hotels like the **Shangri la** (Talk of the Town), the **Dusit Thani** (Bubbles) and the **Ambassador** (Flamingo), there are a few mega-palaces whose clientele is mostly students. The most impressive of these is **NASA Spacedrome** on Ramkhamhaeng Road (turn left at the end of Phetburi New Road).

Spasso, at the Grand Hyatt Erawan, offers live music most evenings. The pride of the gay scene is just around the corner. Straights and gays are welcome at the trendy **Rome Club**, off Thanom Silom, with its hipper-than-hip music and decadent decor. A Pattaya-style transvestite revue, **Calypso**, has opened in its own large theater on Sukhumvit Road near the Washington cinema; either of the two nightly shows costs around 300 baht.

Cafés Finally, you may be tempted to try out one of the many cafés, a very Thai institution. Off the tourist track, entertainment is provided by a roster of male and female singers in elaborate evening dress. They sing requests and are rewarded by garlands of jasmine—altogether very civilized!

Drinking Licensing laws are nonexistent, and almost any little restaurant can oblige with either beer or Mekhong whiskey (foreign liquor being mainly confined to the pubs and discos). Check out the rumlike Saeng Thip, with Coke, for a smoother drink than Mekhong, which can have lethal aftereffects. Of the beers, Kloster lacks the formaldehyde tang of the more popular Singha.

■ Never really an art form for mass entertainment, the traditional *khon* performances survive mainly thanks to the Fine Arts Department. Each takes the form of a masked dance-drama and can last for up to eight hours when the fuller versions are staged. Designed originally for performance at court for the pleasure of the king, *khon* drama, like all classical performances, can be a bit heavy, even for the Thais. However, the program is leavened with music, from classical (both Thai and *farang*) to folk and popular, and the costumes are very extravagant. Actors will happily pose for photographs after a performance. ■

National Theater This is a large building where plays and *khon* drama in Thai are staged. As befits the theater's status, the performances are most often adapted from such literary classics as *Phra Lor* or the *Ramakien* epic, the Thai version of an Indian legend (the *Ramayana*). There are tales of battles and even comedy where various colorful characters act out the parts. One of the all-time favorites is the monkey god Hanuman, easily distinguished by his white face. The troupe regularly participates in the joint Asian Ramayana festival. The dancers move with slow, deliberate formality, and it is an interesting spectacle, but hard—even for those who understand a little Thai—to follow. The theater itself is large, its lush decorations and facilities mainly patronized by schoolchildren being dragged through their required texts, although the material of *Phra Lor* is very earthy.

Entry to the National Theatre is around 100 baht, and

Bangkok's National Theater

English-language programs can be obtained from the Thailand Cultural Center. These also contain a wealth of other "arty" activities, current details of which can mostly be found in the *Bangkok Post* and the *Nation*.

The Cultural Center This is way east of town on Ratchadaphisek Road. It offers much more accessible attractions such as recitals, mime, ballet and singing contests. Here they also stage performances of *Likay*, a lively piece of folk theater. This is much more in the popular vein of entertainment and relies on pratfalls and bawdy lyrics rather than on long or complicated dialogue. The comedy of the early evening gives way to more risqué material, and the air is thick with double meanings until the small hours of the morning. It is easy to see *Likay* in its spontaneous environment all over the country at provincial temple fairs.

Khon Sot (fresh) is halfway between *Likay* and court *khon*. Charity concerts, featuring music from the current Thai hit parade and old crooning standards, are sometimes televised.

Thai classical music performances are put on at the beginning of every month. These ensembles, which may seem to be somewhat cacaphonous to the untrained ear, make music that is based on a seven-note scale and much improved by vocals.

A more accessible musical evening for a visitor may be a *Luuk Thung* performance. This folk-with-modern-instruments gives concerts of old favorites that are sung by the top commercial stars.

Other cultural activities
In Bangkok a diverse program of events centers on the British Council, the American University Alumni, the Alliance Française and Germany's Goethe Institut. The Alliance puts on some excellent films, while the others encourage modern Thai artists of all disciplines.

Plastic arts
The Visual Dhamma Gallery (Soi Asoke 44/28 Sukhumvit) is where to catch the best of the plastic arts. Universities and hotels likewise plug the high-culture gap; the Imperial and the Monthien in particular stage regular concerts and plays, while the Auditorium of Chulalongkorn University presents a similar program to the National Theater.

Traditional Thai dance

Boutique hotels

A recent phenomenon in Bangkok's accommodation scene has been the development of "boutique hotels." These small, luxury establishments offer immaculate standards of service and facilities and are predictably pricy. Geared more to independent business travelers than to groups, they offer a more personal, intimate atmosphere than large international hotels. Examples include the Evergreen Laurel, the Somerset, the Swissotel and the Mansion Kempinski. The newly opened Sukhothai inclines toward chic Thai minimalist decor.

Looking for a bed

Anyone with the misfortune to find himself stuck at an unplanned stop in the back of beyond can take comfort from the fact that every province and many districts can be relied on to have at least a small hotel, often under Chinese management.

Bangkok offers a full range of accommodations, from inexpensive guest houses to high-rise, high-comfort luxury hotels.

Since the river affords the easiest way of getting around and many of the major sights are close by, it makes obvious sense to base yourself near it.

Despite the quantity of accommodations, these places fill up alarmingly quickly in high season; advance booking (easier for hotels than for guest houses) is advised.

There are disappointingly few places to stay that have real Thai character, although some of the hotel towers have breathtaking views from the upper floors.

Guest houses The popularity of the guest house is explained by a combination of low prices and informal atmosphere. Budgeteers now have a huge variety to choose from, and newer developments have raised the general standard.

Ten years ago, Khao San Road was an ordinary thoroughfare in the heart of Bangkok's historical district. The first guest houses, such as the VS and PB, were basic affairs—cheap but welcoming. The road's heart is a row of wooden shop houses and a few leftovers from the old days, which now compete for space with upmarket tailors.

New guest houses, cafés, shops and money changers open almost monthly, and souvenir stalls line the sidewalks. Khao San Road itself has become saturated, and the guest houses have taken over adjoining streets, mainly around Wat Chana Songkhram up to the river. They are moving north up Samsen Road and east along Ratchadamnoen Road.

Shop houses on Tanao Road soi (west) have opened as guest houses recently. The guest houses around Khao San Road are convenient for the Express Boat pier at Tha Phra Athit.

Other budget areas In Bangkok, these include Thonburi (around Pata Pin Klao) and Rama IV Road. While the former area is a Khao San offshoot, the latter dates from Vietnam War days.

A communal toilet—including a pot and water to use instead of toilet paper

The **Grace** and **Malaysia** hotels in particular are surviving icons of the era. However, this area is inconvenient as a base for exploring the city.

As a base for provincial travel, the guest house scene has one major advantage over conventional hotels. Up-country relatives of the proprietors usually advertise in them with enticing notices and business cards, thereby providing a ready-made pointer for somewhere to stay farther down the line.

This way, too, there is more chance of finding an English-speaking place that understands how Westerners like to relax.

Moving upmarket Above all, the Thais are keen hoteliers and so the choice is great. Hotels in the moderate-to-expensive bracket are scattered about the city in a bewilderingly random fashion. If you find yourself in Banglamphu, the **Viangtai** is a comfortable choice.

Moving downtown, many moderate hotels have the advantage of being open 24 hours a day. One such is the **Reno** in Soi Kasemsan, Rama I, which also has a pleasant swimming pool.

The **Honey Hotel** (Sukhumvit Soi 11) and the **Rex**, prominent on the south side of that road, are establishments of very similar caliber.

At the top end Of the upmarket hotels, the **Oriental** is an attraction in itself, its original building carefully preserved with details of the famous writers who have stayed there, such as Joseph Conrad and Somerset

109

Maugham. The tradition is kept alive with an award ceremony every year for writers in the Southeast Asian languages.

Even if you are not staying here, do try to sample the ambience, maybe by stopping by for cocktails at sunset (respectable dress is required).

Gargantuan riverside neighbors include the **Shangri-La**. Farther from the river lie the **Siam Intercontinental**, the **Regent**, the **Imperial**, the **Dusit Thani**, the **Montien**, the **Ambassador** and international chains such as the **Hilton** for five-star diners or guests. The Regent has a light and airy lobby, and the Hilton has refreshingly green gardens.

The cool, spacious lobby of the Imperial Hotel is typical of Bangkok's top international hotels. No expense is spared on decor, furnishings and facilities

Thai boxing

Thai boxing is supposed to have developed from hand-to-hand combat with the Burmese. King Naresuan the Great was himself a skilled fighter and made it compulsory training for his troops in the 16th century.

Muay thai

"Vicious and little controlled" was how one visitor described Thai boxing, and certainly it is not hard to believe that only 60 years ago muay thai—as it is known to its adherents—was illegal. Until the 1930s, horsehair strappings were used instead of gloves, and rules were nonexistent.

The apparent savagery of Thai kick-boxing may alarm Westerners, but there are some rules. Elbow-stabs and drop-kicks are far more common (and effective) than punches

Thai boxing The main stadiums for this part-sport, part-martial art are Ratchadamnoen and Lumphini. The audience will bet furiously but won't take a farang wager.

There is a lot of bleeding and lost consciousness, with legal blows including such charming moves as the elbow-thrust and drop-kick. Looking at the fanatical level of interest in this national sport today, it comes as no surprise to discover that when it was outlawed prior to the 1930s, an unregulated underground scene flourished. Eventually a set of rules was adopted: a fighter can use his feet, elbows, legs, knees and shoulders, in fact almost any part of his body. However, butting, biting, spitting and kicking an opponent when he is down are all forbidden. Kick-boxers fight in bare feet and are drenched with buckets of water in between rounds, when they are also pummeled by their masseurs almost as hard as by their opponents.

The kick-boxing ring has proved a successful training ground for regular boxing: Thai fighters consistently taking world honors in the lighter-weight divisions. Junior bantamweight champion Khaosai Galaxy stayed the course longer than most. The Isan lads produce *muay thai* champions like Rambo. Size is not a decisive factor and is not necessarily a measure of potential. Skill and dexterity are more important, and a well-delivered kick can floor an opponent.

Tension is heightened by a band that plays drums and the oboe-like *pii chawa*. Before a fight commences, fighters pay homage to their teachers and then start with an elaborate dance. When the fists start flying, the band crashes with the action. There are usually five three-minute rounds, and the referee has the authority to stop the fight if one of the contestants is seriously injured.

If you want to sample the frenzied atmosphere of a bout, Lumphini on Rama IV Road is open Tuesdays, Fridays and Saturdays, while the stadium on Ratchadamnoen Nok is open on the other days. Tickets for home games are hard to come by. Ticket prices vary from 500 baht or more for a ringside seat to 150 baht for the outer ring.

Colorful kites brighten the skies above Sanam Luang when the south winds blow in spring. Traditionally this is a time of leisure for rural workers after the rice harvest is over

Flying bomb kites

Kite-flying is now entirely recreational, but when Sukhothai was the capital of the first Thai kingdom (13th–15th centuries), kites played a deadlier role in warfare. The heads were packed with gunpowder, and the long tails were set alight to act as fuses. Other kites were used to ward off evil spirits, or as festive elements In great state occasions. Nowadays, kites are still sometimes used in rural areas as bird-scarers.

Kites Kite-fighting as a sport survives today from its origins in the Sukhothai period. Nowadays it tends to be an after-work activity that starts at around 4:30, when the larger offices close for the day.

The large star-shaped "male" *julaa* is pitted against several smaller square "female" *pakpao*. The julaa are sometimes as long as 6½ feet and take up to ten men to fly; the pakpao are smaller and faster and can usually be flown by an individual. For the purposes of a contest, the "male" and "female" teams face each other from opposite ends of the field. The object is to force the opponent out of the sky. The *julaa* tries to cross the boundary and capture the *pakpao*, bringing it to the ground back in its own territory. This is achieved by flying a series of skillful loops and sometimes by putting powdered glass on the strings.

Although the days of grand tournaments sponsored by kings are now over, the mecca for Bangkok fliers is Sanam Luang, the Royal Field. This is a large open expanse between the Grand Palace and Ratchadamnoen Avenue. Ornamental and specialist models are hung up across the paths for sale.

Prime season for kites is from March through May, when the southerly winds are blowing regularly. Watching this colorful spectacle is really a very pleasant way to pass the time.

The best vantage point for watching these kites in action could well be the benches that are found under leafy shade to the north of Sanam Luang. The ubiquitous mobile snack-sellers are usually on hand close by to ply the visitor with hard-boiled eggs and chili fish-broth noodles.

The children, too, have kites of their own, usually in the form of dragons and bats, which they fly for the sheer fun of it, leaving the serious fighting to the grown-ups.

Kite-fighting

First records of kite-fighting as a recreational activity traditionally come from the Sukhothai period. Ramkhamhaeng's father, Sri Intharadit, was a major enthusiast. Legends tell how he met the daughter of Phaya Eua while retrieving a kite from her roof in the dead of night.

SPORTS

Sword fighting
Three levels of the sport of sword fighting are practiced: with real weapons, with toy weapons for a striking game, or with decorated toy weapons for a dancing game.

Tagraw
Tagraw is a national sport that men of all ages play in their off-duty moments. Skilled players make the movements look effortless and dancelike as they use different parts of their bodies to keep the ball in the air.

There is no shortage of participants for Thai boxing matches. Despite the jasmine good-luck charms, the prize will go to the most skillful and determined fighter

Sword fighting Hand-to-hand combat with swords has been successfully turned into a very popular spectator sport by the exponents of fencing and a little-known variant with the traditional Thai battle sword, called *krabee krabong*. Also involved are the long, spearlike *ngaao* and the stave, *phlorng*, which gives it a resemblance to *Tai-kwondo*.

The sword (the straight-handled *daap*) is used double-handed or with a shield. The *krabee* with its proper hand-guard is used alone. The *mai san* are short shields for the forearms, which link the sport with Thai boxing. Other similarities are the band that accompanies the fighting, as well as the ceremonies at the start of a bout that pay respect to the masters.

In the sport version, players are arranged in suitable pairs, often matching one weapon against another of a different type: the stave may be pitted against the arm-shield, for example. There is no firm deciding test of victory—the players attempt set pieces in the roles of "attack" and "defense."

Many children still learn the art at school, and demonstrations are included in cultural shows put on for tourists at such places as the Rose Garden.

Tagraw or *takraw* is a sport in which a special touch-sensitive rattan ball is volleyed between two teams who face each other over a badminton-type net. The object of the game is to keep the ball aloft, and to this end any part of the body, such as elbows, shoulders and the back of the head, can be used except the hands. Whether the game originated in Thailand or Malaysia is a moot point. Malays take it very seriously; their word for it, *sepak* (kick), is added in the combined name *sepak-tagraw* in the Southeast Asian games.

Formal matches can be watched at Hua Mark or the National Stadium on Rama I, although it is very much a participatory sport, with matches going on everywhere. Another version, *takraw buang*, resembles basketball. Those without equipment stand around in a circle, and anyone who wants to develop his skills can join in.

Other sports

Boat racing Numbered among the many popular minor sports in Thailand, boat racing involves crews of 20–100 paddling brightly bedecked hardwood canoes. The occasional Thai *vs.* Lao contest on the Mekong River is a far cry from Oxford and Cambridge universities' crews battling it out in the annual boat race on the River Thames! Inside Thailand, the Phichit Regatta at the beginning of September is well known, but there are races in provinces as far afield as Nan, Buri Ram, Ratchburi and Korat (Phimai).

Fighting fish Buddhist fish-lovers may be appalled at the bizarre fighting fish, which tear each other to pieces in a jam jar to satisfy a wager. On their own they are quite attractive and show no signs of their aggression potential, but it is a different story if they are allowed to see one another. Two fish in separate jars must be shielded from each other's view.

Golf The Thais are great fans of this Western sport. While their soccer fields struggle with floods and droughts, golf courses are well looked after. Courses spring up everywhere as the focus for suburban development. Golf is tremendously popular with the leadership elite.

Recommended courses in the Bangkok area include the **Navatanee** at Bang Kapi (par 72), **The Rose Garden** at Nakhon Pathom (par 72), the **Royal Thai Air Force** at Don Muang (par 68) and the **Krungthep Kritha** at Hua Mark (par 72).

Of provincial courses, the **Royal Hua Hin** (par 72) is the oldest, having opened in 1924. The **Thaai Muang** (par 72), north of Phuket in Phang Nga province, features an 18th hole that is parallel to the beach.

Back in the city, a driving range has been built on Rama IV Road at Soi 26, where it is possible to practice your swing without the tedious long walk afterward.

Snooker This billiards-like game went through a boom here after the success of James Wattana Phu-Ob-Orm in Britain (see panel). For the less talented, a casual frame can be had at the PB Guesthouse on Khao San Road.

Thai chess The board-game fanatic may well enjoy a board of Thai chess (*mark rook*), which is often played on the sidewalk. The moves are played faster than in the Western version of the game.

Thai bullfighting
Bullfighting takes place in the south, but the Thai version is bull versus bull, rather than man versus bull.

Snooker star
James Wattana, or "Tong" as he is known in Thailand, was the country's first snooker player to have major success in world tournaments. In 1986, at the age of 18, he beat three former world champions— Steve Davis, Denis Taylor and Terry Griffiths—to win the Camus Masters' Trophy. He scored the highest break in the 1992 British Open Tournament.

113

Whatever the weather, golfers in Bangkok pursue their sport with every bit as much enthusiasm as their counterparts in the West

Practical points

Taxis and *tuk tuks*
If you are traveling by taxi or *tuk tuk*, it is useful to have a good map with you, as some drivers are woe-fully or willfully ignorant of the city's geography. Ask your hotel to write the name of your destination in Thai for you to show the driver. Always negotiate and agree on the rate before you set off in a *tuk tuk.* Many taxis now have meters; check that it is set at zero when you start your journey.

Getting about In Bangkok, it can be a nightmare. Pollution is high on the list of the city's troubles; it is worsening, and masks are now a common sight on the streets.

As traffic increases, the roads can't cope, and road budgets are a political football. Trying to drive in Bangkok itself is an unpleasant experience—slow, dangerous, smelly, confusing and best avoided. Getting out of the city is a blessed relief. Up-country driving has its drawbacks, but jams are not often among them, although there is a shortage of two-lane roads.

Driving at night, especially motorcycles, is best avoided. Cars must put up with heavily insect-smeared windshields, particularly around dusk, and motorcyclists must put the visor down or endure a diet of flies.

The river bus (see page 95) is the quickest way of getting between places within easy reach of the river. For travel from the airport, see pages 256–257.

Motorcycle taxis, whose drivers know the back streets and can squeeze down alleys, are cheaper than renting a car, and although the bikes are not all that powerful, they are usually quicker than taxis.

Tuk tuks, as a practical form of transport, do not rate highly, being uncomfortable, dangerous (unless you are wedged in), noisy and polluting. They are good, though, for loads such as backpacks and giant baskets of fruit.

Taxis are clean and air-conditioned and have drivers who will often complain in English about the traffic. They can get expensive.

Songthaews are pickups or low trucks with two long benches. Nowadays these ply along sois rather than the main roads.

City buses are improving. Bangkokians cram them-selves into the buses, but the cost-effectiveness of such low fares (between 3 and 30 baht) for the route's entire length cannot be denied. Even the little green buses, a backup system that operates for the normal routes, are usually quite packed.

The air-conditioned buses, identified by the Thai letters saying *por*, are the most comfortable. They can also fill up to bursting, but by getting on near the beginning of the route, you should be able to get one of the precious seats.

Crews personalize their vehicles with Buddhas, and Buddhist monks have an unassailable right to the back seats, so leave these alone. Many frown on the backpackers' habit of blocking the gangway with their backpacks.

The system shuts down around 11 PM. However, there are a few all-night buses. A useful one is the No. 2 from Sanam Luang all along Sukhumvit Road.

Some of the more useful air-conditioned buses are: 6 Sanam Luang, Indra Vihan, Nonthaburi, Pak Kret; 11 Sanam Luang, Ploen Chit Road, Sukhumvit Road, Ekamai (which is the eastern bus terminal); 12 Sanam Luang, Phetburi Road, Ramkhamhaeng Road, Bang Kapi; 44 Sanam Luang, Phaholyothin Road, Chatuchak, Morchit (northern bus terminal), Lat Prao Road; 7 Phrakhanong, Rama IV Road, Lumphini, Hualampong Station, Sanam Luang, Thonburi, Saai Tai (southern bus terminal).

An indispensable aid for the visitor is the latest edition of the Bangkok Bus Map, which shows all the bus routes in the city.

Provincial buses (see also pages 271–272). Operated by a sprawling state enterprise calling itself the Transport Company, the Thai system is cheap and extensive. If you are trying to get out of Bangkok, the three main terminals are sensibly sited on the major routes out of the city.

North/Northeast terminal
Morchit, Phahon Yothin Road
Destinations served: Ayutthaya, Bang Pa-in, Khao Yai, Lop Buri, Nakhon Nayok, Nakhon Sawan, Petchabun, Saraburi, Suphan Buri, Chiang Mai, Chiang Rai, Fang, Kamphaeng Phet, Lampang, Mae Hong Son, Mae Sai, Mae Sot, Nan, Phitsanulok, Phrae, Sukhothai, Tak.
From a separate northeastern terminal: Khon Kaen, Loei, Mukdahan, Nakhon Ratchasima, Nong Khai, Roi Et, Sakhon Nakhon, Surin, Ubon Rachathani, Yasothorn.

South terminal
Sai Tai, Nakhon Chaisri Road
Destinations served: Damnoen Saduak, Hua Hin, Kanchana Buri, Nakhon Pathom, Phetcha Buri, Cha-am, Chumphon, Hat Yai, Krabi, Nakhon Si Thammarat, Narathiwat, Phang Nga, Pattani, Phuket, Prachuap Khiri Khan, Ranong, Songkhla, Sungai Kolok, Suratthani, Trang, Yala.

East terminal
Ekamai, Sukhumvit Road
Destinations served: Chantha Buri, Ko Samet, Pattaya, Si Racha, Trat.
Additionally, numerous travel agents in and around Khao San Road offer bus services; these include frequent minibuses to the airport.

Microbuses
A recent addition to Bangkok's complex hierarchy of bus services is a smart, zippy little red vehicle known as an executive microbus. These are more expensive than the ordinary buses, but with air-conditioning, on-board telephones, newspapers, fax machines, and a guaranteed seat, they are understandably popular with Bangkok's hapless commuters, who frequently spend hours in choking traffic jams. Place the flat fare (currently 30 baht) in the box near the driver.

Traffic lights
Everybody wants to get somewhere quickly. The traffic light sequence in Thailand is red—stop (or when it's clear of other cars and police—go); yellow—go; green—go . The normal response to a changing green-to-red signal is to speed up. Only the traffic jams are effective in bringing vehicles to a halt.

115

CENTRAL THAILAND

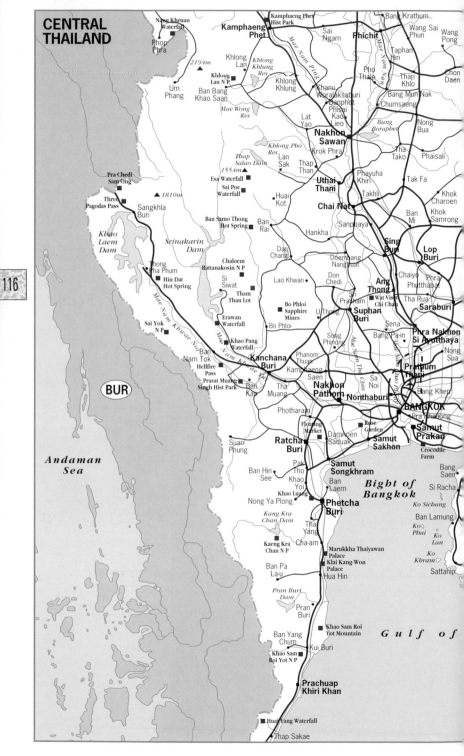

CENTRAL THAILAND

Nang Khruan Waterfall
Phop Phra
Um Phang
2194m
Khlong Lan
Khlong Lan N P
Ban Bang Khao Saan
Mae Wong Res
Khlong Khlung Res
Khlong Khlung
Khanu Woralaksaburi
Banphot Phisai
Lat Yao
Nakhon Sawan
Krok Phra
Kamphaeng Phet
Kamphaeng Phet Hist Park
Sai Ngam
Mae Nam Ping
Phichit
Wang Sai Phun
Bang Krathum
Wang Pong
Pho Thale
Taphan Hin
Thap Khlo
Bang Mun Nak
Chon Daen
Chumsaeng
Bung Boraphet
Nong Bua
Tha Tako
Phaisali
Phayuha Khiri
Tak Fa
Khok Charoen
Pra Chedi Sam Ong
Three Pagodas Pass
Sangkhla Buri
1810m
Khlong Pho Res
Lan Sak
Thap Salao Dam
1554m
Esa Waterfall
Sai Poe Waterfall
Uthai Thani
Takhli
Ban Mi
Khok Samrong
Huai Kot
Chai Nat
Sanphaya
Khao Laem Dam
Srinakarin Dam
Ban Samo Thong Hot Spring
Ban Rai
Hankha
Dan Chang
Doembang Nangbuat
Don Chedi
Sing Buri
Lop Buri
Chaiyo
Phra Phutthabat
Thong Pha Phum
Hin Dat Hot Spring
Chaloem Rattanakosin N P
Si Siwat
Tham Than Lot
Lao Khwan
Bo Phloi Sapphire Mines
U Thong
Si Pracham
Ang Thong
Wat Visit Chi Chan
Tha Rua
Saraburi
Suphan Buri
Erawan Waterfall
Bo Phloi
Sena
Bang Pa-in
Nong Sua
Khao Pang Waterfall
Sai Yok N P
Ban Nam Tok
Hellfire Pass
Prasat Muang Singh Hist Park
Kanchana Buri
Mae Nam Khwae Noi
Mae Nam Khwae Yai
Phanom Thuan
Kamphaeng Saen
Song Phinong
Bang Pa-in
Phra Nakhon Si Ayutthaya
Pathum Thani
BUR
Ban Kao
Tha Muang
Nakhon Pathom
Nonthaburi
Bang Khen
BANGKOK
Pra Pradong
Samut Prakan
Crocodile Farm
Photharam
Floating Market
Rose Garden
Samut Sakhon
Andaman Sea
Suan Phung
Ratcha Buri
Damnoen Saduak
Ban Hin See
Pak Tho
Khao Yoi
Samut Songkhram
Ban Laem
Bight of Bangkok
Bang Saen
Si Racha
Ko Sichang
Ban Lamung
Khao Luang
Nong Ya Plong
Kang Kra Chan Dam
Tha Yang
Cha-am
Phetcha Buri
Ko Phai
Ko Lan
Ko Kbram
Sattahip
Kaeng Kra Chan N P
Ban Pa La-u
Marukkha Thaiyawan Palace
Klai Kang-Won Palace
Hua Hin
Pran Buri Dam
Pran Buri
Ban Yang Chum
Khao Sam Roi Yot N P
Kui Buri
Khao Sam Roi Yot Mountain
Gulf of
Prachuap Khiri Khan
Huai Yang Waterfall
Thap Sakae

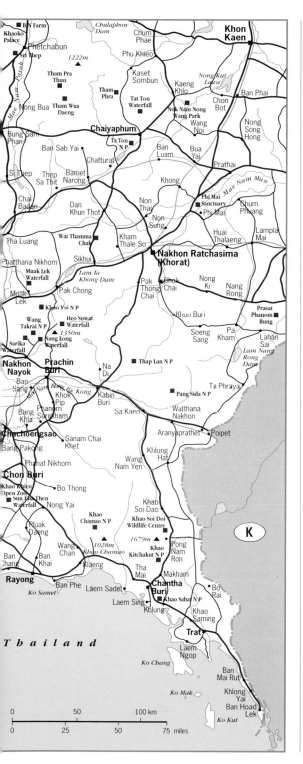

CENTRAL THAILAND

CENTRAL THAILAND

Bangkok's hinterland, the Chao Phraya basin, is the most densely populated and agriculturally productive of the country's main rural regions. For the purposes of this book, it includes the eastern coast of the Gulf of Thailand.

The **central plain** is drained by the Chao Phraya, the Tha Chin and the Bang Pa Kong rivers and is very fertile. When the Thai people first arrived here from the north, they found civilizations that offered them useful lessons in city-building, administration and statecraft.

The 9th-century Dvaravati culture passed on the branch of Theravada Buddhism that remains Thailand's official religion. Some say Nakhon Pathom may have been the chief city of Dvaravati, although most visitors come to see the 19th-century *chedi*.

A Buddha's head encased by a tree in Ayutthaya

Rice growing
The central plains are the rice bowl of Thailand, which is still the world's leading exporter of top-quality rice. During the dry season, farmers plow the land and plant the new crops before the rains. Through the summer, the rice paddies turn from green to gold. The whole community helps with the harvest in November. Modern technology has changed this annual cycle very little in over 700 years.

When the Mon withered under Khmer pressure, Thai chieftains took the lead. During this time, Lop Buri was a Mon-Indic center offering valuable tutelage. The foundation of Ayutthaya soon afterward hastened the Thai adoption of Indic rituals and mythologies.

The name Siam dates from the Khmer (10th–11th centuries), who employed Thai mercenaries. Khmer sanctuaries are scattered far to the west. For 400 years, the focus of Siam was Ayutthaya (although King Narai decamped briefly to Lop Buri). Although it weathered innumerable vicissitudes, the Burmese finally put an end to its dreams. Rallying quickly, the Thais drove them out, and Bangkok replaced Ayutthaya as the regional trade hub.

Ayutthaya, Phetcha Buri and Lop Buri are the most striking of the ancient cities of the region. In the far west, Kanchana Buri stands out as a rewarding area for its history and natural beauty and is easily accessible from Bangkok. Meanwhile, the coast is a well-established pleasure ground, with Hua Hin and Cha-am popular among weekending Thais. Farther east, Pattaya is a capital of sleaze and sex, but Ko Samet is an idyllic, though much discovered, tropical island.

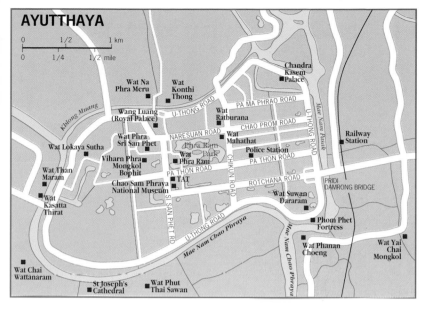

AYUTTHAYA

▶▶▶ Ayutthaya

47 miles north of Bangkok. Trains, boats and buses (northern terminal) from Bangkok

A pleasant day trip from Bangkok, especially by boat or train, the ancient city is littered with the remnants of its former glory. In its heyday, Ayutthaya was one of the biggest cities in the world, the center of a civilization that had diplomatic relations with Louis XIV of France. (His Jesuit mission built Thailand's first observatory.) This vast area, now a large modern town, is really too much to attempt on foot, but there are fleets of *tuk tuk* drivers on hand to guide people around for half a day.

History In 1350, when it was newly founded, Ayutthaya was just another Thai city-state in the Chao Phraya basin. There was Lop Buri, still a center of Mon-Indic culture, and there was politically dominant Sukhothai. Less than 100 years later, in 1438, Ayutthaya wrested control of the lower Chao Phraya basin from Sukhothai and did not yield it for another four centuries. Whereas Sukhothai represented a rebellion against the Angkor (Khmer) yoke, Ayutthaya's kings, in particular King Boromtrailokanat, sought to consolidate their power through the reimposition of Khmer social controls such as slavery.

By the early 16th century, the first voyages of exploration had led to the establishment of European trading settlements. The remains of these can be found to the southeast. The Portuguese and Dutch were the most persistent settlers, although the English and French had an important presence.

It is quite easy to imagine Ayutthaya as a bustling city at the hub of an empire. Tourists come to see the ruins, but may be disappointed with the sandstone stumps— all that remained after the Burmese had finished with the capital; their destruction of the city in 1767 was total.

Boat trips
Many visitors like to visit Ayutthaya from Bangkok via a cruise on the *Oriental Queen* river boat (see page 95), with a stop-off at Bang Pa-In summer palace. This is a slow but delightful trip; the train and bus provide useful alternatives for getting back.

Ayutthaya's heyday
The weathered ruins at Ayutthaya give little inkling of the city's former glory. From the mid-14th century until its catastrophic destruction by the Burmese in 1767, Ayutthaya enjoyed enormous prestige. By the 17th century it was a cosmopolitan trading center of world renown, with a populace composed of 40 different nationalities and a population numbering more than London at that time. Merchants and diplomats from East and West alike marveled at its golden temples and splendid pageantry.

Wat Yai Chai Mongkol

Suriyat Amarin Hall
King Narai built the Suriyat Amarin Hall, to the north of the city, to review boat races. Banyong Ratanat Hall was built by his son, Phetracha, a few years later in 1688.

The monuments There are altogether the ruins of some 375 monasteries, 29 fortresses and 94 city gates. (Certain sites charge an entrance fee). At the heart of the city is the huge compound of **Wang Luang (Royal Palace)►►►**, attributed to King Boromatrailokanat. Here are the spectacular remains of **Wat Phra Sri San Phet:** a trio of chedis lined up together contain ashes of Ayutthaya kings. This was the most important temple in the palace, and although the Burmese torched the standing Buddha, you get a good idea of its former glory. Farther south is the 40-foot-high bronze Buddha image at **Viharn Phra Mongol Bophit►**. **Wat Phra Ram,** begun in 1369, retains some stucco work displaying *nagas*, *garudas* and other mythical beasts; elephant gates can be seen in the walls.

Wat Mahathat (1384), with its tall Khmer-style tower, is picturesquely reflected in the pools of centrally located **Phra Ram Park**. Nearby is impressive old **Wat Ratburana** (1424).

Another monument to Ayutthaya's past is **Wat Lokaya Sutha**, with its large reclining Buddha, recently renovated in gleaming whitewashed cement.

The oldest temple is **Wat Phanan Choeng**, to the south of the city, which predates the city's founding by 26 years. Nearby, and also beyond the river, is **Wat Yai Chai Mongkol**.

On the north side of the city, **Wat Na Phra Meru**▶▶ is worth a detour because it was the only temple that escaped damage. Built in 1503, the *bot* has typical Ayutthaya-period features; there is a wonderful seated Buddha image beneath a gorgeous red and gold ceiling. Just over a mile northwest, on the very edge of the city, **Phu Kao Thong (Golden Mount)**▶ is a large, slightly leaning *chedi*; if you can bear the heat, climb to the top (the upper portion is restored) for an extensive view of the pancake-flat countryside.

Samurai
King Narai the Great had a bodyguard of mercenary samurai. The Japanese built their own village in the same area, which is now marked with memorials.

Museums There are two national museums in the city, both with exhibits from Ayutthaya. The **Chandra Kasem Palace**▶▶ (*Open* Wed–Sun 9–noon, 1–4. *Admission charge*) is a beautiful pavilion-style building. It was built by the 17th king of Ayutthaya and reconstructed by King Mongkut as a royal residence. **Chao Sam Phraya museum**▶▶▶ (*Open*—see Chandra Kasem Palace above) has a dazzling array of treasures as well as displays relating to outside influences on Thai art.

Workers make intricate models of historical figures in Ayutthaya. The city's illustrious past gives them plenty of subject matter

Queen Sunanda

An obelisk at Bang Pa-In commemorates Sunanda, the favorite queen of King Chulalongkorn. She drowned in a boating accident in 1881. Her boat capsized in full view of many horrified onlookers who could easily have rescued her, but in those times it was strictly forbidden for a commoner to touch any member of the royal family, on pain of instant execution. After this tragedy, the laws of *lèse-majesté* were swiftly reformed in Thailand.

Creative topiary at Bang Pa-In

▶▶ Bang Pa-In

Buses (northern terminal) from Bangkok; boat from Maharaj Pier at 8 AM, returning at around 5–5:30 PM
Open: daily 8:30–5. Admission charge

The famous **summer palace** of King Chulalongkorn was originally built by King Prasat Thong of Ayutthaya and abandoned when the city was sacked. King Chulalongkorn used the place to indulge his love of eclectic style. The formal Thai element jostles with Greek, Italian and Chinese influences.

Most bizarre of all is perhaps **Wat Niwet Thamprawat**, reached by a cable car, which proves that the beauties of Gothic cathedral architecture can just as well be used to praise Buddha. The place is nonetheless somber and unsettling—Westerners may expect to see a black-clad minister in this setting, but all around are monks in their orange robes. The grounds are pretty.

Cha-am

Buses from Bangkok (southern terminal), Hua Hin and Phetcha Buri. Off Highway 4

Like Hua Hin (see page 125), Cha-am is a resort with a history—though its future is perhaps looking even more high-rise. A mere 12 miles north of its royal neighbor, Cha-am's beach lies half a mile off Highway 4.

The long beach here is the closest west of Bangkok, which probably accounts for its rapidly developing popularity. Around the back you will find a small fishing port where you can watch boats steaming out to sea. The **Rung Arun Bungalow** on Ruamchit Road is at the bottom end of pricey resorts.

▶ Chantha Buri

Buses from Bangkok (eastern terminal) and Pattaya

This ancient port is about 205 miles from Bangkok, south along Highway 3 on the eastern coast. Popularly known as Muang Chan, it is replete with natural resources. The rainy season feeds the waterfalls and the lush forest; the dry season is the time to take to the province's beaches; and the best time of all is the fruit season.

The town itself is interesting and includes Thailand's largest Catholic cathedral, built by an emigré Vietnamese community.

Somdet Phra Chao Taksin Maharaj Public Park is a 148-acre public park in the center of Chantha Buri town (opposite the provincial court). Boats can be rented for punting. In the middle of the park is an island with a

Not many gems are left in Thai mines these days. Most of the rubies and sapphires on sale are imported from Cambodia and Burma

123

statue of King Taksin, who rallied Siamese troops here in their darkest hour against the Burmese.

The gem industry "Chan" (as Chantha Buri is locally known) is famous for its position as a center of Thailand's booming gem industry. The most convenient gem-mining region for the casual visitor is **Tha Mai**. It is reached along Highway 3, and day tours are organized from Pattaya. Seven miles along the route is the small peak of **Phloi Waen**, with **Wat Khao Phloi** at the top. Thai miners have more or less worked out the reserves; jewelers say the last big area for rubies is Phailin, in Cambodia. Beware of the rip-offs and false guarantees that plague the gem trade; see page 260.

Laem Sadet Khung Kraben has long, clean beaches. It is off Sukhumvit Road (Highway 3) at km 301, a right turn 30 yards along a laterite road. Coconut palms add to the tranquil atmosphere, and many of the restaurants have bathing rooms for swimmers.

Laem Sing, too, is worth a visit, on the left of the river mouth. It can be reached in 10 minutes by boat from one of the fishing villages. A walkway passes **Phai-rii Phinat,** one of several ancient forts, and there are fine views to be had from this hill. To the west of Laem Sing is a clean yellow beach with great views of the islands **Ko Chula, Ko Nom Sao** and **Ko Pehrit**; a pair of old cannons remains by a sentry post. In town, there are several budget hotels awaiting independent travelers.

Along the road to Laem Sadet Khung Kraben, bear right at a fork to reach the smaller beach of **Khung Wiman**. Just before the beach is a large standing Buddha, "subduing the ocean."

Panning still continues in some areas for the few gems that are left. You may be one of the lucky ones if you join a prospecting tour of the old mining areas

CENTRAL THAILAND

*Damnoen Saduak's
floating market is
one of the most
photogenic sights in
Thailand*

National parks Khao Khitchakut National Park is about 17 miles northeast of Chantha Buri, off Route 3249. It is mostly forest, and spots well worth visiting include the nine-level Krathing Falls. Great care should be exercised when climbing the levels.

There are two national park dormitories, capable of sleeping 10–15 people each; a large camp here takes 100 people. A fee is collected on the way in.

Wat Khao Sukrim, a further 6 miles from Krathing Falls and about 10 miles from Chantha Buri, is a "reformist" *wat* offering a 24-hour supply of free food and a library for overnight stays: a *wat* for the devotee rather than the tourist.

Phliw is a particularly charming, three-stage waterfall at the end of a paved road 10 miles from Chanta Buri. There are some chedis 650 feet up, dating from the reign of King Rama V, and a pyramid contains the remains of one of his queens who drowned tragically at Bang Pa-In.

About 2½ miles farther on are **Trork Nong Falls**. The "twin peaks" of **Khao Soi Dao** are thickly forested, with beautiful mountain views, and a vast wildlife reserve is home to Soi Dao Falls, a 16-level waterfall said to be the biggest and most beautiful in eastern Thailand (40 miles north on the Prachin Buri road).

▶▶▶   Damnoen Saduak

65 miles southwest of Bangkok; bus service 78 from southern terminal

Buses run regularly to Damnoen Saduak, a popular tour destination, starting at 6 AM

Visitors go to see the floating market—most popular of the many that have grown up in the region. All over the navigable system women paddle their little boats, selling food to householders on the banks. The market is held early to avoid the midday heat. The classic Thai peasant's straw hat is much in evidence among the women, who mostly trade in fruit and vegetables; visitors look on from the bridge spanning the canal.

▶ **Hua Hin**

South on Highway 4, about 140 miles from Bangkok
Hua Hin is a historic resort, the site of King Rama VII's palace, Klai Kang-won, or "Far from Worries." Of period interest are the royal golf course, the railway station and its hotel, which are now in private hands. The spacious Edwardian verandas are quite impressive.

Hua Hin is well endowed with other hotels and guest houses—budgeteers can shop around for a homely atmosphere—but maybe this "endowment" has gone too far, as blocks of flats and apartments crowd out the skyline; Hua Hin is bidding to become Pattaya without the nightlife but with hill tribe trekking. The beach is pleasant enough, but lacking in shade.

▶ **Kaeng Kra Chan National Park**

Off Highway 4, Phetburi (Phetcha Buri) province
Covering an area of 1,160 square miles, Kaeng Kra Chan is Thailand's biggest national park, located 37 miles from Phetburi (Phetcha Buri) town. The park office is a further 5 miles from Kaeng Kra Chan dam, built to service a smaller dam farther down the Phet River. Its reservoir has 20–30 islands and supports waterfowl and fish. Rental boats can carry 10–12 people.

The Thor Thip waterfall Boasting 18 stages, this dramatic spectacle is to be found 9 miles from Khao Phanoen Thung, the tallest peak in the park at 3,960 feet; the peak is 12 miles from the park office.

Walkers might go another 61 miles along the dam to the Paa Son Khao Thammachat, a mountain pine forest. Rewards take the form of viewpoints, cliffs and rock gardens. The park is not greatly developed, and treks off into the jungle are best undertaken with national park guidance. Very little English is spoken.

Staying over There is an accommodation service at usual national park rates, and it is advisable to make a reservation on 02/579 0529 or 02/579 4842. As with similar places elsewhere in Thailand, the accommodation gets most heavily booked at weekends.

Pa La-u
Pa La-u, a Karen tribe village a 17-mile jaunt from Hua Hin, has two stunning waterfalls. If camping, take every precaution against malaria. Attractive features in town include a thriving night market. Walkers can try climbing the stairs up Khao Tagiap ("Chopstick Mountain"), which has a monastery, a band of monkeys and tremendous views of the coast.

Hua Hin—tranquility under threat from development

■ **Thailand has suffered huge losses of natural habitats in the second half of this century. It is still rich in wildlife, from the exotic insects that you can see in town gardens to the giants of the jungle. But many creatures—tigers, elephants and the Sumatran rhinoceros, which is now believed to be extinct—are visibly under threat from the destruction of jungles and other habitats, a far-reaching problem that Thailand is at last trying to counter.** ■

Thai wildlife: fighting a losing battle? A female fire-tailed sunbird ...

126

Wild elephants

The number of wild elephants roaming the forests of Thailand has fallen dramatically in the last few years. It is estimated there may be fewer than 2,000 left, mostly in the national parks of Khao Yai and Khao Sok. The number of domestic elephants, too, has dwindled rapidly. There were over 100,000 working elephants in Thailand at the turn of the century. Now perhaps 5,000 remain, many relegated to the role of entertaining tourists, rather than their traditional task of hauling timber.

Threats Loss of habitats is not the only threat to Thailand's wildlife: in settled, heavily populated regions, it's neither safe nor convenient to have large, potentially dangerous animals wandering around. Hunters and poachers take a huge toll; the rarer some species become, the more desirable they are to unscrupulous collectors, and the prizes to be gained are therefore very great. Several species of mammal, bird, plant and even insect have been brought close to extinction by poachers and collectors. Trading in the meat of wild creatures is commonplace, as you can see by visiting the Chatuchak weekend market in Bangkok. Not only are wild birds and wild pigs sold for their meat, but even protected species like barking deer. The Wildlife Protection Division, which has only a handful of permanent officials, faces a grave shortage of funds and manpower to carry out its job.

Variety Thailand is at a geographical crossroads and has "captured" species from the Indian subcontinent, northern Asia and Australasia, as well as southern Asia. This diversity is particularly noticeable in its bird life; around 900 species have been recorded, making this one of the most exciting places in the world for bird-watchers.

When it comes to insects, the species are literally innumerable. It is possible that they become extinct even before they are recognized, as forests tumble under the loggers' chainsaws.

Wildlife

Optimism The Thai authorities are eager to preserve and enhance the country's wildlife, if for no other reason than its appeal to tourists. Already there are more than 80 or so national parks, protecting more than 15,440 square miles of unspoiled areas. One of the best and most accessible is Khao Yai (see pages 134–137), which covers a huge area of tropical rain forest. The rain forests are Thailand's greatest natural treasures, with staggering diversities of plants and creatures. Also of great interest and beauty are the coastal regions, with mangrove swamps, forested islands, salt pans, marshes and beaches.

Elephants The elephant is Thailand's most revered animal and a national symbol, once featured on its flag. But that doesn't deter the poachers. A chief warden at a national park recently committed suicide in desperation because his rangers were repeatedly attacked by elephant poachers armed with M-16s and other sophisticated military weaponry. The maximum fine for poaching is so small as to be derisory.

At the beginning of the century there were about 100,000 domesticated elephants here. They were used in war, to carry logs and to open up virgin forest. You will still see them used commercially even in the towns. A very small proportion of them are "white" elephants. These are not actually white all over but have lighter patches of skin here and there.

Thailand's flag
The former flag of Thailand was unintentionally flown upside down at the Versailles Peace Conference, and people said it looked like "a small domestic animal," so King Vajiravudh changed it for stripes.

Bears' paws
In 1991, a raid on a wildlife farm in Damut Prakan province revealed a grisly haul of 40 bear's paws. These are a particular delicacy in the Chinese and Korean cuisines and are believed to enhance sexual prowess.

... and white water buffalo, which, like most of Thailand's larger mammals, hover on the verge of extinction, along with many other species

CENTRAL THAILAND

Railroad trip to Nam Tok
Three trains daily make this two-hour trip from Kanchana Burialong the 48 miles that remain of the Death Railway. Booking is not possible. Near the end, the train grinds slowly along a wooden viaduct with views over the river and surrounding mountains. At Tham Krasae, it is possible to break the journey and have lunch at the bungalow resort below. At the end of the line, songthaews leave Nam Tok for Sai Yok Yai, a roadside waterfall. There are frequent buses back to Kanchana Buri.

The Bridge on the River Kwai, immortalized in the movie by David Lean, evokes one of the most harrowing events of World War II

▶▶▶ Kanchana Buri Province

Highway 323 west of Bangkok. Buses (southern terminal) and trains run daily from Bangkok (Noi station)
Kanchana Buri province offers grand scenery, with waterfalls, caves and rugged hills accessible within an hour or two of Bangkok. The **train journey**▶▶▶ from Bangkok, which takes three hours, is a real pleasure, passing lush wetlands, forests and rice paddies; the same train continues to Nam Tok (see panel).

Kanchana Buri Town▶▶, 80 miles west of Bangkok, has strong associations with World War II, but today the ghosts of the town's grim past seem exorcised, and it is a pleasure resort popular with residents of Bangkok, who during weekends frequent the food stalls by the river and party all night on fancifully designed rafts.

Beyond a bland town center (bus station and TAT office), older streets toward the river retain characterful wooden shop houses with balconies, and the city gate still stands. A number of waterside guest houses are relaxing and attractive, although the all-night weekend discos on the river can be irritating.

The Bridge on the River Kwai▶▶ Two miles from the town center is a grotesque remnant, symbolic of the traumas of the Death Railway, built by POWs in World War II (see pages 132–133). Only the two central pairs of girders—the straight-topped ones—are original. (The others are post-war replacements). Today trains make special stops at this macabre tourist attraction, and souvenir stalls sell plastic models of the bridge. It is possible to walk across between the rails, but there are unguarded drops. Two original locomotives are preserved here, and boat trips leave for the Floating Nun Cave (see below), the JEATH museum and the Chung Kai cemetery. In November/December, a strange weekend sound-and-light spectacular takes place here, culminating in a mock-up of the Allied bombardment on the Death Railway in 1945, complete with flashes and explosions.

Nearby are the **Japanese War Memorial** and the **World**

War II Museum and Art Gallery (*Open* daily 9–4:30. *Admission charge*). The latter's bizarre exterior is adorned with life-size statues of historic warriors and figures from World War II. Count Winston Cherchill (*sic*) bears a remarkable resemblance to Mussolini!

Chung Kai War Cemetery This is located on the west bank and most easily reached by long-tailed boat from the bridge or from the pier near the old city gate. Buried here are the remains of 1,750 prisoners.

Kanchana Buri War Cemetery►► Opposite the town's train station are the gates to these well-tended burial grounds, where 6,982 POWs are interred. An alphabetical register pinpointing locations of graves is kept in the office on the far left-hand side of the site. It is a moving place.

JEATH War Museum► (*Open* daily, 8:30–6. *Admission charge*) This museum was established by the chief abbot of the adjacent wat. JEATH is an acronym for the main nations involved: Japan, England, America, Australia, Thailand and Holland.

The museum is at the far south end of town and is reached by boat from the bridge or by samlor. It consists of a reconstruction of a POW *atap* hut and houses a modest but sobering display—objects from the camps, photographs, press cuttings and a series of paintings based on prisoners' sketches that resemble medieval depictions of hell.

Kanchana Buri Province
Wat Tham Monkorn Thong *4 miles west of Kanchana Buri town on Highway 3429*. This cave temple is of minor interest—consisting of a staircase leading to a meditation cave—but is celebrated for the Floating Nun, who sometimes meditates afloat in a pool and blesses the audience by blowing candle smoke over them.

Prasat Muang Singh Historical Park► *Follow Highway 323 westward, turning left onto Highway 3229, then right onto 3455 as indicated*. On the way you pass the turning for Ban Kao Museum, devoted to the archeology of a neolithic site in the area.

Prasat Muang was a Khmer outpost sited on a scenic loop of the Kwae Noi River. The major shrine dates back

---

Excursions and tours
Kanchana Buri is a great excursion center. Raft and boat trips with swimming and candlelit dinners and treks to waterfalls or caves are immensely popular. Bicycles can be rented if you want to see the countryside independently, but it is easier and safer to take an organized tour through a reliable local agent. Ask the tourist office for advice, as tour companies are subject to frequent change. Many operate directly from Bangkok.

The War Cemetery at Kanchana Buri

129

The Death Railway
A recent proposal to extend the reconstructed Death Railway as far as the Burmese border as a tourist attraction has offended survivors of the notorious prisoner-of-war camps and their families. Allied P.O.W.s and Asian laborers who died of ill-treatment while building the line for the Japanese lie along the original route, and many feel it should be left un-disturbed as a war grave.

The River Kwae, near Kanchana Buri, is a hive of activity as tour boats and ferries ply past innumerable bamboo raft bungalows. Despite the peaceful scenery, it can sometimes be quite noisy

Hog-nosed bat
Lawa Cave, in Sai Yok National Park, is one of 21 such cave sites in Kanchana Buri province, which is home to the kitti, or hog-nosed bat, *Craseonycteris thonglongyai.* This is the world's smallest mammal. Looking no larger than a butterfly, it weighs just under one-tenth of an ounce. Only 2,000 have been recorded, and the bat is one of the world's 12 most endangered species.

800 years, its form pierced by four gateways. A shelter by the river houses 2,000-year-old skeletons, discovered in 1979; clay pots, as well as bracelets of bronze, shell and bone, are still in situ.

Highway 323 to Three Pagodas Pass A road notorious for its smuggling, this pass leads into Burma through scenery characterized by sugarcane fields and curiously shaped limestone hills. This is an unstable and unpredictable area—there have been border skirmishes in the past—and you would be wise to seek local advice before traveling there.

A bus from Kanchana Buri to Sangkhla Buri takes five hours; there are morning *songthaews* from there to Three Pagodas Pass. The main sights on the highway are:

The Hellfire Pass Memorial▶, *signposted at the 66 km stone.* This is a short circular trail incorporating a section of abandoned track from the Death Railway. Begun by Australian POWs in April 1943, the pass was completed in 12 weeks and earned its nickname from their nighttime campfires. The trail opened in 1987 and some rails have been relaid.

Sai Yok National Park▶, *at the 82 km stone, 2½ miles off the highway.* (There is no bus service.) The park is best known for its bat cave (see panel), which can be reached by boat from the pier here, and the Sai Yok Noi waterfall.

Hin Dat Hot Spring, *a right turning at the 108 km stone.* This spring is a pleasant 104°F—a little above normal body temperature—and can be combined with a cool dip in the adjacent stream.

Sangkla Buri▶▶, *beside the vast Khao Laem Reservoir.* Here the forest has been submerged, but eerie tree stumps can still be seen above water level. A spectacular matchstick-like wooden bridge straddles the water and leads into the adjacent Mon settlement. Above this there is a hilltop *wat*, which offers a good view of the lake.

Three Pagodas Pass▶ Along the dirt road to Phra Sam Ong, the route heads past three modest pagodas at the border. It is often possible to walk into the Burmese village of Payathonzu▶, but cameras must be left behind at the border post. Across the border it is strikingly primitive, in contrast to Thailand. This is a remote and often dangerous area: only the very intrepid tend to travel here (see panel).

Tham Than Lot Cave▶▶ North of Kanchana Buri, this is one of the province's finest caves (electrically lit), with a waterfall nearby. There is no direct bus.

Erawan Waterfalls▶▶ These are to be found on Highway 3199 and can be reached by hourly buses and additional excursion buses.

The splendid falls have seven stages; a wet, enjoyable walk to the top takes between three and four hours to do the sight justice. There are pools for swimming, limestone encrustations, tufa and petrified logs. Overnight accommodations are available nearby.

Farther north, **Huay Khamin Waterfall▶▶**, remote but majestic, is reached by boat across Sri Nakharin Dam from Takadan pier.

The waterfalls of Erawan National Park are among the most beautiful and popular in Thailand

Burmese border tensions
The border region around the Three Pagodas Pass (Sam Phra Chedi Ong) has long been the scene of ethnic tension between the Burmese regime and the two hill-tribe peoples who dominate the area—the Mon and the Karen. During the past 50 years the three groups have struggled for control of the troubled hinterland and the consequent gains from illegal logging, smuggling, and drug-running.

■ **Made famous by David Lean's movie *The Bridge on the River Kwai*, the Death Railway commemorates one of the most appalling episodes of World War II. In the midst of the war in Southeast Asia, the Japanese saw the need for a rapid land route to get troops and supplies into Burma, as the voyage by sea across the Strait of Malacca, followed by a cross-country journey from Rangoon to Moulmein, was slow and hazardous. In January 1942, they decided to build over 250 miles of track over some of Asia's most inhospitable terrain.** ■

The Bridge on the River Kwai
David Lean's famous Hollywood movie was a fictionalization of these events, based on Pierre Boulle's novel. Among the cinematic inventions were the blowing up of the bridge by Allied commandos (when in fact it was bombed by the RAF), the use of British engineering skills to construct the bridge (the Japanese knew perfectly well what to do) and the efforts of the Allies in building as quickly and well as possible (they botched it wherever they could).

Forced labor Allied prisoners of war captured in Malaya, Borneo, Singapore and Indonesia were brought here to build the railway, and 16,000 of them died. Asian laborers were also enlisted, some from foreign companies in Malaya that had closed because of bombing; others came from India, Thailand, Indonesia and Burma. Many were press-ganged into service. They were regarded by the Japanese as totally expendable and were treated even worse than the POWs; the death toll among them was in the region of 100,000—roughly one man dead for every sleeper laid.

The initial task for POWs was to construct camps at Kanchai and Ban Pong (near Nam Tok). Priority was given to completing the Japanese guards' accommodations, then workhouses and working parties' huts, and lastly the buildings for sick prisoners.

Work began at Thanbyuzayat in Burma on October 1, 1942, and a little later at Ban Pong in Thailand. The two parties met at Nieke in November 1943, and the 263-mile line was completed in December. Reconnaissance flights by Allied forces began in 1943 and bombing followed; POWs were now working on patching up and maintenance, cutting fuel for the locomotives, handling stores and building roads. By the end of October, Japanese troops and supplies were getting through to Burma, and bombing intensified. Conditions for the prisoners temporarily improved in the spring of 1944 as the Japanese began to worry about world reaction to the heavy POW casualties, but things got worse from May until the end of the war.

Appalling conditions Malnutrition, disease and torture were the main causes of the high mortality rate. Food deliveries were erratic, and what got through was often rotten or infested. Many prisoners came to regard maggots as a vital protein source, and some even went to the length of washing the contents of Japanese officers' latrines to retrieve beans that had passed through their captors' digestive systems. Red Cross parcels were often held up by the Japanese, who sometimes deliberately let new food consignments rot.

Malaria, dysentery, vitamin deficiency and cholera were rife. POW camp doctors had to make do with what few medical supplies they had brought with them. Equipment was ingeniously improvised; drips were made from bamboo. Only the sick could tend to the sick; even some of these were forced to work. Prisoners became walking skeletons. Tropical ulcers gnawed them to the bone; rotten flesh was "cleaned out" by fish, which ate the loose material.

Hours were long and bamboo lashings frequent. Japanese and Korean guards devised sadistic tortures for those who were in breach of discipline or not working hard enough. Offenders were suspended by the thumbs from a branch with their feet only just touching the ground, or they were tied to trees with barbed wire. They were forced to hold heavy stones above their heads, or made to kneel on sharp sticks while bearing weights.

The shadow of death was always close, and despair crept into many prisoners' minds. Many died in Allied bombing raids, as they were forbidden to build a white triangle on a blue base, the international recognition symbol for a POW camp.

After the war American corpses were repatriated, but those of other nationalities were transferred from the camp burial ground to three war cemeteries—one in Burma and two in Kanchana Buri. Mass graves are still discovered from time to time in the jungle.

Fate of the line
In 1945, the British dismantled 2½ miles of track at the border and two years later gave the remaining 185 miles to Thailand. Thai authorities dismantled the line from Nam Tok westward and upgraded the rest. The line reopened in full in 1958.

133

Memorial to the victims of the Death Railway at Kanchana Buri (top), and (bottom) the line itself

IN HONOURED REMEMBRANCE OF THE FORTITUDE AND SACRIFICE OF THAT VALIANT COMPANY WHO PERISHED WHILE BUILDING THE RAILWAY FROM THAILAND TO BURMA DURING THEIR LONG CAPTIVITY
THOSE WHO HAVE NO KNOWN GRAVE ARE COMMEMORATED BY NAME AT RANGOON SINGAPORE AND HONG KONG AND THEIR COMRADES REST IN THE THREE WAR CEMETERIES OF KANCHANABURI CHUNGKAI AND THANBYUZAYAT
I will make you a name and a praise among all people of the earth when I turn back your captivity before your eyes, saith the LORD

▶▶   **Khao Chamao National Park**

Off Sukhumvit Road (Highway 3) at km 274 and a further 10 miles up to Ban Nong Nam Sai

Located in the Klaeng district of Rayong province, Khao Chamao's 32 square miles were declared a national park in 1975. Waterfalls are plentiful; on the list to see are Khao Chamao, Nam Pen, Khlong Paa Kan, Khlong Hin Phloeng and Khlong Phra Jao. Khao Chamao, also known as Khlong Nam Sai, has very beautiful rock formations. Look out for the big fish in the rock pools, especially the Pla Phluang at Wang Matcha.

Many of the caves at **Khao Wong** have extensive systems of caverns, some of which are very deep. Waai li Lo, Thong Phra Rong, Phra and Sa Song have plenty of stalactites and stalagmites, and some caves shelter pools of water (complete with fish). Khao Wong can be reached by turning off Sukhumvit Road at km 286 and continuing for 7 miles. It is a laterite road: tough going in the rainy season.

▶▶   **Khao Sam Roi Yot National Park**

Reach by private transportation or by tour. South of Pran Buri off Highway 4, the turnoff to this national park is found at Kuiburi, by the 286 km post, but it is quite difficult to spot. About 25 miles south of Hua Hin

This is a most impressive, desolate moonscape over flooded rice paddies, with the mountains clearly visible.

The park office has refreshments and very helpful staff. Park beds are available for about 100 baht, and groups can rent a dormitory house for around 500–1,000 baht.

A canal behind the office can be explored in a long-tailed boat. Between the office and Khao Daeng summit, birds and monkeys abound on all sides. The park is also home to the *serow*, an endangered goatlike animal.

Modest Samphraya beach, 4 miles north of the park headquarters, has tents for rent. The more remote and beautiful **Laem Sala beach** (10 miles) is accessible either by boat or by vehicle. Here, King Rama V built a glittering little pavilion at Phraya Nakhon Cave to catch the sun.

▶▶▶   **Khao Yai National Park**

Highway 1 to Saraburi, then Highway 2. A bus leaves from Bangkok Northern Bus Terminal at 9 AM, returning at 3

Thailand's richest national park for wildlife lies just over 125 miles to the north of the capital, and extends across 836 square miles, straddling four provinces and rising to 4,431 feet. The road up to the top (Highway 3182) has a signed viewpoint looking across the park.

Park wildlife The park encompasses a diversity of habitat—tropical rain forest, hill evergreen, dry evergreen, dry deciduous forest and grassland—that gives rise to over 2,000 plant and 300 bird species. Bird checklists and trail maps are on sale at the park headquarters. It is easy to get lost here, and you would be well advised to hire a guide or take a tour.

Each evening at 8, trucks leave on night safari from the park headquarters and restaurant. The trucks beam spotlights over the adjacent jungle, and there is a slight

Khao Yai National Park

Hornbills
Hornbills are among Thailand's most spectacular birds. Large, noisy, and colorful, they are easily detected crashing about in the trees or swooping for food. Khao Yai offers refuge to four of Thailand's 12 different species of hornbill. Most striking of all is the great hornbill, with vivid yellow and black plumage. The Indian pied hornbill is black and white. The others are the wreathed and rhinoceros hornbills. They breed from January to May.

chance of spotting one of the park's 200 elephants, which are attracted by salt licks near the road. Samba deer are the largest deer species and display magnificent antlers. Porcupines, palm civets (small, spotted cats), gaurs (wild black cattle) and slow loris are commonly seen, and a watchtower in the grassland is well placed for a rare view of Khao Yai's two dozen tigers.

Park trails Khao Yai has 12 marked trails through tropical forest, thick with winding creeper and luxuriant ferns. Look out for gibbons, civets and monkeys. Exotic birdsong haunts the forest; the birds themselves often remain tantalizingly out of sight, but with patience you should get the odd sighting, maybe of the great hornbill, the park's largest bird.

Haew Suwat is the most accessible and popular of the park's many waterfalls and has a beautiful pool where you can swim behind the curtain of water.

The **Million Bats Cave** is off the Pak Chong road (outside the park at the 21km stone, by a *wat* and a sign to Forest Hill; fork right after 1¼ miles to reach a parking area). A steep path leads up to a small cave where a dark swirl of countless wrinkled-lipped bats leaves at dusk. They hunt for eight to 10 hours and trap 6,000 mosquitoes each night. Their guano is collected for fertilizing fruit trees and for use in gunpowder manufacture.

Conservation pressures Khao Yai missed out on gaining World Heritage Site status because of illegal encroachment around its peripheries, a highway slicing through its very heart and a recurring threat of a major dam construction on a site partly covered with virgin forest and inhabited by elephants. Recently, in the interests of conservation, a hotel has been demolished and a golf course has been abandoned. The campsite has been retained. Guides should be arranged in advance through the Forestry Department (tel: 02/579 0529).

Walk 6-mile circular walk in Khao Yai: trails 1, 3 and 4.

A five-hour walk through dense jungle. Tread quietly to enhance your chances of spotting wildlife. The paths are shown with paint marks and, despite the luxuriant vegetation, are mostly well beaten.
Start at Pha Kluai Mai (Orchid) Campsite.

Turn right out of the campsite, along the road. After 350 yards, take the trail on the left marked Gong Gheo Waterfall (4 miles) and follow Trail 3 (red and yellow paint marks).
The jungle here is usually very quiet, although gibbons can sometimes be heard. Much of the birdlife can only be seen high above. Civets may be spotted on the ground, and elephant dung often litters the paths.

After 1¼ hours turn right at path junction (Trail 1; orange paint marks). The left path is signed to Visitor Center. Ignore another left turn for Visitor Center 10 minutes later. After another hour's walking, continue on to Haew Suwat at the junction, ignoring the left turn to Haew Praton.
The final section has fine waterfalls (excellent for swimming), and there is a well-sited restaurant.

Fifteen minutes later, Haew Sai waterfall is reached by a short, steep path to the left, or by continuing along the main path. Both routes unite near the foot of Haew Suwat waterfall, from which it is an easy 1½-hour riverside stroll on Trail 4 to the campsite.

Getting there Khao Yai is about three hours by road from Bangkok. Two-day tours from nearby Pak Chong are offered by **Khao Yai Wildlife Tour** (tel: 044/313 0545) and **Jungle Adventure** at 752/11 Kongvaksin Road Soi 3, Pak Chong (tel: 044/313836. Both leave daily, and no booking is required. Additionally, many travel agencies in Bangkok can arrange trips. There are four buses an hour from Bangkok to Pak Chong.

King Narai (1656–88), who presided over one of Ayutthaya's most glorious periods, spent more than half his time in Lop Buri, his second capital

▶▶ Ko Samet

Off the eastern coast of Rayong province, in the Gulf of Thailand. It is easy to drive or get a direct bus to Ban Phe, the supply port, then take one of the regular boats. The bus stops at Samet harbor, and the walk around to the beaches is not arduous, but a pickup service is available. There are also tour buses.

Also known as Ko Kaew Phitsadan, "The Enchanted Crystal Island," Ko Samet inspired some of the writings of the classical Thai poet Sunthorn Phu. Its beauty, however, has been under threat, and this is another national park (like Khao Yai) where the authorities have felt compelled to reinforce the national park status in the wake of massive surreptitious development. Toward the end of 1990 and again in 1992, the island was officially closed in a tense standoff between the government and bungalow operators. The bungalows were allowed to stay, but an unrepentant government refused to rescind the ban. Maybe the operators realize the insecurity of their investment and are unwilling to increase it. Cynics doubt the government's sincerity, suspecting them of wanting shares of a bigger pie.

None of these political considerations seems to affect Ko Samet's popularity as an island retreat for Bangkokians. Despite the fact that boats stop running in the evening, despite limited well water and unreliable electricity, the weekends in particular see hundreds of Thais coming to "hang out in the air," or *tak agat*. It gets very busy in August, December and January.

After you pay the national park fee, it is an easy matter to walk down to the beach at Hat Sai Kaew. This first beach is popular with Thais, who have built restaurants and bungalows here. At Ao Phai beach, Sea Breeze and Naga bungalows are recommended. Beyond a charming little cove is Ao Wongdeuan and some upmarket developments. Forest trails run west from the track, linking this string of beaches to another beach and coves, where there are splendid sunset views.

▶▶ Lop Buri

North of Bangkok on Highway 1. Buses and trains (Chiang Mai line) from Bangkok

The town of Lop Buri lies 96 miles to the north of the capital. Note that buses take you to New Lop Buri, which is of no intrinsic interest; take a *samlor* to the ruins, as it is much too far to walk. The train station is within a few minutes' walk of all the historic sights. Lop Buri has considerable appeal for its compactness and modest demands, although it hasn't the wealth of historical remains found in Ayutthaya or Sukotai. Sites of interest can be toured on foot comfortably in half a day.

During the Dvaravati period of the 6th to 11th centuries, Lop Buri was named Lavo and was a major center. In the 10th century, it became part of the Khmer empire, but its heyday occurred during the reign of King Narai in the 17th century, when it was the second capital after Ayutthaya.

King Narai's city wall fortification still encloses the old city, although it is little more than a rough bank. A town gate survives on the south side.

Narai Rajaniwet Palace►► (*Open* Wed–Sun except national holidays, 8:30–noon, 1–4:30. *Admission charge*) The walled palace dominates the town center. It was built between 1665 and 1677 for King Narai, who died here in 1688. French architects assisted in its design, which shows European as well as Khmer influences. Numerous European emissaries stayed here. The palace stands partly ruined in a pleasant park setting of shady lawns.

Entering through the main gateway, the path leads past a former reservoir, on the left, which once supplied the city and which was fed by terracotta pipes from a source 12 miles away. The long red-brick building behind is the old treasure house. Over the path ahead, a pointed arch shows clear Islamic influences.

Beyond, a complex of three pavilions houses the **Lop Buri National Museum**, a substantial collection, with objects from the Dvaravati period onward, including fine Lop Buri–style religious artifacts found locally.

Behind this is the roofless audience hall, where Narai received the ambassador of Louis XIV, the Chevalier de Chaumont. Arched doors and windows hint at the European connection, although others are traditional Thai tapering oblongs.

Wat Phra Sri Ratana Mahathat► Opposite the train station, this impressive site dates from the 12th century. Its central *prang* is Khmer in style; later additions include *chedis* in the Ayutthaya and Sukhothai styles. There is an admission fee.

Phra Prang Sam Yot► By the railway line 656 feet north of the station, these three giant laterite and sandstone *prangs* show both Hindu and Buddhist influences and represent the quintessence of Lop Buri style. They denote Brahma, Siva and Vishnu, the Hindu sacred triad.

Across the tracks, San Phra Kan is a modern Hindu shrine abutting an ancient laterite mound. Well-fattened monkeys and docile goats frequently visit the compound, feeding on temple offerings. The "monkey feast" every afternoon at 4:30 is a lively scene.

Lop Buri style
Khmer (Cambodian) influences on art in the central and northeastern regions from the 10th to the 14th centuries produced a distinctive style generally known as "Lop Buri." Buddha images dating from this period can be seen in many Thai museums, though some fine examples have been smuggled out of the country. The main characteristics of the style include broad, flattish faces, a pronounced bump on the head (signifying enlightenment), and courtly robes and a diadem.

The Khmer temple of Sam Yot is a good example of provincial art. The prangs (towers) are decorated with stucco friezes

Vichayen House
This was built for the Chevalier de Chaumont and was later the residence of Constantin Phaulkon, Narai's chief minister from Greece. Phaulkon was the only farang to hold such a post in the Thai court and was killed in a coup by Phra Phetracha, who subsequently moved the court to Ayutthaya. Remains of a chapel and hall of residence are visible. There is an entry fee.

Thongs are popular and convenient in a country where it is customary to remove shoes on regular occasions, such as before entering a wat

Princess Chumbot's garden

The botanical gardens at Wang Takrai Park were established by Prince and Princess Chumbot (see Suan Pakkard Palace in Bangkok) during the 1950s. Princess Chumbot was a skilled and knowledgeable horticulturist, and she imported many unusual varieties of plants and trees discovered on her travels abroad. When her husband died in 1959, she opened the gardens to the public in his memory. A stream flows through the park, adding to its pastoral air.

"Newsmen, young ladies, senior citizens—why be slow? Happiness awaits in Nakhon Nayok. Cast off your sadness into Wang Takhrai falls. Boost your morale at Sarika—where can compare with our house?"—Thai promotional leaflet.

▶ **Nakhon Nayok and Wang Takrai**

North from Bangkok along Highway 1, then Highway 305. Buses from Bangkok (northern/northeastern terminal)

About 87 miles from Bangkok, Nakhon Nayok has a scattering of nearby attractions within a couple of hours of the capital.

Follow Route 3049 northeast across the main intersection in town to get up the mountain to **Wang Takrai National Park▶**.

Sarika waterfall▶ is reached by a 2-mile turnoff to the left on Highway 3049. This popular beauty spot is close to a number of prettily designed bungalow resorts such as Chor Mamuang Cottage, Sut Jai and Po Daeng Wang. These will serve the fainthearted, while the energetic will find, above the headwaters of Sarika, the **Mae Plong waterfall**, which must be trekked to and camped at. Nang Long waterfall is a short drive to the east.

Takrai Resort was one of the first bungalow resorts built in Thailand. The **Sidari Resort** offers accommodations at Nang Long waterfall, toward the road's end.

The Chumphot-Phanthip botanical gardens These were founded in 1952 by Princess Chumbot and named after the lemon grass that grows here in abundance.

Dong Lakhorn To the south of the city are the ruins of this settlement, which dates from the Dvaravati period until the time that the Ayutthayan influence made Nakhon Nayok preeminent. It was abandoned to the forest 100 years ago.

Ironically, today the surrounding forest is all rice paddies, and Dong Lakhorn itself is now a last refuge for many forest species. Of special interest among the artifacts uncovered are glass beads and small earthenware pots.

► **Nakhon Pathom**

*West along Highway 4 about 33 miles from Bangkok.
Buses (southern terminal) and trains from Bangkok*
Believed to be the oldest city in Thailand, Nakhon
Pathom's name is derived from the Pali expression
Nagara Pathama, "First City."

Phra Pathom Chedi►► (*Open* daily 6–6) The whole city
is dominated by this huge tower, which can be seen for
miles around. At 417 feet, it is the highest Buddhist
monument in the world. The original *chedi* was a much
more modest affair, built during the Mon empire and the
oldest Buddhist monument in the country. Nakhon
Pathom was then one of a loose collection of city-states
that flourished between the 6th and 11th centuries.
When the town was beseiged by King Anawrahta of
Burma in the 11th century, the *chedi* was destroyed and
the town left in ruins. Restoration was begun by King
Mongkut in the mid-19th century, but eventually these
attempts had to be abandoned as the building's
structures proved to be so unstable. Instead, a new one
was built over the original site. This new temple fell
victim to a particularly bad period of rain and storms and
was finally completed by King Chulalongkorn as the
magnificent structure seen today. It commands an
appropriately large park setting and is surrounded by
trees. Dance drama is sometimes performed next to the
outer walls, and a fair is held in the temple grounds each
November.

A nearby museum (*Open* Wed–Sun 9–noon, 1–4.
Admission charge) contains some interesting sculpture.

► **Nakhon Sawan**

*North off Highway 117, 150 miles from Bangkok. By bus
and train (Chiang Mai line) from Bangkok*
Nakhon Sawan town is situated at a major river
confluence, where the rivers Nan, Ping, Wang and Yom
unite to form the great Chao Phraya. Central and North
Thailand meet here, adding significance to this large
town, whose sights include Wat Chom Kiri Nak Phrot,
towering over the plain and offering a huge view.

At the Chinese New Year, a lively dragon procession
draws crowds from miles around.

Legend of the *chedi*
Legend has it that the
original 128-foot *chedi* at
Nakhon Pathom was built
as an act of contrition by
a Mon prince who unwit-
tingly murdered his father,
thus fulfilling the prophecy
that had caused him to be
abandoned at birth. After
dispatching both his
tyrannical father and the
unfortunate women who
had adopted him (whom
he blamed for his patricidal
tendencies), he built the
first *chedi* to expiate his
sin.

141

*The immense gold
chedi at Nakhon
Pathom is the most
recent version of
several tombs on the
same site built over
the course of a
thousand years*

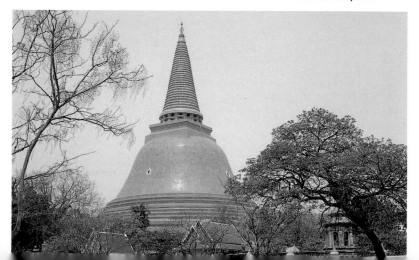

Pattaya

Off Highway 3 on the eastern coast of the Gulf of Thailand. Buses from Bangkok (eastern terminal)

The legend of Pattaya is well known. From a few G.I.s sleeping on the beach grew a city to rival its political master, Chon Buri. Starting out with attractions aimed at the young single military man, the settlement soon added other items for family clients, as the new tourist resort turned to the deutsche mark as the main incoming foreign currency. The days of R & R are still far from over. The U.S. Navy rewarded their Gulf War personnel with an extended binge in a town that might be likened to a latter-day Sodom or Gomorrah.

Garish signs and billboards vie for the attention of potential customers along the noisy, neon-laden streets of downtown Pattaya

Islands
The sleazy artificiality of modern Pattaya is inescapable. To enjoy a faint glimpse of the unspoiled tropical paradise those war-weary U.S. troops discovered when they first landed here on leave from Vietnam, visit the coral islands just offshore. Despite some pollution and damage to reefs by dynamite fishing, the tropical sea life is still abundant. There are excellent spots for divers and snorkelers on the remoter islands of Ko Sak, Ko Lin, and Ko Pai.

Rapid growth Development has been fast, furious and mainly unplanned, to the extent that the "Pattaya syndrome" has been specifically avoided everywhere else, even in Phuket. As at Patong in Phuket, some visitors may feel uneasy in a place that is almost no longer "Thai," but for jaded urban decadence, Pattaya is heaven. The foreign-food restaurants are a prime example, offering a Babel of menus that easily rivals Bangkok's.

Nighttime entertainment, besides the "bar-beer" joints, includes nightclubs and discos, of which the Palladium is the largest.

Building sites litter the place, and this is a town where seediness is endemic. The disadvantages of carelessly disposed waste are painfully apparent, as swimming becomes an unpleasant obstacle course. However, wide publicity about Pattaya's unsavory aspects has not discouraged the visitors, and, to be fair, it is a lot more appealing than some cold and wet European cities.

The beaches There are two beaches: **Pattaya,** named after a sea breeze, and the larger **Jomtien** to its south. The former area, a "ladder" of parallel sois, is where the night action takes place in noisy bars. Jomtien is a more pleasant venue for just enjoying the beach, although it is not clean, and sitting in the wrong place can mean constant harassment by a stream of vendors.

The package tourists generated Pattaya's second spurt of growth. Water sports by day are of most kinds—parasailing, waterskiing, windsurfing and game fishing. Pattaya scores over Phuket, with dinghy sailing encouraged by the king, whose Royal Varuna Yacht Club is in nearby Jomtien with single-handed Laser dinghies for rent.

Leaving early in the morning are tours to **Ko Lan** with the glass-bottomed boat excursion. Less than an hour away, there is a regular ferry, although most people book a tour. Farther out, and for divers only, are **Ko Sak**, **Ko Lin** and **Ko Pai**, the last having an old shipwreck.

Packaged fun Water World, at the Pattaya Park Beach Resort, is the perfect water palace, with huge slides. A death-defying bungee jump has been installed, said to be the highest in the world. Kids may love a little ride on a water scooter; away from the beaches, the scale-model **Mini Siam** and the zoo, orchid farm, culture shows and handicraft demonstrations at **Nong Nooch Orchid Wonderland** are popular.

Ka-toeys
Thailand's transsexuals use hormones and are so convincing that it is a challenge to spot them. The *ka-toey* is generally understood to be a passive homosexual who has long had a role in the traditional village burlesque or *Likay*. In Pattaya, they make serious money by titillating coachloads of package tourists with lip-synch cabaret routines. The phenomenon has spread from there to Bangkok and recently to Patong beach in Phuket. The shows are genuinely entertaining, with an eclectic menu of Chinese, Thai and Western songs. Pattaya's pioneering shows, still going strong, are called Tiffany's and Alcazar.

143

Water pollution
Water pollution has been one of the main environmental problems caused by the unplanned escalation of Pattaya into a major resort. For years raw sewage was simply pumped into the bay, with the result that swimming close to the shore became a distinctly unsavory prospect. Coastal bacterial counts rose to alarming levels, but eventually the government announced plans for a clean-up and invested a large sum in water treatment plants. Things are gradually improving.

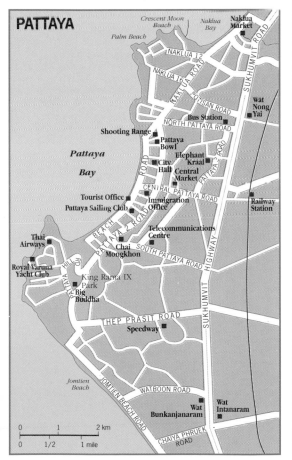

The tall white tower of Wat Mahathat at Phetcha Buri dominates the skyline for miles around. The bot contains rich murals and fine statues

▶▶   Phetcha Buri (Phetburi) Province

102 miles south of Bangkok, on Highway 4. Trains and buses from Bangkok (southern terminal)

The provincial capital of Phetcha Buri (Town of Diamonds) is a comfortable two-and-a-half-hour journey from Bangkok. Phet's proximity to the capital makes it very popular with Thai weekenders; it is worth a visit with a stopover, to take in the many worthwhile sights in and around the capital. The town itself is haphazardly and quaintly laid out. Rivers and canals abound, and the growth of the concrete shop house has been at least partially arrested.

Phetcha Buri town An ancient *wat* of Mahayanist inspiration, **Wat Mahathat▶▶** has an impressive sister temple in Nakhon Si Thammarat. The largest of five white *prangs* (rounded spires) can be seen from quite a distance away. This important temple is always a hive of activity.

Wat Yai Suwannaram▶▶ has strange murals in a windowless chapel associated with Phra Jao Seua, "the tiger king."

Well worth a visit is **Wat Kamphaeng Laeng▶**, a complex of temples that as a whole is in good condition. Indicative of a Khmer presence a millennium ago, there are four red sandstone *prangs* from the reign of Woraman VII in Bayon style. In 1956, a statue of Umadevi was found inside a broken *prang*. On Kamphaeng Laeng Road in town, the original walls remain.

On the west side of the city is the major landmark of **Khao Wang▶▶** (*Open* Wed–Sun 9–4. *Admission charge*). It is the site of King Mongkut's palace and hilltop settlement known collectively as **Phra Nakhon Khiri** (Holy City Hill). A cobbled path leads up the hill, or you can take the cable car. The vista spans the city, the surrounding river and rice fields and even the border with Burma to the west. The walk up is harder than it looks

Marukkha Thaiyawan Palace
In 1924 the teak palace of Marukkha Thaiyawan, designed by an Italian, was dismantled and moved on the orders of King Rama VI from its original location on Jao Samran beach near Phetcha Buri to the southern outskirts of Cha-am just down the coast. It has been under renovation for many years but is usually open to visitors.

Mongkut's palace
King Mongkut (Rama IV) built the palace of Khao Wang in 1858 as a holiday retreat and its eclectic style combines Oriental and Western architecture. Views from the hill reward the steep ascent. When the king came to stay, he lodged in the summer house (now the museum) and spent many nights stargazing from his nearby observatory (see page 134).

and is usually completed with monkeys looking on from their vantage points in the trees and surrounding walls.

The site is now a National Historical Park. There is a national museum on the site with 1½ miles donated to the royal family.

Beaches Once a favorite haunt of 16th-century King Naresuan, **Jao Samran beach** has now been well developed with hotels and eateries. The wide choice of places to stay includes Jao Hut bungalow (in the budget range), Wong Jan bungalow (moderate to expensive) and Hat Jao Samran hotel.

Hat Beuk Tian is another clean, wide beach 4 miles to the south of Jao Samran. The broad white sands are reached by the Phetkasem highway, turning left at Thaa Yaang. Accommodations at Beuk Tian Villa range from budget to expensive.

Out of town Some 3 miles out of town, **Khao Luang** is a famed Buddhist shrine, where a big cave has a tree-lined entrance secured by a door. In the illuminated caverns, locals have installed images and a footprint. Opposite the entrance is **Wat Bun Thawoo,** with striking designs by its former artisan abbot. The legend of nearby **Tham Klaep** caves tells of a secret door leading to a mysterious land that is populated only by young maidens.

Khao Bandai-it is about 1¼ miles west of Khao Luang. Vehicles have easy access to the mouth of this pretty Phetcha Buri cave system with its Ayutthaya-period religious accoutrements. Beyond the elephant statues by the entrance lies a labyrinth of limestone caverns crammed with hundreds of Buddha images.

Khao Yoi, another cave system, in the isolated mountain area, is 14 miles out of town (but accessible by train) and boasts a reclining Buddha, 32 feet in length. This was a favored meditation spot of Rama IV when he was a monk.

E-Ko mountain, to the north of Khao Yoi district, has an important *chedi* and customary "merit walk."

Egg custard
If you have a sweet tooth, you will enjoy Phetcha Buri. This town is famous for its sugary egg custard (*khanom maw kaeng*), made from coconut-palm juice and mung beans. Local shops, restaurants, and foodstalls sell this specialty, which is still very much a cottage industry. A custard festival takes place each year, featuring a coconut-picking comp-etition between men and monkeys (the monkeys generally win).

145

Offerings of gold leaf and rich cloth adorn the Buddha images at Wat Tham, near the caves of Khao Yoi, west of Phetcha Buri

Bird life in Prachuap
Prachuap Khiri Khan province is an excellent area for birdwatching. It lies at the intersection of several important migration routes between Asia and northern Europe, and between 200 and 300 species have been spotted here. The peak birdwatching season is from September through November, and the best place to see them is in the national park of Khao Sam Roi Yot (The Mountain with Three Hundred Peaks—see page 134), a haven for waders and songbirds.

Prawn farming
The brackish marshes north of Prachuap Khiri Khan were extensively exploited for prawn farming in recent years, and much of the environment in the national park was damaged as a result. The prawn farms did not flourish because of endemic disease, and steadily the marshes are reverting to their natural state. As King Mongkut's unfortunate experience in 1868 shows, however (see page 134), malarial mosquitoes thrive in this region, so take appropriate precautions.

Mysterious islets loom from the waterline just offshore from Prachuap Khiri Khan. The view is taken from Khao Chong Krajok, one of the best vantage points in the area

▶ **Prachuap Khiri Khan**
Off Highway 4, 56 miles south of Hua Hin. Buses from Bangkok (southern terminal) and Hua Hin

Thailand is only 6 miles wide at the narrowest part of this slender lifeline linking Bangkok with the south. Attractive beaches are dotted down the coastline, which makes up a large part of this province.

Hua Hin is a favorite Thai resort (see page 125), while **Pran Buri**, a small town just over 14 miles to the south, is trying to emulate its northern neighbor.

The nearby beaches of **Suan Son** ("Casuarina Garden") and Khao Tao are good for swimming. Just off Suan Son is Ko Singto, from where boats can be hired for diving and fishing.

Prachuap Khiri Khan town has an attractive waterfront, a glittering panorama of harbor and mountain. Conveniently close is the walkway up **Khao Chong Krajok**▶▶ ("Mirror Mountain") to a *chedi* and pleasant viewpoint, taking in nearby Burmese mountains and the town laid out below. The "Mirror Mountain" earns its name from a hole in its side that seems to reflect the sky. Halfway up, look out for the guardian monkeys. Apart from this, Prachuap is a typical quiet provincial center with several budget /moderate bungalows.

Fourteen miles south of Prachuap Khiri Khan, **Wanakon** is a long casuarina-lined beach with clear and shallow water, fine for swimming. Kasetsat University Forestry Department has a bungalow that it rents out (tel: 02/579 0520).

Three miles farther on lies **Huai Yang Waterfall National Park**▶, refreshing and fish-filled. South again from this is **Thap Sakae**. The moderately priced Chanruen Hotel, right on the end of Thap Sakae beach (tel: 032/671890), has spotlessly clean bungalow units, but the overall atmosphere is a bit bleak. The budget Chavalit (tel: 032/671 010) is a small hotel reached by a

right turn off Highway 4. The beach is not very suitable for swimming.

The last district before Chumphon is Bang Saphan Noi, where **Pa Klang Ao** is a preserved forest campsite only 1¼ miles away.

The port at Ban Pak Khlong services **Ko Thalu**, which has fine shallow beaches: a great camping spot. Near the end is **Ao Bor Thong Lang**, a pretty, crescent-shaped rocky bay.

Saraburi Province

North of Bangkok on Highway 1

Saraburi is an unremarkable central province with three main attractions.

Thailand's most famous Buddha footprint, **Phra Buddhabat▶**, 17 miles north of Saraburi town on the road to Lop Buri, is housed in a most impressive pagoda.

Muak Lek waterfall▶ is fine for swimming and is easy to find in Muak Lek district on the road and train to Khorat (Nakhon Ratchasima).

The remarkable **Wat Tham Krabawk▶** is a Buddhist response to drug addiction. At the Krabawk cave monastery, addicts undergo an intensive course of herbal emetics to clean out their systems. The success rate is higher with Thais, because of their respect for the monkhood. Reformed addicts put on displays to warn schoolchildren, and herbal products are on sale.

Si Racha

Southeast of Bangkok on Highway 3. Buses from Bangkok (eastern terminal)

Exactly 62 miles along an upgraded highway from Bangkok, Si Racha is in the middle of government efforts to develop the Gulf of Thailand's eastern seaboard as a manufacturing base. This is not really a tourist destination, rather more a fishing port that is passed through en route to the island of Ko Si Chang.

South of the provincial center of Chon Buri is **Ang Sila** and its distinctive *wat*. Many Thai tourists head for the beach resort at **Bang Saen**. Serious efforts have been made to clean up this beach, which at times is clogged up with plastic bags and pieces of rope. On the plus

Si Racha is a great center for seafood, as its industrious fishing fleet indicates. These colorful boats are searching for squid, which is dried on the waterfront

Bang Saen legend
At Bang Saen, a shrine stands on Monkey Hill in memory of Chao Mae Khao Sammuk, a Chinese girl who drowned herself during the 18th century when her parents forbade her to marry her chosen suitor. It is a favorite pilgrimage for members of the local Chinese community, who believe that by paying homage to Chao Mae Khao Sammuk, their own love lives will be more fortunate.

Jao Por
The route to Si Racha passes the provincial center of Chon Buri, headquarters of the increasingly influential Jao Por, or Chinese mafia. It is said they arrange assassinations at bargain-basement prices.

Scandal
Ko Sichang has recently been the center of an embarrassing scandal, in which overzealous quarrying caused much of the island to collapse.

148

Pepper water
Si Racha is famed for its seafood and even more for the powerful spicy sauce called *nam phrik* (pepper water), a condiment that no Thai kitchen would be without. There are several different kinds, but the one manufactured in Si Racha is considered to be the best. Made from the ferocious crushed "mouse-shit" chilis and fermented shrimp paste—blended with pepper, garlic, onions and lemon juice—it is an acquired taste for Westerners.

side, there are deck chairs, food stalls and showers for swimmers.

Si Racha is not a swimming center, although there are two small beaches. But the town has a "coastal" appeal all the same, unlike the rushed, modern Pattaya. Prime spot of the market/fishing town is pretty **Ko Loi**, a small island with a fetching Thai-Chinese temple on it. Sitting at the end of a long causeway, it cuts a pretty silhouette at sunset.

About halfway between here and Si Racha there are clear signposts to **Khao Khio open zoo**, an 11-mile detour inland. A variety of species roam over a wide area. Perhaps this is the best place to appreciate gibbons; elsewhere, domesticated animals are kept on chains, and in the wild, mothers are shot for their babies.

Ko Sichang►► This is one of the closest islands to Bangkok. The boat there takes approximately 45 minutes and costs about 20 baht. It leaves from Tha Jalin, left of the intersection coming in from the main road to Si Racha.

The island has one town, where the boats arrive, and a hilltop temple overlooking it. The system of roads is toylike and not suitable for cars; however, there are motorbike taxis available. The island is small enough to walk around, and a stroll to the far side will take you to several beaches.

Khao Khaat (Hin Klom) beach, on the other side of the mountains from the port area, is amazingly clean for this area, powdery grey sand and shallow waters making it ideal for swimming. It is somewhat inaccessible by road and involves a climb down the rocks. There is another beach at Laem Nguu, but not as good.

Other attractions on the little island include the overgrown remains of the **summer palace**, whose site still has atmosphere even though the best of it was moved to create Wimanmek in Bangkok. The hilltop wat looks out over the developed, low-lying side of the island, at its base an impressive Chinese arch. The **Chakraphong caves** here hold Buddha images.

Besides beaches, the hilly western coast has Tham Phang (cave), Hin Tukata (rock formations) and the garden of Kratok Rok. Pick-up services are available. The oldest established bungalows on the island are half a mile from the boat jetty.

Staying at Ko Sichang Thiw Phai Guest House is a lively place, well known to travelers but some way from the beach. Prices are moderate and facilities good, making it an excellent budget choice. There is a popular restaurant (see **Directory**, page 279). Day trips are organized to nearby Ko Khang Khao from 10–5. The cost per group is in the region of 1,000 baht. Activities include fishing, snorkeling, swimming and sunbathing.

Benz Bungalow is another bungalow-accommodation site near the dirt track that leads up to the beach (see page 279). Alternatively, there are simple rooms and guest houses in the town.

Suphan Buri

Northwest of Bangkok and about 43 miles northeast of Kanchana Buri on Highway 340. Buses from Bangkok (northern terminal)

Suphan Buri town is at the apex of a triangle with Bangkok and Kanchana Buri. A moderately sized, prosperous center, it is fairly typical of others in central Thailand, although it is not high on the list of tourist destinations.

It does have its attractions, not least of which is its long history, dating back to the Dvaravati period between the 6th and 10th centuries. However, the town today is modern and dull, and probably only worth seeing if you are changing buses here.

On the outskirts of town is **Wat Palalai►**, the town's most notable and biggest attraction—biggest because of the tall whitewashed walls around the *bot*. Their height was necessary to accommodate a huge, 50-foot seated Buddha image, which draws hundreds of believers daily to pay their respects and to worship. Many of the surrounding buildings are very old, having been built originally in the U Thong period. To complete the scene, goats wander around outside the temple.

Nearer the Suphan Buri River and the center of town is **Wat Phra Si Ratana Mahathat**, set a little way back off Malimaen Road. Most impressive is the Khmer *prang*, which contains a chamber at the top of a staircase housing a replica of another *prang*.

To the west of Suphan Buri is the war memorial and famous battle site of **Don Chedi►**. It was built to commemorate the defeat of the prince of Burma in 1582 and the freeing of Ayutthaya by Prince Naresuan and his forces, riding on elephants.

The site fell into disrepair and was eventually lost and forgotten. It was rediscovered in 1913, after Rama V had tried and failed to find it, but was not restored until the 1950s.

During fair week (see panel), buses run from Suphan Buri and, at other times, from the Northern Bus Terminal in Bangkok. Transportation can also be arranged via travel agents in the capital.

Celebrations
Don Chedi Monument Fair is held annually during the week that includes Armed Forces Day, January 25. As part of the celebrations, there is a reenactment of the battle of the princes and their elephants.

U Thong National Museum
Suphan Buri's considerable history is documented in the U Thong National Museum (4 miles west of town on Malaimaen Road), housing a collection of artifacts dating back to neolithic times. The Bronze Age and several eras of Buddhist sculpture are also covered, and a special section is devoted to the culture of the Lao Song people, a local ethnic minority. *Open: Wed–Sun 9–4. Admission charge.*

It may take a while to get used to the strength of Thai condiments. Be cautious with the chili sauces, and keep a glass of water handy as you experiment

▶　　　**Trat Province**

*Southeast from Bangkok down Highway 3. Buses from
Bangkok (eastern terminal)*

Trat province is on the border with Cambodia, 250 miles
southeast of Bangkok. Its strange shape dates from
Thailand's most serious tussle with France, when Rama
V gave up swathes of the north to remove French troops
from this strategic shoreline in the late 19th century.

Malaria still plagues the province, so take good
precautions as you go east. To prevent mosquito bites, it
is as well to use several methods of protection (e.g.,
screens, net, repellent, coil) simultaneously.

Owing to Cambodia's troubles, and also because of its
remoteness, some unpleasant incidents have given rural
Trat a poor reputation for safety. Traveling alone is not to
be recommended. Tension in this area seems to be
easing, but take the local advice before venturing into
remote regions.

*Thailand's east coast
is an intensely fertile
region, full of fruit
orchards, rice
paddies and rubber
plantations.
Coconuts are another
important crop*

The gem markets Northern Trat, like Chanta Buri, is a
famous ruby-mining area. The province's most important
gem market is in Bo Rai district, found by taking one
of the many roads about 30 miles north toward the
Cambodian border. It takes a trained eye to tell the value
of a raw stone. Use the afternoon market on the road to
Khlong Yor for small souvenirs, bearing in mind that it is
possible to be taken in by some of the wares. An added
attraction at Bo Rai is the nearby **Khao Salak Dai
waterfall**.

Trat town is best used as a starting point for trips to the offshore islands. Its large market is well suited for stocking up with equipment and provisions. All the boats to Ko Chang leave from Laem Ngop district, 12 miles southwest of the town of Trat.

Incurable sightseers will want to see the 300-year-old Wat Bupharam, off the road to Bangkok. In the older quarter, too, are some reminders of the brief French occupation. Several beaches on the coast along from Trat town are excellent for swimming, such as Mai Rut, where purple shellfish litter the beach. On the western side of the Trat estuary is remote but beautiful Ao Tan Khuu, found by continuing west from Laem Ngop.

Khlong Yai▶▶ Frequent *songthaews* leave from Trat to this atmospheric fishing port close to the Cambodian border. It is a memorable place, with a pier, stilt houses and lots of atmosphere, and the journey to reach it passes through magnificent mountain scenery.

The offshore islands Trat's 39 islands are becoming increasingly well known; this whole area is a marine national park. **Ko Chang** is the country's third-largest island and, together with other coconut- and fishing-based paradises like its neighbors **Ko Mak** and **Ko Kut**, it is now experiencing tentative development, although it is still distinctly quiet. Water is scarce; even the park accommodations have shared washing facilities. May to October can be very stormy, and many facilities close down in that period.

Ko Chang▶ Here on the Khlong Mayom, whose beauty attracted kings, there are some beautiful waterfalls. The park office is at the khlong mouth, and a passable road links settlements on the northern coast. The **Thanmayom** waterfall is a rewarding sight, as is **Nonsee** waterfall, opposite Tha Dan Mai jetty.

Three budget resorts are sited next to beaches. Spots to head for are **Hat Sai Khao**, an easy 1¼-mile stroll from the jetty at Ao Khlong Son, and **Chaichet**, nestling inside a headland about 3 miles farther on. On the south side, **Bang Bao** is recommended. This place marks the end of the trail some 12 miles farther south, where a beach stretches over the mouth of a stream. Unfortunately, the island's beaches are plagued by sand fleas.

Ko Kut This island has become the next victim of development. The trip takes six hours, if you can talk your way onto a fishing or coconut boat in town. The boats leave several times a month. It is better, perhaps, to travel east down the province's thin tail (Highway 318) to get a (quite expensive) long-tailed boat at Ban Ta Neuk, from where the trip takes an hour.

The exclusive Ko Kut Island Resort is the most luxurious development, but there are simpler choices on **Haat Taphao** ("Turtle Beach"), a short distance by dirt track from where the boats pull in.

Ko Mak is an Israeli-managed, expensive resort, which is fun if you can afford it.

Khao Lan refugee camp
Halfway to Khlong Yai at Aranyaprathet, the Khao Lan refugee-camp museum documents a period of history many local people would rather forget. During the late 1970s, Cambodians fled across the border into eastern Thailand to escape the violence of Pol Pot's regime. Khao Lan was the largest of the Red Cross camps operating in Trat province. A decade later, the refugees were mostly resettled and Thai policy has changed: Cambodian refugees are now classed as illegal immigrants.

151

Thai-Cambodian border
Continuing farther south from Ban Neuk, Khlong Yai is the last district before the Thai border melts into the gulf, surrounded by Cambodia. A border market is conducted near here, and there are some budget/ moderate hotels. Not so far away on the Khmer side is Pailin, whose underdeveloped ruby mines are some of the best left. Exports from Cambodia are mostly handicrafts exchanged for everyday Thai consumer goods. Khlong Yai is just one of many markets on the Thai–Cambodian border now thriving in a tentative post-civil-war atmosphere.

NORTHERN THAILAND

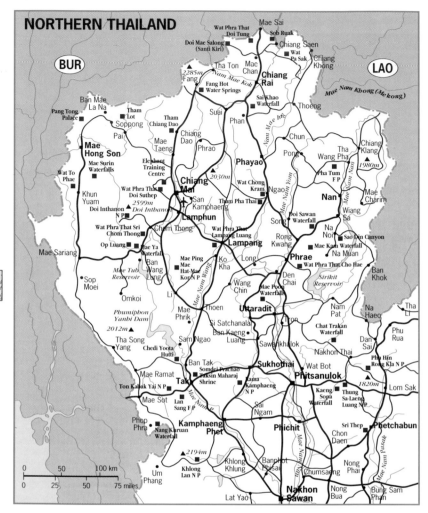

NORTHERN THAILAND

BUR

LAO

Mae Sai
Wat Phra That
Doi Tung
Sob Ruak
Chiang Saen
Wat
Pa Sak
Chiang
Khong
Doi Mae Salong
(Santi Kiri)
Tha Ton
Mac
Chan
Chiang
Rai
2285m
Fang
Nam Mae Kok
Fang Hot
Water Springs
Sai Khao
Waterfall
Thoeng
Mae Nam Khong (Mekong)
Ban Mae
La Na
Pang Tong
Palace
Tham
Lot
Soppong
Tham
Chiang Dao
Suai
Phan
Chun
Pong
Nam Mae Ing
Pai
Mae
Taeng
Chiang
Dao
Phrao
Phayao
Tha
Wang Pha
Chiang
Klang
1980m
Mae
Hong Son
Mae Surin
Waterfalls
Elephant
Training
Centre
2030m
Pha Tum
F P
Nan
Mae
Charim
Wat To
Phac
Khun
Yuam
Wat Phra That
Doi Suthep
2599m
Doi Inthanon
Chiang
Mai
San
Kamphaeng
Wat Chong
Kram
Tham Pha Thai
Ngao
Doi Sawan
Waterfall
Wiang
Sa
Na
Noi
Sao Din Canyon
Na Muan
Doi Inthanon
N P
Lamphun
Song
Mae Nam Yom
Wat Phra That Sri
Chom Thong
Chom Thong
Wat Phra That
Lampang Luang
Rong
Kwang
Mae Nam Nan
Op Luang
Mae Ya
Waterfall
Lampang
Phrae
Mae Kam Waterfall
Ban
Khok
Mae Sariang
Mae Tub
Reservoir
Ban
Wang
Lung
Mae Ping
Mae
Hat-Mae
Kor N P
Ko
Kha
Long
Den
Chai
Wat Phra That Cho Hae
Sirikit
Reservoir
Sop
Moei
Omkoi
Li
Wang
Chin
Mae Poen
Waterfall
Phumiphon
Yanhi Dam
2012m
Mae
Phrik
Thoen
Uttaradit
Nam
Pat
Na
Haeo
Tha
Li
Tha Song
Yang
Chedi Yoota
Hutti
Sam Ngao
Si Satchanalai
Ban Kaeng
Luang
Sawankhalok
Chat Trakan
Waterfall
Dan
Sai
Phu
Rua
Nakhon Thai
Phu Hin
Rong Kla N P
Ban Tak
Somdej Phra Rao
Naksin Maharaj
Shrine
Mae Ramat
Tak
Rama
Kamphaeng
N P
Sukhothai
Wat Bot
Phitsanulok
1820m
Lom Sak
Mae Sot
Lan
Sang F P
Kaeng
Sopa
Waterfall
Thung
Sa-Laeng
Luang N P
Ton Kabak Yai N P
Sai
Ngam
Phop
Phra
Nang Kuruan
Waterfall
Kamphaeng
Phet
Phichit
Sri Thep
Chon
Daen
Phetchabun
Mae Nam Pasak
2194m
Um
Phang
Khlong
Lan N P
Khlong
Khlung
Banphot
Phisai
Chumsaeng
Nong
Phai
Bung Sam
Phan
Lat Yao
Nakhon
Sawan
Nong
Bua

0   50   100 km
0   25   50   75 miles

National museums
Thailand's Fine Arts
Department operates the
excellent National
Museums found in Bangkok
and many provincial capi-
tals, especially in areas
with important historic or
archeological sites. There
are more than 35 museums
all over the country. Most
have similar opening times
(Wed–Sun 9–4). Admission
charges are generally very
moderate.

The green, intricate folds of Thailand's northern
mountains merge into the wilds of Burma and Laos.
Teak forests and patchworks of slash-and-burn
agriculture dominate the highlands above the pancake-
flat rice plains and prosperous-looking cities. High up, hill
tribes subsist in villages of bamboo huts roofed with
palm thatch or corrugated iron. Waterfalls, hot springs
and bat-inhabited caves exist in profusion.

Northern Thailand is still culturally distinct. It retains its
own dialects, cuisine and architecture. Temples in
particular show legacies of ancient Lanna and Burmese
styles. Much of the best of the region lies in unmarked
obscurity. Fortunately, the north is well endowed
with tour agencies and trekking companies that get to
places that an individual would never find. Tortuous
dirt tracks winding up into remote jungle make
exciting but demanding driving. Given the very real
dangers of the notorious Golden Triangle, one of the

world's foremost drug-producing regions, it is best to go with a guide.

Chiang Mai is likely to be most visitors' first stop in the north. Though smaller than a number of other large industrial centers, Thailand's second city makes a good starting point: accommodations are plentiful, including top-class hotels, eating out is wonderfully varied and the range of Thailand's famous souvenir shopping is comprehensive.

It is well placed for Doi Inthanon National Park and for organized trips to see waterfalls and elephant shows. Yet there are indications that the city has become too commercialized. Many tourists find that for all its packaged convenience it has lost its innocence; the real rewards for exploratory travel lie elsewhere.

Mae Hong Son and Chiang Rai provinces offer fine scenery and hill-tribe culture (although the main towns are nothing special) and are gaining popularity. Seekers of the real back of beyond should also sample the Mekong River east of the Golden Triangle or the highlands of Nan province.

The lower north has a trio of historic ruined cities, of which Sukhothai is the undisputed pearl. Westward, Mae Sot is on the edge of some of the grandest mountains in the country.

Lisu women in northern Thailand

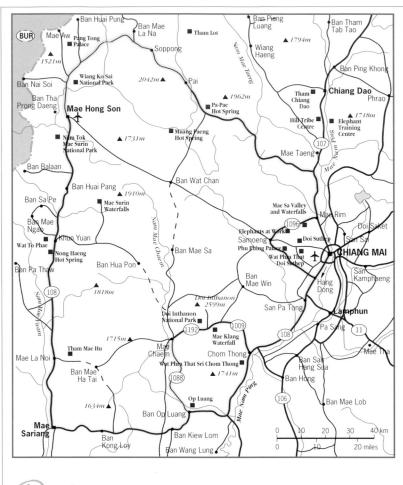

Drive — A circular route starting at Chiang Mai

The wild northwest is an area of complex mountain ridges, thickly cloaked in forest and laced with waterfalls, caves and hot springs.

Allow four to seven days for the circuit, including a few side trips. Take warm clothes in the cool season; unsurfaced side roads are prone to flooding in the rainy season. Those not starting from Chiang Mai are better off omitting the city, as the busy roads leading from it are devoid of interest.

From Chiang Mai▶▶▶, Highway 108 heads southwest through straggly villages. Just before Chom Thong▶▶

turn off up Highway 1009 to see the natural wonders of Doi Inthanon National Park▶▶▶ (see pages 167–168). Either continue on Highway 1192 to Mae Chaem to Highway 1088, or retrace your steps to Highway 108.

Just east of the junction of Highways 1088 and 108, **Op Luang National Park Office** is visible, with a pretty gorge▶ crossed by a wooden footbridge just behind. Carpets of wildflowers interrupt the green monotony—the most diverse blooms appear before the rainy season, while in winter, bright orange swathes of sunflowers make a fine show. In the section of road between Chom Thong and Mae Sariang, the Chaem River is a prominent feature. **Mae Sariang** is of little interest but makes a pleasant enough stopover.

Continue northward on Highway 108.

Northward the scenery is unvaried; a hot sulfur spring (emphatically not for bathing) near the 256-km post can be spotted by the lawn and restaurant. Slash-and-burn agriculture has denuded some hills, which are being reforested with teak and pine. Dirt roads head off into the jungle to remote hill-tribe villages. Soon the road makes a dramatic plunge into **Mae Hong Son►**, a noted center for organized treks. The province of Mae Hong Son is peopled by an ethnic mix of Shan, Tha Yai, Karen, Hmong, Lisu, Lahu and others; only about 2 percent of the population is Thai.

Continue along the main road to Soppong, forking left up a dirt track to visit Tham Lot►►►, one of Thailand's finest caves. Back on the main road, continue southeast to Pai, another good trekking center. The road, proceeding now like a roller-coaster, is a scenic treat. Between Mae Hong Son and Pai, there are some magnificent views to be seen.

Continue toward Chiang Mai. Highway 1096 bypasses the city to the west (see Mae Sa Valley►►, pages 164–165). Loop around from Mae Rim along Highway 1096 and turn south at Samoeng to rejoin Highway 108.

Recommended overnight stops
Doi Inthanon National Park is worth an extended stay, and there are park bungalows available there for stopovers. **Mae Sariang** provides a basic hotel and a few guest houses. **Mae Hong Son** has a wide range of accommodations available, while **Soppong**, **Tham Lot** and **Pai** each have guest-house accommodations. There are also resorts along Highway 1096.

Public transportation *Buses from Chiang Mai to Mae Hong Son take about 9–10 hours, but the journey can be split up by overnighting at Mae Sariang, Soppong and Pai. There are no buses along Highway 1096. Songthaews to Doi Inthanon leave only intermittently from Chom Thong on weekdays (the service is better at weekends), and it is necessary to return to Chom Thong for buses along Highway 108.*

Lisu hill-tribe girls at the rice harvest

The corner bastions of Chiang Mai's city walls are in excellent condition, though extensive restoration has taken place since the 13th century

▶▶▶ Chiang Mai

From Bangkok: by bus, journey time of 9 to 12 hours; by train, 12 to 14 hours; domestic flights, 1 hour

Thailand's second city, dubbed the "Rose of the North," is about a fortieth the size of Bangkok. With a more agreeable climate and less volume of traffic, it is undoubtedly easier to live in and is most people's first destination in northern Thailand. It has a fine legacy of temples, and its Night Bazaar is one of Asia's greatest street markets.

History In 1296, the city superseded Chiang Rai as the capital of King Mengrai's Lanna kingdom, following the capture of the Mon city of Haripunchai (Lamphun) 15 years earlier. It prospered as a cultural and commercial center, initially with its southern and eastern boundaries secure thanks to alliances with the kings of Sukhothai and Phayao. However, it suffered centuries of hostilities with Ayutthaya.

In 1556, it became a vassal state after it was invaded by Burma. Despite liberation by King Taksin in 1775, the centuries of warfare had sapped its spirit, and its citizens deserted to Lampang. Twenty years later, the population started to return to the abandoned city, which gradually became the major northern outpost of the newly formed kingdom of Siam.

The old city used to contain the palace and nobles' quarters, but now the most visible reminders of its past are the temples. There are dozens of them, many exhibiting signs of Burmese and Lanna influences. A particularly distinct piece of evidence of the past is the neat square of the old moat that nicely frames the area

of the old city. Five gateways exist on this fortification, but on closer inspection it can be seen that they are all reconstructions.

Times have changed The old-world Shangri-La found by visitors in the earlier part of this century has altered beyond recognition. Far from being fossilized in exotic charms, Chiang Mai is now developing faster than any other provincial center. The first phase of egg-box architecture occurred in the 1950s and '60s, and today high-rise condominiums are a 1990s addition to the increasingly prosperous-looking skyline. Residents complain that the traffic, worse every year, is developing a Bangkoklike intensity, and the city has graduated to Los Angeles-style smog.

Chiang Mai's popularity with both visitors and Thais stems from its manageability and unsticky climate. The city is now sophisticated, commercially geared and visibly prosperous. A cultural mix is diluting the cultures of the hill tribes—a feature that is probably accelerated by the numbers of tourists.

In the city, the number of *farangs* is immediately noticeable. The choice produced by this cultural mix is almost bewildering, particularly in the variety of its eating places.

There is an extraordinary choice of souvenir shopping, ready-made opportunities for hill-tribe treks (not the cheapest in the north), a vast amount of accommodations from top-class hotels to world-travelers' guest houses, and a bustling street life and nightlife.

Getting about Chiang Mai's simple geography, aided by the prominence of the river and moated area, make it an easy place in which to find your bearings. The huge form of Doi Suthep, the sacred mountain, looms over the city, a reminder of its proximity to the country's upland region.

Chiang Mai used to be a city to walk around, but the increasing traffic is making it tough going. However, cycling and motorcycling are feasible, though a bit scary; rental shops proliferate along Mun Muang Road.

The city's bus system operates only until 7 PM; fares are cheap. Slightly more expensive are the *songthaews* or pickups, and it's potluck whether one is going your way. Easiest by far are the *tuk tuks*, whose drivers have been migrating from Bangkok since 1987. Most rides are about 30–40 baht. Finally, pedaled *samlors* are fine for short journeys.

There are city tours organized by dozens of agencies and hotels, as well as excursions to places outside Chiang Mai, such as the Golden Triangle.

The downtown area This stretches between Mun Muang Road by the eastern moat to the Mae Nam Ping River. Mun Muang Road itself has been largely given over to the tourism industry. There is a great concentration of trekking-tour operators (for which the city is famous), guest houses, Western-food restaurants where travelers swap stories over milkshakes, and ethnic fabric shops. The many nightclubs add to the downtown's reputation as something of a red-light district.

Songkran Day
The Thai love of *sanuk* (fun) is much in evidence in the exuberant spirit in which festivals are celebrated here. During the three-day flower festival in early February and the boisterous festivities of Songkran Day on April 13 (Thai New Year), not many people escape a comprehensive dousing in water by hoses, water pistols or even water-filled condoms; the elderly get a gentler treatment, with a sprinkling of jasmine-scented water, but be prepared—*farangs* are prime targets.

157

Samphet market
A visit to Samphet market makes a good early morning or early evening stroll. A whole new world opens up here: there are exotic fruits and lady stall-holders serenely skinning frogs or hacking up live fish. Farther to the east, there are several ugly and noisy main roads linked by quieter *sois*. This is the area of the Night Bazaar and Warorot Market.

Khantoke

Khantoke dinners are a Lanna-Thai specialty, formerly given only on ceremonial occasions. You sit down at low tables and are served by waiters or waitresses attired in traditional costume; Lanna dancing accompanies your meal, and diners are invited to join in at the end. The most popular places are the Old Chiang Mai Cultural Center and the Diamond Hotel.

Thai boxing

Thai boxing (see also page 110) is a sport where anything seems to go in a free-for-all. The atmosphere is one of frantic excitement and terrific energy. The Thais take this very seriously, and many baht are won and lost at an evening spent watching this explosive sport. Contests take place on Friday and Saturday nights at the boxing stadium on Khong Sai Road near the train station.

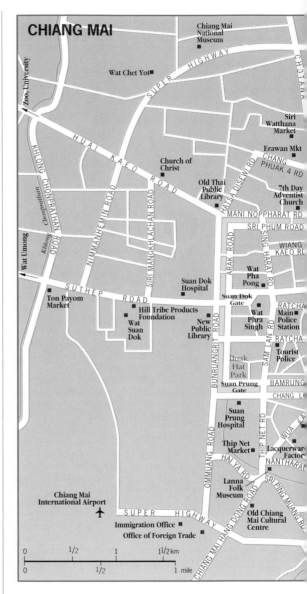

City sights

Chiang Mai National Museum▶▶

Superhighway (Highway 11, north of the center)
Open: Wed–Sat, except national holidays, 9–4. Admission charge

A notable collection of religious art, dominated by an enormous Lanna head. Upstairs there is an entertaining miscellany, including hill-tribe gear, musical instruments, domestic equipment, looms and some spectacular elephant howdahs, as well as a mosquito-proof bed, which was built for a 19th-century king of Chiang Mai.

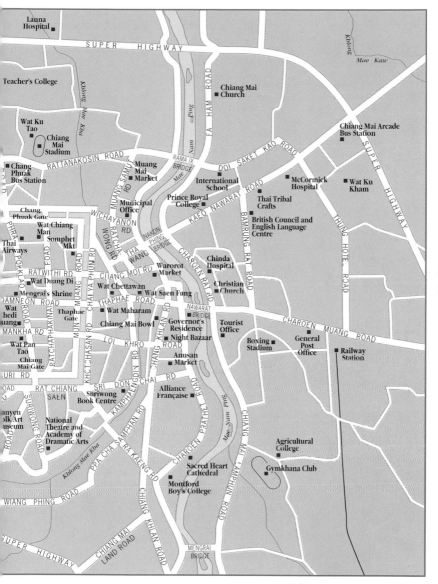

Chiang Mai Zoo▶

Huai Kaeo Road
Open: daily 8–5. Admission charge
Thailand's best zoo has a semijungle setting and adjoins a large arboretum. Minibuses for Doi Suthep pass by the entrance.

Lanna Folk Museum▶

185/3 Wualai Road
Open: daily except Thu, 10–4. Admission charge
Opened by the Siam Society, this modest display gives a rare glimpse of the interior of a traditional Lanna house

Chiang Mai's flower festival
The celebrated Chiang Mai flower festival takes place on the first weekend in February, with a parade of flower-laden floats and a host of beauty contests drawing big crowds to the city.

King Mengrai's memorial
The city pillar near Wat Chedi Luang commemorates the spot where King Mengrai was supposedly struck by lightning—his memorial is on the opposite corner of the Ratchadamnoen /Phra Pokklao intersection.

Wat Phra Singh's Buddha
The Buddha Phra Singh in Wat Phra Singh is regarded as the original despite the fact that two identical ones exist at Nakhon Si Thammarat and Bangkok. The head of this one was stolen in 1922 and a replacement was made.

built in the latter part of the 19th century. Note the octagonal stilts on which it is built and the walls sloping inward as they rise—both typical features. The guide prepares crushed betel leaf in the time-honored manner for visitors to try out.

Tribal Research Center▶
Chiang Mai University Campus (3 miles west of the city)
Open: Mon–Fri 8:30–4:30. Admission charge
Part of the interest here is finding the place, poorly signed on the large campus. Perseverance is rewarded by the presence of a small but informative museum on hill tribes, explaining the lifestyles of the major tribes.

Wat Chedi Luang▶▶
Phra Poklao Road
Apart from the splendid *naga* (dragon-headed serpents) flanking the steps to the wiharn, the main interest here is a vast *chedi* built in the 15th century and later enlarged by King Tilokaraja. The restored structure is an impressive sight. According to legend, the city will stand as long as the eucalyptus tree on the grounds does.

Wat Chet Yot▶
Off the superhighway (Highway 11) just southwest of the National Museum; look for the sign for the Rajamangala Institute of Technology
Built in 1455 to house the relics of the monk Phra Mahathera Uttamapanya, the *chedi* retains outstanding stucco reliefs of cross-legged figures giving a *wai*. Wat Chet Yot is a copy of Buddha Gaya in India, where the Buddha attained enlightenment under a bo tree; the seven spires referred to in its name represent the seven weeks he spent there.

Wat Chiang Man▶
Ratchaphakinai Road
Built by King Mengrai in 1296, this is thought to be the city's oldest wat, known for two small but much venerated Buddha images: the 8th-century marble Phra Sila, thought to be from India or Sri Lanka, and the Crystal Buddha, supposedly presented to the queen of Haripunchai in the 7th century.

Wat Pan Tao▶
Phra Pokklao Road (next to Wat Chedi Luang)
A fine, untampered-with example of a Lanna *wiharn*, retaining its original paneled walls.

Wat Phra Singh▶▶
Sing Harat Road
This absorbing temple in the old city was founded in 1345 to house the ashes of King Kham Fu. It has a new *wiharn* dating from 1925, a wooden *bot* behind and a late Lanna wiharn (*c*1806–11) that contains the celebrated Buddha Phra Singh. The walls are decorated with murals depicting legends and scenes of old city life. Look for the textiles and tattoos that were popular at the time.

Wat Suan Dok▶
Suthep Road

Virtually next door to the Hill Tribe Products Foundation, this contains the burial ground for many of the Chiang Mai royalty. The wedding-cake stucco on the *chedis* housing the remains presents a dazzling show. A central *chedi* contains a Buddha relic that was brought by a white elephant, so the story goes, hence the White Elephant Gate—Pratu Chang Puak—in the city wall. Herbal massage is on offer here.

Wat Umong▶
Off Suthep Road (road signs)

Located on an obscure soi in the extreme west of the city, this forest wat dates from 1296 and is perhaps the city's quirkiest temple. A multitude of signs moralize from every tree: "Time unused is the longest time"; "Love is a flower garden to be watered by tears." You can hardly see the woods for the wisdom.

Monks' bungalows are scattered around the forest, which opens onto a lake fringed with banana palms. At the top of the site, an emaciated Buddha image sits contemplatively close to a *chedi*, his ribcage sunken inward as the result of fasting. Immediately below is a labyrinth of subterranean meditation chambers: English-language sermons on meditation are given. They begin at 3 PM on Sundays and go on until about 6.

Environs
Wat Phra That Doi Suthep▶▶▶

This much-visited temple of Doi Suthep stands on the sacred mountain that towers over Chiang Mai. The white elephant that carried a Buddha relic to Wat Suan Dok (see above) is said to have fallen and died on this spot. From the road where jade and ivory factory showrooms do a roaring trade, a 300-step staircase flanked by a pair of huge *nagas* leads to the top. There is also a cable car that glides up in seconds very cheaply.

Wat Phra Doi Suthep was founded by King Ku Na in 1383 and contains an exquisite courtyard with a gold *chedi* housing a Buddha relic and intricate gold parasols. Signs announce "Don't shake the bells" and "Dress impolite can't enter this temple." The view on a clear winter's day extends over a seemingly infinite plain, making Chiang Mai look surprisingly compact.

continued on page 164

The spectacular temple of Wat Phra That Doi Suthep is a glittering assembly of intricately carved wood and gold filigree

Chiang Mai shopping

■ **There are dozens of shops between the Night Bazaar and Mun Muang Road selling ethnic clothes and crafts. Of the hill-tribe products, everyone has a personal favorite. The many designs are made into anything that will sell: oven mitts, jackets, cushion covers, knapsacks, fanny packs and even baseball caps. Other ethnic goods include attractive Lanna-style cotton and silk fabrics, and Burmese-style souvenirs, many of which are actually made in Thailand.** ■

Umbrellas
Umbrellas are a specialty product of the village of Bo Sang, 5 miles from Chiang Mai on the San Kamphaeng road, a popular venue for handicraft tours. It is fascinating to watch them being made. Cane stems are cut and trimmed for handles and bamboo strips are assembled into frames. Various materials are used for the canopy: fabric, paper, or thin bark from the *sa* tree. The umbrellas are decorated with traditional designs of bricks, flowers, butterflies, and foliage.

Hill-tribe products Of the many different styles, Yao textiles are characterized by intricate cross-stitch embroidery, those of the Hmong by larger, coarser stitchwork, Akha fabrics by long stitches (bright diamonds and triangles on black) with silver bangles and medallions, Lahu by bright colors and sequins, Lisu by colorful bands and squares.

There is an assortment of highly idiosyncratic souvenirs, including opium pipes, Karen *sung* banjos, Akha bamboo musical blowpipes, double-sided drums, lacquered buffalo horns and Yao dolls.

Burmese-style souvenirs The wall hangings are spectacular. There are cushion covers, typically with embroidered elephants, peacocks and scenes from Burmese folk tales sewn onto velvet. The better ones use silver for the sequins and quartz for the beads.

Silk Thai silk is justly famous for its quality and is sold in plain colors, check patterns or printed with designs. It is still manufactured using wooden hand looms.

Wood carving An age-old tradition, as a glimpse at virtually any temple in the city will tell. Ban Tawai, southwest of the city, is a major center.

Basketry Straw, rattan and bamboo basket products of all kinds are made at Hang Dong, 8 miles southwest of Chiang Mai on Highway 108.

Umbrellas These are made of cotton, rice paper and bamboo and are hand-painted in bright colors.

Ceramics Celadon, a high-biscuit finish with a pale green glaze, is much prized by collectors and comes in plain light green or mid-blue; beware of imitations. Benjarong, which means "five colors," is a low-biscuit finish that lends itself to richer decoration, including 12-karat gold.

Silverware This is hand-hammered before being given its final luster by an application of tamarind. Beware of base-metal substitutes.

Lacquerware A three-month process of repeated coatings of clay and lacquer sap is the traditional method; this is followed by careful painting or the addition of a gold-leaf design. Burmese lacquer tends to be made on a bamboo base (as opposed to a teak one), which is less brittle.

Where to buy There are two excellent nonprofit shops selling hill-tribe products, where all the money goes directly back to the craftspeople making the goods: the government-run Hill Tribe Products Foundation, 21/17 Suthep Road, and Thai Tribal Crafts, 208 Bamrung Rat Road (not to be confused with Northern Tribal Crafts a few doors along).

The Night Bazaar►►► Situated in Chang Khlan Road, this is one of the great markets of Asia, for both its range and its atmosphere—indeed, part of the attraction is the people-watching. Virtually nothing carries a price tag, and haggling is the order of the day.

Fake designer-label clothes, pirated cassette tapes, while-you-wait artist portraits, wooden toys, hill-tribe gear and inexpensive jewelry are good buys for those who bargain hard enough. Beware of fake silver, jade and gems, and don't expect those 800-baht "Rolex" watches to last more than a few months.

Home industries (factory tour)►►► Straggling along Highway 1006 on the eastern outskirts, the "villages" of Bo Sang and San Kamphaeng are really a huge industrial zone, where workshops produce handmade crafts in great quantity—notably leather, umbrellas, lacquerware, silverware, silk and ceramics. A bargain-price *tuk tuk* tour (the driver picks up commissions regardless of whether you buy anything) lasts three to four hours, and you can stop off wherever you like.

Prices are often fixed and there is no hard sell beyond the occasional hovering attendant, and someone always appears to explain the production process. Mailing services are provided for large items. It is great entertainment, even if you don't buy a thing.

Shopping advice
As with everything in Thailand, all that glistens… polyester may masquerade as silk, molded resin looks very like carved teak, and those handmade hill-tribe products or precious antiques may prove to be mass-produced junk. Shop around, look closely at what you're buying, and bargain hard. Except for gems or jade, the sums you are likely to spend are not large. Avoid buying products made from endangered animals— ivory, ebony, or tortoiseshell. They're probably fake anyway.

163

It is sobering to imagine how many teak trees have been sacrificed to supply Chiang Mai's ancient wood-carving industry, now largely devoted to the production of tourist trinkets

continued from page 161

Phu Phing Palace▶ (*Open*—grounds only—weekends 8–4 when the king is not in residence) The king's northern palace, 2½ miles farther along the road from Doi Suthep, can be viewed from outside. Although it is nothing remarkable architecturally, its temperate rose garden and neat lawns seem evocatively English (so too does the winter air— bring a sweater). The gardens are open to the public on weekends and holidays.

The roads hereabouts are bordered by masses of wild sunflowers.

Ban Doi Pui About 2½ miles past Phu Phing Palace, reached by a very bumpy track is this spectacular example of a tourist trap (see panels), with stalls stacked up with imported souvenirs and villagers dressed in Hmong tribal costume posing for cameras for a few baht. The half-hearted Hill Tribe Museum scarcely merits the entrance charge.

If this is regarded merely as a sociological insight into the decline of the hill-tribe culture, or as a shopping trip, then the village might be worth a visit. At least the wood-smoke smell, free-running chickens and dirt roads are authentic, and the view from the waterfall is a good one.

Mae Sa Valley▶▶
Take Highway 107 north from the city, turn west at Mae Rim (10 miles) onto Highway 1096
Highway 1096 has been developed for the tourist industry and is a popular half-day visit from Chiang Mai. The road is quite scenic, and there are a number of attractive bungalow resorts, such as Mae Sa and Erawan resorts, with beautifully maintained gardens and views of the hills. Accommodations tend to get booked up at weekends.

Mae Sa Snake Farm▶ About 25 types of snake that are native to Thailand are kept here; daredevil antics with them are performed daily at 11:30, 2:15 and 3:30. The performance lasts about 30 minutes. Admission charge.

Mae Sa Waterfall▶▶ *4 miles along Highway 1096; 300m access road.* Entry fee for cars, less for pedestrians. A mountain stream tumbles down a ravine over a series of 10 waterfalls, which provide delightful shady pools for swimming. The trail along then gets rockier and noticeably quieter on the ½-mile trek to the top.

Butterfly and orchid farms▶▶ (*Open* daily 8:30–5. *Admission charge*) The Sai Nam Phung Orchid and Butterfly Farm (one of several similar attractions) has a fine selection of both cultivated hybrids and native species. Butterflies flit around the indoor tropical gardens and end up as framed souvenirs, which are sold in the entrance shops and in Chiang Mai's bazaar.

Ban Doi Pui
The downside of tourism is seen in the effect it has had on the people of this Hmong village. Their lives today are geared to the tourist industry, and this has given them a keen eye for profit. Their knowledge of English extends to phrases such as "you buy" and "no profit." These once nomadic people used to depend on opium as a cash crop until the government tried to steer them into less harmful ways of subsistence.

Hmong and Meo
The hill tribe that inhabits the village of Ban Doi Pui is variously known as Meo (the Thai name which means "barbarian") and Hmong (which means "free"). Understandably, the tribespeople prefer the name Hmong, but the term Meo is still sometimes used. There are two main groups: the Blue Hmong, who live west of Chiang Mai, and the White Hmong, who live to the east. Some are refugees from Laos who fled during the Vietnam War.

Elephant Shows►►► (*Open* shows daily at 9:30 and 11 AM. *Admission charge*) Ten miles along Highway 1096 on the Fang road there is one of several elephant shows around Chiang Mai (the others are near Chiang Dao and Lampang). Elephants bathe, perform logging activities and obey commands. Shows take place in the morning, but in order to see the elephants' bath time, get there as early as possible. Although it is contrived and commercialized, it is an impressive spectacle, full of photo opportunities. One of the most popular is

Elephants at Work, at Chiang Dao, on the road from Chiang Mai to Fang (a bus route).

Tham Chiang Dao► (*songthaew* from Chiang Dao) is a popular cave system that contains much Shan statuary; at the entrance to the main cave, *chedis* and an ornamental royal barge in a pool serve to enhance the mystical atmosphere.

Lamphun►► *Frequent buses from Chang Puak bus station in Chiang Mai.*
Located 16 miles south of Chiang Mai, the area around Lamphun is famed for the beauty of its women, for its *lamyai* (longan) orchards and for its silk products.

The main road from Chiang Mai passes along a fine avenue of *yang* (rubber) trees; pegs are placed on the trunks to facilitate regular pruning.

Lamphun was founded in AD 660 as the capital of the great kingdom of Haripunchai, the center of Mon culture. It was ruled by the Mons up until the 13th century, when infiltration by King Mengrai, monarch of the Lanna dynasty, eventually led to its downfall: the story runs that the king sent Ai Fa, an officer, to undermine the enemy's defense minister and viceroy, deliberately wasting the city's resources and whittling down its defenses, thus paving the way for rebellion and subsequent takeover by Mengrai's forces.

Wat Phra That Haripunchai►► No visit to Lamphun should miss Wat Phra That Haripunchai. Located in the town center, this is one of the most interesting

Wooden elephants
Most of the handicraft shops in Chiang Mai sell wooden elephants, ranging from half-life-size to those that could fit into a match-box (many made of teak).

Working elephants having their daily bath: get there early to see this part of their routine in the shows near Chiang Mai

Teak logging
After five years of training, elephants work for 50 years, reaching peak efficiency around their 40s. Thai law dictates a retirement age of 61, after which they typically live another 20 years. Elephants make excellent loggers because of their night vision, their near-perfect memory of jungle trails and their ability to carry loads of up to 660 pounds. Teak logging now faces a government ban, and it seems likely that the elephants' future role will be as tourist attractions.

Pasang
About 7 miles southwest of Lamphun is the village of Pasang, famed as a cotton-weaving center. The high-quality product is sold in lengths of cloth or made up into garments. You will find the products all over Chiang Mai, but at Pasang you can see the cloth actually being woven, and you may get a better deal at the local cloth market, which also sells batik, silks, and other typical handicrafts.

Be vigilant
One sure way to have a vacation ruined is to have something stolen. It goes without saying that constant vigilance is need-ed, but beware: even supposedly secure places are not always so. There have been reports of items going missing even from guest house safes, so get an itemized receipt when-ever possible.

temples in the region and dates from AD 897. It is dominated by a dazzling gold *chedi* (the model for the infinitely more visited Doi Suthep), and surmounted by a nine-tiered umbrella made of 14 pounds of solid gold. The library is a handsome example of early 19th-century Lanna style, and a *sala* shelters an elaborate Buddha footprint (four prints, one inside the other). Also to be seen here is northern Thailand's largest temple gong, cast in 1860.

National Museum► (*Open* Wed–Sun, except national holidays, 9–noon, 1–4. *Admission charge*) Just across the road from Wat Phra That Haripunchai is this briefly interesting museum in a building that looks as if it were designed for something more comprehensive. There are good specimens of Lanna art, figures and silverware and also some inscribed stones mostly of the 15th and 16th centuries.

Wat Chama Thevi (Wat Ku Kut)► Follow the minor road to the left of the museum, cross the main road and continue for half a mile until the *wat* is reached on the left; the walk is rather dull, so it is a better idea to take a samlor to the *wat*.
Known for its late Dvaravati-style *chedi*, which stands 69 feet high and rises five tiers with trios of Buddha images (not the originals) in niches on each level.

►   Chiang Rai
Buses from neighboring cities; domestic flights; boats daily from Tha Ton (Tha Ton is a four-hour bus trip from Chiang Mai)
Chiang Rai was founded in 1262 as the capital of the Lanna kingdom, but despite its history and the mush-rooming growth of new hotels and guest houses, there is little to see. Much of the city's recent boom is a result of the upgrading of the highway north of Mae Sai and through Burma, which will make a major land route into China. As a base for exploring the surrounding countryside, it serves well enough. You need only walk down the main street to find something to suit your requirements.

Hill Tribe Museum and Handicrafts Shop► *Population and Community Development Association, 620/25 Thanalai Road.* (*Open* Mon–Fri, 8:30–5) The association gives practical aid to local people in matters as diverse as water supply and family planning. The Chiang Rai branch helps tribespeople in particular and has set up a small museum of tribal artifacts and a craft shop (proceeds go directly to fund its projects). An English-language slide show gives an excellent introduction to hill-tribe culture.

Boat trip from Tha Ton to Chiang Rai►►► Rafts make a five-hour journey along the Mae Kok River, which is so shallow that the boats often run aground and the passengers have to get out and push them free. An isolated attack by bandits a few years ago has fueled interest in the journey as an adventure outing.

The trip winds past hill-tribe villages set beneath angular mountains. Possible stopovers include a Lahu village, a hot spring and a cave, although accommodations are best organized through a trek offered at one of the guest houses at Tha Ton village.

Tha Ton itself is a peaceful village sited on the riverbank. Steps to the left of the bridge lead up to a hilltop *wat*, which gives fine views of the river.

Fang *Bus from Chiang Mai, minibus to Tha Ton.* For most visitors this is just a bus change en route to the boat trip to Chiang Rai. At Ban Muang, 6 miles northwest, a hot sulfur spring gushes out of the ground at temperatures close to boiling point.

►►► Doi Inthanon National Park

Head southwest on Highway 108; turn off north near the 57-km post. Buses from Chiang Mai and Mae Sariang to Chom Thong. A songthaew service makes a tour of the main attractions. The service is sporadic during the week but frequent at weekends.

The park takes its name from the highest peak in Thailand. This statistic is just one of many exceptional features. Attractions are signed in English and listed in the order they are passed. Some 30 Hmong and Karen villages are dotted around the area.

The scenery varies from unspoiled lowlands to rugged, partly wooded highlands that are being afforested by the government, and a number of fine waterfalls.

Mae Ya Falls►► Indicated by a sign on the left almost immediately after leaving Highway 108, the 15-minute drive affords magnificent views over rice fields set beneath the backdrop of the mountain range. The falls, a short walk from the parking lot, plummet dramatically a full 820 feet.

Mae Klang Falls► Close to the road, easy access has been made to these, the most visited feature in the park. A battery of souvenir and food stalls has inevitably grown up as a result. Close by, the visitor center sells a useful map of the park and a booklet detailing the bird species found here.

Varchiratharn Falls► Signed by the road, this majestically graceful single fall involves a steep 10-minute walk down to its base. The effort is amply rewarded.

Park headquarters Inquire here for accommodations (bungalows are available, plus a campsite, at the 31km mark). To reserve a place, phone 02/579 0529. Just before the park headquarters, a right turn (marked "Tribal Silverware") leads via a left turn to the ½-mile path to **Siriphum Falls►**. On the way the route leads through a commercialized Hmong village. American Express is accepted at the silverware stalls, and the women hard-sell everlasting flowers and chrysanthemums. The latter are grown in greenhouses visible below—part of the government scheme to introduce cash-crop farming among the tribes in an attempt to safeguard conservation interests.

Rafting
Rafting can be arranged at Tha Ton village, and 10-seater boats can be chartered from Chiang Rai pier for exploring the river (about 1,700 baht for a day).

Fang
Fang's strategic location has made it an important trading base for centuries. In recent years it has functioned as a conduit and warehouse for Golden Triangle opium, which, refined into less bulky heroin, finds its way to many parts of the world. Government attempts to persuade the local hill tribes to concentrate their attentions on the fertile agricultural land near Fang have had a degree of success. But cabbages have their limits…

167

Mae Kok Elephant Camp
Reached by boat or bus from Chiang Rai, the camp operates elephant treks; for details, contact the office near the Wangcome Hotel in Chiang Rai (tel: 053/711897).

Birdlife

Doi Inthanon is outstanding for birds. A species list of 380 has been recorded for the park, including the Inthanon ashy-throated warbler and the green-tailed sunbird.

Inthawichayanon

Marking the summit of Doi Inthanon is a shrine to Inthawichayanon, after whom the mountain was renamed in a shortened form. In the 19th century, he prophesied the dangers of loss of tree cover in this great watershed area and requested his remains be placed here.

Siva

A prize exhibit in Kamphaeng Phet's museum is a fine bronze statue of the Hindu god Siva, cast in 1510 in Khmer style. In 1886, a deranged German decapitated the image and removed its hands, saying he wanted the bits for the Berlin Museum. An awkward diplomatic incident was averted by astute King Chulalongkorn, who arranged for an exact copy of the statue to be sent to Germany. The original has since been restored to its former glory.

The summit of Doi Inthanon offers magnificent views of the surrounding hilly countryside and the national park, especially at sunrise and sunset

Drive to the summit of Doi Inthanon►►► A good road winds up to the very top of Thailand's highest mountain (8,512 feet). As the road ascends, views open out over distant ridges extending far to the southwest and east.

A modern octagonal pagoda, Napamaytanidol Chedi enjoys the most enthralling panorama of all, best on a clear winter's day, but unfortunately all too often obscured by mist.

The summit itself, chilly in the extreme in winter, is an anticlimax, with trees almost completely obscuring the view and a huge air-force radar installation dominating the scene. A sign gives the mountain's height to the nearest millimeter!

Walk back down the road a few paces and turn right on a path signed in Thai leading to the only site in Thailand of *Rhododendron delavayi*. This thrives in the temperate climate and produces red blooms from November through February.

Environs

Chom Thong *Chiang Mai–Mae Sarang bus passes by.* This is a small town on Highway 108, 36 miles southwest of Chiang Mai. On Saturday mornings, the cattle market presents an animated scene.

On the left side of the main street approaching from Chiang Mai, **Wat Phra That Sri Chom Thong►►** dates from 1451 and displays Thai and Burmese features. The wiharn dates from 1817 and has wood carvings characteristic of the period. Carved tusks surround the central reliquary, which contains a Buddha relic. The *bot*, built in 1516, is a charming example of the Burmese style.

► Kamphaeng Phet

Intersection of Highways 1, 111 and 115
Built by King Ki Thai in the 14th century, Kamphaeng Phet city was a replacement for Chakangrao, the garrison town for Sukhothai, sited on the west bank of the nearby Ping River.

Road signs from the city center point to the museum and historical park, which covers a large area, both inside and outside the ancient moated fortification.

Buses from Sukhothai and Phitsanulok pass the historical park, sited half a mile northeast of the modern city. Ask to be dropped off at the *muang kao* (old city) at Lak Muang Shrine. Cars can go into the historical park.

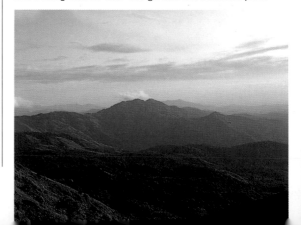

National Museum► (*Open* Wed–Sun, except public holidays, 9–noon, 1–4. *Admission charge*) This features art styles from the Dvaravati period onward and numerous terra-cotta fragments found in the old city.

Wat Phra Khaew► *Opposite the museum. Entry fee covers all sites; free map from the entry booth.* The old royal temple for the (largely vanished) palace still retains its elephant-buttressed base and three Buddha images.

Wat Phra Si Iriyabot► *From the modern Lak Muang Shrine, follow the main road east through the ramparts and branch off left as signed.* The signs explain the sites hereabouts; few are more than piles of laterite rubble. This one has four much-weathered Buddha images in different postures.

Wat Chang Rob►► *Farther along the same road.* This is flanked at its base by 68 stone elephants; steep steps give access to a fine viewing platform over the surrounding countryside.

►►   Lampang
Intersection of Highways 1 and 11. Reached by bus, train and domestic flights
Lampang will never be a major tourist attraction, but it is of interest for its Lanna- and Burmese-style temples.

This is the north's second-largest city, and it has a distinctly prosperous air; rich Thais come here when they are ready to retire. The river that forms the geographical middle is leafy and unspoiled, and the old part of town clustered on the south bank is characterized by wooden shop houses and well-kept teak residences set in lush gardens.

Only the square base of Kamphaeng Phet's Elephant Shrine, Wat Chang Rob survives. Carved from laterite and stucco, the sacred elephants are fittingly decked in ceremonial regalia

Horse carriages
Unique to Lampang are the horse carriages that take visitors and residents for pleasure trips around town. These appeared in Lampang in 1915, having been in use as VIP transport in Bangkok until cars were imported from Europe for the purpose. The whole operation— carriages, drivers and horses—was transported by the newly opened railway. Many of the carriages are original, although the colors are not!

The ornate Burmese mondop in the court-yard of Lampang's Wat Prakeo Don Tao is flanked by a bell-shaped golden chedi, reputed to contain one of the Buddha's hairs

Ban Sao Nak *Radwattana Road.* (*Open* daily, 9:30–5:30. *Admission charge*) Built on 116 pillars, this dark teak mansion is worth a short visit for those wanting to see inside a typical wealthy home built in the northern Thai/Burmese style. The two main rooms are filled with a briefly absorbing collection of antiques.

Wat Pongsanuk Tai▶ *Pongsanuk Road.* A modern *wat* encloses the raised platform, which retains an excellent example of a mondop (temple building for lay people) built in Lanna style; a tiered roof shelters four Buddha images gathered around the sacred bo tree.

Wat Prakeo Don Tao▶ *Prakeo Road.* The city's oldest major temple is known mostly for two Buddha images that are now elsewhere: the Emerald Buddha is now in Wat Phra Keo in Bangkok's Grand Palace (see page 79), and Don Tao is now at Wat Phra Luang. The temple possesses a square *mondop* of 1909 in Burmese style, with a typical multitiered roof. An adjacent museum displays mostly Lanna-style wood carvings.

Wat Sri Chum▶ *Sri Chum Road.* Unfortunately, only the ornate porches remain of one of Lampang's loveliest temples after a disastrous fire in 1992. Some of the monks here are Burmese.

Environs
Wat Phra That Lampang Luang▶▶▶ *Reached by songthaew as far as Kho Kha, followed by a 2-mile walk or a change to another songthaew. It is possible to charter one at a cost of about 200 baht for the round-trip.* Sited 11 miles south of Lampang, this is the sole survivor of one of four fortified satellite settlements built in the Haripunchai period to serve Lampang. A triple rampart with moats still encloses a farming village clustered around the *wat*, itself a supreme example of the Lanna style and in an excellent state of preservation. The main *wiharn* dates from 1496 and contains early 19th-century murals of nobles in Burmese costume. Another *wiharn* displays intricate mosaic-inlaid gables. An open-sided *wiharn* dating from the early 16th century is thought to be the oldest wooden building in Thailand.

Young Elephant Training Center▶▶▶ *22 miles west on Highway 11, on the Lampang–Chiang Mai bus route near Ban Thung Kwian*
This elephant show, similar to the Elephants at Work near Chiang Mai (see pages 164–165), is one of the best and most authentic places to see elephants being trained for logging work (*Open* daily shows at 9 and 11. *Closed* on Buddhist holidays. *Admission charge*).

▶▶▶ Mae Hong Son
End of Highway 108. Buses from Bangkok, Chiang Mai, Mae Sariang, Soppong and Pai; domestic flights
Lying in a valley amid densely wooded mountains and tucked away in Thailand's northwest corner, **Mae Hong Son▶** has recently changed its image from a remote

small town to a booming resort full of guest houses and trekking agencies.

A thick morning mist shrouds Mae Hong Son, adding drama to the town's pretty **Chong Khum Lake**, fringed by neat lawns and shrubberies. Two adjacent Burmese-style temples make a splendid backdrop to the water; both look best from the outside, although **Wat Chong Klang** contains interesting wooden figurines and painted glass panels brought from Burma in 1857.

Perched on a steep hill, **Wat Doi Kong** presides over the town and is the place to make for at sunset. The 15-minute walk up can be started near the Mai Tee Hotel (take the road opposite Singhanat Bumrum Road, fork left and continue until the temple steps appear to your right). Back in town, there is a lively morning market (6–8 AM); hill-tribe people come to buy and sell.

The best guest house locations are by the lake or in Phachachon Uthit Road.

Environs

Motorbikes, mountain bikes and jeeps can all be rented in town. Inquire locally before making any independent trips—border fighting, treacherous roads and lack of road signs are major hazards.

Tour agencies offer trips to hot springs, caves, waterfalls and tribal villages. One excursion heads east to **Tham Plaa▶** ("Fish Cave," inhabited by catfish) and climbs the rough road to Mae Aw—a Kuomintang (see page 182) Hmong village now on the Burmese border—passing the king's summer palace (Pang Tong). Trekking, elephant riding and rafting are also on offer. Trips to see the long-necked Pa Dong tribeswomen are much-touted and overpriced. The women wear rings around their necks to attain a swanlike beauty. Most of the money allegedly ends up in the pockets of their quasi captors.

Tham Lot▶▶▶ *Reached by taking a bus to Soppong, where it is possible to get a songthaow or make the 1½-hour walk.* A fork at Soppong leads through the village

continued on page 175

The entrance to Tham Lot, where swifts and bats enter and exit, respectively, at dusk

■ **The rugged, forested limestone hills of northern Thailand are home to a mélange of some of the most colorful tribal peoples in the world. The Lao, Karen, Hmong (or Meo), Mien, Lahu, Akha and Lisu minorities are a fascinating example of a vibrant preindustrial way of life. They originated in Tibet and south China and live on the migration route that the Thai people themselves traveled 1,000 years ago. Indeed, the Lao are sometimes referred to in Thailand as "the Thai that have not yet come south," and their culture is unlike that of the other hill tribes.** ■

Roots The Lahu and Akha came via eastern Burma and northern Laos, beginning to cross over into Thailand in the early decades of the 20th century. The Lisu migrated from the headwaters of the Salween River in China via Kang Tung state in Burma. To this day only a minority of these peoples live in Thailand, the majority remaining in Burma and China's Yunnan province. The Hmong (or Meo) and Mien came across the Mekong River from Laos after siding with the royalists in their vain attempt to prevent the communist takeover of Laos in 1975. They were settled at first in refugee camps on the border and have since moved into Thailand's northern forests.

The Karen are the biggest tribal grouping of them all, numbering by some counts over 4 million. Their precise origins are shrouded in mystery, but their culture contains Burmese, Mon and Thai elements.

Long-necked Pa Dong woman: the brass rings actually squash down the collarbone rather than lengthen the neck (see page 171)

(see page 171)

Separate tribal identities Karen culture centers on a sophisticated fallow agricultural system, and its feasts and rituals celebrate harmony with the natural environment—extended to human society with an unquestioning submission to acknowledged leaders.

The Hmong are fiercely independent. In Laos they expressed this by fighting communism, which threatened to engulf their way of life. Mien culture stresses propriety, etiquette and avoidance of open conflict.

The Akhas' rituals are based upon keeping alive links with ancestors, whom they revere as awesome guardian spirits protecting the continuity of tribal history.

The Lisu are the most competitive in seeking to provide the best singers, weavers—or opium growers.

A typical day in a hill-tribe village begins early as the roosters herald dawn. The women and girls are first to rise; they roll

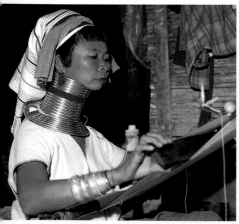

up their sleeping mats to begin pounding the rice to be eaten that day. Children usually collect water, sometimes—if they are lucky—from bamboo aqueducts that carry the water right into the village. Breakfast consists of rice and vegetables from the garden, cooked with roots and jungle spices, served with salt and chili peppers.

The workers returning from the fields at sunset bring firewood and food for the pigs. Families living far from their fields often camp out in the fields for days on end. After the evening meal, the women congregate in groups around smoky kerosene lamps or pitch-pine torches to sew, while the men gather to smoke pipes, drink tea and discuss the day's happenings.

In the dry season, the air is choked with dust and smoke from the burning fields. During the monsoon, the dust turns to sticky mud. Women and children must trudge ever-increasing distances to find firewood.

Crafts Each tribe has its own craft tradition, making jewelry, musical instruments, baskets, tools, utensils, weapons and traps (see page 162). Some villagers become artisans specializing in one particular craft. The highest status is given to the blacksmith, on whom the villagers depend for making and mending their tools and weapons. In recent years, Thai crafts that were previously practiced only for domestic use have become much in demand from tourists. That demand has spawned a whole new breed of skilled entrepreneur tribesman who purchases handicrafts from the villages and sells them at the colorful night bazaars of Chiang Mai, Chiang Rai or Bangkok.

Society The extended family is the most important social unit. Most tribes are patrilocal, including the families of married sons in the household, with the exception of the Karen and the Lahu, where it is common for daughters also to set up families in their parents' household. Marriage is usually monogamous, but polygamy is also acceptable in all the tribes except the Karen.

Communication
The main tradition of tribe communication is an oral one. This is entering a new era with the introduction of radio. Radio stations broadcasting to the tribes now transmit from Chiang Mai and Mae Chan.

Hill tribes

The religions of the hill tribes are sometimes described as "animist," but this is an oversimplification. The Lisu and Akha beliefs show extensive Chinese influence, while the Mien practice a form of Taoism. Most villages have two types of religious specialist—a priest for performing the rituals and a shaman for communicating with the spirit world.

There is a village headman, who must have an understanding of the mythology and rituals of the tribe but who must also represent the village effectively in its dealings with the provincial and central governments of Thailand. Conflict arises, for example, when officials try to get a fluent Thai speaker appointed as village headman when he may not have the confidence of the villagers in other respects.

King Bhumiphol first became interested in the plight of the hill tribes in the 1960s when he was hiking in the forests around his hill palace of Phu Phing. He came across a desperately poor Hmong village with pathetically scraggy pigs. He patiently demonstrated to them how to raise a better breed of pig—and then became drawn into combating their "bad habit" of growing opium poppies.

Realizing that the successful eradication of opium could not just be imposed legalistically, King Bhumiphol initiated a program of research into alternative crops that could be profitably grown to replace opium. He set up an experimental orchard at Kasetsart University, which showed that roses, lilies, chrysanthemums, coffee, apples, peaches, strawberries, Brussels sprouts, mushrooms, turnips and cabbages could be satisfactorily grown in these areas. For a time the tribes took to these new crops, but there has been a degree of reversion to opium.

For the marketing of opium, villagers rely on heavily armed convoys of Yunnanese traders. Because of the illegality of the trade, tribespeople are powerless to avoid exploitation and intimidation by these middlemen.

The main crops are rice and corn, supplemented by melons, squash, cucumbers, tomatoes, onions, beans and cabbages. The most common livestock are chickens and pigs. Cattle and water buffalo are highly prized, partly as a status symbol and also as a real asset that can be sold in hard times. The buffalo are used for plowing and harrowing.

Bartering is still common. A blacksmith may often be paid in rice or corn, and a family might provide labor in a neighbor's field in return for some pork. When the villagers travel to the nearest market to stock up on supplies, they take handicrafts, vegetables, charcoal, broom grass and bamboo shoots to sell. Health care is primitive, and caring for opium addicts creates an even greater burden. Illiteracy is widespread, and the hill tribes suffer the indignity of being laughed at by townspeople and gawked at by tourists. The building of new roads confers great benefits but also produces tension when villagers' interests are overlooked and the pressures of modernization come too fast and insistently along the road from the town.

Tribal fashion

The hill tribespeople wear beautiful and elaborate clothing. The showiest garments are worn by young people of marriage-able age. The styles worn by each tribe are not unchanging but rather a result of constant innovation. Teenage girls spend hours weaving, sewing and beading, in the effort to produce the prettiest costume in the village.

Conflict and dilemma

Even more serious is the destruction of the environment in the hill-tribe areas. This is due to the tribal practice of slash-and-burn cultivation, where one patch of forest is cut down for cultivation for a few years until the soil becomes drained of nutrients— when a new field must be cleared.

With increasing population, the pressure on the land has tightened, reducing the period of fallow from 10 to five and sometimes as little as two years. The resulting soil erosion causes bigger floods on lowland rivers. The long-term solution is reforestation of watershed areas, but this has become a major source of conflict between uplanders and the government.

Restrictions on forest clearing threaten the very livelihood of some hill tribespeople, even if they survive the exposure to tourists and city merchants. Their culture is on the edge of extinction

continued from page 171

and 5½ miles up to a Shan village, where signs lead to this superb cave. Guides (about 150 baht per party) and lanterns can be hired at the entrance. The limestone formations and sheer size are impressive, but insist on seeing the third chamber (this involves some wading), where at dusk there is the breathtaking spectacle of huge numbers of swifts and bats entering and leaving the cave mouth.

Nearby, Cave Lodge offers simple accommodations and cave treks.

Pai *Buses run from Mae Hong Son, Soppong and Chiang Mai.* An aimiably dozy small town, with inexpensive trekking and guest houses, Pai is good for gentle excursions. East, over the river bridge, a dirt track leads past a hilltop *wat* 9 miles to a signposted hot spring. Thick-skinned visitors claim the water is not too hot for swimming.

► ► **Mae Sai and Sob Ruak**
(The "Golden Triangle")
Highway 110. Buses from Bangkok, Chiang Mai and Chiang Rai
The town Thailand's northernmost point is a classic border post, where a bridge spans the Mae Kok River and leads into the adjacent Burmese town of Tha Khi Lek. A constant procession of Burmese and Thais cross over for the markets on either side. Foreign nationals may enter Burma for a day trip, or for longer stays to visit the town of Kengtung, 100 miles from Mae Sai. Several agencies can arrange this tour, but a substantial immigration fee is payable.

Mae Sai excels as a place for people-watching; hill-tribe children, some of them just Thais dressed for the part, pose for tourists' cameras, a blind beggar holds out a metal tankard, while a wizened brown-skinned woman puffs a fat cheroot.

On Buddhist holidays, a fascinating market takes place on the bridge itself. At other times, Burmese crafts (string puppets, wall hangings, wooden musician figures and lacquerware) and jade are on offer—much of it brought in from Chiang Mai.

Mae Sai's modern main street is wide and drab, but a string of bungalow-style guest houses by the river entice a few days' stay.

Opposite and to the left from the Top North Hotel, 207 steps lead up to Wat Doi Wao, which faces into Burma.

Mae Sai lies in a district known for its cultivated strawberries, sold from stalls along the main road in the winter months.

Motorcycles can be rented in Mae Sai for exploring the area.

Environs
Sob Ruak (the Golden Triangle)► ► *Hourly minibuses from Mae Sai, morning only, and all day from Chiang Saen, from where boats can be chartered*
A huge new luxury hotel and a plethora of souvenir stalls

Casinos
An additional lure for Thais to the Golden Triangle is a recently opened casino in the Burmese border town of Tha Khi Lek. Casinos are illegal in Thailand, but gambling remains a popular pastime for many Thais. Despite protests by the Thai government, this controversial, privately funded enterprise, tacitly permitted by the Burmese government, has aroused great interest.

Entering Burma
Foreign visitors are allowed to cross into Burma at Mae Sae on a day trip. Check current regulations before you travel. You have to pay a fee ($5) for a border pass and surrender your passport. Make a photocopy of the photo and visa pages in advance (local photo shops can arrange this). Over the bridge you can visit the Tha Khi Lek market, the Chinese cemetery, and a small *wat*. Many Burmese speak excellent English.

Little China in Thailand
Formerly known as Mae Salong, Santi Kiri ("Hill of Peace") has existed since 1961 as a refugee village for Kuomintang soldiers and their families following the 1949 Chinese Cultural Revolution. After settling in Thailand, they involved themselves in smuggling and in the opium trade. The Thai government has launched a reeducation program and persuaded them to switch to growing tea, coffee, herbs, fruit and corn. Thai language classes are given, and a loudspeaker broadcasts information on taxation matters and health education.

Fearsome temple dragons reveal the strong Chinese influences in this part of Northern Thailand, seen most clearly in Santi Kiri

pander to the needs of the hordes of tourists who come here to be photographed in front of a hideous concrete sign announcing this to be the Golden Triangle. Except on postcard racks, there isn't an opium poppy in sight; the growers of the illicit plant discreetly raise their crops elsewhere, and the altitude is too low anyway. But despite the tackiness of the place, this is a view to remember—the confluence of the Mekong and the Mae Ruak rivers at the meeting of Thailand, Burma and Laos, with mysterious mountain ranges stretching into the distance. **Wat Phra That Phu Khao**, perched on a hill, gives the best panorama, with excellent views over the whole area.

Unfortunately, the Burmese have recently constructed a casino in the middle of the river to lure Thais to gamble their baht and prop up an ailing Burmese economy (casinos are banned in Thailand).

Chiang Saen►► *Buses from Chiang Rai.* Nicely situated on the Mekong River, this sleepy small town lies to the east of Sob Ruak. Around the neat grid pattern of streets are dotted a number of ancient ruins from the old town, which was founded in the 13th century and retains its 14th-century fortifications. The Burmese briefly controlled it in the 16th century, and Rama I later destroyed the town, fearing a repeat capture might occur. Chiang Saen remained in an unoccupied state until the time of King Rama V.

The National Museum► (*Open* Wed–Sun 9–noon. 1–4. *Admission charge*) is on the main street, which leads away from the river. This contains hill-tribe artifacts, inscribed stones, ceramics, Buddha images and Lanna objects.

Close by is the 190-foot-high octagonal *chedi* of Wat Chedi Luang, built in 1290.

Wat Pa Sak► Keep along the main street and turn right as you cross the town wall for a ruined forest *wat* among the trees that retains some of its fine stucco decoration. Wat Pa Sak (the "Teak Forest Temple"), with its magnificent stuccoed *chedi*, is the most impressive monument in Chiang Saen.

Continuing along the road for half a mile, with the moat on the right, brings you to **Wat Chom Kitti►**, which is approached by a long staircase and provides a good view across to Laos.

Chiang Khong *Buses from Chiang Rai; songthaews from Chiang Saen.* The village is also on the Mekong River, which is the sole feature of interest. Riverside guest houses and bungalows make the most of the view (more than in Chiang Saen, where accommodations are not particularly good).

Doi Mae Salong/Santi Kiri►► *Frequent buses run between Chiang Rai and Mae Sai; get off at Basang for a songthaew. Sporadic service*
Perched high on the Mae Salong mountain, 22 miles from the main road, Santi Kiri is an extraordinary place, inhabited by Yunnanese and completely Chinese in

character. Yunnan is spoken; the shops sell strange herbal liquors, litchi and prune wines and locally grown tea. Stalls along the street sell noodles; at daybreak Akha women conduct a lively produce market. A *wat*, a mosque and a Haw Chinese shrine serve the community.

Stay overnight and experience the early morning life: there is a range of accommodations above the village.

Doi Tung►► *Frequent buses from Chiang Rai to Mae Sai; get off at Highway 1149 for a songthaew for Doi Tung* The paved road winds up past Shan, Akha and Lahu villages to the 5,576-foot summit 15 miles from the main road, where Wat Phra That Doi Tung and its vast assemblage of bells of varying pitches look far into the surrounding hills.

Simple bungalows are available on the way up. Views and rural atmosphere can hardly be bettered. You would only be wise to trek in this area if you are accompanied by a guide.

The hilltop setting of Wat Doi Wao in Mae Sai provides an excellent vantage point over the town and the hills of Laos across the Mekong River

► ■■■■ **Mae Sot**
Off Highway 105. Frequent buses from Tak
The westernmost town in Tak province lies close to the Burmese border and is a smuggling post for teak and jade. The streets throng with Chinese, hill-tribe people smoking cheroots, Burmese in sarongs and dark-skinned Muslims in lace skullcaps. The town center is punctuated with Burmese-style *wats* whose golden chedis glint in the hard sunlight.

Mae Sot is a good base for exploring hill-tribe villages, Burmese refugee camps and the mountainous border areas in the vicinity. Among several tour companies that organize trekking tours is the Mae Sot Travel Center (tel: 055/531409).

Environs
Songthaews leave frequently from various locations around town to these and other destinations.

Rim Moei Market►► *Ten minutes' drive west on Highway 105.* This border market town is on the River Moei, now a major crossing point with the completion of the Thai-Burma Friendship Bridge in 1996.

The market is full of Burmese wares—lacquer products, jade, rubies, embroidered vests, Burmese currency and even school slates.

"Death Highway" to Um Phang►►
Songthaews; journey time about five hours. Highway 1090, south from Mae Sot, earned its nickname in the 1960s and '70s when communists held the area and attacked road builders.

Today it is moderately safe (there is a police check-point, so bring your passport) and the magnificent road looks over huge areas of scarcely inhabited terrain, including Thailand's second-highest mountain, Khao Kha Khaeng (7,872 feet).

Um Phang, 102 miles from Mae Sot, is one of Thailand's remotest villages within reach by good road. Several guest houses offer simple accommodations and organize one-day raft trips and three-day treks (dry season only) to **Tee Lor Sue►►**, one of Thailand's largest and more dramatic waterfalls.

Closer to Um Phang, guides will take you to **Tham Mae Klong Cave►**, a 3-mile-long cave with limestone formations, a bat colony and a hermit monk; and **Doi Hua Mod** ("Bald Mountain"), which has a spectacular sunrise view.

Twenty five miles from Mae Sot on this road, a signposted track leads 2,296 feet to **Pha Charoen waterfall►**, which tumbles down a 93-step natural staircase.

►► Nan
End of Highway 101. Frequent buses from Bangkok, Chiang Mai, Lamphang and Phrae. Daily bus from Chiang Rai; domestic flights
The town Relatively remote and considered a dangerous area until recent years, Nan is far from being the most

---

Burma (Myanmar)
This former British colony has suffered brutal repression from dictatorships since 1962, when General Ne Win wrested power in a coup. In 1988, student demonstrations against the government were met with atrocities, and many fled to Thailand, settling around Mae Sot. Despite a crushing electoral defeat by the National League of Democracy in May 1990, General Sauw Maung refused to cede power. In recognition of Burma's struggle for democracy, Suu Kyi, the democracy leader, was awarded the Nobel Peace Prize while under house arrest.

178

Silverware
Silverware bargains can be had in Nan. Prices are about 25 percent cheaper than those in Chiang Mai and 50 percent less than those in Europe. Look out also for superb local textiles.

visited part of the north. However, many visitors stay on longer than they intended, captivated by the town's laid-back atmosphere. The most exciting bus-route approach is on Highway 1148 from Chiang Rai, along a tortuous single track for five and a half hours, traveling past mountains, Hmong villages and opium fields.

The National Museum►► *Pha Kong Road.* (*Open* Wed–Sun 9–noon, 1–4) Erected in 1903 as a palace for the feudal lord, this houses one of the best provincial museums in Thailand.

Wat Phumin►► (see panel) Opposite the museum, this 16th-century *wat* is memorable for its Lanna-style wood carvings and superb murals depicting scenes of old Nan.

Environs
Nan province is relatively undiscovered, with time-warp villages, mountain scenery and good views. Guest houses and the Youth Hostel (tel: 054/710322) organize trekking and tours. Motorcycles and bicycles can be rented from shops near the Devaraj hotel.

Doi Phukha National Park►► *Highway 1256 northeast of Phua (north of Nan), road signs in English.* The highest point in the province (6,494 feet), the park abounds with waterfalls, views and caves. One of the world's rare Chompu Phuka trees, which produces pink flowers, is here. Non-Thai speakers will need a guide. A day trip could take in salt mines at Bor Klua and weaving and silverware villages.

Wat Phumin
On the murals in Wat Phumin, note the women wearing the local costume and the men adorned with tattoos and period hairstyles.

Sao Din Canyon
The weird landscape of wind-eroded earth pillars in the extraordinary valley of Sao Din, south of Nan in Na Noi district, off Route 1026, has been used as a setting in a number of Thai movies. To reach the canyon by public transportation, take a bus to Na Noi, then charter a taxi or *songthaew.*

Wat Manee Pasi Son, in Mae Sot, has a very unusual construction. Dozens of small chedis *rise in tiers around a central spire, each containing a Buddha statue*

King Naresuan
Phitsanulok is no more than a provincial capital these days, but like several other northern cities, it had its days of glory. In the late 15th century, it was the capital of Siam. A century later, it became the birthplace of one of Thailand's greatest kings, Naresuan, who reigned from 1590 to 1605. In his youth, Naresuan ruled the principality as a "training excercise" before ascending the throne of Ayutthaya on his father's death.

Pak Nai▶ *Bus from Nan, changing at Na Noi and Na Muan.* A few hours' drive south from Nan is this peaceful fishing village, built on stilts over the huge Sirikit Reservoir, which is bounded by hills. Simple, inexpensive raft-house accommodations and boat hire are available here.

Some 6 miles south of Na Noi, a turn leads to Sao Din, a curious area of pinnacles and pillars formed by water erosion.

Wat Khao Noi▶ *Just south of Nan, signposted off Highway 101.* A minor road leads to the hilltop *wat*; the statuary is garish in the extreme, but the view over the rice paddies of the Nan Valley and surrounding hills is satisfying enough.

▶▶   Phitsanulok
Intersection of Highways 12 and 117. Buses from Chiang Mai, Bangkok and neighboring towns, trains and domestic flights
Most tourists visiting this friendly city are passing through en route to Sukhothai, but there is enough here for a leisurely half-day exploration. The tourist office at Borom Trailokanat Road has helpful handouts, including maps of the area and a recommended town walk.

Phitsanulok looks its best by night along the Nan River—venue for annual boat races in October or November. Houseboats with rusting tin roofs and tottering TV antennas line the banks; amid them are a number of floating restaurants, one of which even has a boat attached for evening dinner cruises. Many of its traditional wooden buildings were destroyed in a fire during the 1960s. The night bazaar brings after-dark animation, with cheap food and clothing stalls.

Wat Yai (Wat Mahathat)▶▶▶ *Phuttabucha Road.* This contains a revered and beautiful image, Phra Buddha Chinnarat, much copied (see panel on page 181).

Folk Museum▶▶ *Wisuthikasartri Road.* (*Open* daily, 8:30–noon, 1–4:30. Donations welcome) Unprominently signed in a sleepy back street, this two-story house is crammed with the personal collection of retired Sergeant Major Tawee Booranakate. All kinds of bygones are here, mementos of a lifestyle that Thailand is fast shedding. Among them are utensils, plows, homemade toys and vicious-looking traps.

Buddha Foundry▶ Roughly opposite the Folk Museum and even less prominent (it's the door to the left of the Music School), this is run by the same person. Visitors are welcome to look around and watch the production process, where wax images are coated in clay and sand prior to casting, then the cast image is covered with lacquer and gold leaf.

Environs
Kaeng Sopa Waterfall▶ *Highway 12, 45 miles east of Phitsanulok (signs in English); 2-mile access road from main road. The Phitsanulok-to-Lom Sak bus*

passes along the main road; Kaeng Sopa is about 2 miles from here

A waterfall rushing down three steps strewn with massive boulders, Kaeng Sopa is the best-known feature of **Thung Sa-Laeng Luang National Park**, a large area of forest and wilderness, 5 percent of which has been illegally depleted. The park is home to many species of animals, from elephants and wild boar, to buffalo and the occasional tiger or panther.

The flying vegetable
At the night bazaar in Phitsanulok, you can see the city's most eccentric claim to fame, *pak boong loi fah* (the "flying vegetable"), where morning glory is tossed high from the wok to be caught across the street by the waiter.

Phra Buddha Chinnarat
Cast in bronze in 1357, Phra Buddha Chinnarat is a magnificent example of the late Sukhothai style. In 1631, King Ekathotsarot of Ayutthaya melted down some of his gold and personally coated the image. In 1756, King Boromkot donated the doors inlaid with mother-of-pearl. Murals of the Buddha's life and a Jataka tale were added at this time. The image is the most important in Thailand after the Emerald Buddha in Wat Phra Keo in the Grand Palace.

Houseboats, illegal elsewhere in Thailand, make a picturesque spectacle along the peaceful banks of the Nan River, in Phitsanulok

■ **The opium poppy was introduced to the Orient by Arab traders during the Mongol invasions of the 13th century. Minority hill tribes in southern China grew it as a cash crop to pay their taxes to the Chinese emperor. They took it with them when they migrated south to Thailand and Burma.** ■

Victims
The victims of opium include the hill tribes who cultivate the poppies, as well as Thailand's 500,000 heroin addicts. There are no millionaires living in the hills. Few families average more than $300 or $400 a year. The profits are all cornered by warlords, middlemen and international heroin syndicates.

Right: a Lahu woman smoking opium

The Golden Triangle The commercialization of opium and its more lethal refined form, heroin, in Southeast Asia is a direct result of the tangled recent politics and warfare of the region. Its use by American G.I.s during the Vietnam War dramatically increased the demand for it, while also providing outlets to the world market. The illegal trade bolstered the power of opium warlords. The whole inaccessible area between Thailand, Burma and Laos became known as the Golden Triangle.

Drug barons and cash flows The "king" of the opium warlords is Khun Sa. In the 1950s, with U.S. backing, he used opium to finance the futile rearguard battles of the Chinese Nationalists against Mao Zedong. By the late 1960s, however, he was in fierce competition with his erstwhile comrades. The battle for the opium trade escalated into a full-scale war in 1967 in which one of his convoys of opium was napalmed. He survived this and a score of other violent clashes with the Thai and Burmese armies.

Countermeasures Nowadays the government prefers to wean hill tribes away from opium to produce other cash crops. This is part of the broader hill-tribe development program launched by King Bhumiphol. There has been some success; checks are made and large opium fields destroyed, although villagers still grow opium on a small scale for their own use, as many are addicts. However, Thailand now accounts for less than 2 percent of world opium production.

Addicts are increasingly being sent to treatment centers rather than jailed. One such detoxification program is in a Buddhist monastery run by Phra Chamroon Parnchand (see page 147), who administers an emetic to addicts that induces spectacular ritual vomiting. He claims to have cured more than 60,000 addicts since 1959.

Border problems

■ **Continual battling with neighboring tribes and peoples has played a significant part in forming the identity of the Thai people. The Shan of northeastern Burma (Myanmar) and the Laotian people are ethnically related to the Thais, while the Cambodians and Malays have both experienced some degree of Thai rule.** ■

Border history Colonialism in the 19th century revealed the need for strictly defined geographical boundaries. Although Thailand was never colonized, its present boundaries reflect its role as a buffer state between the British in Burma and the French Indo-Chinese empire.

Burma The Golden Triangle, along the border with Burma (or Myanmar, as it now calls itself), is notorious for its rebels, bandits and opium trade. Neither government has full control over the border area.

Because of the practice of slash-and-burn cultivation, many of the hill tribes who live in Thailand frequently move over into Burmese territory and vice versa.

Laos Problems along the Laotian border mounted when the Vietnamese-backed Pathet Lao came to power in the 1970s. Many anticommunist royalist factions resisted from bases within Thailand, while refugees flooded across the border to be housed in camps (they are now being repatriated).

Much of the border is the Mekong River, which is also the main transportation artery of Laos. Trade has increased since a bridge was recently built across it.

Cambodia Thai fears over the border with Cambodia reached a high point after Vietnam invaded Cambodia in the late 1970s.

Tensions eased following the 1991 peace settlement in Cambodia. But the potential for trouble remains. Thais have in the past claimed the Cambodian provinces of Battambang and Siem Reap.

Malaysia Even the short border with Malaysia is ill defined. Until recently one bus journey between two Malaysian towns used to pass through Thai territory. Nine Malaysian forestry officials were arrested recently, accused of logging inside the Thai border.

Radical solution
In 1989, the Burmese government tried to cut off the finance to the Karen rebels by selling teak concessions to the Thai army. The Burmese junta were quite happy to see Burma's rain forests destroyed if it reduced cover and hiding places for the rebels.

183

The opium trade
Khun Sa is one of the world's biggest drug-traffikers. Financed by opium profits, he presides over the world's largest source of heroin. Once he enjoyed American support for his anticommunist activities, but now he has a hefty price on his head in Burma, Thailand, and the United States. With much local approval, Khun Sa campaigns vigorously against the Burmese military junta with his rebel Muang Tai army.

Burmese and Thai shoppers meet at the border market of Rim Moei near Mae Sot. Burmese handicrafts and jewelry are on sale, but not everything is a bargain

NORTHERN THAILAND

The Mrabri

Seldom seen even by local people, Thailand's most primitive tribe, the Mrabri—known also as the Phithong Luan ("spirits of the yellow leaves")—pursue a nomadic lifestyle on the borders of Phrae and Nan provinces. These humble and gentle people wear loincloths and have no use for money, preferring instead to barter. Now numbering less than 100, they face extinction as deforestation continues apace. Their corpses are not buried, but placed on trees to be pecked to pieces by birds. They are excluded from the Thai social system but have become a tourist attraction in the worst zoo tradition.

Time-worn Buddha statues encrusted with patchy gold leaf contemplate enlightenment in the peaceful temple precincts of Phrae

▶▶▶ Phrae

Highway 101. Buses from surrounding cities, domestic flights

Phrae city has little to offer the tourist except as a base for exploring the surrounding uplands. The name of Phrae is associated with the indigo work shirts *seua maw hawn*, much worn by farmers, samlor drivers and even local schoolchildren and teachers—it becomes the Phrae school uniform on Fridays. Made at Ban Thung Ong, north of the city, these hard-wearing garments are on sale throughout town; a shirt will cost you about 100 baht, and you can get jackets and pants made of the same material.

Downtown Phrae is blandly modern, but the adjoining old part of the city retains traces of its moated fortifications and has a maze of peaceful streets of old-style wooden houses.

Wat Chom Sawan, on the northeast side of the city, is a Burmese-style temple, with multitiered tin roofs and a good deal of creaky, old-world charm.

Environs

Phae Muang Phi▶▶ *11 miles to the northeast; take Highway 101 toward Nan, branch off right as signed in English after 7 miles. There are no buses.* This translates as "Ghost Land": soil erosion has left a surreal moonscape of earth pillars, best seen in the early morning when the shadows create some strange effects.

Tham Pha Nanloi▶ *19 miles to the northeast, on Highway 101 toward Nan. On the Nan–Phrae bus route.* An electrically lit cave with limestone formations, this is used as a Buddhist shrine and extend is 656 feet into the hillside.

It is the setting for an ancient and famous legend of a king's daughter who is saved by a soldier from drowning. She elopes with her savior and has his child. The king, furious at their behavior, sends men after them to ambush the soldier as he leaves the cave. Unaware of his death, the princess waits eternally for his return; a rock in the cave is said to represent the princess and her child.

►► Phu Hin Rong Kla National Park

Off Highway 12 east of Phitsanulok. Buses between Phitsanulok and Lom Sak; change at Ban Yang for bus to Nakhon Thai; change for songthaew to the park

Approached by a road that rises through rugged highlands and passes remote Hmong villages, Phu Hin Rong Kla has a magnificent setting—best appreciated from the knobbly rock pavement known as **Lan Hin Boom**, perched on a cliff above a hair-raising drop. Deep rock fissures harbor ferns, lichen speckles the boulders and orchids and white rhododendrons are among the diverse flora.

Today the park is visited for its solitude and quiet beauty, yet from 1968 to 1982 it was the stronghold of the Communist Party of Thailand (CPT). Remnants of that era survive today (there are probably unexploded shells around, so keep to the trails).

Following the road westward from the park headquarters (toward Nakhon Thai) for 300 yards, a left turn near the park sign leads on to a trail across the rock plateau. The memorial on the right near the road commemorates those who died in a major KMT (Kuomintang) conflict.

Eastward from the park headquarters on the main road, a cluster of signs in English points to three KMT relics. The air-raid shelter is a deep natural rock crevice, explored by a short circular trail that leads up and down ladders. Close by, a waterwheel survives, fed by a wooden chute. This was constructed for the purpose of grinding rice for CPT consumption.

Farther along, on the other side of the road, are the remaining huts of the **Political and Military School**, the camp training center.

Adequate bungalow accommodations, starting from 100 baht per person (book in advance: 02/579 0529), and tents at around 40 baht for one or two people are provided. Of the two restaurants, Dungjai's is better; the proprietor's *som tum* (spicy carrot salad) has won her TV appearances. The park headquarters gives away free but basic maps and maintains a small KMT museum.

CPT

Huts, air-raid shelters, bunkers, an abandoned digging machine, a flagpole, some graves being rapidly overgrown and a simple memorial are reminders of a period when the Communist Party of Thailand fortified itself in one of the country's most impenetrable areas. From the 1940s, Hmong tribes settled in this virtually unpopulated region. They planted opium and many were arrested over the next decade. As the Hmong's relationship with central government deteriorated, the CPT took up their cause. In 1982, the government weakend the grip of the CPT until it gave in. The park was established in 1984.

For centuries, Phu Hin Rong Kla's rugged terrain offered a safe hiding place to bandits and insurgents. Now its most peaceful inhabitants include rare orchids, ferns and mosses

The kilns of Sawankhalok
At the Sawankhalok kilns, north of the Historical Park, you can visit some of the excavated kilns that produced world-famous ceramics in the 14th and 15th centuries. The typical grey-green glaze was often decorated with fish or chrysanthemums. Beware fake "antiques"—a local specialty!

▶▶ Si Satchanalai Historical Park

Intersection of Highways 101 and 102, 1¼ miles to the south of the new town of Si Satchanalai and ½ mile off the Sukhothai–Phrac bus route
Open: daily 8:30–4:30

Cars are not allowed in the park itself, but elephant rides are available from the entrance, and bicycles can be rented from the pink entrance gate to Wat Phra Si Rathana Mahathat, 1¼ miles from the park. There is a small entrance fee.

The old city of Si Satchanalai coexisted with Sukhothai and was ruled by Sukhothai princes. It flourished as a center for Sawankhalok celadon ware, first produced by Chinese potters; old kilns dot the area, and the industry

---

Walk A walk in Phu Hin Rong Kla

Allow 1½ to 2 hours for this 2-mile walk.

Start at the parking lot signed "Communist Headquarters" from the main road, 2 miles east of the national park headquarters. Take the path at the bottom of the parking lot. Fork left at the Thai signpost after 650 feet. Ignore a small path joining from the left and cross a rock pavement. Notice the pockmarks in the rock caused by shelling. (You will return to this point; to the right is your eventual continuation.) Keep to the left of the gun and take the right-hand of two paths signed in Thai.
The left-hand path leads to the former huts of the Political and Military School, where it is a short walk left along the road for signed turnings to the waterwheel and air-raid shelter.

Immediately fork left again and reach a hut on your right, formerly used for pounding rice.
Just ahead lie the former CPT headquarters and wooden-barred jail.

Take the path by the hut. It leads through another air-raid shelter (a natural rock crevice). Walk on and rejoin the main path, keeping left on it to return to the rock pavement and the abandoned gun. Turn left.
The path soon leads to Pa Chu Thong, or Flagpole Cliff edge (passing to the right of the Flagpole

Cliff itself), to the rock pavement of Lan Hin Boom. This is the most famous land form in the park.

Retrace steps to a fork; bear left. Later, Flagpole Cliff comes into view, and you pass mushroom-shaped rock formations. At a wooden gateway on the left, a short path leads past the site of a CMT burial ground, where a few overgrown mounds can be discerned.

Keep left on rejoining the main path and return to the parking lot.

Wat Chedi Jet Thaeo, Si Satchanalai

has been revived, with stalls operating near the old city. Over 140 ruins cover an otherwise largely deserted 740-acre area, the center of which is enclosed by fortifications and contains the park. In its extent, it is almost as striking as Sukhothai itself. Sites are numbered, and a map is available at the entrance.

Wat Chang Lom (Site 1)▶
A Singhalese-style chedi with 39 elephant buttresses; similar to its Sukhothai namesake but much better preserved.

Wat Chedi Jet Thaeo (Site 2)▶▶
Opposite Wat Chang Lom, this *wat* has 30 monuments in various styles, including a Sukhothai-style lotus bud *chedi*, and it is thought to enshrine the three princes of Sukhothai.

Wat Nang Phya (Site 4)▶
Early Ayutthaya style; still embellished with intricate stucco on a column and on the *wiharn* wall.

Phaa haat siaw
The village of Ban Hat Siaw, southeast of Si Satchanalai, is famous for its beautiful handwoven textiles, known as *phaa haat siaw*. These are made by a local ethnic group called the Thai Phuan, who fled here from north-eastern Laos during the 19th century to escape a Chinese–Laotian conflict. The cloth produced is patterned in bold horizontal stripes and edged with brocade. Weaving skills are passed on to the women of each generation.

Wat Chedi Jet Thaeo

Wat Khao Phanom Phloeng (Site 8)
Reached by a flight of laterite steps, the ruin is unremarkable, but it commands a large view, partly obscured by the trees.

Wat Si Rathana Mahathat▶ (1¼ miles southeast at Chalieng) Approached from the main road by a rickety wooden suspension bridge, this working temple stands inside a loop in the Yom River and retains a Sukhothai-style seated Buddha image.

▶▶▶ Sukhothai
Intersection of Highways 12 and 101, west of Phitsanulok. Buses from Chiang Mai, Phitsanulok, Bangkok and neighboring towns; domestic flights

Three examples of Sukhothai's many and varied temples include the 13th- to 14th-century Wat Chetupon, built partly of slate...

If you only have time to visit one ancient site in Thailand, it must be the old city of Sukhothai. New Sukhothai, 7 miles east, is a completely separate town, of interest only as a place to stay and eat. There are no inhabited buildings within the old city.

From the new city, cross the main road bridge over the Yom River and take a minibus from just behind the police box on the right. Cars are not allowed in the old city ruins; buses tour the main sites from the museum, and bicycles can be rented from the shop by the bus stop for about 20 baht. Distances are too great to cover on foot. There are admission charges for each of the city's five zones; the historic park is open daily until dusk.

History Established in 1238, when the central plains were inhabited by Mons and Khmers, Sukhothai was the capital of the first large Thai kingdom in Siam and became a vassal state of Ayutthaya in 1365. It was a cosmopolitan kingdom, host to a variety of cultures from Borneo, Ceylon and China, all of which contributed to the diversity of its monuments. King Ramkhamhaeng extended the kingdom with his warrior skills and was responsible for much of the flowering of Sukhothai

Loi Krathong
The colorful festival of *Loi Krathong* is thought to have originated in Sukhothai during the 13th century when a royal concubine placed candles and offerings in a banana-leaf dish and set it afloat on a lotus pond. Today, the custom is revived on the full moon of the 12th lunar month (generally November). At Sukhothai, the festival continues for three nights, with thousands of candlelit *krathong* set afloat on local rivers and lakes.

culture. He brought in Chinese ceramic skills, introducing the Sawankhalok celadon industry to the region. Sukhothai-style Buddha images are unmistakable for their oval heads bearing crowns, their plain torsos and their serene, mystical smiles.

Of more than 90 historic sites, about a third are within the walls, which are still visible and are pierced by four gateways.

The city is walled and threaded by beautiful canals and lakes carpeted with lotus flowers. These waters were supplied by a reservoir built southwest of the city and were both functional and ornamental.

The National Museum►►► (*Open* Wed–Sun, except national holidays, 9–noon, 1–4. *Admission charge*) An excellent introduction to the historic city, including much in the Sukhothai style. Look too for the chart showing the evolution of the Thai alphabet, thought to have been invented by King Ramkhamhaeng; a set of photographs showing the overgrown ruins before restoration in 1953; and a copy of a Khmer stone that has told scholars much about the history of the site.

Royal Palace and Wat Mahathat►►► Only the base of the palace survives, but the royal temple ruins contain 200 structures. The main *chedi* bears a Sukhothai lotus-bud motif and its base bears a frieze of 111 Buddhas.

Wat Trapang Thong and Wat Trapang Ngoen►►► "The Temples of the Gold and Silver Ponds" adjoin the waterside, with a *bot* built on an island. This is the original site of the Loi Krathong festival (see page 228).

Wat Si Chum►► The tallest and most famous Buddha image in the city stands 47 feet high and has eyes of inlaid mother-of-pearl. A passage on the left, bearing *Jataka* inscriptions, is locked off because it would raise climbers above the Buddha's head.

Information Center► (*Open* 9–4) A beautiful modern pavilion overlooking a lake; inside are a pleasant coffee shop and a fine scale model of the city.

Wat Phra Pai Luang► An atmospheric ruin, with partly restored Khmer *prangs*; rather overgrown. It is thought to be at the heart of the original city, whose growth was restricted by the canals.

Wat Saphan Hin►► Turn off just past the sign for a scout camp and you will reach this hilltop *wat*, from where the kings could survey their city and kingdom.

Rama Khamhaeng National Park► *Off Highway 101 toward Kamphaeng Phet at the 414-km post.* A bumpy 9-mile access road finally leads to the national park office and bungalows (which can be rented). People come here to climb Khao Luang mountain (3,887 feet). Views are often misty but can be huge, and tents available near the summit offer sunset and sunrise views.

...Wat Mahathat, the city's most important site and the religious epicenter of the kingdom...

"Sukhothai style"
"Sukhothai style" describes the classic image of the enlightened Buddha, often depicted walking, instead of seated. It is characterized by a precise list of physical features regarded as "marks of greatness," including hands like lotus flowers, a chin like a mango stone, and skin so smooth that dust would not stick to it.

... and Wat Sra Sri

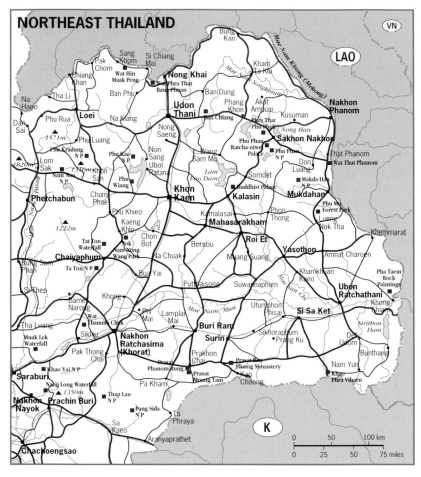

NORTHEAST THAILAND

VN

LAO

Bung Kan · Sang Khom · Si Chiang Mai · Kham Ta Kla · Mae Nam Khong (Mekong) · Pak Chom · Wat Hin Maak Peng · Nong Khai · Mae Nam Songkhram · Nakhon Phanom · Chiang Khan · Ban Phu · Wat Phra That Bang Phuan · Ban Dung · Phang Khon · Amnuai · Kusuman · Na Haeo · Tha Li · Udon Thani · Ban Chiang · Phra That · Phu Phek · Sakhon Nakhon · Dan Sai · Phu Rua · Loei · Na Klang · Nong Saeng · Phu Phan Ratcha-niwet Palace · Phu Phan N P · That Phanom · Wat That Phanom · 1571m · Phu Luang · Phu Kradung N P · Phu Kao N P · Non Sang · Wang Sam Mo · Don Luang · 1820m · Lom Sak · Nam Nao N P · Phu Khon San · 1316m · Phu Wiang · Lam Pao Dam · Somdet · Makda-Han N P · Phetchabun · Chum Phae · Khon Kaen · Kalasin · Buddhist Palace · Mukdahan · Phu Mu Forest Park · 1222m · Phu Khieo · Kaeng Khlo · Nok · Chon Bot · Kamalasai · Mahasarakham · Phon Thong · Lueng · Nok Tha · Khemmarat · Tat Ton Waterfall · Nam Nong Wang Park · Borabu · Roi Et · Yasothon · Amnat Charoen · Chaiyaphum · Ta Ton N P · Na Chuak · Muang Suang · Pha Taem Rock Paintings · Bung Sam Phan · Bua Yai · Khamkhwan Kaeo · Si Thep · Khong · Puttaisong · Suwannaphum · Mae Nam Chi · Ubon Ratchathani · Bamnet Narong · Wat Thammi Chak · Phi Mai · Lamplai Mai · Mae Nam Mun · Utumphon Phisai · Si Sa Ket · Khong · Sirithon Dam · Tha Luang · Sikhiu · Nakhon Ratchasima (Khorat) · Buri Ram · Surin · Sikhoraphum · Prang Ku · Det Udom · Buntharig · Muak Lek Waterfall · Pak Thong Chai · Prakhon Chai · Pluang Monastery · Nam Yun · Khao Phra Viharn · Saraburi · Khao Yai N P · Phanom Rung · Prasat Muang Tam · Kap Choeng · Nang Long Waterfall · 1350m · Prasat · Prasat Ban · Nakhon Nayok · Prachin Buri · Thap Lan N P · Pa Kham · Sa Kaeo · Pang Sida N P · Ta Phraya · K · Chachoengsao · Aranyaprathet

0   50   100 km
0 25 50 75 miles

Economic migration
The infertile soils and sparse rainfall of the northeast combine to produce the poorest region in Thailand. Poverty and unemployment reduce many Isan people to the state of economic refugees. Many migrate, at least seasonally, to large cities to look for work. Saddest of all are the young women (often barely more than children) who head for the bright lights of Bangkok or Pattaya and end up working as prostitutes to support their families.

This region is known as Isan by the Thais, and natives of Isan's 19 provinces are justly proud of their region's distinct identity. Khorat and Khon Kaen have been earmarked for industrial development, but agriculture is still the basic occupation of the majority of people. Nature here is a harsh master, with yearly droughts or flooding.

With the Mekong River and the Laotian Peoples' Democratic Republic to their north and east, many Isan folk identify themselves culturally as Laotian, although their political allegiance to the Thai crown is still very strong.

Isan is famous for its food—the sticky-rice staple, papaya salad and barbecued meat. Its folk music tradition, *mor lam*, is also special.

In a recent chapter of the region's history, thousands of American troops fought in the second Indo-China War, in Vietnam. Later upheavals have come in the wake of the Cambodian civil war.

Poverty here is such that the peasants who scratch a living from the soil supplement their diet with frogs and insects. The per capita income is still the lowest in the country, a paltry few thousand baht per year. Government attempts at development have been partially successful. The birthrate is falling, and increasing numbers of buffalo are replaced by the *E-taen*, a low-slung vehicle that can serve a multitude of purposes, which include plowing, pumping, threshing and transporting people about.

For the visitor There are plenty of attractions for the visitor. Be prepared for a trip through a land that, although barren at times, has much to amaze—both natural and cultural.

The northerly provinces of Loei and Nong Khai have stunning scenery along the Mekong, Loei being particularly mountainous; southern Isan, with its strong Khmer (Cambodian) flavor, has a wealth of remains from the days of Angkor's glory; and Surin is famous for its elephants.

Warm welcome One thing immediately noticeable in the more obscure provinces of the country is the open curiosity and generosity of the local people. If you drive around, you will find yourself constantly waving and smiling in response to roadside greetings. The famous Thai welcome to strangers is possibly warmer here than anywhere else.

NORTHEAST THAILAND

Temple ruins at Suwannaphum

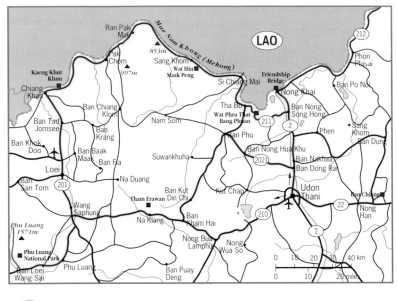

Drive A tour around Udon Thani, Loei and Nong Khai

This tour is best spaced over five days.

Suggested schedule
Day 1: Early morning, leave Udon Thani. Optional detour to Ban Phu. Arrive in Phu Luang National Park around twilight. Stay overnight in park accommodations booked in advance.
Day 2: Leisurely drive to Chiang Khan. Stay in guest house.
Day 3: Leisurely drive to Sang Khom. Stay in guest house.
Day 4: Leisurely drive to Nong Khai. Stay in hotel or guest house.
Day 5: Short drive to Udon Thani. Day excursion to Ban Chiang.

Start in Udon Thani, with its handi-craft markets. To arrive in Loei before sunset, take the main Highway 210 west. Alternatively, take Highway 2 (the Friendship Highway) north.
A diversion to **Ban Phu**▶▶ at the well-signed Highway 2021 will mean arriving at dusk, especially if time is taken to explore the rock garden and cave systems of **Phra Putthabat Bua Bok**. This is not signed in Ban Phu district.

On arrival at the crossroads, go straight across by the market and look for Highway 2348.
The road down to Highway 210 and Loei from Ban Phu is not particularly remarkable; there are a few interesting *wat*s (temples) back from the road. Mountains of awe-inspiring scale start at the border of Loei province as the road climbs gently upward.

Highway 210 swings 90 degrees right at Wang Saphung district to become Highway 201; keep an eye out for the turnoff to avoid plunging into the paddies.
Jeep drivers may have time for the very well-signed 12-mile trip south from Wang Saphung to **Phu Luang National Park**▶, where there are accommodations. Phu Luang mountain can be seen from the road here, a gray stone leviathan dominating smaller neighbors.
  The short approach to Loei in the other direction is no less scenic. Loei town may not amount to much, but it has a ring of mountains and all the amenities of civilization, such as guest houses and hotels.

Continue to Chiang Khan district 30 miles due north.
This is an excellent spot to rest before contemplating the 125-mile drive along Highway 211 into Nong Khai, where guest houses taking advantage of the riverside ambience are plentiful.

Sang Khom is a modest target from Chiang Khan; Highway 211 sticks to the Mekong River for very long stretches. Khut Khuu Rapids is a short and reasonably signed left-hand detour just out of Chiang Khan. The scenery is formed by the meandering middle-aged river. The water level can go down so far in the dry season that it is unclear where the border actually lies. Shoals of rocks and extensive bogs dominate the view.

The 37 miles to Sang Khom are more of the same marvelous Mekong moonscape. The road scales a series of cliffs passing some viewpoints in order to cross the well-marked provincial boundary. Shortly afterward, **Than To waterfall**▶ is prominently indicated by the blue tourist signs as seen earlier on the road to Phu Luang. **Sang Khom** provides a leisurely stopover to relax peaceably by the now broad and clearly defined river. There are budget guest houses here. Nearby is Wat Hin Mak Peng, an atmospheric spot enhanced by an interest in meditation.

Alternatively, travelers may press on a further 25 miles into Si Chiang Mai. Shortly after Si Chiang Mai, the road swings away from the river and you are back into dusty, featureless Isan. The road becomes wider as it approaches Tha Bo.

Highway 211 cuts across the flat fields past Wat Bang Phuan to link up with Highway 2, a full 6 miles short of Nong Khai. Note that following the white signs all the way will lead into Nong Khai.
A dirt track turning left about 3 miles out of Tha Bo returns to the river all the way into **Nong Khai** train station, but the turning is difficult to locate. It will be easy to find a room in Nong Khai, although Highway 2 back into Udon is very fast. From Udon Thani it is a 30-mile drive (Highway 22) to **Ban Chiang**▶▶, where excavations have revealed bronze and clay artifacts thousands of years old (see page 194).

A Bronze Age skeleton from the Ban Chiang burial pits

Crude, mass-produced modern versions of the famous Ban Chiang pottery compete with convincingly antique-looking fakes. To see the real thing, head for the National Museum

▶ ▶ ▶ Ban Chiang

Off Highway 22. Buses from Udon Thani

The otherwise fairly nondescript province of Udon Thani made the headlines when pottery and bronze artifacts discovered in Ban Chiang were dated to the 3rd millennium BC, contemporary with Sumer, suggesting that metalworking was discovered independently in Southeast Asia.

Village crafts are largely reproductions of ancient Ban Chiang ware in all shapes and sizes. The native Thai Lao weaves and embroideries are also on display in the museum.

Archaeological finds Little is known of the early Ban Chiang people's language and ethnic origins, but the large and beautiful pots which were found as well as the metal tools and weapons, are a rich testament to their technical sophistication.

We also know that they farmed rice, domesticated animals, wove their own clothes and eventually progressed to working iron. The find stimulated research in geographical history, which showed a decrease in water sources.

Pottery The ancient pottery-making techniques of Ban Chiang are essentially the same as those used by modern villagers selling cheap reproductions. The patterns show an evolution through the period of the culture (*c.* 3600 BC–AD 300), the primeval inhabitants favoring the highly distinctive burnt-ochre whorl pattern. From about 2,000 years ago the potters incorporated figures of animals and people into their designs, and by the later period they had developed a process of printing patterns onto the pot with the aid of wooden discs.

Metalwork The metallurgy, too, shows a progression through a long period of experimentation. The search for minerals, the control of temperature, the greater admixture of tin for a shinier finish and a "lost-wax" molding process were all well developed. It appears that bronze was first cast from around 2000 BC onward. Ax heads, spear tips and arrow tips bear this out. The people of Ban Chiang had discovered techniques of smelting iron by 800 BC, and the stronger metal came to be used for heavier implements. Bronze came to be used for mainly decorative purposes, such as arm bangles and household objects like ladles.

Modern Ban Chiang The area was settled by an inward migration of the Thai Lao about 200 years ago. Like their forebears here, who were subsistence rice farmers, they built Wat Po Si Nai, which is one of the excavation sites.

The National Museum (*Open* Wed–Sun 8:30–5, except public holidays. *Admission charge*) Some of the choicest finds from the site are displayed in the modern National Museum. A *songthaew* (small pickup truck) drops passengers here from the main bus station in Udon for a few baht. Visitors are greeted on the stairs by a skeleton disinterred from a long sleep.

As with ancient cultures everywhere, burials supplied the greatest amount of cultural information. Bones reveal that life expectancy was as low as the early 30s, while the relative scale of the burials indicates a social structure.

The main Princess Mother building, which opened in 1987, houses an exhibition that once toured the world and is now on display at the National Museum in Bangkok. There are the fascinating details of the discovery, which was authenticated by a team from Pennsylvania University led by the late Chester F. Gorman. The other smaller building contains more artifacts.

Ban Chiang finds
In any terms, the archeological finds of Ban Chiang are remarkable, not least on aesthetic grounds. But the exact significance of the discovery has been hotly debated by experts. At first, Ban Chiang was dated at around 3000 BC, thus predating earlier evidence of the Bronze Age found in Mesopotamia. Later tests on the material revealed that it was not really so old. Nonetheless, it seems that Thailand developed smelting techniques well before China.

195

Archeological work
Locals soon cashed in on the Ban Chiang booty, collecting the pots by the carload for worldwide distribution, and by 1973, when an organized archeological dig at last got under way, the site had been sadly depleted of its treasures. But some artifacts were still to be found, most importantly the bronze that was to change archeologists' understanding of the development of metalmaking. Fortunately, the looting ceased, and much archeological work on the site was carried out by Thai volunteers.

The main characteristic of the Ban Chiang style of pottery is a swirling pattern in burnt ochre. Many of the pots were associated with burial rituals

196

The rocks of Ban Phu have provided local inhabitants with a blank canvas for thousands of years. These paintings reveal the artistry of early Buddhists

▶▶ **Ban Phu**

Intersection of Highways 2021 and 2098. Songthaew from Udon Thani or Nong Khai

This obscure corner of Udon is great for bush walkers. Bring some water for the arduous tramp. Getting there is relatively straightforward, and it is a feasible day trip from Udon Thani, Nong Khai or Sang Khom. While the final part of the route is a bush track, paved roads and buses run into Ban Phu, where there are motorbikes for rent, making it feasible to go another 6 miles to **Nam Som.**

The mazelike rock gardens of Ban Phu were recently designated the Phu Phra Bat Historical Park. They have cave paintings dating back approximately 4,000 years. It is fascinating to trace the rise and fall of civilizations and cultures through their sculpture.

Local legends grew around some of the stranger formations such as Hor Nang Usa, "Usa's Bedchamber," Usa being a woman who followed her lover here. Humans have arranged circles of stones, and there are curious formations caused by natural erosion. An imitation of That Phanom stands at the top of the hill. Wat Phra That Phra Putthabat Bua Bok, with relic and footprint, points the way along a path to the cave paintings and the mushroomlike sandstone "bedchamber."

Rock painting of early Buddhists

▶ **Khon Kaen**

Intersection of Highways 2 and 12. Buses from Bangkok (north terminal), Phitsanulok and Khorat; trains from Bangkok and Khorat; domestic flights

Officially a "development center," Khon Kaen is a large commercial and administrative city. Rapid industrial growth has been fostered by Khon Kaen University, the biggest in the region. The city's name came from Phra That Kham Kaen in Wat Jetiaphum, 19 miles north of town. According to legend, it was here that a tamarind log (*kham kaen*) began sprouting new shoots.

Attractions start with two large lakes, **Beung Kaen Nakhon** and the larger **Beung Thung Sang**. The cool atmosphere makes these popular picnic spots, even if the views are nothing out of the ordinary. Stalls sell Isan food such as *som tam* salad and barbecued chicken.

The Khon Kaen National Museum▶ (*Open* Wed–Sun, 9–noon, 1–4. *Admission charge*) has Dvaravati artifacts from Muang Fa Daet in Kalasin.

Environs
For palaeontologists, **Phu Wiang** is a detour worth making off Highway 2038 to see the bones of a Cretaceous-period dinosaur.

Tham Pha Phuang▶, Chum Phae district, is a 2½-mile turnoff some way along the road to Chum Phae. The huge cave here is an indirect walk from the parking lot. There is a terrific view from the cave mouth, but it is probably better to drive on to Phu Kradung National Park just over the boundary in Loei province (see page 198).

The name of **Pha Nok Khao** (Owl Cliff) on the border of Loei province refers to the strange shapes that can be seen on the Pong River. They can also be seen from Mt. Phu Kradung, which is visible in the distance.

Pong Neep (Ubol Ratana Dam), 16 miles out of town, is the biggest multipurpose dam in the northeast. Completed in 1966, it created a reservoir of 158 square miles and makes electricity for eight provinces.

Chon Bot *Off Highway 2. This district of Khon Kaen is reached by a turnoff at 248 miles, Ban Phai. Follow the road for another 7 miles.* Chon Bot is famous for the locally tie-dyed *mut mee* silks. The silk is cheap, and there is a good selection available. There are plenty of factories, busily serving markets in Chiang Mai and Bangkok. They are small, informally run and welcoming to visitors.

Mut mee
Isan is famed for its textiles. One of the best-known types is *mut mee*, a tie-dyeing process that produces a soft, subtle blend of colors and textures. *Mut mee* cloth is made from both silk and cotton yarns, the finer silk ones being more expensive. The geometric designs are based on natural patterns—flowers, snakes, etc. The revival of this traditional industry has been encouraged by Queen Sirikit, and by the growth of tourism.

197

The silkworms of Thailand expend their yellow labors for what is now a vast industry. Many Isan towns are important textile centers

Cotton Blossom Festival
Loei province is an important cotton-growing region and a good place to buy cotton goods, including sweaters and cushions. Heavy cotton quilts are another specialty, designed to ward off the chill of the cooler months in this mountainous area, which has the coldest winter in Thailand and occasional temperatures below freezing. A Cotton Blossom Festival celebrates the local product in February, with decorated floats and a beauty contest.

Phu Kradung's flora
Because of the cool temperatures, Phu Kradung has an unusual range of flora, including orchids and temperate species such as roses. Elephants frequent the pine forests. Pha Nok Aen is the place to go for sunrise views. There are numerous waterfalls.

▶▶ **Loei Province**

Highway 201; a border province with Laos. Regular buses from Udon; buses from Bangkok (northern terminal)

Temperatures can plummet below zero in this mountainous province, which is the coldest in the country. Have warm clothing at hand.

Loei town is a cotton center, and goods are on sale in town at reasonable prices. There are many hotels here, of which **King's Hotel** is the most luxurious while still remaining in the moderate price range. **Muang Loei** guest house is typical of the type of budget accommodations on offer.

Northwest of Loei town, an ancient city waits for discovery at **Ban Khok Doo▶**, while **Wang Saphung** district, a short way south out of town, has a few spots worthy of a visit amid a ring of mountains. On the Udon Thani road are the **Erawan caves▶**, where a long tunnel through a mountain is full of limestone formations.

National parks Loei's mountain national parks—Phu Kradung, Phu Luang and Phu Rua—are breathtaking in their scope and are centered on the mountains that lie to the town's south and west.

Heavily visited, **Phu Kradung▶▶** (sometimes closed during the rainy season) is best appreciated on weekdays. It is 52 miles south of Loei town on Highway 201. There are 30 miles of well-marked trails to explore across the forested plateau. The southern trail runs along a precipitous edge where gibbons can be heard calling from below. Park headquarters are on the summit, a tiring 5-mile climb. The trail up the table mountain leads past fields of colorful wildflowers and carnivorous pitcher plants hidden in the grass (see panel). Wildlife includes wild boars, wild dogs, giant black squirrels, langurs, macaques and herds of elephants. Restaurants and bungalows are available to help you get your strength back.

Beds can be booked on tel: 02/579 0529 or tel: 02/579 4842. Stalls selling soft drinks are set up along the trail but are closed during weekdays in the off-season.

Phu Luang▶ lies southwest towering behind Wang Sapung district, from where it is signed. It is worth the trek up to the plateau for waterfalls, stone gardens and forests of flowers.

Phu Rua lies 25 miles west of Loei, but drivers must skirt the thickly forested mountains after leaving Loei, turning right on Highway 203. *Phu Rua* means "Boat Mountain" and is so named because of its unusual prowlike summit.

There is a paved road up Phu Rua, but no regular public transportation. The progression of vegetation from lush tropical to the more barren temperate varieties is as well defined as in a geography textbook. Early morning mist makes a breathtaking spectacle around the mountain. If you want to stay, the park bungalows are about halfway up the mountain.

Accommodations for any of the parks can be arranged through the national park central booking service in Bangkok, tel: 02/579 0529 or 02/579 4842.

The border with Laos Driving west from Phu Rua, you reach Dan Sai district and Na Haeo near the Laotian border. Turn right off Highway 203 as it swings down toward Petchabun.

Passing Dan Sai, follow an unprepossessing sign right to **Ban Muang Phrae▶**. This village is where it is possible, technically, to cross into Laos. There is a large sign bearing the inscription "The end of Siam," and a little wooden bridge with the legend "Lao-Thai friendship will endure." See the Lao town hall and rickety little mudpile of a temple, dark inside with guttered wax. Walking farther is not recommended as the area is still sensitive, and there are military checkpoints on the border road.

The important *wat* in Dan Sai cemented a Thai–Lao pact in 1560, with *chedi* (pagoda where relics are kept) Phra That Sri Song Rak. Around May and June, there is dancing for the rain god in papier-mâché masks that have a striking resemblance to African art, the dancers becoming fearsome *Phi Takone* ghosts.

Chiang Khan district, in the north, is an excellent starting point for a long scenic drive along the mighty Mekong River. The delightful small town of Chiang Khan is on the Laotian border, in a large valley surrounded by mountains where Highway 201 becomes 2186. The road goes to the east past narrow rapids at Khut Khu and continues on to Pak Chom. There are a number of *wats* in Chiang Khan. The oldest is 17th-century Wat Mahathat, in the center of town.

For accommodations, the **Nong Ball** has farang- (foreigner-) friendly services and an English-speaking owner, its restaurant having a fine Mekong-side ambience.

Border villages
The Tha Li district is one of the most beautiful parts of Thailand, and one that Western travelers rarely visit. Villages similar to Ban Muang Phra can be found all the way to Pak Chom, following the banks of the Heuang River, which forms the border with Laos and flows into the Mekong near Chiang Khan. Cross-border trade is steadily increasing as relations ease between Laos and Thailand, but the district remains a lawless and troubled zone.

199

The simple wooden huts of this Loei village indicate something of the standard of living in rural areas of the northeast. Many people live below the poverty line

The Mekong River

■ **The Mekong, which forms the border between Thailand and Laos for more than 465 miles, is one of Asia's great rivers. It springs from the high Tibetan plateau, and then stretches more than 2,800 miles to the South China Sea to become the world's 12th-longest river.** ■

River boats
On the Mekong River you will see the extremely simple Lao boat called "three planks," which translates into Lao as *sampan*.

See how it runs The Mekong River first pursues a turbulent course through the high Chinese mountains of Tibet and Yunnan, then flows parallel to the Yangtze and the Salween through Yunnan province. The river forms the border between Burma and Laos, and then between Laos and Thailand. Even in its upper stretches it is, in some places, more than 1¼ miles wide.

Along its way, it irrigates vast areas of land, supporting villages with rice, coconuts, sugar cane and fish, and provides miners with small finds of gold.

Passing Vientiane and Phnom Penh, an eventual 475 billion cubic meters of water per year burst into the sea in a Vietnamese delta. When it is in flood, the water can rise by 50 feet; yet in the dry season the flow is reduced to a trickle, and the people of northeastern Thailand can walk across the riverbed into Laos.

The river's banks are heavily forested, except in the drier areas of northeastern Thailand. Thick bamboo grows, as well as kapok and banana trees. Crocodiles are rare these days, but monkeys, pythons and the ubiquitous mosquitoes abound.

Embarking to cross the Mekong

Hydroelectric power Laos uses the Mekong for hydropower; a dam at Nam Ngum generates 150 MW. Half of the electricity generated can be exported to Thailand, whose booming economy is hungry for power, but deforestation and resultant erosion is making the reservoirs silt up.

Several dams have been built across Mekong tributaries, and others are under construction or being planned to supply the country with energy.

River language The people on both banks of the upper Mekong speak the same "northern language"; there are eight times as many Lao-speakers as there are in Laos itself.

For the people The river is a source of food—fish, shrimps, crabs and frogs—to supplement the staple diet of *kao niew*, or sticky rice.

The Mekong has given its name to a fierce rice liquor, Mekhong whisky. When it is drunk on the river a mweasure is sometimes poured into the stream for the water spirits.

FOCUS ON *Poverty*

■ **When the World Bank annual meeting and the Miss Universe Pageant were held in the new $90 million Queen Sirikit Convention Center in Bangkok in 1991, the Thai government moved to another area some 7,000 slum dwellers thought to be too visible to those foreign eyes.** ■

Rich and poor Thailand's rapid economic progress during the past two decades has placed it firmly among the success stories of the Pacific Rim, such as Singapore and Taiwan. Indeed, overall wealth just in Bangkok is close to the level of some of the poorer European countries, such as Portugal. But in the kingdom as a whole there is an enormous gap between rich and poor, and extreme poverty still exists. A good quarter of the population falls below the poverty line defined by the World Bank. The rapid growth of the late 1980s has actually widened the gap between rich and poor.

Isan in the northeast, where 40 percent of the Thais live, is one of the most poverty-stricken regions of the country. Across the large, arid plateau stretching from Nakhon Ratchasima all the way to the Laotian border, millions scratch out a living growing rice and tapioca.

Almost all but old people and children move away from home to search for work in the central plains region or in Bangkok itself. Some travel farther afield, to the rubber plantations of the south or to man Thailand's fishing fleet. They return to the villages only for the planting and harvesting seasons.

Solutions There are many new schemes to help the very poor, from land-sharing to commercialized agro-industry, village adoption to cooperatives. In the past five years, hundreds of millions of baht have been poured into the region by the government, and some improvement is noted. But the overall phenomenon of poverty remains.

Isan
Isan still suffers from malnutrition, landlessness and poor infrastructure. Children are still forced to cut short their education to go to work. Many of the poor and landless end up in one of Bangkok's numerous slums, where they lack the support of a village community.

201

Making a living from the sale of watermelons in the poverty-stricken northeast of Thailand

The weird, mushroom-shaped rocks of Phu Pha Thoep National Park in Mukdahan province make curious landmarks amid the surrounding dipterocarp forest

Phu Pha Thoep National Park

The small national park of Phu Pha Thoep lies south of Mukdahan, near the Laotian border. A remote, hilly area of dry forest and strange rock formations, it is renowned for its fossils and prehistoric finger paintings. Near the park headquarters is a cave stacked with dozens of small Buddhas brought by local villagers. The park is an important habitat for wildlife, including barking deer, civets, and monkeys. It can easily be visited on a day trip from Mukdahan.

►► Mukdahan

Highway 212, on the eastern border with Laos. Buses from Nakhon Phanom and Ubon Ratchathani

This province has one chief tourist attraction—views along the Mekong River. In Mukdahan town, a laid-out riverside walkway extends from the customs checkpoint, and car ferries work their way back and forth over the river. Across the river on the opposite side is the important Lao center of **Savannaket**. A little farther upriver is Kaeng Kabao, a dry-river islet.

The southern road is mountainous. Not far out of Mukdahan is **Phu Manorom**, a brisk climb up ending in a chedi and a pavilion. A good diversion off Highway 212 in this direction is **Phu Muu Forest Park**, near Nikhom Kham Soi. Rich in forestry, wildlife and water, the area has rest shelters on the mountaintop with good views of the plain below. Near town, on Jom Nang mountain, are "red-handprint" caves, which are similar to those at Pha Taem.

The area boasts a jumble of colorful Thai subtribes, such as Phu Thai, Saek, So, Khaa, Yor, Kalerng and Kula. January 9–15 is when the local people stage the Thai Tribes of Mukdahan festival. The end of a special Buddhist spiritual season is marked by a boat race.

►► Nakhon Phanom Province

Off Highway 22, near the Laos border. Buses from Nong Khai; possible to travel by bus from Udon (journey time over seven hours)

Nakhon Phanom town► itself has a seductive charm, with its fine legacy of dignified public buildings and old-fashioned houses. A memorable view of the Mekong River can be enjoyed from a number of restaurants and hotels. The main attraction in Nakhon Phanom province is **That

Phanom►►, a striking *chedi* of great antiquity, located 47 miles to the south of town. On the site there is a museum containing relics, including one of the Buddha, reputed to be a collar-bone, and a festival is held there every year, in January/February.

Renu Nakhon, near the provincial capital, is a similar structure on a more modest scale.

► Nakhon Ratchasima (Khorat)

Highway 2, 155 miles northeast of Bangkok. Regular buses from Bangkok (northern terminal); trains from Bangkok; domestic flights

Khorat is a day's drive by car from Bangkok and is an important railroad junction for Nong Khai and Ubon Ratchathani.

The moated city has long been a Thai redoubt against aggressive Lao and Khmer. It is often described as "the gateway to the northeast," and indeed, traffic to most Isan provinces must pass through Khorat. **Silver Lake Park** is an artificial lake just outside Khorat, off Mitraphap Road, with an aviary, flower garden and swimming pool.

The city owes its present plan to King Narai, who hired a French architect in the 17th century. A worthwhile sight on the outskirts is **Wat Salaloi►**, representing a ship beating against the waves. Ceramic tiles used to roof this innovative modern *wat* were made in **Dan Kwian**, a stopover easy to spot on the southwestern road to Phanom Rung. Special black clay characteristic of Dan Kwian pottery gives the distinctive "latticework" patterns a bright metallic sheen.

No visitor to modern Khorat can fail to notice **Khunying Mo** (or **Thao Suranan**), one of Thailand's martial heroines. This scourge of the Lao, who rallied the women of the town during an invasion in 1826, is immortalized on a terrace in front of the city's main gates, and a parade in her honor is held every March. Near her effigy is **Maha Weerawong** museum containing a hodgepodge of exhibits.

Environs

Ban Prasat has been continuously inhabited for several thousand years. Skeletons have been found here of a Bronze-Age culture which produced patterned red pots. A museum, opened in 1991 on the road from Khorat, just before the turning to Phi Mai, contains finds believed to be second in importance only to those of Ban Chiang (see pages 194–195).

A southbound turning just before Ban Prasat leads to another important Khmer sanctuary, **Prasat Hin Phanom Wan**. There are many other Khmer sites in the area around Khorat.

Staying over In a fine spot by the moat in Khorat, in an atmospheric green, wooden building, is the rather basic budget **Muang Thong Hotel. Faah Sang** is a budget alternative near the main station. There are plenty of moderate and expensive hotels, of which the central **Anajak** is moderate with good service (credit cards accepted).

Mut mee
Pak Thong Chai is a silk-weaving center due south on Highway 304—a day trip from Khorat. Once famous for the men's silken lower garment *pha jong kraben*, it went into decline as trousers gained wide popularity. The area has since revived, and the royally-promoted *mut mee* patterns are woven here. Plenty of workshops reveal the secret of this temperamental fiber.

Khorat disaster
In August 1993, Khorat attracted international attention when the Royal Plaza Hotel collapsed crushing 137 people. Subsequent enquiries revealed the six-story building violated regulations. The top three floors and a number of heavy water tanks were added without permission, far beyond the load-bearing capacity of the foundations. Several Thais were arrested and charged with negligence. They are the tip of a very large iceberg; inadequate planning controls and official corruption are rife.

Waterslides galore attract visitors to Silver Lake Park, on the western outskirts of Khorat

204

Wat Phochai
Wat Phochai, at Nong Khai town's eastern end, is the focus for festivals. The complex has a tall bell tower, and the main image is solid gold.

A restaurant sign in English and souvenirs on sale indicate a strong farang *presence in the frontier town of Nong Khai, much visited since the construction of the Friendship Bridge into Laos*

Spanning the Mekong
The Thai–Australian Friendship Bridge at Nong Khai is the first of several bridges to span the Mekong, finally linking Thailand and Laos after decades of hostility delayed construction. Financed by $30 million of aid from Australia, it opened in April 1994 with wide-reaching implications for the governments involved and for tourism, as well as for the local people. Increased trade and travel have already brought greater prosperity to the area.

▶▶▶ Nong Khai

Highway 2, near Vientiane on the Laotian border. Buses from Bangkok (northern terminal: journey time nine hours); trains from Bangkok

Like the province, the town of Nong Khai is long and thin, clinging to the Mekong River. The town preserves its old wooden houses by the riverbank and along Meechai, the "main drag."

After an independent Vientiane had been crushed, King Rama I established controlling lordships, one of whom was based here in Nong Khai. The currents of history swept Marxism to power in Laos, and until recently, Nong Khai has been the most communist-influenced of Thailand's provinces, with many Russian goods available, such as watches, cameras and fur hats.

An enduring legacy of the earlier French presence in Laos is freshly baked baguettes. Once these were imported, but prohibitive taxes forced the Thais to bake them for themselves.

Orange robes are prominent in Nong Khai: there are many novices studying in colleges here. The classic spot for visitors, **Tha Sadet** (the jetty), is on Rim Khong Road. There are some quaint shops here selling filigree silver jewelry and Lao weaves. Locals are secretive about the market where Lao traders dispose of their goods.

Near here is a cooperative called the **Village Weavers**, a handicraft center that weaves indigo-dyed *mut mee* cotton. The cooperative was set up in response to the lack of off-season opportunities, which causes many locals to go off to find new work in Bangkok.

Take a pleasant stroll among the wats and houses, looking across at Laos and the river views. Here, more than anywhere, Laos seems poised to open up to the outside world. In 1994, the bridge linking Nong Khai and Vientiane (pronounced "Wiang Jan") was completed. Thai–Lao trade will boom as a result of this, but the status of Western tourists is uncertain. The Lao authorities are still very grudging with visas, and group tours are favored. The situation changes rapidly; check at the Lao embassy in Bangkok. Australians might have special rights as their government funded the bridge!

Nong Khai is now rather overwhelmed by civil works. The rising water table led to the loss of a few houses recently, and a concrete bank was constructed. Just west of the jetty are some riverside restaurants with a very pleasant ambience. From here, you can see a sunken *chedi*—under water for 150 years—but only in the dry season.

Nearer the town's center, about halfway to the train station, there is a monument to a failed rebellion of Haw Chinese outside the town hall.

In town, the spread-out and informal **Mut Mee** guest house is a mine of local information. There are now many moderately priced hotels for those unwilling to rough it.

Provincial Nong Khai is very pleasant, with the Mekong saving the province from the fate of its more barren southern neighbors.

Take Highway 211 west of Nong Khai to pass the chedi at **Wat Phra That Bang Phuan**, said to contain the Buddha's chestbones. The spectacular scenery starts around Sri Chiang Mai on the river, where Vietnamese make spring rolls; there are budget bungalows here.

Farther on in Sangkhom district is Than Thong, a waterfall-cum-river feeder and popular stopping point. Among budget bungalows in Sang Khom town is the **TXK Guesthouse**. Its bamboo balcony is pure relaxed tranquillity and the atmosphere is engagingly informal, even if the place is short on modern facilities.

Wat Hin Mak Pheng, near Sang Khom, specializes in *Thudong*, a voluntary ultra-asceticism. Its teachers and fine riverside setting attract visitors.

Along the border nearly 125 miles to the east along Highway 212, **Wat Phu Tork** is reached by a spiral walkway around a strangely shaped mountain. The Hideaway Guesthouse in Ban Ahong (60 miles east) makes a good touring base.

Wat Khaek
No-one should miss Wat Khaek, just a short way out of Nong Khai town and a good stop for children. The eccentric Luang Puu in charge has built a garden of extraordinary statuary, loosely based on Buddhist and Hindu iconography. It often slides into the bizarre: dogs driving a car, or the latest addition, a seven-headed snake. All the town *tuk tuks* will urge you there.

205

An old fashioned tuk tuk plies for custom in Nong Khai, still an engagingly traditional and relaxing town despite increasing numbers of tourists

Kala
The lion head of Kala adorns many Khmer sanctuaries in Isan. Kala was the god of time and death, the most feared of all the planetary gods, powerful enough to swallow the sun and the moon. Lunar and solar eclipses caused great superstitious terror among many Thais until comparatively recent times. King Mongkut did much to assuage this fear by his accurate predictions of eclipses, showing they were entirely natural and explicable events.

Khmer ruins at Phanom Rung

Architectural terms
Several specific technical terms relate to Thai temples. A brief fglossary follows:
wat—a Buddhist monastery
prasat—a Khmer shrine or temple sanctuary
pagoda—a Burmese temple
prang—a Khmer temple tower (shaped like a corn-cob)
chedi (also called a *shipa*)—a bell-shaped relic chamber with a tapering spire
mondop—an ornate cube-shaped reliquary tower found in Burmese temples
bot—a central chapel or ordination hall of a *wat*
wiharn—an assembly hall in a *wat*

▶▶ **Pha Taem (Rock Paintings)**
62 miles east of Ubon Ratchathani on the Laos border. Reach by private transport or tour
Take Highway 217 from Ubon east along the river (Mae Nam Mun), cross the rapids along Route 222 into Khong Chiam at the confluence of the Mun and the Mekong rivers. Turn right at Route 2112 through a strange rock garden to arrive at Pha Taem (see photograph on page 210).

This is a magical place. Layers of different civilizations are represented—Thai, Khmer, Mon, Ban Chiang—going back 4,000 years to when people first inhabited this lonely cliff overhanging Laos. Was it their art gallery or temple? Pha Taem is the largest of many sites all over Isan where motifs of hands appear on the cave wall, made by spraying paint over the hands from the mouth. There are also representations of fish, swimming elephants and people pouring water into long-necked pots.

▶▶ **Phi Mai**
37 miles from Nakhon Ratchasima province; off the Friendship Highway (Route 2). Buses from Khorat
Open: daily 7:30–6. Admission charge
This sanctuary in the small district town of Phi Mai is set in a luscious garden of red sandstone with delightful

pools of water. Evidence points to construction in the reign of King Jayavarman VI (1082–1107), and its dominant religion is presumed to have been Mahayana Buddhism. Four intricately carved porches surround a tall central *prang* (tower). Because it is so convenient to visit, the sanctuary is often used as a set for dance troupes. Recently restored, it is Thailand's best-known Khmer shrine and attracts a never-ending stream of visitors.

▶▶▶ Prasat Phanom Rung

Accessible in a day from Khorat, Buri Ram or Surin; turn off Route 24 at Ban Tako
Open: daily 8–5. Admission charge

Set a long way out in dusty Buri Ram, this temple dedicated to Siva has a remarkable setting on an inactive volcano rearing up from bare, scrubby plain. Seven-headed serpents flank a long avenue that leads to the main *prangs* (towers), in a series of terraces rising out of the crater.

The earliest inscriptions are 9th century; the story given in the stones tells of Hiranya, a religious leader who was ordained here and enlarged the sanctuary. One of the inscriptions in Sanskrit expounds the phallic dogmas of the Hindu Pasupat sect.

Aspects of Khmer belief can be seen in the cruciform main prang—such as the monstrous Kala head, representing Eclipse, the most fearsome planet god. A lintel of Vishnu, recently returned here from the United States, attracts many Thais, who lobbied for its return.

Before leaving, it is worth taking a look at the smaller **Prasat Muang Tam**, 5 miles south.

Phi Mai carvings
The carvings at Phi Mai mingle Hindu and Buddhist mythology in a riot of energetic stonework. If you look closely over the entrance lintels you will see Krishna lifting Mount Goradhana, Siva dancing, and battle scenes from the *Ramayana*. Inside, the themes are mainly Buddhist, showing Buddha vanquishing Mara (the Evil one), preaching, and sheltering from the flood waters beneath a protective *naga* (dragon-headed snake).

The Khmar temple complex at Phi Mai was probably used as a model for the Cambodian temple of Angkor Wat

Banyan tree
Just outside the town of Phi Mai stands Thailand's largest banyan tree, a magnificent specimen covering an area half the size of a football pitch. It is known locally as Sai Ngam. Beautifully set on an island in a lake, it makes a delightful shady spot for a picnic or an evening stroll.

Khaen music

The *Khaen* is one of the most recognizable sounds of Isan folk music. A reed instrument originating in Laos, it consists of a series of bamboo pipes arranged around a central sound box. Roi Et is one of the principal *khaen*-making towns of the northeast, where the instruments are widely on sale. It is a major component of the typical northeastern folk music called *mor lam*, a fast-paced style featuring vocal and instrumental elements.

Wax Castle ceremony

The Wax Castle ceremony takes place each year in Sakhon Nakhon at *Ok Phansa*, the end of the Buddhist season of spiritual exercises (October). This custom is associated with a local ethnic group called the Phu Thai. Elaborately designed and intricately detailed models of *wats* are molded from beeswax, filled with Buddha images, and paraded through the streets of the town, accompanied by folk music and dancing, and general joie de vivre.

An anti-AIDS sign on a Sakhon Nakhon hotel door

► ####   Roi Et
Highways 23, 214, 215, southeast of Khon Kaen. Buses from Ubon Ratchathani

Roi Et means "one hundred and one" in Thai. The town has modest ancient remains and a cool, refreshing lake full of fish. But the surrounding plain is not so blessed. The barren, salty region of Thung Kula Rong Hai, ravaged by a harsh climate, is one of the poorest in Thailand. Huge amounts have been invested in land-improvement schemes, but rural depopulation is still a major problem as farmers commute to cities for work in the dry season.

At **Wat Burapha**► there is a massive standing Buddha up on a hill; the view there is panoramic. Climb up inside the statue and look over his right hand. At **Wat Neua**, in the northern part of the town, there is an old *chedi*. The city shrine is unmistakably phallic.

The best place for souvenirs is the nonprofit Community Development Center at the back of City Hall. Not least among local crafts is the *kaen*, a kind of bamboo harmonica. All over Isan, its reedy, jumping wail accompanies the *mor lam* singers. Also on sale are cushions, silks and basketry in the excellent market on Padung Panit road, near the *wat*.

Roi Et celebrates the **Bun Pha Water Festival** in March, including a parade with flags and 101 floats.

Sakhon Nakhon
Highways 22 , 213, 223, east of Udon Thani. Buses from Udon, Nakhon Phanom, Khorat, and from Bangkok (northeast terminal)

This province in the northeast of the Isan region is home to the sacred Wat Phra That Choeng Chum, one of the most sacred in the country. The new 80-foot-tall *prang* was erected on top of an earlier Khmer one, and the *wiharn* houses a statue of a seated Buddha. Two meditation masters, Achan Man and his disciple Achan Fan, lived in Sakhon Nakhon. Their remains are at **Wat Pa Sutthavat** and **Wat Pa Udom Somphon**.

Giant **Nong Han** lake has islands such as Don Sawan, reachable by boat. Worthy of a visit is **Phu Phan Rachaniwet**►, a palace open to visitors when the royal family is not in residence.

West of town near the crossroads at Phang Khon district (the road to Udon Thain) is **Nam Oon** dam and reservoir, where fish frolic in a whirlpool.

▶ Sikhoraphum

Highway 2080. Trains and buses from Surin
On the main road (and railroad line) from Surin to Si Sa Ket and Ubon, in the south of Isan, Sikhoraphum is a comfortable morning's tour from Surin.

The main sight, a five-*prang* 12th-century Khmer ruin, is a ½-mile trek from the station. Standing on an 80-foot-long terrace, it creates an attractive picture set against a backdrop of trees. Inside are two fine Buddha statues. A ride on a trishaw might save you from dehydration.

The craftsmanship of the carving here is delicate and entrancing. The Thais converted Sikhoraphum into a wat around the 16th century, and a gnarled old tree adds character to the compound.

▶▶ Surin

Highway 214, in the south of the Isan region. Songthaews connect with Tha Tum
The villages of **Ban Ta Klang** and **Krapoe** provide all the elephants for the famous roundup in Surin town (see panel). The Suay (called *"Kuy"* in Thai) tribe catches, rears and trains them with a special "spirit language."

Accommodations are hard to come by at round-up time. The **Saeng Thong** (tel. 044/512099) is a large budget hotel with cheap rooms on the roof. At the **Phirom Guesthouse** (tel: 044/515140) on Krung Sri Nai Road, budget facilities are supplemented by friendly personal tours to local sights. On weekends Thais barter Khmer handicrafts near the border for food and essentials.

The southern border with Cambodia near Surin is still a troubled zone and best explored with a guide. A cluster of Khmer temples lie near the border. Passing the eerily deserted refugee camp, ask for the *nam tok* (waterfall) and you can walk down the track to a tremendous panorama of Cambodia's flat, dense forest.

Surin

Normally placid Surin town comes to life in November's roundup, when two teams of elephants, urged on in a tug-of-war by their drivers, take over the football field. The best time to visit Surin is in late afternoon, when the elephants return to their stables. Do not approach an elephant without its mahout present. The Suay consider it a sacrilege to kill an elephant for his ivory, but a few chips off the end of tusks are taken and intricately carved.

209

Adorned from top to toe, elephants prepare for the Big Parade in Surin's annual round-up. Thousands of visitors converge for this colorful event

Betel chewing

Betel-chewing is a widespread habit among older people in rural communities in the northeast. The main ingredient of this complicated substance is the fruit of the areca palm. When chewed with betel leaves spread with limestone ash, it acts as a mild narcotic stimulant. Betel trays were once prized possessions used by all ranks of society and given as dowries. Now, stained teeth and continual spitting are considered less appealing social assets.

This strange cliff at Pha Taem on the Laotion border has witnessed aeons of Thai history. Many different peoples have left their mark on the rock faces since prehistoric times

▶▶   Ubon Ratchathani

Highways 212, 23 and 24, bordering Laos and Cambodia. Buses from Nakhon Phanom and Bangkok (northern terminal); trains from Bangkok; domestic flights

The end of the road east and sited on the scenic Mun River, Ubon is a crossroads of Thai, Lao and Khmer influence and is one of the largest provinces in the northeast.

Many old wats in town, such as **Wat Thong Si Muang▶**, itself graced with a teak library built on stilts over a pond, become festive in late July. Locals parade giant carved beeswax candles symbolizing the onset of Phansa, Buddhist Lent, which burn for the duration. The national museum▶▶ (*Open* Wed–Sun 9–4.30. *Admission charge*) is an entertaining Isan miscellany, with crafts, geology, musical instruments and other displays.

Midstream in the Mun River is **Hat Wat Tai island**, with a rickety wooden bridge and Isan food. For a night of traditional Isan music, go to the **Pathumrat** hotel in town, which is both authentic and entertaining. Way out of town to the southwest is the famous farang **Wat Pa Nanachat**, where most of the monks are from the West and the abbot is a Canadian.

The incredible ruined temple of **Khao Phra Wiharn▶▶▶** stands on the Thai–Cambodian border, accessed from the Thai side only (passports not required). Because of fighting by Khmer Rouge guerillas, the site is sometimes closed. Seek advice before traveling. Approximately 800–1,000 years old and built on a limestone escarpment, it is approached by a straight pathway made of hand-hewn blocks, over a half mile from bottom to top. There are three huge gatehouses on the way up. A special train service runs from Bangkok to Khao Phra Wiharn. Admission charge (hefty for *farangs*).

► **Utumphon Phisai**
Highway 2028. Trains from Surin
The district of Si Saket, on the highway and railroad line to Surin, is the site of two Khmer ruins. **Prasat Hin Wat Sa Kamphaeng Yai** is on a high hill 1¼ miles from Utumphon Phisai; the entrance is well signposted. It was constructed by Suryavaraman I (c. AD 1042). Renovation by the Fine Arts Department is almost complete. Its younger sister, **Sa Kamphaeng Noi**, is less impressive but worth a stopover on the trip back into Si Saket town, 9 miles from Utumphon Phisai.

► **Yasothon**
Highway 23, east of Roi Et. Buses from Ubon Ratchathani and Khorat
"Yaso" is famous for its rocket festival. The province is not one of Thailand's natural beauties, being mostly flat, its former forests decimated. **That Kong Khao Noi** stands out for its ancient *chedi*, the site of a matricide over a "little lump of rice" (*kong khao noi*). A Ban Chiang culture site, Tat Thong, is on Highway 23 to Ubon.

A rocket-float passes by Yasothon's Bang Fai *festival, a time when locals let their hair down and have fun*

Heading north on the main road to Mukdahan is **Phu Tham Phra►**, a mountain cave system with weird rock formations, still difficult to reach. **Tham Kheng**, completely shut off from the elements, is favored by wandering meditators. Yaso handicrafts are exemplified by the *morn khit*, or embroidered cushion, such as those made in the village of **Sri Than** in Patiw district (Highway 202 east). The triangular cushion has become a Thai symbol, the design passed on by an elderly nun.

The rocket festival When May comes, the northeast is scorchingly dry and the rains are eagerly anticipated. Around the 10th, Yaso folk try to tempt Phya Thaen, a rain deity, in the Bang Fai ceremony. The fireworks are quite powerful; wealthy and corporate sponsors build decorated firework floats that bear a local belle on top, dancers leading the way; and locals are liberally daubed with mud. The place is packed, and the two local budget hotels, **Yot Nakhon** and **Udomphon**, fill up. Phya Thaen public park was built with income from the festival. Out of season, it is a pleasant green space.

Historical parks
Thailand's Fine Arts Department has developed a number of historical parks at major sights, many in the north or northeast. The aim is to defend the sights from theft and vandalism, and to protect visitors from the miscreants who once plagued remote places of interest. The more famous sites, such as Ayutthaya and Sukhothai, are well known, but other antiquities, such as the ruins of Utumphon Phisai, are also protected.

SOUTHERN THAILAND

Gulf

of

Thailand

Andaman

Sea

BUR

MAL

212

Arguably the most popular of Thailand's four regions, the south gently woos its visitors with a predominantly seaside atmosphere. Sun-worshipers, swimmers, divers and boat-lovers need look no further.

The coasts The Indian Andaman Sea washes the shores of the western provinces of Ranong, Phang Nga, Phuket, Krabi, Trang and Satun. Pacific provinces are Chumphon, Suratthani, Nakhon Si Thammarat, Songkhla, Pattani and Narathiwat.

Classic tropical islands float off both shores, and a few, such as Samui and Phi Phi, welcome the Western traveler with open arms.

This is a region inhabited since early times. The Buddhist

kingdom of Srivijaya blossomed here, while yet more ancient Negrito tribes such as the Sakai still survive.

Inland there are many national parks—and some are real gems. The farther away from civilization you get, the wilder it becomes—mountains and waterfalls abound, along with whatever wildlife can stand up to the constant incursions of development.

The borderlands These are the provinces of Satun, Yala, Songkhla and Narathiwat. The Federation of Malaysia is Thailand's friendliest land neighbor, and Westerners can come and go with little formality. However, smugglers, Muslim separatists and logging disputes keep security tight.

Islam has made some headway in the Malay-speaking extreme south, but it is not of the most fervent kind.

Economic activity Rubber is the south's number-one cash crop. Other popular crops are cashew nuts and durians. Offshore, Thai fishing fleets are rather too efficient for their own good and are now being sent farther into Burmese and Vietnamese waters.

Meanwhile, tin mining, once the mainstay of Phuket and Phang Nga, has declined somewhat, mainly as a result of market forces. Tourism is the rising star. Everyone wants a piece of the action, but official policy tends toward plush development.

Bungalows (simple thatched huts with not much more than a thin mattress and a mosquito net inside), which started Phuket on its road to world fame, are now a rare sight there. This standoffish attitude to budget travelers is unfortunate for the small operators, but the small-scale, laid-back ethos is still easy to find off the beaten track. Nowadays it just means having to look slightly harder.

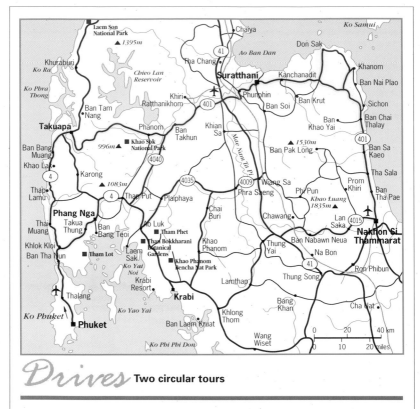

Drives Two circular tours

A tour from Phuket

Allow four to five days for the round trip. It is possible to skip Suratthani, but the roads are treacherous and stopovers are a bit too far apart. Highway 4040 linking Phanom and Phang Nga town is recommended for a vehicle that can cope with dust, mud and potholes. Highway 4118 is for dry weather only. In either case, the tour can take a mere two days from Phuket, with an overnight stay in either Khao Lak or Khao Sok.

Start at Phuket▶▶. Phuket to Takuapa is an unhurried drive of 80 miles up Highway 4. Accommodations can be had on the first night at Khao Lak (see Phang Nga, pages 238–239).
Plenty of waterfalls and beaches line this road.

From Takuapa, take Highway 401 toward Suratthani.
An early start will make it possible to reach **Khao Sok National Park▶**. Look out for **Art's Jungle House** for accommodations. The road here is spectacular as it climbs up into the watershed of the Tapi River. Passing the turnoff for Art's, the scenery is stunning almost all the way into **Suratthani**, where the next night can be spent in a hotel. A trip to **Ko Samui▶▶** could be taken from Suratthani, as there is a car ferry.

Carry on out of Suratthani, still on Highway 401.
The road goes past the attractive beaches of **Khanom** district down into **Nakhon Si Thammarat▶**, where the next night can be spent.

An early start is recommended for the next day; the destination can be Phang Nga or Phuket. Take Highway 4015 west on the main road out of Nakhon Si Thammarat.
The scenery around **Khao Luang National Park▶▶** is stupendous and there are many diversions.

*The aim now is Highway 41, west at
Jan Dee across the railroad track.
North up the fast if rather bleak 41,
look out for a left at Wiang Sa,
Highway 4009, becoming 4035.
Wind through the rubber plantations
to Ao Luk.*
Accommodations can be found here,
advisable if night has already fallen.
The smooth main Highway 4 goes
through the lovely karst mountains to
Phang Nga►►► and eventually
crosses the Sarasin bridge to return
to Phuket.

A day trip from Chumphon

This can be accomplished in a day,
but a more relaxed pace is also
possible with a night in Ranong,
which has several hotels, including
the Jansom Thara.

*Start in Chumphon. The first half of
the route runs west along Highway 4
via Kraburi and Ranong.*
This part of the trip offers marvelous
sea views as the mountain chain is
crossed at Kraburi►. Waterfalls can
he seen from the road, and the
approach road to Ranong► is
impressive. (This area is thinly
populated, and it would be a good
idea to get well equipped in Ranong
for the journey ahead.)

*Signs for the Jansom Thara stand
out well, but 19 miles out of town,
the left turn at tiny Ratcha Krut is a
bit harder to spot.
Recross the mountains while
avoiding herds of cows on Highway
4006 (tarmac but substandard
surface).*

*A left turn at the intersection with
Highway 41, near Lang Suan, is easy
to spot, and from here it is a quick
journey alongside rice paddies back
into Chumphon.*

*Nai Harn Beach, at the tip of Phuket,
was once a favorite haunt of hippies*

216

Betong

Highway 410. Buses from Yala town

This town on the Malaysian border, some 83 miles from Yala, has been developed on a par with the average provincial capital. The big market sells cheap Malaysian goods brought in on the major highway. There has been violence in this area—Muslim separatists are active here, and there has been border disturbance.

At the end of a 6-mile dirt road from Betong are hot springs, *bor nam rorn*, in a village of the same name. Betong is otherwise famous for the biggest mail box in Thailand (over 13 feet) and for the annual invasion of swallows from September to April. They darken the sky, crowd telephone wires and rain their droppings down, fortunately only at night!

►► Chaiya

Off Highway 41. Trains and buses from Suratthani

Chaiya district of Suratthani province is famous for two temples: **Wat Phra Boromthat**, one of the oldest in the south, a classic survival from the Indo-Javanese Srivijayan empire; and **Suan Mokapalaram**, or Suan Mok.

Suan Mok Buddhadasa Bhikkhu, the founder of Suan Mok (the Garden of Liberation), initiated a reform movement in the *sangha* (Buddhist order of monks) that is still working itself out. It is one of the several temples in Thailand that have attracted a significant number of Western devotees and accept laypeople on ten-day retreats.

Meditation through concentration on breathing and a vow of silence are on the program, which follows the strict regimen of the monks. Visitors of either sex are welcome to stay in dormitories and sample the simple life. Offerings of cash or food are readily accepted.

Wat Suan Mok is on the left off main Highway 41 going north from Suratthani—its imposing entrance arch cannot be missed. Buses run directly here from Suratthani.

Wat Phra► This temple lies on the western edge of town. It dates from the Dvaravati period (AD 500– 700), and a life-size Buddha image remains. The main *chedi* (pagoda where relics are kept), in a pool surrounded by clusters of images, was erected by the Srivijayans (AD 700–1000), whose bronzes of the Bodhisattva Avalokitesvara are in evidence.

The many red sandstone images are of Ayutthaya vintage. The Burmese overran the temple in the reign of Rama II, but it was fully restored in the reign of Rama V. There is a small museum opposite the entrance (*Open Wed–Sun 9–4. Donation requested*), where Srivijayan artifacts predominate.

► Chumphon Province

Highway 4. Buses from Suratthani and Bangkok (southern terminal); trains from Bangkok

Most travelers know Chumphon only as a midnight-supper stopover on the way to or from Phuket. It came to the public eye when Typhoon Gay tore through it in 1989. Almost completely restored now, the province has quiet beaches and islands, all of which are just waiting to be discovered. Thai and Burmese fought here, and in World War II, volunteers repelled a Japanese amphibious assault.

Sights Pharadornphap Beach is near Pak Nam Chumphon, some 8 miles southeast Chumphon town. At adjacent **Sai Re** is a ship encased in concrete, a monument to Admiral Krom Luang Chumphon. Students of herbal medicine may be interested in the admiral's Thai herbal garden. He is most remembered, though, for re-creating the Royal Thai Navy as a modern fighting force.

Another such shrine graces the beach of **Arunothai** in Thung-Tako subdistrict farther south. Like Sai Re, it is a jumping-off point for long-tailed boat tours of the offshore islands.

Corals around here took a heavy beating from Typhoon Gay, such as those off the islands of Ko Raet (named for its rhinoceros-like form), Ko Lak Raet, Ko Thalu, Ko Jorakhe, Ko Mattra and Ko Lawa. The last three also have pleasant beaches.

Pathiu district to the north has long beaches at **Phanung Tuk**, 5 miles out of town, **Ao Bor Mao** and nearby **Laem Thaen.** This last beach is ideal for camping. Best of all is **Thung Wua Laen**, 7 miles north. South of Chumphon there are some famous caves in **Lang Suan. Khao Ngern** cave near town is home to a group of monkeys. A further 11 miles to the south is **Khao Kriap** with a large sunlit cavern.

Swallows
Beware! Long, narrow Ko Maphrao, like the more famous island of Ko Phi Phi Le, has a swallow colony prized for its nests. Tourists are scared off the long white beach with a shotgun. Ko Ngaam Yai and Ko Ngaam Noi also have swallows' nests, and landing to sunbathe or snorkel could also be dangerous here.

Wat Phra Boramthat, in Chaiya, is a fine and rare example of the Srivijayan style, reminiscent of some of the temples in Java

217

Bird's nest collecting

■ **Birds' nests have been eaten in China for at least 1,500 years, and their export by the collectors of the Malay Peninsula and southern Thailand was well established by the early 18th century. Nowadays, the largest market for them is Hong Kong, which consumes 100 tons of them, worth $25 million, every year. A perfect white nest can fetch as much as $1,200.** ■

Gang rivalry
Gangster-style killings have occurred as rival gangs fight over scraps of nests left behind after the season.

Conservation
Nest collecting has unfortunately taken its toll on the numbers of swiftlets, whose nests are often overharvested. Many former nest sites on open cliffs have been abandoned because they were too accessible to gatherers. Another, and undoubtedly more serious, threat to their survival is the destruction of the inland rain forests where the swiftlets breed.

What nest? The nest of the swiftlet *Collocalia esculenta* is edible, prized by the Chinese as a powerful pick-me-up tonic and typically ingested at the banquets of the rich in the form of bird's-nest soup. It is said to taste like noodles by those who have tried it. The nests themselves are tiny translucent cups about the size of a small egg. They are made by the male brown-rumped swift from glutinous threads of its own saliva, which it weaves into a cup that dries to become thin and translucent like fine porcelain.

Chinese feed bird's-nest soup, cooked with chicken broth or coconut milk, to their children in the belief that it will improve their complexion, promote growth and generally act as a restorative.

Recent research has indeed shown that the nests do contain a water-soluble glyco-protein that may promote cell division in the immune system. Some have even speculated that it may help combat the immuno-deficiency in AIDS.

Collecting the nests Nests are collected in spring and fall. This is skilled and dangerous work, high up on the ceilings of caves, which abound on the Thai coast and its offshore islands. The intrepid collector shins barefoot up rickety trellises of bamboo scaffolding, ropes and bridges, tapping as he goes to make sure the bamboo is sound. He lights his way in the black caves with a torch of bark soaked in resin held between his teeth, and he uses a special three-pronged tool called a *rada* to harvest the nests.

To use bare hands to pick a nest would be considered stealing from the gods and would anger them. If a man happens to forget his rada, he will descend at once, taking it as a sign from the gods that it would be dangerous for him to climb that day.

The collectors work from sunrise without food or water until sunset, when the cave is filled with flocks of bats and roosting swiftlets. Sometimes nest-gatherers have to swim underwater to reach a submerged cavern, or squeeze through tiny blowhole passages to reach the cave ceiling.

The caves themselves are often spectacular cathedrals of stalagmites and stalactites, covered in thick carpetings of guano, and seething with golden cockroaches.

Big business Collecting nests is a lucrative business and is tightly controlled. The Finance Ministry grants five-year concessions to competing private groups, the taxes from which can yield over $600,000 in one year. The nests are so precious that the islands are virtually off-limits, protected by armed guards during the season to deter robbers who might harm the baby swiftlets—which would affect the next year's supply of nests. They are also paid to protect the birds from natural predators such as snakes, cockroaches and eagles.

In spite of this protection, attempts are made to bribe guards. In Thong Thum district in 1987, one gang of poachers began to encroach on other gang networks. The gang leader and his wife were sprayed with machine-gun fire at their home.

Ladders against the cliffside where swiftlets nest in Ko Phi Phi Le

SOUTHERN THAILAND

Guest House
The budget Cathay Guest House is a short walk from the station and its old steam engines. It has a welcoming guest house aspect, right down to the crowded noticeboard.

Malaysian trips
Trips to nearby Malaysia can easily be arranged from Hat Yai. The border lies just 30 miles away. The idyllic island of Penang is a popular destination, most conveniently reached by a shared taxi (they run regularly every morning from Hat Yai and are not expensive). Comfortable air-conditioned buses also provide a regular service. Make sure your official documents are in order; you can renew your visa at the Thai consulate in Penang.

Hat Yai is a great shopping center. In local market stalls, Malaysian batik, electronic gadgetry and dried fruit are especially good buys

Hat Yai
Highway 4. Buses from Songkhla and Bangkok (southern terminal); trains from Suratthani and Bangkok; domestic flights

Hat Yai grew on border trade, rubber and, latterly, sex. Hat Yai's "night industry" generates a higher-than-average level of associated diseases. There are plenty of all-night cafés and lounges. The town itself is drab, a forced stopover for destinations farther south. Hat Yai is an important railroad junction; trains were instrumental in the town's growth.

Sightseeing The Chinese presence here is evident in Channiwet Road, where **snake farms** make a strange concoction by slashing open a live snake and squeezing the blood out. It is often mixed with whiskey and honey, which almost mask the taste.

Local farmers have established Hat Yai as a center for southern Thai **bullfighting**. Khlong Wa stadium by the bus station alternates with others in the area in staging the frenetic bull-against-bull contests. Entry is around 120 baht for three rounds of bulls, and the atmosphere is alive with manic betting and sizzling food.

Also on the edge of town but in a completely different direction is the **Thai Cultural Village▶**, which stages dancing shows. The little theater is set in rolling parkland, which also has a small zoo.

People who are attracted to the bustle will enjoy Hat Yai's **markets** and nightlife, which are both distinctive. It is here that all goods from Malaysia are unloaded. Smugglers once thought that if they made it to Hat Yai they were safe, but a recent police campaign has been giving them second thoughts.

A little way out of town, off Phetkasem Road, **Wat Hat Yai Nai** is remarkable for its very large reclining image of Buddha in white stucco. A curious contraption nearby has ten plaster-cast monks bolted to a revolving platform, a novel way of making merit.

A scenic ride out of town is **Tone Nga Chang Falls▶**. The "elephant tusks" of its name are formed at one of the higher stages where the fall splits into two. The road does not go anwhere else, but the waterfall is in a wildlife preservation area.

►► Ko Lanta

Access by boat from Krabi town; or from Ban Hua Hin (a songthaew ride from Krabi)

The relatively little-known Lanta Islands, approximately 30 miles off the southwest coast of Krabi province, have the status of a distinct district. The district takes in a total of 52 islands, of which only a few are inhabited. The geography of the islands is mostly forested mountains (highest elevation 1,614 feet), with not much in the way of flat land.

There are three main islands: Lanta Yai and Lanta Noi are almost one, being separated by a narrow 220-yard channel. Boats travel from Ban Hua Hin to Ban Khlong Mak on Lanta Noi and from this island to Ban Sala Dan on Lanta Yai. Access to the western beaches for the tourist landlubber is best from Chao Fa pier in Krabi town, a few yards north of the Phi Phi pier. This regular boat takes three to four hours. Closer to Ko Lanta, a turning south from Highway 4 leads to Bo Muang, starting point for a much shorter ride.

Tourist development is fairly low-profile but steadily increasing, and the beaches are long and idyllic. The longer beaches are on the west coast.

A favorite spot for yachts, the northern anchorage has bungalow accommodations. The natives mostly live off the sea, and their villages dot the coast, most densely at this northern end.

National Marine Park
Fifteen of Ko Lanta's southerly islands have recently been declared a National Marine Park, which may place a partial brake on the hasty and ill-conceived tourist development has blighted some of Thailand's most beautiful islands. Despite the tourism, there are indications that the local "sea gypsy" inhabitants wish to retain their traditional way of life. Land speculation, however, is increasing on the inhabited parts of Ko Lanta.

In some parts of the south, the traditional ways of life on the water have not been entirely supplanted by tourism

221

Phuket to Phi Phi
A traveling schedule that may appeal to the independent traveler involves a trip from Phuket to Phi Phi, at least a night or so in one of the island's many reasonable accommodations, followed by a boat ride into Krabi town. There are usually three services a day (fewer in the monsoon season), taking 2–2½ hours. Avoid the trip in rough weather.

►►► Ko Phi Phi

Boats from Phuket and Krabi town

This pair of islands, blessed with natural beauty, is now perhaps one of the most absurd examples anywhere of a marine national park. Some observers have already written it off as thousands of tourists swarm all over it, the vast majority being day-trippers from Phuket, threatening the fragile ecosystem. The main island, Phi Phi Don, is quite developed, and strenuous efforts are made to keep it clean.

Yet the attraction is easy to understand; nothing short of an earthquake would destroy the stunning natural formation of the back-to-back Loh Dalam and Ton Sai beaches, only 164 feet apart. Their clear waters are particularly inviting to swimmers and are enhanced by the optical effect of the shallow sea floor, which gives a beautiful turquoise color.

Getting there The island communities' needs are served with a regular boat service from Krabi, which takes two hours. The islands are almost equidistant from Phuket, and many companies there offer the day tour from around 700 baht upward, depending on the degree of luxury of the boat used. Top-of-the-line cruisers with every amenity ply the route daily. All the tours include lunch in one of the resort restaurants by Ton Sai Bay on Phi Phi Don.

Life on a tropical beach beneath coconut palms is the stuff of dreams for overstressed Westerners. In southern Thailand, it is a reality

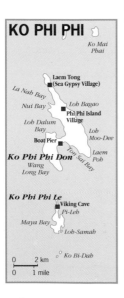

223

Phi Phi Don Accommodations on Phi Phi Don are very comfortable, with well-equipped bungalows thick on the ground.

A general view of the island can be had from several mountain viewpoints east of Ton Sai. One path leads down to the beach of Loh Bagao, now site of the expensive Phi Phi Island Village.

Laem Tong, where Phi Phi Don's last remaining "sea gypsies" rub shoulders with wealthy guests of an exclusive resort, lies on the extreme northern tip of the island, accessible only by boat. A very worthwhile glass-bottomed boat tour leaves from here, as at Ton Sai—an opportunity not to be missed by nonswimmers.

Phi Phi Le Neighboring Phi Phi Le has many fine corals such as those at beautiful Maya Bay and Pi-Leh. Spectacular turquoise inlets offer wonderful swimming. Boat tours invariably stop at Phi Phi Le's "Viking Cave," where mysterious unexplained paintings of boats (believed to be Chinese junks) adorn the walls near the entrance. The cave is also home to a swallow colony whose nests are harvested for the famous bird's-nest soup (see pages 218–219). The smell of swallow droppings is quite overpowering! Because of the birds' nests, no one may stay overnight on the island.

Fishermen are well served around Phi Phi Le. All types of fish await the intrepid angler. A group can charter a long-tailed boat for this purpose from about 800 baht for six to eight hours or 500 baht for a half-day trip.

Boat paintings in the "Viking Cave" at Phi Phi Le

Lush vegetation clings to the rocky cliffs of Phi Phi Le, rising sheer from the waterline. The limestone foundations of Thailand's Andaman Islands are unforgettable

Drug omelets
Ko Samui used to be famous for mind-expanding drug omelets, but after several notorious incidents that were too much even for the liberal and tolerant Thais, the local police were forced to act.

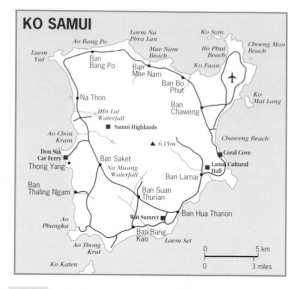

KO SAMUI

Laem Na
Phra Lan
Ko Som
Ao Bang Po
Mae Nam
Bo Phut
Beach
Beach
Choeng Mon
Beach
Laem
Yai
Ban Bang Po
Mae Nam
Ban Mae Nam
Ko Faan
Ban Bo Phut
Ko Mat Lang
Na Thon
Ban Chaweng
Hin Lat Waterfall
■ Samui Highlands
Ao Chon Kram
Chaweng Beach
▲ *635 m*
Don Sak Car Ferry
Ban Saket
Coral Cove
Thong Yang
Na Muang Waterfall
Lamai Cultural Hall
Ban Lamai
Ban Thaling Ngam
Ban Suan Thurian
Ao Phangka
Wat Sumret
Ban Hua Thanon
Ban Bang Kao
Laem Set
Ao Thong Krut
0   5 km
Ko Katen
0   3 miles

Boats, beaches and a turquoise sea create endlessly photogenic subjects on Ko Samui. Despite increasing tourism, there are still plenty of places to photograph scenes like this

▶ ▶ ▶   Ko Samui Archipelago
Off the east coast. Buses from Suratthani connect with ferries to Ko Samui; domestic flights, tour buses from Bangkok

A first stop for many visitors, Ko Samui has a laid-back atmosphere even for Thailand. As with most other currently booming destinations, it was the much-maligned backpackers who discovered it first. This is a luscious tropical island with coconut palms, squeaky-clean sands and idyllic villages; it almost looks too good to be true. There's a vibrant party scene, but it is also possible to find peace and quiet.

Express boats to and from Suratthani moor up at the Na Thon jetty in the northwest.

Although the airport is now busy with regular daily flights, Ko Samui is still a paradise for young people who

want to enjoy themselves relatively cheaply. Rents have been creeping up, but bargains are still there to be had, away from the popular Chaweng and Lamai beaches. Expect to pay anything from 150–200 baht upward for a room.

The island's natural beauty remains much as it was and is not unduly spoiled by the development here, which has been low-rise, though not on a modest scale. Beach activities by day are combined with Thailand's most popular nightlife of disco and bar. It proves that a farang tourist area need not be crawling with prostitution, although Ko Samui has inevitably attracted its fair share.

Around the island The concrete road circling the island is only 30 miles long, and you can travel around the whole island in a day. As in Phuket, scooters are ideal, being slow and safe. Newer models have power to take on the bigger hills. Rent a scooter at Chaweng and follow the road south to Lamai, taking in the tremendous panorama as the road twists round past Coral Cove.

In **Lamai** you might check out the bizarrely designed **Mix club.** Lamai's landmark is the unmistakably phallic **Hin Ta,** or Grandfather Rock, and its female companion, **Hin Yai.** The beach is fairly clean, given the number of visitors, although it certainly isn't as clean as it used to be.

Out of Lamai to the south the road forks. To the left it cuts across the south of the island, past **Na Muang,** a spectacular waterfall. The right fork veers around the tidal coast of **Ao Thong Krut.** Boats here service the small **Ko Katen.** Farther on is a long dirt road turnoff for the small, sweet and quiet **Phangka Bay.** There are modest facilities here on locally owned land.

A fishing boat at Ko Samui tilts on the beach as the setting sun is reflected in mirrorlike water. In the monsoon season, the scene can look very different

Ko Samui's coconuts
Ko Samui has more to it than beaches. Before the tourist boom, islanders' income came exclusively from coconuts, and the tall palms are still the dominant vegetation.

SOUTHERN THAILAND

North out of Phangka, the road takes in wonderful views of distant shimmering sea before you get to the Don Sak car ferry terminal turnoff. Inland from here are two of Ko Samui's other waterfalls, **Hu Nam** and **Wae Khwai Tok**. The track up to them is quite difficult.

Na Thon is the district seat and as such has a market, post office, banks and other essential services. The road out north yields a fantastic view (if you ignore the municipal tip in the foreground).

Ko Phangan, the other main island in the archipelago, is visible from all along Ko Samui's northern shore. Of the three main beaches along this shore, it is **Bo Phut** that has become the most popular. On the others, Mae Nam and Bang Rak, tourist facilities are still in the process of hasty construction.

Very prominent is the long causeway linking Bang Rak and Ko Fan, where, in the temple of Hin Ngu, the so-called Big Buddha looks out over the sweeping bay.

Next on the circuit are roads leading to Ko Samui's airport; flights from here to Bangkok take less than an hour and a half.

Turning south, the route reaches the top end of **Chaweng**. At 2 miles it is the longest beach on the island, and developers have made the larger projects a feast of traditional teak architecture. Because of its sheer size, Chaweng has been able to absorb the feverish rush for the tourist dollar so far—as is usually the case, a balance must be struck between creature comforts and an unspoiled atmosphere.

Ko Phangan Boats from Ko Samui and Suratthani land at Thong Sala on the island's southern coast. Phangan is now taking Ko Samui's overspill, and although the beaches are just as good, the level of infrastructure here makes Ko Samui seem urban. Roads are unpaved but a dirt bike is still useful.

Bungalows line the beaches, being concentrated on the double-backed Hat Rin, home to a lively travelers' society. Boats ply the shoreline.

Waterfall fans may take in **Than Sadet▶**, where kingly visitors have carved their initials in the stones. The journey upstream is still as hard as it was in their day.

Ko Tao ("Turtle Island") is only 5 miles long, and the nearest land is well over the horizon. It can be reached from either Chumphon or Phangan. The former is a grueling five-hour ride, costs about 200 baht, and is available only in the high season.

The latter trip, from Thong Sala pier, takes three hours for around 150 baht. When exploring Thailand, remember that remoteness and inaccessibility are usually related to degree of unspoiled beauty. **Sai Ri** and **Mae Hat** are the main beaches lining the west coast. Jungle trails beckon.

A short boat ride from Mae Hat leads to the natural marvel of **Ko Nang Yuan,** where three islands are linked by sandbars. It is even possible to stay overnight here. As on Ko Tao, little bungalows are available and are still very reasonable.

Road safety
Extreme caution is advised if you rent a car or scooter on any of the southern islands. Both roads and vehicles may be in poor condition, and the standard of driving is appalling. Many horrifying accidents are caused by tourists driving under the influence of alcohol or drugs. Phuket and Ko Samui have the highest road fatality rates in Thailand—an unenviable record. Bear in mind that local insurance coverage is minimal or nonexistent.

227

Express boats set out from the Na Thon jetty, on the northwest coast of Ko Samui

■ **Sometimes life in Thailand seems like one festival or traditional ceremony after another. Some are rites of passage for the events in the lives of individuals, such as birth, puberty, ordination, marriage and death. Those linked with traditional farming rituals are concerned with the seasonal rhythms of nature, while others commemorate important events in the history of the nation.** ■

The sky rocket festival
Bun Bang Fai, a festival of the northeast, usually takes place in May or June. With its crude sexual pantomimes, it is performed to celebrate the generative forces of nature and the coming of the rains.

228

Songkran
Songkran begins sedately with Buddhist merit-making ceremonies and offerings to elders and monks. Then it explodes into water-splashing, beauty contests and tippling of Mekhong rice whiskey. Everyone gets splashed, even foreigners—all in good fun.

Loi Krathong
Loi means "to float," and *krathong* means "leaf cup." The use of polystyrene for floats was recently banned because of the river pollution it caused.

Most festivals are fixed by the lunar calendar, so the dates vary from year to year. The Buddhist holiday of *Maga Puja* is celebrated in February, and the **Chinese New Year** usually falls within this month too. Festivities for the latter usually last three days. Gifts are exchanged; food is offered to ancestors via the ancestral tablets. Altars are set with the tablets and images of benevolent deities, and candles and joss sticks are lit. Chinese shops close for several days. See also pages 94 and 268.

Songkran This is one of the great festivals—the old Thai New Year, which falls in mid-April. It is a time when everyone goes in for water splashing, April being the hottest month in the year. The *Songkran* water-splashing festival was originally an occasion to pay homage to one's elders by pouring scented water over their hands and making offerings to the ashes of ancestors.

Loi Krathong This most unforgettable celebration is in November, after rice planting has been completed, when toy boats made of molded leaves carrying a lighted candle and incense stick are floated along rivers and canals, which are swollen with rain and sometimes flooded at this time of year, to honor the water spirits. Everyone goes to the riverbank in the evening to see the flickering lights on the water, and fireworks are let off.

Rites of passage One recurring feature of personal Thai ceremonies is the tying of white thread around the wrists. It has been described as a kind of "spiritual telegraph" between the participants. At weddings the thread joins the heads of the marrying couple, while at funerals the thread is carried around the crematorium three times.

In their early '20s, many Thai men spend a short period as Buddhist monks, regarded as a rite of passage into adulthood. Before the formal ordination there is a lay ceremony called *sukhwan nak*. The man's head and eyebrows are shaved (to show freedom from vanity and sexuality) and the ordination candidate, or *nak* (meaning "dragon"), is dressed in white robes, garlanded with flowers and bank notes. The friends and relatives of the nak gather in a circle around him while a song recalling the pain and suffering of his mother in giving birth and stressing his filial obligations is sung—sometimes for up

to four hours. Around him, holding a ring of white thread, sit the nak's relatives and friends. They pass three sets of lighted candles around in a clockwise direction to protect him while he is in the vulnerable position of being neither a layman nor a monk.

The following day, the ordination ceremony takes place. Inside the wat, the new monk kneels before his father, who presents him with the saffron robe of the monkhood before approaching a quorum of monks and asking to be admitted to the sangha.

Songkran *water-splashing festival starts at a sedate pace and then takes off into mayhem...*

Diving

The Similan Islands are rated among the best sites for diving in the world, with clear, unpolluted waters and a wealth of marine life. Each island has a different ecosystem. Many companies organize diving trips, mostly from Phuket. If you are not an experienced diver, you can learn locally. Check your instructor's qualifications. Harpoon-fishing is carried out by some unscrupulous operators, but it causes immense damage to the reefs and is officially banned.

Strange fish

Deep-sea divers (at a cost of around 2,500 baht per day) can see such strange creatures as the star feather and the gross puffer fish off the Similans.

Turtles

Thailand's turtle population is rapidly diminishing, and the four native marine species are now officially classified as endangered. The loggerhead turtle is already locally extinct. Deliberately hunted for their shells, meat, and eggs, turtles are also incidental victims of trawler nets, pollution, and the disturbance caused by tourism and developement. Belatedly, several of Thailand's principal turtle habitats have been declared marine parks, and serious efforts are at last being made to protect them.

The densely wooded islands of the Ko Ta Ru Tao archipelago contain a great variety of wildlife habitats, from mangrove swamps

► Ko Similan

Access by boat from Takuapa or by tour from Phuket
This archipelago, far over the horizon to the west, forms a national park famous for its underwater diving opportunities. There are pleasant beaches that are used by snorkelers, swimmers and picnickers. Spearfishing is officially prohibited by the national park authorities.

The Similans are so called because there are nine islands (Malay *sembilan*, "nine"), of which number 8, Ko Similan, is the largest. They are low-lying and forested, uninhabited before the park wardens brought in regular supplies of fresh water. The park station is on Ko Miang, where there is a campsite with bungalows and a restaurant.

Islanders have come here to fish for a long time. Recent years saw the appalling practice of dynamite fishing, when a whole coral reef would be blasted, dead and stunned fish then rising to the surface. Tourists, both day-trippers and yacht sailors, have scared off the dynamite fishermen, but in their turn have brought litter, which they leave on the beaches.

An average tour from Phuket costs around 2,000 baht. Alternatively, a boat can be chartered from Tap Lamu in Takuapa. The Similans are being increasingly used as stepping stones to other remote islands. Dive boats run regularly to Ko Surin, Ko Bon (an honorary "10th" Similan) and Ko Tachai.

Ko Miang, island number 4, has beautifully set bungalows run by the Royal Forestry Department. **Ko Ba Ngu**, number 9, has tents for rent at normal park rates. If you want to book, which is advisable, the national park office responsible is at Moo 1, Lamgan, Thai Muang (Phang Nga) (tel: 076/411914). Weekdays are less crowded.

► Ko Surin

Ban Hin Lat in Khuraburi district, almost on the border with Ranong province, is the jumping-off point for a five-hour voyage to Surin Marine National Park. (The five islands are actually part of Ranong province.) Again, most people go to dive. The main islands have places to stay and great lobster fishing.

Trips to Malaysia
Long-tail boats from Tam Ma Rang service Pulau Langkawi, a larger Malaysian island to Ta Ru Tao's south. The service runs Satun–Langkawi–Kuala Perlis, a small town connected by bus to the rest of Malaysia. You must make sure that documents are in order—Thai immigration will stamp them as you go out in Satun town; a Malaysian official will stamp them in Kuala Perlis.

Ko Adang, one of the larger islands of the Ta Ru Tao, consists almost entirely of wild rain forest and coconut palms, but there are a few places to stay

231

►► Ko Ta Ru Tao

Off Satun province. Boats from Pak Bara

The Ta Ru Tao archipelago is made up of 50-odd islands, from the largest, Ko Ta Ru Tao, down through Ko Rawi, Ko Adang and the smaller islands of Ko Lipe, Ko Hin Ngam, Ko Khai and Ko Rang Nok. Ko Ta Ru Tao is only about 3 miles from the Malaysian island of Pulau Langkawi. These islands are not geared to tourists; facilities are basic, and transportation is unpredictable.

Thickly forested with a peak of 2,309 feet, Ko Ta Ru Tao must count as one of the most unspoiled of the country's marine national parks; this one was created in 1974. For overnight stays or camping, it is possible to reserve a park space from Bangkok (tel: 02/579 4842 or 579 0529).

Ta Ru Tao, a penal colony during World War II (see panel), now has an exhibition center and aquarium. The region's famous powdery white sand can be found at Ao Son (Ta Lo Lii Ngai) on the western coast, a beautifully curving bay with clear and shallow waters that has been established as a sea turtle conservation center. Walkers can get a good view from the top of Khao Topu.

Ko Khai is a small island with white beaches and a rich community of coral and fish. Turtles come ashore to lay their eggs. **Ko Hin Ngam**, off Ko Adang, has lines of smooth, even, sleek rocks rounded by the sea, whereas next-door **Ko Rawi** has beaches. The area is populated by "sea gypsies," who build their houses on stilts; tiny **Ko Lipe** hosts a community of 600. Unfortunately, a great many trees have been felled here.

Diving is a popular activity among visitors to the archipelago. On the bigger islands there are interesting caves and waterfalls to visit. Long-tailed boats service the park office from Pak Bara harbor, Langu district, a long day's drive from Hat Yai or Trang (60 miles south of Trang). The flimsy long-tailed boats get tossed about on the open sea, so the time to go is in the more clement months of January to April.

Pirates
The penal colony established in the tropical paradise of Ko Ta Ru Tao in 1939 may have seemed no bad place to spend a world war, but as hostilities increased in Southeast Asia, food supplies to the prison became more and more erratic. Eventually the starving prisoners and their equally desperate guards teamed up for survival and formed a very successful band of pirates. After the war, the British navy was sent in to restore order.

The karst (limestone) scenery of Krabi province produces strange and memorable landscapes. This overhanging cliff is dripping with vegetation and riddled with caves

232

▶▶▶ Krabi

Highway 4, south of Suratthani. Buses from Phuket and Phang Nga

Krabi town is a fishing harbor, giving access to over 100 offshore islands. Ferries arrive here from Ko Phi Phi, entering a mangrove-lined bay before mooring at the centrally located jetty on the broad Krabi River. A gaggle of touts greets passengers as they disembark from the boat.

Krabi town It is a mere minute's walk to the picturesque Uttarakit Road, parallel to the river and the town's main street. Guest houses and hotels of all standards have sprung up here. Krabi ("Fighting Sword") town has not got much going for it besides its views and bike rental shops. The night market, which opens after sundown, looks over the river.

Krabi province▶▶▶ is quite another thing. Besides the famous Ko Lanta▶▶ and Ko Phi Phi▶▶▶ (see pages 221–3), other interesting islands among Krabi's total of 130 include the pretty **Ko Mai Phai▶**, "Bamboo Island," accessible from Ko Phi Phi Don. The local squid fishermen are greatly bemused by the increasing numbers of day-trippers from the larger island.

The **Por-Da archipelago** (Ko Dam Hok and Ko Dam Khwaan) is very well worth visiting. It is only 5 miles off Ao Nang, south of Krabi town, from where boats to the islands can be chartered.

Mainland beaches in Krabi are quite fascinating. **Laem Phra Nang▶▶** is cut off by mountains, so the strange arrangement here of three beaches and cliffs can only be reached by boat—45 minutes from Krabi town or a mere 10 minutes from neighboring Ao Nang.

Nopparat Thora Beach lies 13 miles west of Krabi town. Its beautiful setting (part of the Phi Phi Marine National Park) makes it popular with Thai picnickers

Local legend
According to a legend that is still told by locals, food used to appear by magic at the mouth of Phra Nang Cave, which looks out on to a gently curving lagoon.

Sights Sa Phra Nang ("Princess Pool") is a geological oddity—a saltwater lake high among the cliffs. The strenuous walk up to it leads through a series of roofless caves. **Ao Nang►►**, a magnificently sited but rapidly developing beach, is only a short *songthaew* ride out of town.

The inland karst (natural underground cavities) along the road makes bizarre scenery. **Nopparat Thora** beach, just west of Ao Nang, has little Ko An straddling a river mouth. Dense casuarinas and coconut trees provide shade on this beach, which is also the headquarters of the marine national park that includes Ko Phi Phi.

Palaeontologists may wish to stop off at the Susan Hoi or "**Shell Cemetery►**," one of only two or three such sites in the world. Here, tertiary-period fossilized shells which have been compressed into slabs, jut into the sea like a causeway. Many *songthaews* going to Ao Nang pass the site.

Other points of interest within easy reach of Krabi town include **Huay To waterfall►** in Phanom Benja, 12 miles due north. The fall is in 10 stages, each stage with a large natural pond. Another road leading north off the main highway leads to **Wat Tham Seua** ("Tiger Cave Temple"), a meditation monastery with grim paintings as reminders of mortality.

Ao Luk is a small town on the road to Phang Nga, also with the strange inland karst. Regular buses to Phang Nga and Phuket stop there.

The nearby port of Laem Sak connects to **Ko Mak Noi** (actually in Phang Nga province), an island surrounded by beach. Only five minutes from Laem Sak is the **Chong Talat archipelago►**, Ko Pai and Ko Klui, graced with the usual—but still beautiful—corals, beaches, caves and mountains.

Caves
Ao Luk, in the north of Krabi province, has many caves. Tham Lot and Tham Hua Kalok (Skull Cave) are two neighboring caves that you can reach by chartering a boat from Bo Tho for 200–250 baht. Hua Kalok is well lit by the sun and features paintings 2,000–3,000 years old.

Krabi's traditional fishing fleet keeps local restaurants well stocked with fresh seafood, despite the increasing importance of tourism in the area

▶   **Kra Buri**
Highway 4, north of Ranong
The last district before Chumphon in the north of the southern region is Kra Buri, head of the Isthmus of Kra, which at its narrowest is only about 15 miles wide at 340 miles on Highway 4.

Unsurprisingly in this mountainous territory, there are plenty of waterfalls; **Punyaban▶**, **Bokkrai▶** and **Chum Saeng▶** are three that you can visit as you travel northward from Ranong town. Punyaban, as the most accessible, has the most visitors. **Tham Phra Khayang▶**, a cave in Kra Buri district, 7 miles north of Kra Buri town, is sacred to locals, who believe that "iron flows" here, taking the form of stalactites and stalagmites.

▶▶   **Nakhon Si Thammarat**
Highway 401, east coast. Buses from Krabi, Suratthani and Bangkok (southern terminal); trains from Bangkok
Nakhon Si, as the province is known to southerners, is a paradox: the biggest and most populated southern province, while at the same time relatively unexplored.

Communications are excellent: the town of Nakhon Si Thammarat is a rail terminus and has air and bus connections. A thriving Srivijaya center back in the 13th century, it spread its Buddhist teaching to Sukhothai, seat of the first Thai kingdom. More recently, in World War II, local men repulsed an amphibious Japanese assault; they are commemorated in bronze.

The town's religious focus is the ancient **Wat**

Wet weather
A warning: the rainy season in the provinces of Nakhon Si Thammarat and Ranong lasts longer than elsewhere and can be ferocious.

Gold leaf donated by centuries of devout pilgrims decorates Wat Mahathat in Si Nakhon Thammarat, the most revered shrine in southern Thailand

Local crafts
Local crafts are the delicate Yan Lipao basketry and shadow puppets. At "Suchat's House" the latter are cut from buffalo hide.

Within the side chapels of the great Wat Mahathat in Nakhon Si Thammarat, polychrome friezes illustrate the life of Buddha

Mahathat►►►. The tip of its large *chedi* is topped with several hundred pounds of gold and contains relics, venerated in the third lunar month. A **museum**► in the complex houses an eclectic collection of bits and pieces donated by worshipers. The city wall dates from the Ayutthaya period. There is also a large National Museum► (*Open* daily 9–4. *Admission charge*). Shadow plays are performed during temple festivals.

Highway 401 connects Nakhon Si with Surat, and near the border with Suratthani province (a right turn along Highway 4014; the Khanom bus) are attractive beaches, popular with locals and becoming increasingly discovered by foreigners.

The beaches of **Khanom**, **Nai Phlao** and **Nai Dan** sport many moderate–expensive places to stay, with the budget **Watanyoo Villa** on Nai Dan. Nearer town is Hat Sa Bua, and halfway up is the boulder-strewn Hat Hin Ngam.

Inland, nature lovers will not be disappointed by the scenery around **Khao Luang National Park**►►, skirted by highways 4015 and 4016. There are many stunning waterfalls in the lush green wilderness, best appreciated on a driving tour. The district is famous for durians and prawns.

235

Bullfighting
Bullfighting (bull versus bull) is popular here as in Hat Yai—the best fighters have small testicles or, even better, only one!

The exterior of Wat Mahathat reveals its distinctive Ceylonese style. The massive chedi has undergone much costly restoration to save it from collapse

Narathiwat Beach
Narathiwat Beach, reached by a samlor or taxi from the market, nestles in the shade of casuarinas, with food stalls dotted about. It is an ideal camping spot; 3 miles of broad white sands end in a bar at the mouth of Klong Bang Nara, site of a fishing village.

The Thai-Muslim fishing village in Narathiwat, at the mouth of the Bang Nara River, is lined with special fishing craft called reua kaw lae

▶▶ **Narathiwat Province**
Highway 42; a border province with Malaysia. Buses from Yala, Sungai Kolok and Bangkok (southern terminal)
This border province has a wealth of natural resources with forest, beaches and different customs at the end of a marathon 715 miles from Bangkok. Gold is mined on a small scale. As Malaysia approaches, concentrations of Muslims become denser, but this is Islam with a Thai flavor.

Narathiwat town is not of great interest, but it retains some traditional character. Atmospheric wooden houses abound, and vintage Mercedes Benz taxis ply the streets.

Khao Tan Yong Mas, on the opposite bank of the river from town, has beautiful views and is a popular picnic spot for locals. Nearby is the inaccessible Taksin Rachaniwet Palace.

Ba Joh waterfall▶▶ is on the Pattani–Narathiwat Road. A left out of town on Pattani Highway 42 becomes a dusty (or muddy) laterite road, eventually reaching the fall, which flows off a very high cliff with force. One of the biggest waterfalls in the south, it is located in the Budo mountains and Budo National Park. The park office is in Ba Joh district near the waterfall. Budo National Park is a shelter for endangered rhinos, gibbons and tapir, but there is no news yet of accommodation schemes. Other waterfalls in the region are **Ya Mu Raeney** and **Wang Thong**.

Farther south of town is the **Chatwarin waterfall**▶, reached by turning left at Sungai Padi district hospital. A dry-season track winds through thick forest to the fall, passing To Deng village. A distance of 27 miles makes it a full day trip.

Phra Puttha Taksin Ming Mongkhol▶ is a huge image on Khao Kong mountain in the town district, 4 miles along Highway 42 to Ba Joh. The 79-foot figure is decorated with golden mosaic. The same "Buddhist park" contains a hollow bell-*chedi*, the top of which contains a "relic."

Two *wats* deserve a mention. In **Wat Cherng Khao** (Ba Joh district) the body of a monk, Luang Phor Daeng, lies miraculously undecayed in a glass coffin—the object of great local veneration. **Wat Chol Thara Sing Hey**, near the border, has murals, eclectic southern Thai-Chinese architecture, Hindu statuary, Song dynasty ceramics and a reclining Buddha. However, it is not these features that distinguish it, but its history: this ancient foundation was invoked as the last Siamese territorial stand, when Narathiwat stood out against the British, who threatened to incorporate the region in their Malayan possessions.

Tak Bai district▶ This border location can be an interesting visit in itself. Ban Taba, at the end of the road, has reasonable views over the large mouth of the Golok River, which forms the national boundary. Fishing boats come and go, and it is an easy matter to get the necessary papers stamped and slip out of Thailand and into Malaysia on one of these.

The atmosphere is frenetic, the market prominent. Vehicles must go through a modern passport check and cross over on a car ferry; Malaysian passport officials wait on the other side.

► **Pattani**

Highway 42, east coast, south of Songkhla. Buses from Narathiwat, boats from Songkhla

This old province of the south has a tradition of rebellion against Thai authority, and today it is the focus for Muslim separatist politics. The **central mosque►** just outside town on the road to Yala is the second-largest in Thailand and of great importance to the south's many Muslims. It is a recent construction, opened in 1963. Visitors are welcome from 9 to 3:30.

Seven kilometers out on the road to Narathiwat is the old **Kreua Se** mosque, dating from the reign of Naresuan in the 16th century. The Chinese shrine of Mother Lim Kor Nio nearby is said to have put a curse on the mosque to prevent it being completed. She has a major festival in the third lunar month, when her effigy is paraded and devotees walk on hot coals, as in Phuket.

Wat Chang Hai► is to be found 22 miles from town on the Khok Po–Yala road (Highway 409). At 300 years old, it is distinguished for its huge golden *chedi* visible from far away. Despite being so near Malaysia, the wat is wholly Thai in style.

North of Pattani town is Bang Nara, a picturesque village containing the campus of the Prince of Songkhla University. The **Princess Mother Gardens►**, a newly laid out public park that connects with the campus grounds, is formed from a mangrove swamp tastefully planted with flowers.

Beaches Khae Khae and Panare, 27 miles out of town, are Pattani's most famous beaches. In Khae Khae Valley, they follow the mountain's curve. Boulders and rock formations alternate with wide bays, and the water is clear. The laterite road winds for 5 miles; a limited food service serves a beach that is otherwise unspoiled. Some 33 miles from Pattani toward Sai Buri is Patatimoh beach and the village of Paseyawor, a large fishing community that builds decorative *kor-lae* boats.

Sai Khao National Park►, a Royal Forestry Department park, with its waterfall, is to be found off the Khok Po–Yala road. At the highest stage, the fall drops 26 feet down a cliff on the side of Nang Jan mountain. This is a popular local spot.

237

Batik
A major Malay-craft product on sale in the modern-looking town of Pattani is bright and busy batik.

The people of Pattani are racially and culturally more closely related to the Malays than to the Thais. Pattani was, until recently, part of an independent principality

The bizarre limestone islands off Phang Nga loom out of the water, reaching heights of up to 300 yards. Similar formations occur in Laos, Vietnam and China

The chisel-shaped profile of Nail Rock (Ko Tapu) will be familiar to all James Bond fans from The Man with the Golden Gun

▶ ▶ ▶ **Phang Nga**

Highway 4, west coast, north of Phuket. Buses from Phuket and Krabi

Phang Nga province has two distinct coastlines: the mangrove-fringed bay formed by Ko Phuket and the

long, straight, beach-lined Andaman coast, north of Phuket. Limestone rock formations rise out of the sea at Phang Nga Bay, to dramatic effect. Inflatable-canoe tours are very popular, and rubber dinghies can also be used to enter the island caves, which are like weird "rooms" of water, but canoes are better for silently approaching any wildlife. Of course, the discriminating diver has long known about the Similan Islands some 25 miles to the west, part of Phang Nga province (see page 230).

Boat tours▶▶▶ from Phuket are something of a hackneyed tourist trip but one of the cheapest. Coaches whisk you to a long-tailed-boat jetty from where you snake out of mangrove channels to the open sea. **Khao Phing Kan**▶, not very far out, is a leaning megalith that, with its naillike companion **Ko Tapu**▶▶, was the setting for the James Bond film *The Man with the Golden Gun*. The boats then head back to the unusual village of **Ko Panyi**▶▶, a Muslim settlement built entirely on stilts attached to a tall rock. It is as well to be aware of local customs and sensitivities; the Muslim village does not tolerate alcohol. Photograph the attractive little white and green mosque but show due respect. After a generous repast, the tour re-embarks for the return to base. The coach may take a route around shops and temples in Phuket on the way back.

Phang Nga town, like Phuket, grew up around the tin-mining industry. The small town, set in a spectacular backdrop of mountains containing an assortment of caves, has little nightlife.

Suwan Khuha cave, to the west of town, contains images of Buddha and is important to the Thais.

Phang Nga port, 5 miles to the south, serves the important islands—the largest, **Ko Yao Yai** and **Ko Yao**

Noi, are two hours away. There are beaches and even a pearl farm on Ko Yao Yai, but little in the way of accommodations.

The western coast of Phang Nga province could not be more topologically different from the indentations of Phang Nga Bay. Starting at Khao Pilai off Phuket, the long, straight sands run for a score of kilometers into Thai Muang district. This is the territory where the endangered sea turtle lays its eggs from November to February; the eggs are eaten by some people.

There are plenty of stopovers as you carry on up through **Khao Lampi-Hat Thai Muang National Park. Khao Lampi▶**, opposite the beach side of the road, is a pretty waterfall where a swim in the pool below is possible. **Bang Sak** is a typically inviting large beach, not quite empty, and there are drinks for sale. There is also Tap Tawan beach and Coral Cape; signs for waterfalls are a way off the road.

North of here is **Khao Lak National Park▶**. There are many bungalows and resorts in this park, about 21 miles short of bus-stopover Takuapa. The **Nang Thong Bay Resort** is a typical example, with budget–moderate charges. Clean rooms overlook the ocean with fantastic sunsets, and there is yet another quiet and swimmable beach. Khao Lak is the closest departure point for the Similan Islands (see page 230). Tours can be arranged at several of the local bungalow complexes.

Phang Nga's sights
Other western Phang Nga attractions: Highway 401: Ban Bangklang Spa. Highway 4032: Lam Ru Fall, Laeng Hin Fall, Ban Plai Phu Spa.

The stilt village of Ko Panyi is a scheduled lunch stop for boat tours from Phuket, whose Muslim inhabitants tolerate the regular invasion with remarkable forbearance

230

Thale Luang and Thale Noi
A huge saltwater lagoon known as Thale Luang gives Phatthalung a coastline of sorts, although it lies some 22 miles inland. A peaceful scene, with beach resorts and islands, this land-locked water is now very polluted, and swimming is not advised. Many fish have died because of effluent-dumping. Bird life still flourishes, however. The reserves at Thale Noi and Khu Kat (see page 249) attract thousands of migrant birds, which flock here between January and April.

Phuket
To avoid embarrassment, note that "Phuket" is pronounced *poo-ke(t)*, with an almost silent *t*.

The temple cave of Khuha Sawan contains dozens of Buddha images. Steps lead up to a fine vantage point overlooking rice fields

► **Phatthalung Province**
Highway 4, east of Trang on the east coast. Buses from Nakhon Si Thammarat, Hat Yai, Songkhla, Trang and Phuket; trains from Bangkok
On the route of the main Trang–Songkhla artery, this inland province has its own peculiar attractions, such as a beach on the huge lake of Thale Luang, not far out of Phatthalung town. Dense casuarinas give welcome shade at Hat Saen Sukhrim (Lam Pa), which has a charming view of little islands in the lake.

Also near town are **Khuha Sawan caverns►**, where light floods in through the spacious northern entrance and huge Buddha images, some gold plated, can be seen inside. **Thale Noi Waterbird Sanctuary** (see panel), 20 miles northeast of Phatthalung town, is a large watery swamp that connects with the lake through a canal. It is an ideal waterfowl habitat, and large birds such as cranes and storks can be spotted.

The nine-stage **Khao Khram Falls►**, halfway to Trang, have pools large enough for swimming, and **Khao Pu Khao Ya National Park** spreads over a wild landscape to the northwest. Near the park office in Sri Banphot district are **Matja Pla Won caves►**, with stalactites hanging like a delicate curtain near a large fish pool. Another famous waterfall among the many in the park is **Rien Thong►**, otherwise known as Roi Chan or "Hundred Stages." Stage 13 is the most beautiful, with views over Thale Noi and the mountains, Pu and Ta.

► ► ► **Phuket**
South of Phang Nga on the west coast. Buses from Bangkok (southern terminal; journey time 13 hours) and neighboring towns; domestic flights
Thailand's largest island is crammed with things to see. It is a major package-deal vacation spot, heavily developed in places but with some lovely beaches and fine scenery. Boat trips to Ko Phi Phi► ► ► (see pages 222–223) and Phang Nga► ► ► (see pages 238–239) are popular. Underwater sightseeing is big here; as are diving and snorkeling.

The upper west coast has some beautiful beaches.

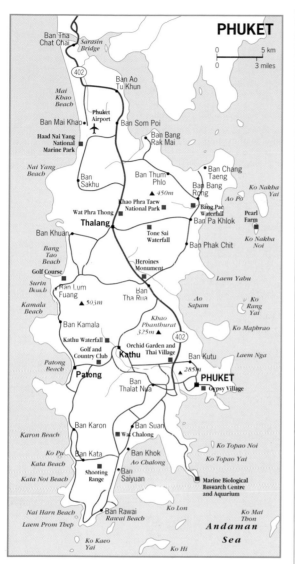

PHUKET

Tin-mining
Phuket's former wealth was founded on tin-mining. The first deposits were discovered around 1640, whereupon Phuket was swiftly annexed by Siam. Chinese traders developed the mines, and an English entrepreneur, Edward Miles, improved extraction methods. In the early 20th century, Phuket was the world's fifth-largest producer of tin ore, but prices fell sharply after World War II, when plastics developed.

Paragliding is popular at many of Thailand's coastal resorts, nowhere more than at Phuket's Patong Beach

Turtles
Marine turtles always return to the beach where they were hatched to lay their eggs, so the destruction of any habit is disastrous. Choosing a cloudy night, they clamber above the high-water mark and dig a nest in the sand, laying up to a hundred eggs in a batch. Once hatched, the babies scuttle for the waves as fast as they can. Very few baby turtles survive their perilous early years into adulthood.

Nai Thon Beach is usually missed by the hordes—probably because access is awkward. From here north up to Sarasin Bridge, which connects Phuket with the mainland, is all Nai Yang National Park. With its beautiful casuarina trees, **Nai Yang Beach** has managed to acquire limited (if exclusive) development. At the long and straight **Mai Khao** (White Trees) **Beach**, conservationists have made real efforts to save diminishing turtle populations, whose females come to lay their eggs from November to February. Past the exclusive resort of Pansea is long **Bang Tao Beach**.

Going south from Bang Tao, access to the privately owned **Laem Sing Beach** is down a path off the road from Surin Beach to Kamala Beach. For such perfection, however, there is a charge in the high season.

Most package tours are catered for on the complexes of Kata and Karon beaches and Patong Beach, big, loud and international. Diving and game-fishing are popular here. **Patong Beach** is where the trend toward mass tourism has gone the furthest, with the proliferation of high-rise hotels and blocks of apartments, but it may yet be some time before even Patong is as crowded as Nice (with which Phuket is officially paired). Also here is a Pattaya-style transvestite show.

Kamala Beach is what Patong must have been like before the feverish speculation started. **Surin Beach** to the north is fronted by small bars, restaurants and souvenir shops. **Karon and Kata**, to the south of Patong, have witnessed rapid large-scale development—in the case of the smaller Kata, with claustrophobic results.

Open-air "bar-beers" similar to those at Patong have mushroomed. The **Club 44** discotheque in Karon is one

Vegetarian festival
Past the market in Phuket town is the Chinese shrine San Jao Jui Tui. During the annual 10-day vegetarian festival in mid-October, Phuket's many Chinese citizens in white costumes bring the shrine to life. Firecrackers explode and dragons dance. Ranong Road becomes a vegetarians' paradise, stalls offering the broad range of Thai culinary goodies minus the meat. The awe-inspiring climax is when *nagas*, or spirit mediums, parade the streets, their cheeks pierced with huge skewers. They also walk on fire and up ladders of blades.

Phuket is a mecca for watersport lovers. Facilities at Patong Beach are especially good, but don't expect to enjoy the place by yourself in high season

Heroines of Thalong
In 1785, the widow of Phuket's governor and her sister fended off a Burmese attack by dressing all the local women in men's clothing, cutting their hair short, and rolling up banana leaves to resemble musket barrels. The invaders were thus convinced that a vast army awaited them. Rama I honored the brave sisters for their actions, and their bronze monument stands at a crossroads on the Phuket–Thalong road.

of the oldest establishments—you can tell by its cheap shedlike appearance—but it has a welcoming atmosphere, drawing both gays and heterosexuals until well after midnight.

The small **Kata Noi** and **Nai Harn beaches** to the south have been the home of lavish resorts that tend to dominate otherwise peaceful beaches.

Few visitors leave without a view of Prom Thep Cape, the island's southernmost extremity. Between it and Nai Harn is the diminutive and charming **Ya Nui Beach**, popular with the locals. Snorkeling is a pleasure, and although corals on the coast have been degraded, there are still some dazzling fish.

Many Thai tourists prefer **Rawai Beach** on the eastern side of the cape, with its restaurants overlooking the water. Boats go from here to nearby islands.

The main road north from Rawai into Phuket town passes **Chalong Bay**, a fine yacht anchorage, and thereby a firm base on the international yachting circuit. The King's Cup Regatta in November is becoming ever more popular, and yacht charters are available for the wealthy.

Phuket Town The town takes its name from the Malay *bukit*, meaning "hill." It became the provincial capital relatively recently.

The island has rich agricultural land and deposits of tin ore. Mining and smelting have been continuously carried out by Europeans and Chinese, and much of the town's architecture dates from the last century. The terraces of Krabi and Thalang roads in particular are very quaint.

The modern town is centered on the market traffic circle where blue buses leave for the beaches. The grassy hill called Khao Rang dominates the town; a paved road goes to the summit, where the view takes in offshore islands and much of the flat eastern plain. Another good trip is to the **Marine Biological Research Center**, at the end of Laem Phanwa (Phanwa Cape), 9 km south of town, where you can see a whale's skeleton and many varieties of the colorful reef fish.

Other sights The island's central landmark is the unmistakable **Heroines Monument**▶, at the road intersection for the upper west coast beaches. The two militant ladies in stone are Thao Thep Krasatri and Thao Sri Sunthorn, who saved Thalang from the Burmese in 1785. Next door, and well worth a visit, is the **National Museum of Thalang**▶ (*Open* Wed–Sat, 9:30–4). The displays are skillfully thought out and visually appealing.

The route north to Thalang passes the rather gaudy **Wat Phra Nang Sang** with its massive image of Guan Im, the female Bodhisattva. Nearby is the buried Buddha image of **Wat Phra Thong**, which not even a Burmese army could dig up. It was discovered by a buffalo boy who tethered his buffalo to the image's head. The gables and windows of the temple exhibit rich carving.

Back at the museum, the road east leads to **Khao Pra Taew National Park**▶ with Phuket's two waterfalls, Tone Sai and Bang Pae. Farther on is Ao Por, the port for trips to the pearl-farming Naga Noi island.

Ko Ban Yee
The village of Ko Ban Yee near Phuket town is one of many built on stilts in and around the mangrove swamps. There is another at Rawai Beach. The *Chao Le*, or Sea Gypsies, who inhabit these villages have their own Malay-related language, *Moken*. The Sea Gypsies, originally from Malaysia, are fishing folk who once led a nomadic existence.

Prawn farming
The mangrove swamps of Southern Thailand have suffered serious degradation in recent times because of a sudden boom in prawn farming. Many coastal rice paddies were converted into prawn ponds during the 1970s. The resulting salination and pollution from pesticides and prawn feed has made fertile land useless, and damaged the fragile ecology of the mangroves, a habitat for many unusual species. Local lakes and water systems have also been contaminated.

The mangrove swamps of Phuket Island's eastern shores are a fascinating habitat for many kinds of wildlife, including the strange amphibious mudskipper

■ **The quality of Thai rice has been internationally renowned since the 1930s. Apart from rice, the other traditional exports for which Thailand is famous are rubber, tin, teak and gems. Each of these has traditional export markets in different parts of the world.** ■

Rice The distinctive quality of Thai rice is still recognized across the world. People might buy cheaper rice from other countries, but would prefer the more expensive Thai rice if they could afford it.

The first Rice Experimental Station was set up, with the encouragement of the king, in 1916. Over 4,000 domestic varieties of rice were studied, of which the Pin Kaew variety won first prize at the World Grain Exhibition in Canada in 1933.

Rubber The southern provinces of Thailand were traditionally dominated by the production of rubber and tin. Rubber trees are cultivated principally by Thai, Thai-Malay and Chinese landowners, and the industry was mainly developed after World War I. Production is primarily for export, and has boomed since World War II, especially in sales to the U.S. market. Annual production exceeds one and a half million metric tons a year.

A tree planted today can begin to be tapped for rubber within about six years. Raw sheets can then be sold or smoked in a smokehouse, which costs the buyer more; the buyer is invariably a Chinese merchant.

Today the development of synthetic rubber has challenged natural rubber production, and the planters face problems, although new, higher-yielding methods of cultivation since the 1960s have helped rubber to be more profitable.

Tin Tin-mining goes back to ancient times. By the end of World War II, most mines had come into the hands of British, Australian and local Chinese mine owners. The tin used to be exported, but now the canning industry for tuna and other food products has created a domestic demand. Entitlement to all mineral rights is vested in the king, allowing the government to control tin mining.

Teak This is also an important export product, shared with neighboring countries, particularly Burma. Thai and Burmese teak are considered to be the highest quality in the world market.

Tapping for rubber

Teak plantations were first set up in Thailand in the middle of the 19th century, and there has been an annual planting program since 1942. Teak trees intended for timber export are usually replanted every 70 years, so this is a long-term business.

A new method of vegetative propagation of teak trees using tissue-culture techniques has been tried. This means that one single bud from a mature elite teak tree can be mass-propagated to produce millions of plantlets of the same genetic makeup.

Teak is a quality hardwood used for specialty carving and a durable finish wherever wood is used as a material. The demand is such that the recent logging ban, imposed for ecological reasons, has sent Thai exporters into neighboring countries for concessions. Thai teak is particularly valued for shipbuilding purposes.

The trees grow in the northern part of Thailand, and the logs are brought down by waterways. The teak forests belong to the state, and short-term leases are given. Some European companies have concessions.

Two years before a teak tree needs to be felled, its trunk is girdled by a ring cut through to the heartwood. This kills and seasons the wood slowly and makes it sufficiently dry to float. Felling takes place during the rainy season, and elephants drag the logs down to the nearest stream.

Gems In Bangkok you will see hundreds of shops selling gems and ornaments, another Thai specialty. Both unset gems and finished jewelry are popular buys in the Bangkok markets.

Jade, rubies and sapphires are the most popular stones, traditionally produced in Thailand but also found in neighboring countries. Thailand is very much a center of the gem trade in Asia.

The mines for these gems are often small, employing fewer than 40 people, sometimes only five. In some areas they have to be dug out from more than 50 feet below the ground. The gemstones can then be heated to a high temperature to improve their brilliancy and coloring for market purposes.

Nowadays locally produced gems are supplemented by imports from Laos, Sri Lanka and Australia. There are distinct districts in both Bangkok and Chantha Buri specializing in the gem trade. The trading tables, where the gem dealers sit head-to-head with their customers, can be seen directly inside the shop windows—sunlight being essential in order to examine the stones' cut brilliance and blemishes.

245

Export commodities
Rubber, tin and gems remain important export commodities for Thailand, worth about 14 billion, 1.5 billion and 8 billion baht a year, respectively. Almost half of the rubber goes nowadays to meet the materials needs of Japan's industries, with Singapore, China and the United States providing other important rubber markets. Japan is the biggest customer for tin, and the Netherlands is also a major buyer. Japan, Hong Kong and the United States are the principal markets for Thai gems.

SOUTHERN THAILAND

The Kra Canal
North of Ranong, the southern peninsula constricts to its narrowest point—only about 30 miles wide near Kraburi. For many years the prospect of digging a canal across the Kra Isthmus to link the Gulf of Thailand and the Andaman Sea has been a tantalizing dream. Tense relations between Burma and Thailand have blocked the idea, and worries about environmental damage have also surfaced. Another idea, to build a canal farther south at Songkla, is still on ice.

Jansom Thara Hotel
Those looking for the last word in luxury may find it in the Jansom Thara Hotel, a half mile east out of Ranong town. Here are featured whirlpools that are filled with natural spring water preheated to 150°F.

At Ranong, a local lad points proudly to a fine display of drying fish. The port is an important base for both Thai and Burmese fishing fleets

Illegal immigrants
Burmese migrants workers hold many of the less attractive jobs around Ranong, for lower wages than Thais. Many do not have work permits, but nonetheless they find life in Thailand more appealing than the restrictions and low standard of living they face at home. Sadly, many are exploited by unscrupulous employers. As elsewhere in Thailand, the brothel trade thrives, along with smuggling, illegal fishing, and a black market.

▶ **Ranong Province**
Highway 4 east of Chumphon, on the Burmese border.
Buses from Chumphon, Suratthani and Phuket
Highway 4 is the main road running through the narrow province of Ranong. Ranong is Thailand's wettest province, and this is evidenced by the lush rain forest. Thousands of tourists pass through, but most only admire its scenery from a bus window on the journey southward to Phuket, Phang Nga and Krabi. They can also catch glimpses of neighboring Burma (Myanmar) and its offshore islands.

The general public can "take the waters" in **Raksa Warin Forest Garden**, 1 mile to the east of Ranong town. This is actually in the compound of a temple, Wat Tapotharam, and the municipality has provided all the requisite amenities.

The three hot springs, Phor, Mae and Luk (Father, Mother and Child), are rich in dissolved mineral salts as they bubble up through the local limestone. A road leads away from here to Som Paen beach some 4 miles distant.

For nature-lovers Coming up by Highway 4 from Phang Nga, the first main attraction reached is **Khlong Nakha Wildlife Sanctuary▶**. Dress for forest walking is essential—stout shoes and covered shins may save a great deal of pain. In recompense are the wonders of a real rain forest that is unlike anything that Europe has to offer. There is a fine waterfall here waiting to be discovered by intrepid walkers: the lovely **Khao Phra Narai** falls near Kapoe district.

Farther north toward Ranong town is the huge (over 115 square miles) **Laem Son ("Pine Cape") National Park.** The road leading to it at the Km 657 stone crosses a vast expanse of mangrove swamps to reach the national park headquarters at Bang Ben. This beautiful and little-visited beach gives access to a number of islands, Ko Kang Khao ("Bat Island"); Ko Kam Noi, known for its aquamarine waters and snorkeling; and Ko Kam Yai with its fantastic coral, among others. Around Ko Chang are some fascinating corals.

There are bungalows on Bang Ben and they must be booked in advance; contact the Forestry Department in Bangkok (tel: 02/579 0529 and 579 4842).

Coastal trips Ngao waterfall is 7 miles south of Ranong town and can be seen from a long way off, lying inside a bend of the road. The *tha reua* or port at Ranong is actually a few kilometers out of town. There is a great fishery here, accompanied by the unmistakable aroma of raw fish. A popular island to visit from here is **Ko Phayam▶** with its beaches, cashew-nut plantations, pearl farm and Chao Le (Sea Gypsy) village. The trip takes two hours.

Another boat from Ranong crosses over to the coast of Burma for about 300 baht. "Prior immigration formality must first be gone through," you are told. Tours organized by the Jansom Thara Hotel offer the chance of a brief glimpse of Burma, enabling you to visit a temple and the market. However, it is possible just to take a look without actually landing; the journey takes about half an hour.

The Thai island of Ko Phi can be visited on the trip. Many Burmese cross over into Thailand looking for work. Men wearing Burmese dress can be seen around the port area; in addition, various signs and notices in the town are written in Burmese script.

Victoria Point (Ko Sawang) is Burma's most southern extremity, and Thais cross over to shop for ivory and gems. Near the village of Pak Nam, opposite Victoria Point and to the northwest of Ranong town, is Charndamri Beach, where it is possible to watch the sun set over the point.

North of Ranong, heading toward Chumphon, the road becomes increasingly idiosyncratic, twisting up and down improbable hills as it passes the district of La-un, where the hulk of a Japanese warship can be seen in the river at low tide.

Ranong province
Ranong became a province in its own right when it was officially separated from Chumphon in 1862.

247

The hot mineral springs at Wat Tapotharam are hot enough to cook an egg. Thermal water is piped through the Jansom Thara Hotel for hot baths and a huge whirlpool

►► Songkhla

Highway 408 south of Phatthalung on the east coast.
Buses from Hat Yai and Bangkok (southern terminal)

A town of ancient heritage, much of which is still largely visible, Songkhla occupies the tip of a peninsula guarding the entrance to the vast **Thale Sap Songkhla (Songkhla Lake)**. The lakeside is busy with the town's port, where huge catches of fish are iced and packed. On the eastern side of the town is open sea with a couple of fine beaches. **Hat Samila** lines the wide part of the peninsula. **Son Orn** ("Casuarina Point") is a sliver of land farther north, which offers only sea, trees, beach and breeze. There are strategically placed restaurants along the road on the port side. The road from the town center passes the stone mermaid inspired by the one in Copenhagen, who sits with her back to the offshore Cat and Mouse islands, a favorite spot for anglers.

You can get a better view of the whole setup from the top of either Khao Noi or Khao Tang Kuan. Khao Noi is easier, as it is possible to drive up.

The beaches are fine for swimming, but this area has a decorous Thai atmosphere, which results in a curious reluctance to take the plunge.

The most relaxed beach is way down toward Kao Seng, well away from the port, with strange rock formations such as "Mr. Raeng's Head," and a Muslim fishing village

Songkhla
Songkhla has a large expatriate community, employed by the oil industry, which exploits the southern gulf.

One of Songkhla's most recognizable monuments, a copy of Copenhagen's Little Mermaid, suns herself on the beach of Laem Samila

that decorates its boats in the colorful *kor lae* style. Hotels are plentiful. The budget **Saen Samran** by the clock tower is clean and comfortable enough. The **Sunday market** gathers near here around Songkhla train station, where groups of old men wait for a train that will never come: the branch was closed in 1972.

Other sights in town include the **National Museum** (*Open* Wed–Sun 9–4), housed in a Chinese mansion that has its own charm, especially the side away from the entrance where there are huge gnarled old trees. It contains a good collection of Srivijayan art. The 19th-century Laem Sai Fort stands to the north of the fishing port.

An extraordinarily cheap ferry connects Son Orn with the lake's top lip, a deep-sea port where the Khao Daeng is a sister fort to Te Noi on the Songkhla side.

Environs

For traveling around, renting a motorcycle is easy in Songkhla town. To appreciate the lake properly, rent a vehicle and head west toward Hat Yai. About halfway there, take a prominent right turn, which leads past a rather barren public park to the first of the **Tinsulanonda bridges**, linking the island of **Ko Yor**, straddling the mouth of the lake at this point, to the mainland. The view from the bridge is fantastic. Thale Sap Songkhla is not a true lake but a long lagoon that is freshwater and boggy at the northern end, becoming increasingly saline towards the south.

The view over Thale Sap Songkhla from Ko Yor is spectacular, looking over the second Tinsulanonda bridge, which links the long thin land separating Songkhla Lake from the sea, with fish corals—bamboo and net structures erected around houses in the ocean—to the leeward side.

Highway 408 north up the coast from Ko Yor to Ranot is a typical Thai country road with villages and wats every few miles. Of the latter, **Hat Sai Keo** is an isolated meditation island on the Pacific side, a right turn shortly after meeting the main road.

The town of Ranot and the ancient temple Wat Pa Kho lie about 37 miles north, served by a regular bus from Songkhla. Halfway there, and the reasonable aim of a day trip from Songkhla, are Wat Jathing Phra, with a 10th-century chedi, and **Khu Khut Waterbird Park**, a conservation area for many species of migratory birds.

A few miles inland, the lake and swampland are very popular with visitors in winter, when many birds are on the wing. Truly dedicated ornithologists can rent a cheaply boat at the sanctuary office, where there is a small amount of information in English.

These colorful fishing boats, known as kor lae, *can be seen in the Muslim fishing village at Kao Seng. Sadly, this traditional craft is dying out*

Ko Yor
It is possible to speed over Ko Yor, but the island has several attractions, such as a weaving indus-try, strange rocks and the Southern Folklore Museum, part of Songkhla University. The exhibits, some of Srivijayan antiqui-ty, illustrate and illuminate the origins and crafts of Songkhla's people.
*Open: Mon–Fri 8–6.
Admission charge.*

■ **The warm, tropical waters surrounding Thailand's islands are a relatively unspoiled paradise of multicolored fishes, underwater marine life, and intricate coral reefs.** ■

Coral

Coral has a special meaning for many people, summoning up images of clear tropical water, white sand and the idyllic island life. But its allure is part of its undoing: it is collected to be used as a decorative item, it is damaged by the keels and anchors of tourist boats, and it is all too easily broken by careless handling or flailing flippers. A particularly destructive way of fishing—dynamiting—is also hastening this destruction. Coral grows slowly and it cannot possibly replace itself more quickly than it is being destroyed, so its future looks bleak.

250

Beautiful but deadly sea anemones are found among the coral reefs in many shapes and colors. The animals use their poisonous tentacles to trap their prey

Underwater swimming is obviously the best way to experience what the sea has to offer; scuba-diving lessons will cost you something like $100 per day, but snorkeling or just using a mask in shallow water can be very rewarding.

Exotic species can be seen surprisingly easily: parrotfish, with their winglike blue fins, and dish-bodied butterfly fish built for maneuvering in tight corners rather than for speed, can both be seen only a little way from the shore.

Coral is fascinating and precious. Like an underwater forest, it harbors many sorts of creatures; like a forest it is a living thing, gradually growing and evolving over the centuries. This treasure can be destroyed very easily by clumsy handling, and in any case a coral splinter is excruciatingly painful—so don't touch. Also beware of the waving tentacles of sea anemones, which are beautiful but pack a painful sting. The boldly striped clown fish has developed an immunity to the anemone's poison and so can lurk in the protective tentacles, safe from attack, but ready itself to seek out its prey.

Other creatures have developed close relationships with one another: for example, moray eels (large, predatory, not friendly) have a following of cleaner shrimps, which feed on their skin parasites. Both species benefit.

Seahorses are among the most endearing of fish and are well worth seeking out. They are much easier to find than the aptly named needlefish, which resembles nothing so much as a stick floating upright. At the other end of the size scale is the plankton-

feeding whale shark, the world's largest fish, which is an occasional visitor to these waters. Marlin are much more frequently seen; these elegant beauties are one of the species most sought out by game-fishermen. Dolphins are often seen and sometimes frolic around boats such as the ones that go to Ko Si Chang on the east coast. This is also a good vantage point from which to look out for flying fish, which sometimes glide a yard above the surface on their elongated fins.

On coastal beaches, you might still see sea turtles, although these huge creatures, which come ashore to lay their eggs, are now at great risk, their nesting areas disturbed and destroyed by tourist facilities. The nests themselves are often plundered for food. Here, pressure from concerned visitors might help to ensure a future for these gentle giants.

The quaint clownfish looks temptingly conspicuous to predators, but shields itself from harm amid sea anemones' tentacles

251

Sungai Kolok

Highway 4056; border town with Malaysia. Buses from Narathiwat and Hat Yai

This important border crossing with Malaysia is 37 miles from Narathiwat.

Sungai Kolok is a newish town and not of itself remarkable. The market is opposite the railroad terminus, and inside the station compound are racks of goods from Malaysia.

There are modern duty-free shops on the Malay side. Pay in the shop and collect the goods from Malay guards on the bridge. If crossing by foot over the old bridge into Thailand, a tuk tuk is recommended for the 2½-mile journey into town.

Suratthani

Highway 401. Buses from Bangkok (southern terminal), Phuket and Nakhon Si Thammarat; trains from Bangkok

The "Land of the Good People" is a huge, sprawling province whose major attraction is **Khao Sok National Park**, along Highway 401. Dam politics have bedeviled the fate of the forests. One scheme inundated millions of acres. Another, however, was thwarted.

For accommodations, besides **Art's Jungle House** (a collection of tree houses charging moderate rates), there are some budget bungalows and national park accommodations. Art's can be booked on 02/279 4967. East of Suratthani town on Highway 401 at Kanchanadit is the "college" where monkeys are trained to pick coconuts (see panel).

► Trang

Highway 404, on the southwest coast. Buses from Hat Yai, Phatthalung and Bangkok (southern terminal); trains from Bangkok; domestic flights

Communications with Trang are excellent, with access by air, rail and road.

Out of town past the airport is **Thung Khai Forest Garden**, and farther along Highway 4 is **Lamchan Waterbird Park**, which is richly endowed with waterfalls.

Offshore islands A train journey to the end of the Trang branch line at Kantang is met by buses to the seaport with its fine views. Ko Kradan is considered the most beautiful of Trang province's many islands, and Ko Hai (which is actually part of Krabi province) has some accommodations. The boat from Hin Pak Meng takes 40 minutes. Ko Libong to the southeast of Ko Kradan is Trang's biggest island. Royal Forestry Department accommodations (total, ten people) are free.

The mainland has many fine beaches. Hat Yao (Long Beach), Hat San (Short Beach) and Yong Ling are all in Kantang district. Behind them is a hot spring. The southerly Palian district has some fine beaches in Samran and Hat Ta Se off Koh Sukorn.

The road up to Sikao district leads to Hat Chang Lang and Hat Pak Meng, with a fine waterfall; camping is permitted. Inland waterfalls, Tone Khlan in Huay Yot and Roi Chan near the Phatthalung border, are fairly difficult to reach.

Superstition

■ **Superstition has woven itself into the fabric of Thai Buddhism, especially in rural areas. For example, Thais take astrology very seriously, and Brahman astrologers are still consulted at the royal court. The Buddhist church in Thailand is divided on these matters, although Buddha himself was only concerned with the compatibility of a belief with the quest for enlightenment.** ■

Astrology and lucky charms The last prime minister, Chatichai Choonhavan, was led by an astrologer to announce the members of his new cabinet before his coalition partners had decided their nominations for cabinet posts.

The Chinese are especially fond of lotteries, and tickets are sold on every street corner. In one village an

anthill was worshiped because it was said to house a ghost who could foretell the numbers which were about to win prizes in the lottery.

Some monasteries earn an important part of their income by blessing lucky Buddha amulets. Amulets were issued by the army to officers fighting in the border areas, and even science graduates wear them as protection from unknown dangers.

Spirits In the animist tradition Thais believe that *khwan*, a spirit or genius that resides in the physical body, reflects a person's essential characteristics and is indispensable to a person's well-being. If the spirit is scared into leaving that person, misfortune or illness will ensue. The very first post raised in a traditional Thai house is known as the *khwan* post. Most woods used for building are said to possess female spirits.

There is a more nebulous realm of spirits or *phi*. A newborn baby is said to have a spirit mother. Three days after birth a child is initiated into the human world in a ceremony that involves buying it with a coin from its spirit mother.

Thais also believe in a spirit companion, called *chetabhut,* which leaves a person during dreams and times of worry. A man who walks alone in the forest, hears footsteps following and turns to find no one there has heard his *chetabhut.*

Spirit houses
Many homes have a spirit house, a cross between birdhouse and dollhouse and always elaborately decorated. Offerings are placed on it every day, and joss sticks burn there continuously.

253

Left: offerings to the spirits

A Bangkok spirit house

The Negrito Sakai

Yala's foremost ethnic minority, the Negrito Sakai, are assumed to be the peninsula's oldest inhabitants. Formerly scattered around Betong and Bannang Sata districts, they were rounded up by the government into one village in 1973. Known simply as Mooban Sakai, the village is 50 miles from Yala town on the road to Betong. The 90 or so inhabitants were given a few hundred acres of rubber to tend, and all took the surname "Sri Than To," in honor of HRH the Princess Mother.

▶ **Yala**

Highway 410, southernmost border province with Malaysia. Buses from Narathiwat, Pattani, Sungai Kolok and Bangkok (southern terminal); trains from Hat Yai, Sungai Kolok and Bangkok

Yala town itself is grand and spacious, the result of careful planning. There are several public parks. One is around San Jao Phor Lak Muang, the city pillar, which was donated by the present king. Rites in respect of the town's tutelary deity occur here at the end of May. Nearby is Suan Khwan Muang, more of a sports ground.

It is difficult to explain the significance of singing doves among southerners, and Yala folk in particular, but entrants in the annual **ASEAN Barred Ground Dove Festival** held here on the first weekend of March come from as far afield as Indonesia and Brunei.

Environs

About 5 miles north of town by Highway 409 to Hat Yai is Wat Khuha-phimuk▶ (Wat Na Tham). Turn left down Highway 4065 to Yaha district. The reclining image in a cave that is part of the temple is presumed to date from AD 757 and is of classic Srivijayan style.

Fish fanciers might stop off at **Beung Nam Sai** in Raman district, famous for its decorative "dragon fish." Widely bred in Southeast Asia, these fish are supposed to bring their owner luck. The village is a further 5 miles from Raman on the road to Ruso district.

Than To waterfall▶, a seven-tiered fall in a forest garden surrounded by mountains, is one of Yala's star attractions. It is to be found in Mae Wat subdistrict, Bannang Sata district, 35 miles down Highway 410 to Betong. Visitors can bathe, and there is easy access for cars. In the immediate vicinity is the Banglang dam over the River Pattani, which generates electricity. Although there are places provided to admire the view, the way up is steep and only recommended for four-wheel-drive vehicles.

Ginseng is grown at the Than To self-built community near the waterfall.

Wat Khuha-phimuk on the outskirts of Yala is one of the most important Buddhist temples in southern Thailand

TRAVEL FACTS

Arriving and departing

Visas U.S. citizens can stay in Thailand for 30 days without a visa, but extensions are not given except in very unusual circumstances. A confirmed onward-travel ticket must be shown.

Those who wish to stay longer must apply—before traveling to Thailand—for a 60-day tourist visa, valid 90 days from the date of issue.

Applicants must hold a passport valid for at least six months from the date of application. Completed forms must be accompanied by two passport photographs; postal applications take up to 10 working days, but personal applications are much quicker.

Nonimmigrant visas, valid for 90 days, are issued to those who can show that they are traveling for business purposes. These can be extended provided that evidence of business or education in Thailand is shown.

> ❏ Visa expiry: There may be a charge of 100 baht per day for every day exceeded, and overstays are recorded on your passport. ❏

Visa extensions Thirty-day extensions of tourist visas (500 baht) can be obtained at the discretion of the Immigration Division, Soi Suan Phlu, Sathon Tai Road, Bangkok (tel: 02/287 3101), or any provincial immigration office, e.g., Phuket. Tax clearance certificates are no longer required.

Visiting another country from Thailand and then returning requires an additional visa for each return visit to Thailand.

Arriving by air Bangkok International Airport (also known by its former name, Don Muang Airport) is one of the major air destinations in Southeast Asia, with over 40 international airlines and a number of charter companies operating flights to the city. A second airport is under construction.

Remember to book flights well in advance.

Money exchange desks (offering the same rates as downtown), a hotel reservation desk, a limousine service desk and a cafeteria are open 24 hours; shops and restaurants are open from 6 or 7 AM to midnight.

The hotel desk does not require a commission (the deposit is deducted from the bill), but only more upmarket hotels are offered.

Travel into Bangkok Allow at least 60 minutes for possibly the ugliest journey in Thailand. The painless way to do it is to go straight to the limousine counter and pay about 500 baht for the **limousine service**.

Across the road from the airport, trains leave for Hualamphong station in central Bangkok—but there are only a few trains a day.

The **public bus** option is of interest only to confirmed tight-budgeters and masochists; the costs are negligible, but first experiences of Thailand will probably be of standing for over an hour with people clambering over your luggage. There are bus stops under the right-hand footbridge over Vipavadi–Rangsit Road as you leave the airport and down the slip-road to the right on the way out of the airport. Buses 4, 10, 13, 29 and 59 head downtown.

From the main road it is possible to flag down a **taxi**. Agree on a fare of around 300 baht before getting in. Official taxis have yellow license

plates and taxi signs on the roof, and taxis with meters are now the rule rather than the exception.

> ❏ Travel to Pattaya: the limousine desk offers a bus service to the beach resort (leaving at 9 AM, noon and 7 PM). There is also a more expensive sedan service. ❏

Avoiding Bangkok Two long-distance trains per day stop at Don Muang station across the road, offering immediate escape from the capital for those arriving before 9 am. Ayutthaya and Lop Buri make interesting first-night stops; trains to Chiang Mai do not stop here. Additionally, the Northern Bus Terminal is easily reached by taxi or limousine bus, and buses run to several places north of Bangkok.

Arriving by train Travelers from Singapore and Malaysia can enter Thailand by taking the train that runs the length of the Malaysian peninsula (1,197 miles) and takes over 34 hours, passing through Kuala Lumpur, Butterworth (for Penang) and Suratthani; second-class sleeping berths are comfortable and must be reserved in advance.

Arriving by road is possible from Malaysia via cheap taxis and minibuses. Malaysia closes the border each day at 6 PM. It is also possible to enter Thailand from Laos, at Nong Khai.

Departing by air Airport flight inquiries, tel: 02/535 1254 or 02/535

> ❏ Malaysia is ahead of Thailand by one hour, so the border closes at 5 PM on the Thai side. ❏

1253. Remember to keep 200 baht for the airport tax, which is payable for all international flights on departure.

Allow plenty of time to get to the airport—two hours should be safe; the train service from Bangkok to the airport takes about 40 minutes, but there are only a few services each day. Tour agencies and guest houses in Khao San Road offer cheap, hourly **minibuses;** book in advance. Even if you have a departure date on your ticket, it is essential to reconfirm 48 hours before travel.

Bookstores
Generally, prices for English-language books in Thailand are high. This short list is a selection of shops with English- and foreign-language titles.

Bangkok Asia Books, 221 Sukhumvit Road; DK (Duang Kamol) Books, 180 Sukhumvit Road and Siam Square (both sell new books). Used books are sold from stalls in Khao San Road. Neilson Hayes, 195 Suriwong Road, is a superb library for residents; 95 percent of the books are in English, and stock is constantly updated. Dating from 1922, the fascinating building alone is worth a visit.

Chiang Mai DK Book Store, 234 Tha Phae Road (new books; hill-tribe trekking and contoured military survey maps, useful for hiking); Book Exchange, 21/1 Rathchamankha Soi 2 (used English-language paperbacks); Suriwong Book Centre, 54/1–5 Si Donchai Road (good range of new books on Asia).

Hat Yai DK Books, Thamnoon Withai Road outside Hat Yai station.
Pattaya DK Books, Pattaya Beach Road, Soi Post Office.
Phuket Seng Ho, Montree Road, (English newspapers and best-sellers).

Camping
Beach camping shouldn't be a problem if you ask permission politely: *Kor thot, khun rop guan mai, ta rao ja gangs dten ti ni?* However, rough camping is not advised: the risk of robbery—or worse—is too high. It always helps to establish a rapport with the locals.

TRAVEL FACTS

Most of Thailand's national parks have campsites. Readily erected two-person tents cost about 40 to 50 baht per night; a small charge is made if you bring your own. Some upmarket bungalow resorts (e.g., near Chiang Mai) also provide tents.

Be warned that camping is a chilly experience in the hilly regions. In some areas, an additional hazard is the wildlife—a wandering elephant has been responsible for trampling a tent and destroying expensive camera equipment (fortunately, the occupants were not inside).

Children

Thais love children, and many visitors bringing young offspring report how easy it is to meet locals as a result. Climate and health hazards are clear drawbacks; sandals are advisable on major beaches where broken glass may by lying around. Some children take to the breakfast fish soup, but few will like chilis (ask for *mai sai prik*—without chili). Western-style **baby food and diapers** are available in Bangkok and other major centers.

Locals love looking after babies, so there is rarely a problem if a baby-sitter is needed. Hotel discounts are given for small children.

Climate

Most of the year the climate is hot and humid, with daytime temperatures in the 86–93°F range, falling to 75°F at night. March to May or June is the hottest and stickiest period, as the temperatures rise to 100°F and the humidity is high—at least 80 percent most of the time.

The rainy season is June or July to October, when most of the rain falls around dusk, and there is widespread flooding. However, most of the day is fine, and, generally, this is quite a pleasant time to travel; there are fewer tourists. Prices are cut, and there are more rooms available, but expect about three rainy days in any two-week period.

By far the most popular time to visit is the so-called cool season, from November to February, when rainfall is low and daytime temperatures are very warm—typically 84–90°F—but rather less oppressive than at other times.

Weather chart conversion
25.4mm = 1inch
°F = 1.8 x °C + 32

❑ Leeches are a problem in forest areas in the rainy season. Do not pull them off but make them let go with salt or a lighted cigarette. ❑

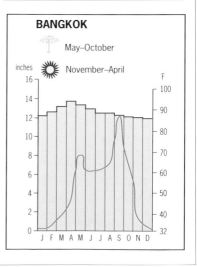

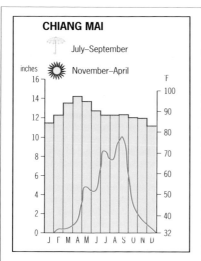

CHIANG MAI

July–September

November–April

inches

16

14

12

10

8

6

4

2

0

J F M A M J J A S O N D

°F

100

90

80

70

60

50

40

32

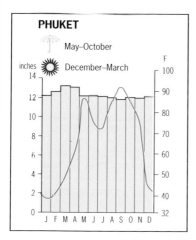

PHUKET

May–October

December–March

inches

14

12

10

8

6

4

2

0

J F M A M J J A S O N D

°F

100

90

80

70

60

50

40

32

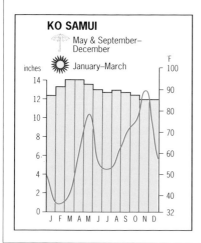

KO SAMUI

May & September–December

January–March

inches

14

12

10

8

6

4

2

0

J F M A M J J A S O N D

°F

100

90

80

70

60

50

40

32

Regional factors If you are visiting the hills in the cool season, be prepared for some sharp drops in evening temperature to about 52°F; wind chill can make it seem a lot cooler, so take a sweater and maybe a padded sleeping bag, too.

Avoid the plains of the northeast region in the hot season, when temperatures are frequently over 100°F. Flooding can extend beyond the rainy season, as the subsoil is saturated for some time.

Monsoon winds can make the Ko Samui archipelago and the southeastern coast unpleasantly wet and windy in November and December, when much of the rest of the country (even the nearby southwest coast) is at its best. Conversely, this coast is dry in Thailand's usual rainy season.

Crime

See also **Emergency telephone numbers** and **Money matters**, below.

Theft The friendliness of the Thai people is one of the country's great assets, but it pays to be streetwise, especially in Bangkok. Take special care of your baggage, particularly in crowded buses where the razor-blade thieves are at work and can remove the contents of a bag or cut through a camera strap without the owner realizing it.

Never leave valuables unattended in hotel rooms. Most hotels and guest houses have safes; be sure to get an itemized receipt for all items left. If you are trekking and will be gone for a few days, make sure you take your credit cards. Stories abound of visitors receiving their next credit-card bill back at home and finding that someone has gone on a spending spree in their absence.

At airports keep an eye on your luggage, and never carry parcels for strangers; you might be unwittingly carrying illegal drugs. Gross overcharging for services such as taxi fares can be avoided by agreeing on the price beforehand.

Beware especially of seemingly friendly strangers offering to take you on a boat trip in Bangkok; this

259

can lead to a huge bill at the end, or even robbery in the middle of the river. The offer of a free can of drink or a bar of chocolate may be harmless enough, but some people have been drugged this way and wakened hours later to find all their belongings stolen.

Fakes Thailand is famous for fake goods—designer clothes that are obviously not the real Benetton or Lacoste represent the more innocent end of the scale. So-called Rolex watches look remarkably like the real thing at a fraction of the price. Those trying on behalf of American film and record companies to crack down on copyright pirating often meet with bribery. More serious are fake gems. As it is possible to go *very* wrong buying gems, it is best not to buy unless you really know what you are looking for. Be sure you get a receipt and a certificate of quality in case of problems; disregard offers of helpful advice from strangers or promises of refunds at embassies.

Customs regulations
Items to be declared Video players, televisions, cassette players, radios, gold and currency (but not traveler's checks) over $10,000.

Prohibited imports Firearms, narcotics and pornography are forbidden. Merchandise is taxable, and you may face a tax bill if several new-looking electronic goods of the same type are brought in. There is no limit on foreign currency brought into Thailand, but large amounts must be declared.

Prohibited exports Thai currency in excess of 50,000 baht and foreign currency in excess of $10,000, if undeclared on arrival, cannot be taken out of the country.
   Permission to export Buddha and other deity images (even reproduction ones, but not small figurines worn as part of a necklace) should be obtained from the Fine Arts Department at the Bangkok National Museum (tel: 02/224 1370); this is seldom granted even for

reproduction images, unless it can be shown they are required for worship by practicing Buddhists.
   The export of other antiques also requires a permit from the Department of Fine Arts; this involves submitting two photographs of the object (maximum five objects per photograph) and a copy of your passport to the National Museum in Bangkok, Chiang Mai or Songkhla; allow three to five days for the application to be processed.

Duty-free allowances 200 cigarettes or 250 g of cigars or pipe tobacco and one liter of wine or liquor can be brought into Thailand. Theoretically only one still camera and five rolls of film can be brought in duty free, but this regulation is seldom enforced.

Driving
Nerves of steel are needed to drive in Bangkok, where factors to contend with include signs written in the Thai language, a complex and congested one-way system and a tendency to ignore lanes.
   Taxis or public transportation in the capital is a better option. In rural areas, public transportation is so cheap and plentiful and driving standards so hair-raising that it is probably wise to forget about driving altogether. However, the Chiang Mai, Phuket and Pattaya areas are not too daunting to explore by car.
   Long-distance country roads are of quite a good standard, but surfaces are patchy on even major highways. Some minor country roads are still unsurfaced, making them a sticky experience in the rainy season; potholes and ruts are frequent hazards.

Accident rates are high, and adequate insurance is essential; most Thais do not carry even third-party insurance. In the event of an accident, foreigners seldom have the benefit of any doubt.
   Usually the police will settle disputes about liability with the witnesses. Both parties will accompany the police to the nearest police station or make an appointment to settle the dispute about damages.

In Bangkok, traffic violations are punished with a fine, instantly payable, of varying amounts.

❏ Avoid traveling alone in the more remote areas of the country, particularly after dusk; travelers are sometimes attacked and robbed. ❏

Driving regulations Traffic drives on the left in Thailand. Visitors driving cars must hold an International Driving License. It is possible to get a Thai license with a letter from your embassy.

Fuel Both leaded and unleaded fuel are available; service stations are Western style and often give free windshield-cleaning service. Other

❏ Speed limits are 80 kph (50 mph) on highways, 60 kph (37 mph) in cities and 100 kph (62 mph) on expressways. ❏

service stations take the form of red drums with little glass meters above them.

A car must have at least "soo-per," whereas two-stroke motorcycles are fine on *thammadaa* (ordinary). Specify the amount needed, and the gas runs out of a hose by gravity.

Garages These are well distributed, and spares and labor are very cheap; standard Japanese vehicles are easier to repair. Insist on spares (*khorng tair*) made in Japan. *Khorng tiam* from a Thai workshop, however, will save at least 50 percent on prices.

Highway police (emergency number 191) can provide much assistance, in the case of both accidents and breakdowns.

Motorcycle rentals are widely available (deposit of passport normally required) and inexpensive by Western standards. It can be a fun way to explore country areas

for those brave enough. A driver's license is not required.

Motorcyclists are very vulnerable to Thai driving standards; use caution and have adequate insurance. Insist on a crash helmet and protect the skin.

Check the vehicle (brakes, tire wear and lights are among the easiest faults to identify), and clarify who is responsible for repairs in case of breakdown. The biggest danger is undoubtedly *sip lor,* 10-wheel trucks. Drivers have punishing schedules, which they keep to with the aid of stimulant drugs. Buses make up for frequent stops with wild bursts of speed and reckless passing. The roads are full of ancient machines, pushcarts and herds of cows. On main roads, signs are in English. Once onto minor roads, Thai script has to be contended with, so it is useful to have destinations written down in both alphabets.

Electricity
220 volts, 50-cycle AC. For those carrying 110-volt appliances, some hotels supply transformers, but if up-country travel is on the itinerary, bring your own or else forget about hair dryers and shavers; towels and disposable razors are adequate substitutes.

Embassies and consulates
Loss of passport or tickets should first be reported to the Tourist Police. Next, present this report to your

261

national embassy or consulate, which will deal with it and other disasters.

Nearly all countries have representation in Bangkok, making it a good place to obtain visas for travel elsewhere.

United States 95 Witthayu Road (tel: 02/252 5040).

Emergency telephone numbers
Fire 199.
Police 191.
Ambulance (Bangkok) (tel: 02/252 2171/5).
Emergency dentist (Bangkok) Dental Hospital, 88 Sukhumvit Road (tel: 02/260 5000).
English-speaking doctors (Bangkok) J.P. Dickson and Partners (tel: 02/252 8056).
Hospitals (Bangkok) Bangkok Nursing Home (tel: 02/233 2610); Bangkok Christian Hospital (tel: 02/233 6981); Bangkok Adventist Hospital (tel: 02/281 1422). (Chiang Mai) McCormick Hospital (tel: 053/240823); Maharaj Hospital (tel: 053/221122); Lanna Hospital (tel: 053/211037). (Phuket) Wachira Hospital (tel: 076/211114); Mission Hospital (private), Thepkasattree Road (tel: 076/212386). (Pattaya) Pattaya Memorial Hospital, Pattaya Road (tel: 038/429422).

Etiquette
(See also pages 26–27.)
Thais do not care for shows of anger or irritation or even raised voices. They respect a *jai yen*, or cool heart. Criticism or blunt confrontation can cause loss of face. Politeness and respect are the rule. Because the head is considered the most honored part of the body and the feet the most base and despised, it is best to be aware of offending, even unwittingly (for instance, sitting with crossed legs might mean pointing at someone with a foot).

Kissing and hugging in public are not acceptable.

On visiting a temple, the shoulders should be covered. Do not wear shorts or revealing dresses. Remove shoes when entering the main shrine and when visiting a private house. Nudity and topless sunbathing among tourists are common on

262

❏ If a banknote blows away in the wind, never trap it with your foot; this is the ultimate faux pas—touching a portrait of the king's head with the lowliest part of your body. ❏

many beaches but offensive to many Thais. First names are used universally. Thais also have nicknames, which tend to be shorter and easier to remember.

Never criticize the Thai royal family in front of a Thai. Each day at 8 AM and 6 PM, the national anthem is broadcast over train station loudspeakers, during which time you should stand and remain silent.

Smoking is banned in theaters, in train cars and in all buses. Never smoke in a wat.

Women travelers should try to avoid touching a monk. If this happens, he will have to go through a complicated and lengthy penance. Never climb onto Buddha images or show any signs of disrespect to Buddha.

Health
First Aid Although virtually all medical supplies are on sale at pharmacies, it is advisable to have a first-aid kit with you equipped with a few basic things:

- Band-Aids and antiseptic cream

- elastic bandages

- aspirin or ibuprofen

- ointment to soothe insect stings and bites

- rub-on cream for muscle sprains

- talcum powder to ease prickly heat

- cigarette lighter or matches for lighting mosquito coils (the coils themselves are too fragile to carry around)

- mosquito repellent

- pills for diarrhea and upset stomach

Heat Thailand's persistent heat can be quite debilitating; avoid over-exertion on the first few days, and steer clear of alcohol in the daytime. Drink plenty of fluids to avoid dehydration. Thirst is not always an accurate guide to the body's needs; do not let urine get too dark. Shower two or three times a day.

A sun hat or parasol will make the midday sun more bearable. Use a high-protection sunscreen to avoid sunburn; remember it is possible to get badly burned while swimming. The heat often depresses the appetite, so make sure protein and carbohydrate intake is adequate; rice is one of the most common sources.

Malaria This is a serious problem in forest areas and certain islands, particularly in the hilly borderlands and on Ko Samet. There is no risk in cities or in the central plains. Malaria is transmitted by malarial mosquitoes; if you are visiting a risky area, be sure to wear clothes to cover arms and legs. Cover exposed skin with mosquito repellent and sleep under a mosquito net. The main danger time is 6 PM to dawn. Malarial symptoms are a headache and fever; if you experience these, contact any malarial control center (found throughout the country) for a 10-minute blood test.

Many visitors take malaria prophylactics. However, these are ineffective against most Thai mosquitoes, and the **Malaria Control Center** (18 Boonrhagjit Road, Chiang Mai) and the Tourism Authority of Thailand do not recommend them. Also, certain pills often have side effects, including skin problems, corneal damage and temporary hair loss. Ask your doctor for the latest advice.

Stomach problems To minimize the risk of stomach upset, avoid unpeeled fruit, unwashed raw vegetables and tap water. Bottled water is on sale everywhere and is safe; many hotels, guest houses and restaurants buy this in bulk, so water set down in front of you to drink is usually fine. Similarly, cylindrical shaped ice cubes are bought in and should be safe. Ice cream bought from street vendors may have melted and refrozen, which could cause problems.

Vaccinations The only mandatory vaccination is yellow fever if you are coming from an infected area, but it is strongly recommended to inoculate against cholera, hepatitis A, polio, tetanus and typhoid; check with your GP before leaving.

VD and AIDS Sexually transmitted diseases, particularly AIDS, syphilis and gonorrhea, are common. Using a condom (*tung yang anamai*), otherwise known as a sheath (*plork* or *mechai*), is the most effective protection; they are on sale in pharmacies throughout Thailand. The English words are usually understood too.

❏ VD clinics abound in Ploenchit Road in Bangkok. One intramuscular injection cures within 24 hours. ❏

Insurance
Don't leave home without it, and shop around for the best price and most extensive cover. Take a photocopy of the insurance document with you and leave the original at home with a list of the items taken. Obtain the coverage as soon as the flight is reserved to insure against cancellation.

The policy should cover:
- delayed departure and delayed baggage
- all reasonable medical, hospital and emergency dental treatment, expenses and flight home by air ambulance
- personal liability
- canceling or curtailment in the event of the illness or death of yourself, your traveling companion or a close relative; or in the event of job loss; or in the event of being called as a witness; or in the event of your home being damaged by fire, flood or storm or being burglarized; the policy should compensate the cost of the vacation
- belongings and money, including sufficient cover for your camera

- items left in a car in daytime or overnight
- any special needs such as motorcycling, waterskiing and rock climbing
- 24-hour emergency telephone number

Points to notice Delays under 12 hours are not normally covered; after a 24-hour delay, you may be entitled to a refund for the full cost of your vacation if you cancel.

There may be a ceiling for the amount you can claim for the loss of an item.

There is usually a small deductible whereby you pay an initial amount of the claim.

Coverage is not provided for preexisting illnesses.

Contact lenses and dentures may need special insurance.

When things go wrong Get written evidence and receipts whenever applicable. Delayed departure of 12 hours or more usually qualifies for compensation, provided you have the length and cause of the delay confirmed in writing by the airline.

If luggage is damaged in transit, get two repair estimates; if it is lost by the airline, get a report form from the airline before leaving the airport, notify the police (if the policy requires it) and keep relevant receipts.

Theft of personal belongings while in Thailand must be reported to the local police within 24 hours; ask for a **certificate of notification** from them.

Keep copies of any bills or receipts for any additional costs if medical treatment is required; many insurance companies give an emergency telephone number.

Language
The Thai language is extemely difficult to master, and even armed with a phrase book and dictionary, you're likely to find intonation a problem. Fortunately, the Thais are helpful in overcoming the language barrier.

Accordingly, it is worth learning a few basic words and phrases; a little will go a long way. English is widely used in tourist areas, including guest houses, hotels and some restaurants, and many Thais have a smattering.

264

Basic phrases

hello	(man) sawat dee krup
	(woman) sawat dee ka
goodbye	laa gorn
thank you	korp koon
sorry/excuse me	kor toh
how much?	tao rai?
too expensive	phaeng pa
where is...?	...yu thii nai?
we want to go to...	...rao yahk bpai
how do I get to?	bpai...yung ngai?
how long does it take?	chai way-lah tao-rai?
that doesn't matter	mai pen rai
what is this called?	nee ree-uk wah a-rai?
yes	chai!
no	mai! chai!
turn right	lee-o kwah
turn left	lee-o sai
straight on	dtrong dtrong
I'm not feeling well	pom (woman: chun) roo-seuk mai koy sa-bai
I understand	pom (chun) kao jai
I don't understand	pom (chun) mai kao jai
do you understand?	kao jai mai?
see you later	pop gan mai

Numbers

1	neung
2	sorng
3	sahm
4	see
5	hah
6	hok
7	jet
8	bpairt
9	gao
10	sip
11	sip-et
12	sip-sorng
20	yee-sip
21	yee-sip-et
30	sahm-sip
100	neung roy
200	sorng roy
1,000	neung phan
10,000	neung meuun

Glossary Common geographical elements in Thai place names; note double *a*, double *i* and *h* are optional, e.g., thani/thaani (city), ko/koh (island).

baht	unit of Thai currency (100 satang = 1 baht)
ban	house, village
bang	waterside village
bot	the main chapel of a wat
chedi	a pagoda, topped by a spire, where holy relics are kept
farang	foreigner
hat, hatsai	beach
hup	valley
khok, don noen	hill
nam tok	waterfall
ko/koh	island
laem	peninsula, cape, promontory
mae, mae nam, lam nam	river
nakhon, muang, thani	city
pa, dong	jungle
paknam	river mouth
pha	cliff
phanom	hill
prang	Khmer-style chedi
nong	swamp
samlor	bicycle rickshaw taxi
songthaew	pickup van that is used as a minibus
tham	cave
tha	port, harbor
thale sap	lake
thanon	road
tuk tuk	motorized pedicab taxi
wai	Thai greeting (hands placed together as if in prayer)
wang	palace
wat	temple/ monastery
wiharn	hall where religious duties are carried out

Pronunciation Thai has five tones: mid, high, low, rising and falling. The differences seem small to the untrained farang ear, but it is a crucial part of speech.

Mispronounce the Thai for "snow" and you may find yourself talking about a delicate part of a dog's anatomy!

To make matters harder still, consonant sounds are slightly different: k, p and t, for instance, are mouthed rather than sounded at the end of a word. For example, the city of Phitsanulok is actually pronounced "Piss-anu-loh." Th and ph are pronounced like simple t and p—so Phuket is "Poo-ke(t)"—and there is even talk of getting the official spelling changed.

Other groups of letters to note:

kh	k
k	hard g
p	plosive bp
r	often silent (e.g., Krathong ="Katong")
th	t
t	plosive dt

Lost property
Contact the Crime Suppression Division of the Tourist Police on 02/225 7758, extension 4.

Maps
Local maps are generally poor and should be avoided. For those who need greater detail than the maps in this book give, or for those who like to compare maps, look out for the following.

For general planning, the **Bartholomew World Travel Map of Thailand** covers the whole country at a scale of 1:500,000.

The Department of Highways puts out a set of four maps of the country that is available from the Tourism Authority of Thailand office in Bangkok or the Highways Department on Si Ayutthaya Road.

Bangkok's labyrinthine street network probably will never be mapped accurately to include the last tiny back alley. In the meantime, the **Latest Edition Guide Map of Bangkok** is indispensable in showing bus routes of as much of the city as is needed by most people, and it also locates points of interest, hotels, embassies and places of entertainment.

Phrannok Witthaya publishes quality maps of Bangkok (**Bangkok Guide**) and most provinces. Its map of Krabi is particularly recommended. For Bangkok and Chiang Mai, Nancy Chandler's hand-drawn color maps are full of comments on where to eat noodles, buy crafts or English-language books, find a doctor and go to early-morning aerobics classes—all in addition to sights and hotels.

For drivers, DK Books publishes a useful road atlas (**Thailand Highway Map**), showing all of the highways and many dirt tracks, with place names in Thai, and major ones in English; there are town plans in the back.

Free local maps are available from tourist offices and many guest houses. While the standard of cartography is not high, these maps are often very useful sources of tourist information.

The best map for the northwest is the PN map of Chiang Mai and area, which has a city plan on the front, and a contoured 1:500,000 map on the reverse.

Measurements and sizes
Although the metric system is widely used, certain Thai measurements are sometimes given, especially when referring to land.
1 *niu*=2 cm; 1 sq *wa*=4 sq m; 1 *rai*=1,600 sq m.

❏ The Thai year-dating system is 543 years "ahead" of ours; for example, AD 2000 becomes in Thailand 2543. ❏

Media
Newspapers The *Bangkok Post* and the *Nation* are English-language newspapers published in Bangkok and on sale throughout Thailand. Both have foreign coverage, although the *Nation* is more parochial and the *Post* has many features taken from such publications as the *Independent, The Economist* and *Rolling Stone*.

The most readily available foreign English-language paper is the Singapore edition of the *International*

CONVERSION CHARTS

FROM	TO	MULTIPLY BY
Inches	Centimetres	2.54
Centimetres	Inches	0.3937
Feet	Metres	0.3048
Metres	Feet	3.2810
Yards	Metres	0.9144
Metres	Yards	1.0940
Miles	Kilometres	1.6090
Kilometres	Miles	0.6214
Acres	Hectares	0.4047
Hectares	Acres	2.4710
Gallons	Litres	4.5460
Litres	Gallons	0.2200
Ounces	Grams	28.35
Grams	Ounces	0.0353
Pounds	Grams	453.6
Grams	Pounds	0.0022
Pounds	Kilograms	0.4536
Kilograms	Pounds	2.205
Tons	Tonnes	1.0160
Tonnes	Tons	0.9842

MEN'S SUITS							
UK	36	38	40	42	44	46	48
Rest of Europe	46	48	50	52	54	56	58
US	36	38	40	42	44	46	48

DRESS SIZES						
UK	8	10	12	14	16	18
France	36	38	40	42	44	46
Italy	38	40	42	44	46	48
Rest of Europe	34	36	38	40	42	44
US	6	8	10	12	14	16

MEN'S SHIRTS						
UK	14	14.5	15	15.5	16	16.5	17
Rest of Europe	36	37	38	39/40	41	42	43
US	14	14.5	15	15.5	16	16.5	17

MEN'S SHOES						
UK	7	7.5	8.5	9.5	10.5	11
Rest of Europe	41	42	43	44	45	46
US	8	8.5	9.5	10.5	11.5	12

WOMEN'S SHOES						
UK	4.5	5	5.5	6	6.5	7
Rest of Europe	38	38	39	39	40	41
US	6	6.5	7	7.5	8	8.5

Herald Tribune. Where? magazine, free from hotel desks and tourist offices in Bangkok, Chiang Mai, Pattaya and Phuket, lists events and restaurant promotions, and is filled with advertizements for shops and night spots.

Radio There is no problem tuning in to rock or Thai pop music. English-language programs (hourly news bulletins, sports and business) are broadcast on 97 FM; 107 FM has news at 7 AM, 12:30 and 7:30 PM, with jazz and pop in between. English-speaking DJs are found on 105 FM. Between 9:30 and 11:30 PM, Western classical music is played on 101.5 FM. BBC World Service and Voice of America wavelengths are complex (depending on the time of day); the TV/radio page of the *Nation* lists these.

Television Cable TV with international channels is available in top-class hotels; it is also possible to get TV news on 105.5 FM for Channel 3, 103.5 FM for Channel 7, 107 FM for Channel 9 and 88 FM for Channel 11 (which mostly broadcasts educational programs and documentaries; news is at 8 PM).

Money matters
Currency The unit of currency is the baht (often abbreviated to B), and this is divided into 100 satang. Rates do not vary much but are better for traveler's checks than for currency. Coins are 25 satang, 50 satang (both copper), 1 baht (currently three sizes; the older designs do not have Arabic numerals), 5 baht (with copper edge) and 10 baht. Paper money has Arabic numerals and is issued in denominations of 10, 20, 50, 100, 500 and 1,000.

Foreign exchange It is not possible to obtain Thai currency outside Thailand, so on arrival at the airport a visit to the money-change desk is necessary. It is open 24 hours and the rates are reasonable.

Most banks will exchange foreign money and traveler's checks; exchange dealers in tourist areas offer competitive rates and are open from 7 AM to 8 or 9 PM. The Bangkok Bank is open daily, even on national holidays, 7 AM–8 PM. Big hotels have exchange desks, but rates are poor.

The best bet is to take checks in a major foreign currency in reasonably large denominations, as commission is charged on each check cashed.

You can also change money using a credit card (MasterCard, American Express, Diners Club and Visa are the most commonly used). Be sure to have details of emergency telephone numbers if a card gets lost.

Keep traveler's-check counterfoils separate from the checks themselves. Make a record of which checks have been cashed, so if some are lost you know which ones to claim for. Collection of new checks can be arranged through any bank.

Haggling *Tuk tuk* drivers and vendors of clothes and souvenirs expect you to bargain over the price. While there are no hard-and-fast rules, common practice seems to be to offer half of what is asked, then settle for about two-thirds. Most Bangkok taxis have meters.

Sometimes the first price offered may be 10 times over the odds, so ask other people—Thais and seasoned travelers—what you should expect to pay. Don't worry about not getting haggling down to a

fine art immediately; the amounts involved are often paltry anyway. Above all, keep cool and smile.

It is sometimes possible to negotiate cheap rates for hotel rooms, particularly outside the main tourist season. Restaurant and street-stall food and items in department stores (except for expensive goods such as jewelry) nearly always have fixed prices.

National holidays

As in some other Asian countries, certain public holidays are calculated according to the lunar calendar and vary from year to year.

Accommodations can be hard to find, especially at the New Year, during Songkran in Chiang Mai and when a holiday forms part of a long weekend. Tourist offices, some banks and all government offices close during these periods; Bangkok Bank (branches nationwide) and hotel money desks are open, as are most shops.

268

Dec. 31 and Jan. 1	New Year
Early to mid-Feb.	Chinese New Year
Mid-Feb.	Maga Puja
April 6	Chakri Day
April 12 to 14	Thai New Year (Songkran)
Early May	Royal Plowing Ceremony
May 5	Coronation Day
May/June	Visaka Puja
July/Aug.	Asalha Puja
Aug. 12	Queen Sirikit's birthday
Mid to late Oct.	Ok Pansa

Oct. 23	Chulalongkorn Day
Dec. 5	King Bhumiphol's birthday
Dec. 10	Constitution Day

Festival days The biggest festivals and their locations are listed below to give an idea of where and when accommodations may be hard to find.

Feb. 7–9	Flower Festival (Chiang Mai)
April	Pattaya Festival (Pattaya)
Nov. 21–22	Elephant Roundup (Surin)
Nov. full moon	Loi Krathong (nationwide, especially Sukhothai and Ayutthaya)
Nov.–Dec.	River Kwae Bridge Week (Kanchana Buri)

National parks

Thailand's 80-plus national parks are dotted nationwide and include mountainous, forest and coastal regions, individual waterfalls and archipelagoes. Many offer accommodations in the form of tents (about 50 baht for one or two people), dormitories (typically 20–40 baht per person) and ten-bed bungalows costing 100–300 baht per person or 1,200–1,600 baht per bungalow.

Reservations are advisable for weekends and public holidays, through the Forestry Department,

Phahon Yothin Road, Bangkok, (tel: 02/579 0529).

Warm clothing is needed in mountain areas, where temperatures can drop to 39°F, and it is advisable to bring a flashlight. Mapped information for walking is generally poor, and it is imperative to keep to the marked paths.

Opening times
Banks Monday to Friday, 8:30–3:30; **Bangkok Bank** (branches nationwide) and foreign exchange counters (in tourist areas), daily, 7 AM–8 PM.
Government offices Monday to Friday, 8:30–noon, 1–4:30.
National Museum branches Mostly Wednesday to Sunday, 8:30–noon, 1–4:30; closed Monday, Tuesday and public holidays.
Tourist offices Daily, 8:30–4:30; closed on public holidays.
Small stores Daily, 12 hours a day.
Large stores Daily, mostly 10–6:30 or 7.

During Chinese New Year, in February, many small shops are closed. Large stores stay open but take a holiday afterward.

Pharmacies
Thai pharmacies are extremely well stocked for the most part; in fact it is possible to buy over the counter many products, such as antibiotics, for which a doctor's prescription would be needed in other countries. Pharmacies are open daily from 8 to 5 or 6 in smaller places, or until 9 in large cities.

There is no all-night emergency service; in case of difficulty, contact a hospital.

Photography
Daylight is very bright, so use a 50- or 100-speed film for best results outside.

Thais are very tolerant of having their picture taken, but it is common manners to point to your camera first (smiling as you do so!); some hill-tribe folk are shyer, and some may demand a few baht.

Many temples display signs in English prohibiting photography inside the main wiharn, and some museums request that exhibits not be photographed. Video cameras are banned entirely from the grounds of the Grand Palace in Bangkok.

Print and slide film is widely available and reasonably priced, and film can often be developed inexpensively within a few hours.

> ❑ Pack silica gel or another drying agent with cameras to counter the effects of humidity. ❑

Places of worship
For non-Buddhists these are fairly scarce, with the notable exception of the significant Muslim element in Southern Thailand (the largest mosques are in Pattani and Yala).

Roman Catholicism is common in some towns with a substantial Vietnamese or Laotian population, particularly in Si Chiangmai in northeastern Thailand (not to be confused with Chiang Mai in the northwest). There is a Roman Catholic cathedral situated in Chantha Buri.

In Bangkok, the following welcome outsiders:
Hindu Wat Khek, Pan Road, off Silom Road.
Jewish Jewish Association of Thailand, 121/3 Soi 22, Sukhumvit Road (tel: 258 2195).
Muslim Darool Aman Mosque, Phetchaburi Road (near Rajtewi Intersection); Haroon Mosque, Charoen Krung (New) Road (near post office).
Protestant Calvary Baptist Church, 88 Soi 2, Sukhumvit Road (tel: 251 8278); Christ Church (Episcopal/ Anglican), Convent Road, (tel: 234 3634); International Church, 67 Soi 19, Sukhumvit Road (tel: 253 2205).
Roman Catholic Assumption Cathedral, 23 Oriental Lane, Charoen Krung (New) Road (tel: 234 8556); Holy Redeemer Church, 123/19 Soi Ruam Rudee, behind U.S. embassy (tel: 253 0353).
Seventh Day Adventist Bangkok Chinese Church, 1325 Rama IV Road (tel: 215 4529); Bangkok Ekamai Church, 57 Soi Charoenchai, Ekamai Road (tel: 391 3593).

Police

The brown-uniformed policeman is a common enough sight; many officers speak a little English, and they often approach lost-looking farang (maybe just to practice their English).

Police boxes (small police stations) are placed at frequent intervals along main roads. For Bangkok, Chiang Mai, Pattaya and Phuket, a special Tourist Police service assists visitors (see **Emergency Telephone Numbers**).

Contact the police in the event of road accidents, theft, lost property, disputes or car breakdowns; they will also help with giving guidance (occasionally as escort) in remote or dangerous areas.

Post offices and faxes

Postal services in Thailand are efficient, and domestic rates are cheap. Approximate times for airmail to arrive are five to seven days for Europe, seven to 10 days for Australia, Canada, New Zealand and the United States.

Large parcels (maximum weight 33 pounds) should be sent by surface mail; this takes 10–12 weeks. Main post offices sell boxes in different sizes and bubble-wrap; some of the largest offices (including Bangkok and Chiang Mai) offer a parcel-wrapping service.

Bangkok Central Post Office is at Charoen Krung (New) Road. It is open Monday to Friday, 8–4:30; weekends and holidays, 9–1. Telephone and telegram services are open 24 hours.

Post offices outside Bangkok are open Monday to Friday, 8:30–4:30; major ones are open 9–1 on Saturdays.

Nearly all of the post offices offer a general delivery service (1 baht per item), by which the mail can be sent to a given post office and then held until th addresse comes to claim it; such mail should be labeled "Poste Restante," and the last name of the address should be underlined

Additionally, many hotels and guest houses are happy to keep mail for guests; in Bangkok particularly, many guest houses have boards with letters for guests attached to them (often with six-month-old postmarks!).

Main post offices, large hotels and some street bureaus have fax facilities. Stamps are sold at some hotels and at many news stands. Aerograms (fixed price anywhere in the world) and postcards are a few baht cheaper to send than airmail letters.

Public transportation

See also pages 48–49 and 114–115. Thailand is well served with a dense network of inexpensive public and semipublic transportation. Some is quite luxurious; much is crowded and uncomfortable. Some forms of travel will leave you aching, hot or cold, while others will entertain with scenery, snacks and sheer downright eccentricity; all of it is part of the experience.

The language barrier can be frustrating (attempts at pronouncing place names often encounter blank looks), but generally bus and songthaew drivers and conductors are helpful about making sure that foreigners alight at their intended destinations.

Embarrassingly, in crowded buses Thais (sometimes elderly ones) may give up their seat for you.

Internal flights If time is short, consider flights as a method of seeing more; it only takes an hour from Bangkok to Phuket or Chiang Mai (compared to a full day or night by bus or train).

Thai Airways flies to Chiang Mai, Chiang Rai, Lampang, Mae Hong Son, Mae Sot, Nan, Phitsanulok, Phrae and Tak in the north; Khon Kaen, Loei, Nakhon Ratchasima, Sakhon Nakhon, Ubon Ratchathani and Udon Thani in the northeast; and Hat Yai, Ko Samui, Nakhon Si Thammarat, Narathiwat, Pattani, Phuket, Suratthani and Trang in the south.

Reserve seats well in advance if you are flying from Bangkok, through Thai Airways (tel: 02/513 0121).

Each of the destination towns has a Thai Airways office where advance bookings can be made.

Train While the railroad network does not serve every corner of Thailand and services are less frequent than buses, for views from the window and for general comfort, the train wins easily over the bus as a means of travel.

There are three classes, from first-class air-conditioned two-berth compartments to second-class air-conditioned reclining seats, to third-class padded bench seats (wooden-slat variety on ordinary trains may need improvised padding).

Generally, unbooked third class is adequate for short journeys, while the other two classes may give a bit more room; first class is about twice as expensive as second, and four and a half times more than third. Sleeping berths on overnight journeys must be reserved in advance (even the berthless carriages get packed on the Bangkok–Chiang Mai and Bangkok–Singapore lines).

The sleeping berths on second class are excellent (berths are arranged so that you sleep in the same direction as the rails, and not across them). On longer journeys there is a restaurant service, with the menu and food brought to your seat.

For long journeys out of Bangkok, it is usually necessary to book several days in advance as trains are often very full, especially on the Bangkok–Chiang Mai and Malaysia routes. Reservations can be made through travel agents or booking counters at most major stations. For Bangkok (Hualamphong) station, tel: 02/223 7010/20.

Holders of international passports can purchase 20-day passes giving freedom of second- and third-class train travel throughout Thailand. The cost is 1,500 baht for a Blue Pass, while the Red Pass covers extra charges (including for Express Train, air-conditioning and sleeping berths) and costs 3,000 baht.

Buses Thailand's excellent bus network fans out from Bangkok, connecting with virtually every town. Services are cheap and frequent; air-conditioned buses are more expensive but less crowded. Tickets are on sale at bus stations or on the bus and can be bought just before traveling, or sometimes in advance.

On long routes the bus stops for toilets and refreshments, and vendors often come on board offering snacks and drinks.

Few buses show where they are going in Western lettering, but farangs always get plenty of assistance. The major **bus stations** for Bangkok are Taladmochit, Paholyothin Road (for journeys north and northeast); Ekamai, Sukhumvit Road (east), and Sai tai, Nakhon Chaisri Road, straight on from the Pin Klao bridge (south).

Private bus operators abound and are a popular budget method of long-distance travel; numerous agencies, particularly in Khao San Road in Bangkok, advertize these.

Driving standards on buses are not that good, and the fact that private companies often race against one another doesn't help. One lasting memory of Thailand will be looking in the driver's mirror and spotting his reflected glance—five seconds on the road alternating with five looking at the video suspended above the garland of everlasting flowers that decorates the window.

Private overnight buses organized for foreign visitors can be a grim experience as the driver turns out the reading lights just as the journey begins ("power failure") and a Thai

271

voice blares out for most of the night, entertaining the driver but no one else.

There have been hair-raising tales of thefts on one or two of these buses where the passengers were given doped Cokes as they boarded and then woke to find everything gone.

Government-operated buses on shorter intercity routes generally run between 6 AM and 6 PM daily. Long-distance VIP and 999 buses are pricier than ordinary ones but are quite comfortable, with reclining seats and reasonable legroom.

Minibuses Known as *songthaews* (literally "two rows"), these are covered trucks or vans with two long, hard benches at the back. They fill up to capacity with passengers squashed together, hanging onto the back and standing on the running board. You seldom see anything apart from other passengers' limbs and shopping baskets, but the songthaew is often the only way of reaching your destination.

Fares are fixed, strictly no haggling, and very cheap. The destination is not advertized, but usually the driver and conductor are shouting it out and will usher you aboard.

Taxis Plentiful in supply, and most now have meters (look for the "taxi-meter" sign on the roof). Drivers seldom speak much English and may not understand your attempts at Thai (or at English) pronunciation. It is useful to have your destination written down in Thai. Air-conditioned taxis are usually 10 baht or so more than ordinary ones.

❏ As taxi drivers seldom speak fluent English, ask your hotel to write your destination in Thai and suggest the fare. ❏

Tuk tuks The less luxurious version of the taxi, also known as pedicabs or motorized *samlors*, these are covered, open-sided two-passenger chariots built around a scooter and unmistakable for their "*tuk tuk*" noise. They are not particularly safe but cheaper than taxis for short distances, and you have to try a ride as part of the Thailand experience. Bargain hard before traveling; short trips are generally in the 30–50 baht range, although there is talk of making fares standardized.

Bicycle *samlors* The unmotorized version of the *tuk tuk* is seen in many provincial towns. Again, agree on the fare in advance; 30 baht is the rule.

Long-tailed boats Besides the service along the Bangkok canals west of Thonburi, there is a new service that runs from Wat Saket to Bangkapi along Klong Saen Saep. Be prepared for a ride in an open sewer, although the trip takes just half an hour as opposed to the two hours by road. Get off at Ekamai and get a 72 bus down Soi Ekamai for the Eastern Bus Station. Reach the Southern Bus Station by long-tail from Tha Chang.

Sports
See also pages 110–113.
Scuba diving and swimming With so many idyllic beaches to choose from, it is no surprise that Thailand has come to the fore as a major destination for sand-and-sea vacations. Scuba-diving boat trips are widely available in places such as Ko Samui, Chumpon province, Pattaya, Krabi province and Phuket. The spectacular array of marine life makes the experience unforgettable. Numerous places rent out snorkels,

❏ Corals grow in profusion but are endangered because of the numbers of tourists who break off souvenir chunks. Do not follow suit—the coral never looks as pretty back home after it has dried out. ❏

masks (often not large enough for the largest farang heads) and flippers, but you can save yourself quite a few baht by bringing your own equipment.

Golf fees are 400–2,500 baht; caddies, usually women, charge 150–300 baht; club rental is 200–450 baht. There are several courses in and around Bangkok, including the popular **Navatanee Golf Course** (tel: 02/374 1034), designed for the 1975 World Cup Tournament, and the **Railway Training Center Course** (tel: 02/271 0130). Courses are also found at Hua Hin, Lanna near Chiang Mai, Phuket, Sattahip near Pattaya and Tong Yai in Songkhla.

❏ A free booklet from the Tourist Authority of Thailand gives details of over 20 golf courses, with reservation information. ❏

Spectator sports Thailand's national sport is Muay Thai (Thai boxing). Also popular are kite fighting, sword fighting and tagraw (see pages 110–113).

Less exotic but also popular are soccer and horse racing. Racing takes place every Sunday from 12:15 PM and alternates between the Royal Bangkok Sports Club, Henri Dunant Road, and the Royal Bangkok Turf Club, Phitsanulok Road.

Telephones
Local calls can be made from any telephone and cost 1 baht minimum; only small 1-baht coins are accepted. Long-distance domestic calls can be made from blue telephone booths, hotels and post offices, or through the operator (dial 101) on older telephones.

While it is generally a straight-forward process to make long-distance calls from Bangkok, smaller places up-country may require a visit to the local post office, where you may have to wait in a line.

Credit-card pay phones do not exist in Thailand; green phonecards (100 baht) can be used in green phone booths.

International calls can be made from some hotels (often with substantial surcharges) and guest houses, from major post offices and from private telephone offices. Hotels with International Direct Dialing telephones often charge 20 percent or more for the service. The International dialing code is 001, followed by the number of the country. The U.S. country code is 1.

Omit the 0 prefix for the city code after dialing the country code. Alternatively, go via the operator (dial 13 in order to get an English-speaking operator service).

Local codes Bangkok 02, Chiang Mai 053, Pattaya 038, Phuket 076. If you need directory assistance, dial 13.

Time
At noon in Thailand it is 3 PM in Sydney, Australia; 5 PM in New Zealand; 5 AM in the United Kingdom and Ireland (6 AM, BST); 9 PM the previous day in Los Angeles, and midnight the previous day in New York.

Tipping
Taxi drivers are never tipped, and tipping is rare in restaurants, although

10 percent is usually appreciated in upmarket places if there is no service charge. For hairdressers and masseurs, 20 baht is fine; 10 baht for porters.

Toilets

The classier hotels have conventional toilets, but if you are intending to stay in guest houses, you will doubtless encounter Thai-style toilets, which involve squatting over a floor-level basin. Initially it seems a feat of both careful balancing and aiming, but as no part of the body is in contact with the basin (in theory), it is quite hygienic.

A hose with spray attachment may be provided for cleaning your nether portions afterward; the water pressure can be ferocious and mildly alarming the first time around. For those who prefer to use toilet paper (which is commonly available), wastebaskets are usually provided as the discarded pieces often block the pipes.

Public restrooms are rare, but most restaurants do not object to noncustomers using their facilities. Simply ask for the *horng nahm*.

Tourist offices

The Tourism Authority of Thailand (TAT) has offices across Thailand; on the whole these are a fairly useful source of local information and free handouts, although even here there is often a frustrating language barrier. TAT offices do not provide a booking service.

TAT offices in Thailand

Bangkok	(Head Office) 372 Bamrung Muang Road (tel: 02/226 0060).
Cha-am	500/51 Phetkasem Road (tel: 032/471005).
Chiang Mai	105/1 Chiang Mai–Lamphun Road (tel: 053/248604).
Chiang Rai	Singklai Road (tel: 053/717433).
Hat Yai	1/1 Soi 2 Niphat Uthit 3 Road, Hat Yai (tel: 074/243747).
Kanchana Buri	Saeng Chuto Road (tel: 034/511200).
Khon Kaen	15/5 Prachasamosop Road (tel: 043/24498).
Nakhon Panom	184 Sootomvijit Road (tel: 042/513490).
Nakhon Ratchasima	2102–2104 Mittraphap Road (tel: 044/213666).
Nakhon Si Thammarat	Sanum Na Muang, Ratchadamnoen Road (tel: 075/346515).
Pattaya	382/1 Mu 10 Chaihat Road, Pattaya City.
Phitsanulok	209/7–8 Surasi Trade Center, Boromtrailokanat Road (tel: 055/252742).
Phuket	73–5 Phuket Road (tel: 076/212213).
Rayong	153/4 Sukhumvit Road; Amphoe Muang, Rayong 21000 (tel: 038/655420).
Suratthani	5 Talat Mai Road, Ban Don (tel: 077/288818).
Ubon Ratchathani	264/1 Khuan Thani Road (tel: 045/243770).

TAT Overseas

Australia	Level 2, National Australia Bank House, 255 George Street, Sydney 2000 (tel: 02/247 7549).
United Kingdom	49 Albemarle Street, London W1X 3FE (tel: (0171) 499 7679).
United States	5 World Trade Center, Suite 3443, New York, NY 10048 (tel: 212/432 0433); 3440 Wilshire Boulevard, Suite 1100, Los Angeles, CA 90010 (tel: 213/382 2353); 303 East Wacker Drive, Suite 400, Chicago, IL 60601 (tel: 312/819 3990).

There are also offices in Australia, France, Germany, Hong Kong, Italy, Japan, Malaysia, South Korea, Singapore, Taiwan and the U.K., but not in Canada, Ireland or New Zealand.

Walking and hiking

If you want to see Thailand on foot, the obvious way is to take an organized trek.

There are trails in national parks, two described in this book, but the nationwide spread of purpose-made walks is rather thin, and the central plain is too monotonous for worthwhile hiking anyway.

The dangers of getting lost in remote areas are very real, and foreign visitors have been attacked in borderlands. Those who plan to do some hiking should take some light boots with ankle support, plenty of water and spare food; be prepared for mosquitoes, leeches and heat exhaustion.

Treks to hill-tribe villages Treks are big business in the north; street bureaus, hotels and guest houses offer packages lasting between two and seven days, where you stay in tribal village homes and trek in the hills on foot, by elephant and by bamboo raft. At best this can offer

exhilarating views and a glimpse into subsistence cultures. However, a poorly run trek, passing zoolike commercialized villages and going through unvarying scenery, can be an expensive disappointment.

Hints

- Recommendation from other travelers is usually the best way to choose your trek. Check exactly what is included (food, first-aid, transportation, itinerary) and what the trek is like.

- Don't necessarily restrict yourself to treks from Chiang Mai; less-frequented places (Mae Hong Son, Chiang Rai, Pai, Mae Sot and Nan among them) may be better.

- Try to meet the other members of your party before you go. Four to eight is a good group size.

- Leave valuables behind (except your credit cards); take only a little cash (but itemize anything you leave in a guest house).

- Walking can be tough work in the hills, elephant rides are uncomfortable and rafts often capsize.

- Travel light; take a backpack, sleeping bag, sweater, washing kit, towel and swimsuit, and rainwear between June and October.

- Ask before taking photos of tribespeople.

- Carry mosquito repellent and take clothes to cover your arms and legs; a mixture of tobacco and water makes a good leech repellent.

HOTELS AND RESTAURANTS

ACCOMMODATIONS

Thailand offers a huge range of accommodations, varying greatly in price. The smartest international hotels in Bangkok or Phuket charge as much as anywhere in the West, whereas at the cheaper end of the market, you can find simple double rooms for unimaginably little money. There is rarely a problem finding a room, except at certain vacation periods. *Tuk tuk* and *samlor* drivers get commissions from guest houses when they bring them and will ask virtually every luggage-bearing *farang* if they need somewhere to stay. Even in nontourist towns there is usually a cheap hotel (not always with an English sign).

Although room rates are fixed in high season, you can get generous discounts on higher-priced accommodations off-season. Local festivals, conferences, etc. may cause a sudden unexpected dearth of bed-space and sharp tariff increases.

Within any one hotel, room rates may vary very widely according to the standard of facilities available. Air-conditioning, or a private bathroom with hot water, will inevitably add to the bill. As a rough guide, price categories in the following listings denote prices for a standard double room:

Budget Up to 500B. Hotels and guesthouses marked with an asterisk (*) fall into the supercheap category, with rooms for two for 300B or less.
Moderate 500–1,500B.
Expensive Over 1,500B.

Luxury
Top hotels are every bit as luxurious as their Western counterparts, and prices are nearly as high. In major cities and tourist areas, the upmarket hotel scene has boomed in recent years. Nearly all the better hotels are modern, typically with marble foyers like airport lounges and comfortable (though not memorably interesting) air-conditioned rooms with private bathrooms. Many have swimming pools, restaurants, laundry service, currency exchange, international telephone and tour desk, and some have business centers. Bangkok's Oriental and the Hotel Sofitel Central in Hua Hin are among the few quality old-style hotels.

At weekends, many rich Thais stay in and party at "resort hotels"— bungalow developments in quiet country areas. Many such establishments pride themselves on their gardening skills: waist-high orchids border immaculate lawns dotted with old-style buffalo carts (every resort must have at least one of these). These places can be wonderfully relaxing, and good for meeting Thais.

Budget
At the budget end of the scale two can stay for under 100 baht per night. Don't expect clean sheets (usually only an under-sheet is provided), and it is wise to take a sheet, pillowcase, bath plug, toilet paper, soap and towels. Showers dispense cold water only, except in the far north.

Most places are noisy—crowing roosters, traffic, music and howling dogs keep all but the deepest sleeper awake; earplugs are invaluable.

Cheap accommodations are either hotels, often bland concrete blocks (many double as brothels) and guest houses. Many of the most basic hotels are depressing; the advantages are private bathrooms (a cold shower and toilet) and a bed (as opposed to a mattress on the floor).

Guest houses
These vary much more in style; many are private Thai homes adapted for the purpose, while some in country areas are thatched bamboo bungalows. Nearly all offer meals, with an English menu. Beds are hard; you may sleep on a thin mattress on the floor.

Guest houses are excellent for meeting other travelers (Thais rarely stay in such places), and often have local tourist information; many offer tours and treks (in Chiang Mai, trekking is a hard-sell business; guests who don't want to go on a trek are often told to leave).

Eating out
This is an essential part of the national lifestyle. Accordingly, food is served on virtually every street corner and prices are low. The Thais are fastidious about food preparation and generally you don't have to be concerned about your stomach.

Run-of-the-mill restaurants tend not to dress themselves up; plastic tables are the norm, and with a lot of places you will find yourself sitting outside. Look for the places which the locals patronize; some will have an English menu, but it is wise to carry a phrasebook. If you get stuck, simply point to a dish someone else is eating and that you like the look of.

Menus are often very long, typically based on stir-fried rice concoctions (rice with chicken and ginger, sweet and sour pork with rice, fried morning glory with rice), seafood, soups and noodles. Sometimes you pay a little more for surroundings; floating restaurants are popular in many waterside towns.

Western food is offered in many tourist areas; prices are substantially higher than Thai food, and the quality will sometimes only tempt the very homesick traveler! But there are numerous places where you can eat as well as back home; many of these are included in these listings.

Upmarket eating establishments are plentiful in the main tourist centers; in smaller, less frequented towns the best are often to be found in the top hotels. Except in big centers, try to eat reasonably early; many establishments tend to close by 9 PM.

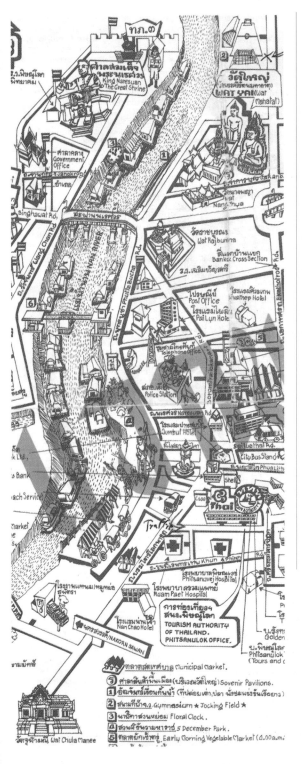

HOTELS AND RESTAURANTS

BANGKOK

Accommodations
Expensive
Amari Airport 333 Choet Wutthakat Road (tel:02/566 1020). Only decent hotel in airport area; short stays available.
Dusit Thani 946 Rama IV Road (tel: 02/236 0450). An elegant hotel overlooking Lumphini Park.
Evergreen Laurel 88 North Sathon Road (tel: 02/266 7223). Small, stylish "boutique" hotel with excellent personal service.
Grand Hyatt Erawan 494 Ratchadamri Road (tel: 02/254 1234). Large well-equipped hotel with a fine collection of modern Thai art.
Holiday Inn Crowne Plaza 981 Silom Road (tel: 02/238 4300). Comfortable, reasonably priced and near river.
Imperial 6 Witthayu Road (tel: 02/254 0023). Extensive grounds in embassy district.
Indra Regent 120/126 Ratchaprarop Road (tel: 02/208 0033).
Marriot Royal Garden Riverside 257/1–3 Charoen Nakhon Road (tel: 02/476 0022). Modern block with excellent pool and good location.
Montien 54 Surawong Road (tel: 02/234 8060). Quiet hotel near Patpong nightlife and market.
Oriental 48 Oriental Avenue (tel: 02/236 0400). An attraction in itself, the old wing carefully preserved.
Regent Bangkok 155 Ratchadamri Road (tel: 02/251 6127). Luxury hotel close to Siam Square.
Royal Orchid Sheraton 2 Captain Bush Lane, Si Phraya Road (tel: 02/266 0123). Restful waterfront luxury with crisp service and multiple restaurants. Shopping center adjacent.
Shangri-La 89 Soi Wat Suan Plu, Charoen Krung Road (tel: 02/236 7777). Superb hotel with riverside views.
Siam Intercontinental 967 Rama I Road (tel: 02/253 0355). Reasonably priced rooms overlooking a charming garden.
Sukhothai Bangkok 13/3 Sathon Tai Road (tel: 02/287 0222). Stylish post-modern interior with pool-filled courtyard and elegant restaurants.
Swissotel 3 Convent Road (tel: 02/233 5345). Small-scale sanctuary.

Moderate
Bangkok Christian 123 Soi Saladaeng, Convent Road (tel: 02/233 6303). Friendly set-up with pretty garden; near Lumphini Park.
Collins International House (YMCA) 27 Sathon Tai Road (tel: 02/287 1900). Remarkable value for the facilities offered, with good pool and friendly management.
Jim's Lodge 125/7 Soi Ruamrudi, Witthayu Road (tel: 02/255 3100). Luxury facilities at moderate prices. A well-known favorite.
Reno 40 Soi Kasemsan 1, Rama I Road (tel: 02/215 0026). Open 24 hours; pleasant swimming pool.

Royal 2 Ratchadamnoen Klang Road (tel: 02/222 9111–20). Famous old hotel, entrance on Sanam Luang.
SV 19/35–36 Soi 19 Sukhumvit Road (tel: 02/253 1747). Small, no extras, clean.
Vlangtal 42 Tani Road, Banglamphu (tel: 02/280 5392). Long-established, comfortable hotel with pool, close to central sights.

Budget
AA 84–86 Phra Sumen Road (tel: 02/282 9631). Large, efficient, hotel-like establishment in Banglamphu.
* Apple 10/1 Pra Athit Road (tel: 02/281 6838). Basic but relaxed atmosphere.
Atlanta 78 Soi 2, Sukhumvit Road (tel: 02/252 6069). Simple but clean and reliable hostelry of great character. European newspapers available in the coffee shop.
C & C 12 Wisuthkasat Road (tel: 02/282 4941). Clean rooms, friendly staff.
Merry V 33–35 Phra Athit Road (tel: 02/282 9267). Small but friendly. Behind the *wat* opposite the west end of Khao San Road.
My House 37 Phra Athit Road (tel: 02/282 9263). Basic but snug rooms with bamboo walls; next to Merry V (see above).
New Siam 21 Phra Athit Road (tel: 02/282 4554). Quiet and clean. Handy location for the river-bus.
Peachy 10 Phra Athit Road (tel: 02/281 6471). Convenient for the Express Boat pier at Tha Phra Athit.
Santi Lodge 37 Sri Ayutthaya Road (tel: 02/281 2497). Quiet, clean and attractive with a good vegetarian restaurant.
Villa Samsen 1 (tel: 02/281 7009). Old wooden house with a garden.

Restaurants
Expensive
Bourbon Street 29/4–6 Washington Square, Soi 22, Sukhumvit Road (tel: 02/259 0328/9). Jambalaya, crawfish pie and other Southern American specialities.
Bussaracum, 425 Soi Pipat 2, Silom (tel: 02/235 8915); 35 Soi Pipat 2, off Convent Road, Silom (tel: 02/235 8915). Top marks for content and presentation; traditional Thai food with traditional musical accompaniment.
Himali Cha Cha 1229/11 Charoen Krung Road (between Surawong and Silom roads) (tel: 02/235 1569). Very good Indian food; book in the evening.
Sorn Daeng Democracy Monument (tel: 02/224 3088). Old-established Thai eatery.
Whole Earth Vegetarian Restaurant 93 Lang Suan Road (off Rama I Road) (tel: 02/252 5574). Appealing if pricey. Meat dishes too.

Moderate
Ambassador Food Center Ambassador Hotel (tel: 02/254 0444). Self-service cornucopia of regional and foreign foods, with all the Thai favorites. Pay by coupon.
Cabbages and Condoms 8 Sukhumvit Soi 12 (tel: 02/299 4610). A local institution with excellent Thai food and planned parenthood fund-raising. Peaceful garden.

Lemon Grass 5/1 Sukhumvit Soi 24 (tel: 02/258 8637). Elegant Thai-style dining area with antiques and a garden.
Mrs Balbir's (Indian) 155/18 Sukhumvit Soi 11 (tel: 02/253 2281/255 4236). Good range, decor and prices.

Budget
Vijit 77/2 Ratchadamnoen Klang Road (tel: 02/281 6472). Traditional café-style Bangkok restaurant with excellent, unpretentious food.

CENTRAL THAILAND

AYUTTHAYA
Accommodations
Budget
U-Thong Inn 210 Mu 5, Rochana Road (tel: 035/242236). Quiet, clean, traditional hotel with good service.

HUA HIN
Accommodations
Expensive
Sofitel Central 1 Damnoen Kasem Road (tel: 032/512021). Old Railway Hotel now in restored splendor.

Moderate
Tananchai 11 Damrongrat Road (tel: 032/511755). Clean, friendly hotel at the quiet north end of town. Coffee lounge serves light meals all day.

KANCHANA BURI
Accommodations
Expensive
Felix Kanchanaburi Swissotel River Kwai 9/1 Mu 3, Tambon Thamakham (tel: 034/515061). Luxury resort newly built on the west side of the river. Abundant facilities in beautifully landscaped grounds, with the world's largest rock garden.

Moderate
Erawan Resort 140 Mu 4, Kanchana Buri–Erawan Road (tel: 034/589056). Handy for Erawan waterfalls.
Kasem Island Resort 27 Rambon Ban Tai (tel: 034/513359). Pretty, island site; thatched-hut resort; tours. Rather noisy at weekends.
River Kwai Cabin Amphoe Sai Yok (tel: 02/433 6688). Bungalows set on scenic river curve below historic train bridge.

Budget
Bamboo House 5 Vietnam Road (tel: 034/624470). Quiet, river views; near the Kwae Bridge.
Jolly Frog 28 Soi Chin, Mae Nam Kwae Road (tel: 034/514579). Set on the river.
***PS Guest House** 84/4 Soi Rongheeb-oiy 2, Mae Nam Kwae Road (tel: 034/513039). Out of the main noise zone; charming sitting room area situated above the river; tours.

***River Guesthouse** Soi Rongheeb-oiy 2, Mae Nam Kwae Road (tel: 034/512491). Rafthouses built on the Kwae; tours.

KHAO YAI
Accommodations
Expensive
Juldis Khao Yai Resort 45 Mu 4, Thanarat Road, Amphoe Pakchong (phone for reservations: 02/255 1712–4). One of several up-market resort hotels outside Khao Yai.

KO SAMET
Accommodations
Budget
Naga Bungalow 36 Mu 4, Phe, Muang Rayong (tel: 01/353 2575). Pleasant layout; amenities include a lending library.
Sea Breeze Bungalow, 23 Mu 4, Amphoe Muang Rayong (tel: 01/239 4780). Self-contained units available.

LOP BURI
Accommodations
Budget
Asia 1/7–8 Sorasak Road (tel: 036/411892). Standard but very clean; located opposite palace gate.
***Nett** 17/1–2 Ratchadamnoen Road (tel: 036/411738). Behind the Asia; has slightly smaller rooms.

279

PHETCHA BURI
Accommodations
Budget
Khao Wang 174/1–3 Ratwithi Road (tel: 032/425167). Good value, simple and straightforward accommodation.
Phetkasem 86/1 Phetkasem Road (tel: 032/425581). Clean and basic; good value.

SI RACHA
Accommodations
Budget
Benz Bungalow Mu 3, Tambon Tha Taewa Wong, Ko Sichang (tel: 038/216091). Sea view from private bungalows.
Thiw Phai Guesthouse Tha Thewawong (tel: 038/216084). Big price range, helpful owner, late-night café.

TRAT
Accommodations
Budget/Moderate
Thai Rungroj 45 Sukhumvit Road (tel: 039/511141). Clean; has air-conditioned rooms.

NORTHERN THAILAND

CHIANG MAI
Accommodations
Expensive
Amari Rincome 301 Huai Kaeo Road (tel: 053/221044). Fine luxury hotel; antiques and tasteful decor.

HOTELS AND RESTAURANTS

Chiang Inn 100 Changklan Road (tel: 053/270070). Comfortable hotel near night market.

Chiang Mai Orchid 100–2 Huai Kaeo Road (tel: 053/ 222099). Celebrated, exclusive and priced accordingly.

Chiang Mai Plaza 92 Sri Donchai Road (tel: 053/270036). Roomy, well-sited; swimming pool, good restaurant; shopping mall.

Mae Ping 153 Sri Donchai Road (tel: 053/270160). Tower block near night bazaar. Has tour desk and many other services; attractively designed.

Rim Ping Garden 411 Charoen Prathet Road (tel: 053/281060). On the river; landscaped garden setting, pavilion-style.

River Ping Palace 385/2 Charoen Prathet Road (tel: 053/274932). Delightful Thai-style buildings in riverside gardens south of town center. Lovely restaurant.

River View Lodge 25 Charoen Prathet Road Soi 2 (tel: 053/271110). Family-run; simple rooms.

Royal Princess 112 Chang Khlan Road (tel: 053/281033). Stylish, light interior; swimming pool, restaurants.

Suriwongse Zenith 110 Chang Khlan Road (tel: 053/270051). Recently renovated, centrally located hotel with cheerful decor and modern conveniences.

Moderate

Erawan Resort (on Highway 1096) 30 Mu 2, Tambon Pongyang (tel: 053/251191–4). Popular hill resort with pretty grounds.

Gab's House 3 Ratchadamnoen Road Soi 4 tel: 053/278140). "Antique house" in a garden haven; traditional teak-built rooms.

Galare 7/1 Charoen Prathet Road (tel: 053/249088). On the river; excellent value and central location.

Kangsadarn Resort (on Highway 1096), Km 18.5, Mae Rim–Samerng Road (tel: 053/232551). Hillside bungalows overlooking waterfall.

Lai Thai 111/4–5 Kotchasarn Road (tel: 053/ 251725). Cheerful if plain; main-road site.

Mae Sa Valley (on Highway 1096) PO Box 5, Mae Rim (tel: 053/297980). Charming bungalows in a hillside resort.

Suan Doi 38/3 Soi Charntrasup, Huai Kaeo Road (opposite Rincome Hotel) (tel: 053/221869). Amid quiet, intimate gardens.

Top North Center 42 Mun Muang Road (tel: 053/210531). Plain and quiet, with a pool.

Budget

Chiang Mai Souvenir 118 Charoen Prathet Road (tel: 053/232355). Private house in peaceful leafy garden.

***Je t'Aime** 247–9 Charoen Rat Road (tel: 053/241912). White houses surround a lawn shaded by palms and longan trees.

Laithai 111/4 Kotchasan Road (tel: 053/251689). Spruce, chalet-style guest house near city walls. Open-air restaurant and garden.

The River Front 43/3 Chang Khlan Road (tel: 053/275125). Antiques, river terrace; quiet location, south of center.

***Saitum** 21 Mun Muang Road (tel: 053/278575). Basic backpackers' bungalows, convenient site. No hard-sell treks!

Top North 15 Mun Muang Road Soi 2 (tel: 053/213900). At the quiet end of a street of bars. Good-value, air-conditioned rooms.

Restaurants
Expensive

Jasmine Royal Princess Hotel, 112 Chang Khlan Road (tel: 053/281033). Leading Chinese restaurant with good *dim sum*.

Le Coq d'Or 68/1 Koh Klang Road, Nong Hoi (tel: 053/282024). Fine continental cuisine; just south of town.

Le Grillade Chiang Inn, 100 Chang Khlan Road (tel: 053/270070). Top French cuisine, top service.

Le Pavillon Chiang Mai Orchid Hotel, 100–102 Huai Kaeo Road (tel: 053/222099). The quality and prices one expects from the city's classiest hotel.

Moderate

Antique House 71 Charoen Prathet Road (tel: 052/276810). Restored 19th-century teak mansion full of antiques and curios. Extensive varied menu.

Ban Suan 51/3 San Kamphaeng Road (tel: 053/242116). Authentic Thai food in a teak house just out of town.

Diamond Hotel 33/10 Charoen Prathet Road (tel: 053/270080). *Khantoke* dinners in an antique hall.

Galae 65 Suthep Road (tel: 053/222235). Nicely set by a lake at the foot of Doi Suthep.

The Gallery 25–29 Charoen Rat Road (tel: 053/248601). Well-prepared Thai food; riverside venue.

Old Chiang Mai Cultural Center 185/3 Wualai Road (tel: 053/275097). Leading *khantoke* dinner venue, popular with tour parties.

Once Upon A Time River Ping Palace, 385/2 Charoen Prathet Road, near Mengrai Bridge (tel: 053/274932). Beautifully restored old houses, period decor, *khantoke* dinners.

Riverside 43/3 Mu 2 Chang Khlan Road (tel: 053/275125). Candlelit ambience by the waterfront in a beautifully decorated teak pavilion.

Whole Earth 88 Sri Donchai Road (tel: 053/282463). Lanna-style house; Thai vegetarian, Indian and Pakistani meals.

Budget

Aroon Rai 45 Kotchasan Road (tel: 053/276947). Plain but good; North Thai cuisine.

JJ Bakery and Coffee Shop Montri Hotel, 2–6 Ratchadamnoen Road (tel: 053/211069). Bright, fast-service, wholly Westernised.

Ta Krite 17–19 Sam Lan Road (tel: 053/278333). Celebrated Thai food; a favorite with locals.

Vegetarian Food 65 Mun Muang Road (tel: 053/278315). Run by an Indian sect; threadbare decor, but appetising food.

CHIANG RAI
Accommodations
Expensive
Dusit Island 1129 Kraisorasit Road (tel: 053/715777). Island site; great views, top prices.
Wangcome 869/90 Pemawiphata Road (tel: 053/711800). A safe bet, in the town center.
Wiang Inn 893 Phahonyothin Road (tel: 053/711533). Modern block; spacious and popular.

Moderate
Saenphu 390 Banphaprakam Road (tel: 053/717300). Good value modern comfort.

Budget
Boonbundan 1005/13 Jedyod Road (tel: 053/717040). Spotless, modern, quiet yet central.
Chiang Saen Chiang Saen–Sop Ruak Road (no tel). Odd but comfortable "wigwam" huts, clean bathrooms.
***Mae Hong Son** 126 Singhakai Road, Chiang Rai (no tel). Characterful but very basic.
Mae Kok Villa 445 Singhakhai Road (tel: 053/711786). Cheap and well-equipped bungalows.

Restaurants
Expensive
Chiang Mai Island Dusit Island Resort, 1129 Kraisorasit Road (tel: 053/715777). Attractive, pavilion-style restaurant serving excellent Thai cuisine.

Moderate
Haw Naliga 402/1–2 Banphaprakam Road (tel: 053/711062). Popular restaurant near the clocktower, with a varied Thai menu.

LAMPANG
Accommodations
Moderate
Asia Lampang 229 Boonyawat Road (tel: 054/227844). Competent if unspectacular.
Lampang River Lodge 330 Mu 11, Tambon Chompu (tel: 054/217054). Individual Thai-style stilt bungalows on banks of the Wang.

Budget
***No. 4 Guesthouse** 54 Pamai Road, Vieng Nuea (no tel). Old-style house with polished teak floors. One of an excellent chain of No 4. Guesthouses in the north.

Restaurants
Budget
Riverside (Rim Wang) 328 Thipchang Road (tel: 054/221861). Fair menu, live country music; on the river.

MAE HONG SON
Accommodations
Expensive
Holiday Inn 114/5–7 Khunlumprapas Road (tel: 053/611390). Comfortable, imposing block just outside town. International cuisine.

Tara Mae Hong Son 149 Mu 8, Tambon Pang Moo (tel: 053/611473, 611272). Located in a teak forest.

Moderate
Mae Hong Son Resort 24 Ban Huai Dua (tel: 053/611406). Secluded resort 4 miles from town. Shuttle to airport.

Budget
***Cave Lodge** Ban Tham, near Tham Lot, (radio tel: 536 11711, ext 822). Finely sited by Tham Lot cave; day treks and cave visits.
***Holiday House** 23 Pradit Jongkham Road (no tel). Plain; nicely sited by Jongkham Lake.
***Jungle Guesthouse** Soppong (no tel). Pretty, if basic, huts above a stream.
Kemarin Garden Lodge Soppong (no tel). Peaceful bungalows on outskirts of center on Pai road.
Maelana Guesthouse Maelana village, off a T-junction halfway along the Mae Hong Son–Pai road (no tel). Very basic, a must for the adventurous.
***Pai River Lodge** off Ratchdamrong Road, Pai (no tel). Riverside location southeast of the bus stop.
***Wilderness Lodge** west of Soppong, 1 mile off main road, at Ban Nam Khong (no tel). Simple paradise for the adventurer.

Restaurants
Moderate
Fern 87 Khunlumprapas Road (tel: 053/611374). Mellow, cane decor, softly lit; very reasonable prices. Thai.

Budget
Inthira 170/1 Mu 2, Wiang Mai Road, Mae Sariang (tel: 053/681529). Popular, cheap; above-average food.
Khai Muk 23 Udom Chaonithet Road (tel: 053/612092). Open-air pavilion restaurant serving excellent Sino-Thai fare. Young, lively staff. Popular with travelers and locals.
Thai Yai 12 Rungsiyanon Road, Pai (tel: 053/699093). *Farang*-oriented café; good wholemeal bread.

MAE SAI
Accommodations
Expensive
Delta Golden Triangle Resort 222 Mu 1, Golden Triangle, Chiang Saen (tel: 053/777001–4). Scenically poised high-rise block at the meeting point of three countries.

Budget
***Ban Tammila** Tambon Wiang, Chiang Khong (tel: 053/791234). Thatched bungalows in tiny garden by the Mekong River.
***Mae Sai Guesthouse** 688 Tambon Wiengpangkam (tel: 053/732021). Wonderful river site looking into Burma.
***Northern Guesthouse** 402 Tumphajom Road (tel: 053/731537). Pleasant riverside bungalows.

HOTELS AND RESTAURANTS

Ruenthai Sopaparn 83 Mu 3, Tambon Wiang (tel: 053/791023). Perched above the Mekong River; carved wood veranda.

Restaurants
Moderate
Rabieng Kaew 256/1 Phahonyothin Road (tel: 053/731172). Lanna-style wooden house serving excellent Northern Thai specialties.

Budget
JoJo 233 Phahonyothin Road (no tel). Popular coffee shop serving visitors with Western breakfasts and great ice-creams; also offers Thai and vegetarian dishes.

MAE SOT
Accommodations
Expensive
Mae Sot Hill 100 Asia Highway (tel: 055/532601). Just out of town; pool; travel center adjacent.

Moderate
Porn Thep 25/4 Prasat Withi Road (tel: 055/532590). Impersonal but adequate hotel near market.

Budget
*No. 4 Guesthouse 736 Indharakiri Road (no tel). Clean teak house ½ mile from town centre.
Um Phang Hill Resort Um Phang (tel: 055/561063). Attractive chalet-style accommodations in lovely waterside setting.

Restaurant
Budget
Pim Hut 415/17 Tangkimchiang Road (tel: 055/532818). Everything from fried frogs to fries and burgers, in a pleasant outdoor setting.

NAN
Accommodations
Moderate
Thewarat 466 Sumon Thewarat Road (tel: 054/710094). The best in town; central.

Budget
*Nan Guesthouse 57/16 Mahaphrom Road (tel: 054/771849). Basic but friendly; good local information.

Restaurant
Budget
Da Dario 37/4 Rajamnuay Road, Ban Pra Kerd (tel: 054/750258). Authentic Italian fare prepared by a Swiss-Italian chef.
Tiptop 2 349/7 Sumon Thewarat Road (no tel). A mix of Thai and Italian fare, once run by the owner of Da Dario (above). Immensely popular with homesick *farangs*.

PHITSANULOK
Accommodations
Expensive
Pailyn 38 Baromatrailokanart Road (tel: 055/252411). Roomy suites and the best views in town.

Moderate
Thep Nakorn 43/1 Sri Thamtripidok Road (tel: 055/244070). Good value, standard hotel.

Budget
*Youth Hosteling International 38 Sanam Bin Road; 15–20 minutes' walk from center (tel: 055/242060). Antique beds and creaky charm; no evening meals.

PHRAE
Accommodations
Expensive
Mae Yom Palace 181/6 Yantarakikoson Road (tel: 054/522904). Pleasant six-story block opposite bus station.

SI SATCHANALAI
Accommodations
Moderate
Wang Yom 78/2 Mu 6, off route 101 to Sawankhalok (tel: 055/611179). Peaceful gardens with rustic bungalows by old city. Simple facilities, but good restaurants in a lovely garden.

SUKHOTHAI
Accommodations
Expensive
Pailyn 10 Mu 1 Jarodvithithong Road (tel: 055/613310). Hexagonal courtyard around a pool; handy for the old city.

Moderate
Ratchathani 229 Jarodvithithong Road (tel 055/611031). Convenient, well located; dining room, coffee shop.

Budget
*No. 4 Guesthouse 170 Ratchathani Road (tel: 055/611315). Prettiest riverside teak house, one of three similar "No. 4 Guesthouses" in town.
River View 92 Nikhonkasem Road (tel: 055/611656). Good river views; fan and air-conditioning.
*Somprasong Guesthouse 32 Pravetnakoly Road (tel: 055/611709). Modern block by river; free bicycles.

Restaurant
Moderate
Dream Café 86/1 Singhawat Road (tel: 055/612081). Antique-laden fantasy interior. Western and Thai food.

NORTHEAST THAILAND

KHON KAEN
Accommodations
Moderate
Kaen Inn 56 Klang Muang Road (tel: 043/237744). A comfortable base.
Muang Inn 41/1–6 Na-Muang Road (tel: 043/238667). A small, recently opened hotel with neat, air-conditioned rooms.

Budget
Suksawad 2/2 Klang Muang Road (tel: 043/236472). Quiet.

LOEI
Accommodations
Moderate
Kings 11/9–12 Chumsai Road (tel: 042/811701, 811783). Best in town.

Budget
Thai Udom 122/1 Charoen Rat Road (tel: 042/811763). Reasonable comfort, central location.

Restaurant
Budget
Savita Bakery 137–9 Charoen Rat Road (tel: 042/ 811526). Pastries, ice cream and simple Thai and Western dishes with good coffee.

MUKDAHAN
Accommodations
Budget
***Huanom** 36 Samut Sakdarak Road (tel: 042/ 611137). Clean; shared bathroom.

NAKHON RATCHASIMA (Khorat)
Accommodations
Moderate
Anachak Hotel 62/1 Chomsurangyart Road (tel: 044/243825). Good service.

Budget
Doctor's Guest House 78 Soi 4, Sueb Siri (tel: 044/255846). Small-scale, with friendly owners and copious local information.

Restaurant
Budget
Veterans of Foreign Wars Café Pho Klang Road (tel: 044/256522). Set up by expatriate G.I.s, this relaxing place offers travelers a venue to eat and meet.

NONG KHAI
Accommodations
Budget
Poonsub 843 Mechai Road (tel: 042/411031). Oldest hotel in town; average Chinese fare.
Sawasdi Guesthouse 402 Mechai Road (tel: 042/412502). Friendly, old Isan house; some air-conditioned rooms.

Restaurant
Budget
Thai Thai Phochana 257/1 Bantherngjit Road (tel: 042/420373). Authentic and cheap Thai and Chinese food.

PHIMAI
Accommodations
Budget
Old Phimai Guesthouse Mu 1, Chomsudasapet Road, (tel: 044/471725). Charming old house, handy for the Khmer sanctuary.

Restaurants
Moderate
Sai Ngam 1 mile northeast of town (no tel). Garden restaurant in the shade of the great banyan tree. Popular with day-trippers.

SURIN
Accommodations
Budget
***Phirom's Guesthouse** 242 Krung Sri Nai Road (tel: 044/ 515140). Friendly owner; tours (see page 209).

Restaurant
Moderate
Country Roads 165/1 Sirirat Road (tel: 044/515721). Engagingly relaxed, open-air bar-restaurant. Music and movies.

UBON RATCHATHANI
Accommodations
Moderate/Expensive
Pathumrat 337 Chayangkun Road (tel: 045/ 241501). On north side of town; best of the bunch locally.

UDON THANI
Accommodations
Expensive
Charoen 549 Phosri Road (tel: 042/248155). Fair luxury; useful base for visiting Ban Chiang (itself devoid of hotels).

283

SOUTHERN THAILAND

CHUMPHON
Accommodations
Moderate
Chumphon Cabana Thung Wua Laen Beach, Saphil (tel: 077/501990; reservations 02/224 1884). Deserted beach, boat tours, diving.
Jansom Chumphon 188/65–66 Sala Daeng Road (tel: 077/502502). Excellent service; comfortable.

Budget
Si Tai Fa Hotel 73–4 Sala Daeng Road (tel: 077/511063). Clean; view of green gardens.

HAT YAI
Accommodations
Budget
Cathay 99/1 Niphat Uthit Road (near railroad station; tel: 074/235044). Guesthouse atmosphere.
Lada 13–15 Thammanun Within Road (tel: 074/220233). Good value, air-conditioned rooms; near railroad station.

KO PHI PHI
Accommodations
Expensive
Phi Phi Island Cabana 201/3–4 Uttrakit Road (tel: 075/612132). The smartest place on the island, with a good (if pricey) restaurant.

HOTELS AND RESTAURANTS

KO SAMUI
Accommodations
Expensive
Chaweng Blue Lagoon Chaweng Beach (tel: 077/422037). Traditional style buildings on quiet beach.
Samui Yacht Club Ao Thong Takian (tel: 077/422400). Charming bay; roomy bungalows.

Moderate
Island Resort 162 Mu 2, Chaweng Beach (tel: 077/230941). Simple rooms as well as air-conditioned luxury; private bathrooms.

Budget
Moon Bungalow Mu 2, Chaweng Beach (tel: 077/422167). Friendly, laid-back and peaceful.
Pearl Bay Bungalow 81/1 Bang Kao Beach (tel: 077/423110). Comfortable huts in quiet, out-of-the-way location.

KRABI
Accommodations
Expensive
Dusit Rayavadee 67 Mu 5, Susan Hoi Road, Ao Phra Nang (tel: 075/620740–3). Exclusive luxury resort in the romantic surroundings of Phra Nang headland.

Moderate
Thai 7 Issara Road (tel: 075/611122). Clean and comfortable; tour services available.

PHANG NGA
Accommodations
Moderate
Phang Nga Valley Resort 5/5 Phetkasem Road (tel: 076/412201). Attractive bungalow complex in lovely setting.

Budget
Nang Thong Bay Resort Ao Nang Thong, Khao Lak (tel: 01/7231181). Well-furnished accommodations in garden setting near the west coast national park.

PHUKET
Accommodations
Expensive
Amanpuri Resort 118/1 Pansea Beach, Tambon Choeng Thale (tel: 076/324333). Expensive and exclusive bungalow development on a peaceful beach.
Kata Thani 62/4 Rasada Road, Kata Noi Beach (tel: 076/330124). Beach complex with excellent facilities.
Phuket Yacht Club 23/3 Wiset Road, Nai Harn Beach (tel: 076/381156). Comes alive in December (racing season); wonderful views.

Moderate
Jungle Beach Resort 11/3 Wiset Road, Ao Sane Beach (near Nai Harn), (tel: 076/381108). Shady, quiet beachside paradise, with every amenity.
Kata Guest House Kata Beach (tel: 076/381627). Good view; simple, basic rooms.

Phuket Fishing Lodge 59/9 Mu 1, Chalong Bay (tel: 076/281003). Every room has a waterfront view (yacht anchorage), and there is good food available.
Phuket Garden 40/12 Bangkok Road, Phuket town (tel: 076/216900). Reasonable rates for its luxuries.
Rawai Plaza and Bungalow 64 Wiset Road, Rawai Beach (tel: 076/381346). Smart and friendly complex on fine beach.

Budget
***On On** Phang Nga Road, Phuket town (tel: 076/211154). Pleasant travelers' hotel.

Restaurants
Expensive
Boathouse Wine and Grill Kata Beach (tel: 076/330015). Renowned restaurant in "boutique" resort, serving Thai and European food of international repute. Good wine cellar.

Budget
Mae Porn 50–2 Phang-Nga Road, Phuket town (tel: 076/212106). Curries and *farang* favorites.
Muslim Restaurant 1/3 Thepkasattree Road, Thaewnam Intersection (tel: 076/223930). Tasty *khao mok kai* with yellow rice, liver curry.

RANONG
Accommodations
Expensive
Jansom Thara 2/10 Phetkasem Road (tel: 077/ 821511). All possible luxuries and facilities, including mineral-water whirlpools.

SONGKHLA
Accommodations
Moderate
Lake Inn 301–3 Nakhon Nok Road (tel: 074/321044). Well-appointed and recently renovated, with lovely lake views.

Budget
Chan, 469 Saiburi Road (tel: 074/311903). Passable, if shabby.
Saen Samran 2 Ramwithi Road (tel: 074/311090). Small but spotless rooms, TV available.

SURATTHANI
Accommodations
Budget
Art's Jungle House Khao Sok National Park (Bangkok reservations tel: 02/279–4967). Tree houses by a pretty stream.

TRANG
Accommodations
Moderate
Thammarin Thammarin Square (tel: 075/211011). The best hotel in town, benefiting from a very Thai style.

Budget
***Sri Trang** 24 Lang Sathani Road (near railroad station) (tel: 075/218122). Some air-conditioned rooms, basic.

Index

Bold figures denote the main entry of a particular subject.

INDEX

INDEX/ACKNOWLEDGMENTS

Publisher's Acknowledgements

The Automobile Association would like to thank the following photographers, libraries and associations for their assistance in the preparation of this book.

RICK STRANGE took all the photographs in this book (© AA Photolibrary) except those listed below:
BANGKOK POST 60b, 62a, 62b, 63a, 65b, 66/7a, 67b, 68b, 69b, 70a, 70b, 71a.
TIM LOCKE 133b, 253c, 256a, 271a, 275.
NATURE PHOTOGRAPHERS 250e (S C Blisserot), 251 (S C Blisserot).
SPECTRUM COLOUR LIBRARY 104, 105.
TOURISM AUTHORITY OF THAILAND 17a, 18 , 50a, 51, 83, 93, 94a, 110a, 121a, 195a, 197a, 202a, 203a, 209a, 210a, 211a, 213a, 215a, 221, 224, 225a, 226a, 229 , 230a, 231a/b, 248.

Contributors

Revision copy editor: Janet Tabinski   **Original copy editor**: Beth Ingpen
Revision verifier: Lindsay Hunt